The Nineteenth Century

With 326 illustrations
88 in colour
238 photographs, engravings,
drawings and maps

EDITED BY ASA BRIGGS

The Nineteenth Century

THE CONTRADICTIONS OF PROGRESS

Texts by

ASA BRIGGS   JOHN ROBERTS   JAMES JOLL

F. BÉDARIDA   F.M.L. THOMPSON

JOHN RÖHL   BRIAN BOND   MARCUS CUNLIFFE

HUGH SETON-WATSON

THAMES AND HUDSON

First published in Great Britain in 1970
by Thames and Hudson Ltd, London
This edition 1985

© 1970 and 1985 Thames and Hudson Ltd, London

Printed and bound in Yugoslavia

CONTENTS

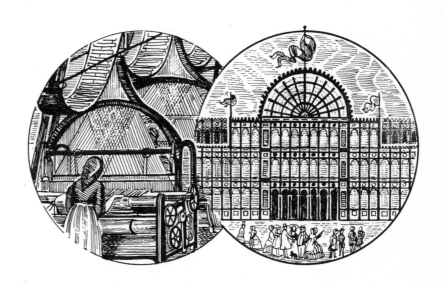

I THE SHAPE OF THE CENTURY

Changing values in art and society

ASA BRIGGS

'I feel within me the rebellious unspoken word.
I will not be old. The horizon enlarges, the sky shifts
around me. It is an age of shocks; a discipline
so strong, so manifold, so rapid, and so whirling that only
when it is at an end, if then, can I comprehend it.'

WILLIAM EWART GLADSTONE, 1860

The romantic spirit,

which seems to epitomize so much of 19th-century culture and history, is easier to recognize than to define. It involved no particular body of beliefs, but was rather a cluster of attitudes, most of which can be traced separately at other periods in the past, but whose association led to a profound change in almost every department of human thought. Even today it is difficult to see literature, the arts, history or even nature through any but post-Romantic eyes.

What are the main elements of Romanticism? A deep and compelling concern for man's inner life; a high valuation of emotion and simplicity as against reason, order and civilization; a love of nature, amounting often to a sense of mystical communion; a fascination with the remote and the strange, in both time and place; and a yearning for the infinite and the unattainable. There were incompatibilities here, currents and counter-currents, but there was usually a commitment to romantic sensibility. English poets in the mid-18th century were already going to natural scenery in search of the Sublime. Thomas Gray's poem 'The Bard' tells how the last of the native poets of Wales, after defying the English invaders under Edward I, threw himself from the top of a rocky crag and died rather than submit to alien rule. Here we have untamed nature; the favoured Middle Ages; violent, uncompromising emotion; and also a strong nationalist sympathy which we noted in Chapter VI as often being linked with Romanticism. The painting (opposite) which the early 19th-century artist John Martin made of Gray's poem emphasizes its Romantic qualities to the point of exaggeration. The landscape is unbelievably precipitous, and the wild bard with his harp confronts the endless line of King Edward's army like a being from another world.

Rousseau had put forward the ideal of 'natural' man as superior to 'artificial', i.e. civilized, man. Goethe's *Werther* had portrayed a hero in whom passion was stronger than life, and had praised rather than condemned him. Wordsworth had seen nature as a moral force. These works were all produced before 1800. Soon after the beginning of the century the first part of Goethe's *Faust* was published, in which man's right to experience and fulfilment becomes the supreme element in life. During the next fifty years the tide of Romanticism carried most things before it. Literature was predominantly Romantic, with Scott, Byron, Schiller, Musset, Hölderlin, Shelley, Keats, Novalis, Vigny, Hugo and many others, but music was in many ways the most Romantic of the arts. With Géricault and Delacroix, painting too freed itself from classical restraints and became chiefly the expression of the artist's feelings or, in Friedrich, Constable or Turner, a means of integrating man and nature. In architecture, various exotic styles were revived, making historical association a prime factor in design.

In the middle of the century the Romantic point of view produced achievements as varied as the modern novel (with its obsession with the emotional life of the characters) and Wagnerian music-drama. Thereafter, the original impetus began to be dispersed. In painting, the Impressionists concentrated on the appearance of the world without endowing it with mystical qualities; in literature and music the quest for the individual led further into introspection, and that for the remote to perversity and neurosis. Architects began to turn their backs on Romanticism altogether. The *fin-de-siècle* represents a time when Romantic ideals, still pervasive, were beginning to be devalued, but no corresponding set of ideals had arisen to take their place.

Contrasts in design throughout the century show three stages of taste – first, Neo-classical elegance; second, an opulent aesthetic free-for-all; and third, either *Art Nouveau* sinuosity or austere modernism.

Beds (*far left*): the top example is Italian, the middle one English (1851), and the lowest (c. 1900) designed by C. R. Mackintosh, a pioneer of modern design.

Clocks (*centre left*): first, the Empire style of Napoleonic France; second, an English clock of 1851; third, a plain British model by Baillie Scott.

Fabrics (*left*) make a more complicated story, since there was wide variety within each period. Top: a French Neo-classical example. Centre: a three-dimensional German pattern of 1851. Bottom: a design of 1884 by Mackmurdo, one of the 'inventors' of *Art Nouveau*.

Ironwork (*right*) closely reflected architectural trends. First, a detail of doors in Berlin by Schinkel. Second, part of a Neo-Gothic choir screen by Sir G. G. Scott. Third, *Art Nouveau* decoration from a Paris Métro entrance by Guimard.

Costume (*far right*) illustrates the same shift in taste. Before 1851 (top, English fashions of 1808) the line was narrow and high-waisted. Mid-century crinolines (centre, France in 1855) emphasized the generous curve. By 1900 (bottom, French), the silhouette was wasp-waisted.

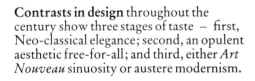

International exhibitions, significant pointers to 19th-century self-consciousness, began with the Great Exhibition in London (*above left*) of 1851. A novel and ambitious undertaking housed in a novel and revolutionary building, Paxton's Crystal Palace, its impact everywhere was immense. Previous exhibitions had been national; London, under the leadership of the Prince Consort, invited the whole world, confident that she could outshine all comers.

Melbourne could demonstrate her coming of age in 1880 by an exhibition (*above*) that equalled any but the largest in Europe. Exhibitions were valuable national advertisements, that at Melbourne stimulating both home trade and foreign investment.

Paris in 1867 staged the largest exhibition up to that time (*left*). The buildings consisted of a series of concentric rings in the Champ de Mars. The outer ring was devoted to machinery, which was shown in motion. Other sections dealt with the progress of civilization, giving unprecedented space to social studies and public education. In the rest of the grounds were buildings in various national styles – a Turkish mosque, a Swiss chalet, etc.

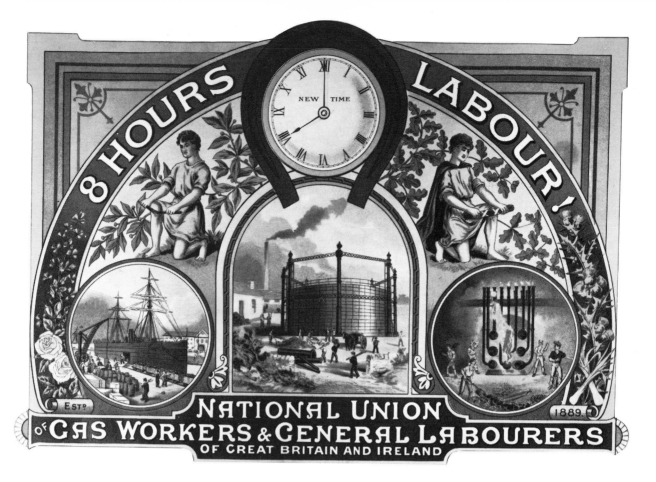

8 HOURS LABOUR!

NEW TIME

NATIONAL UNION ESTD · 1889 · OF **GAS WORKERS & GENERAL LABOURERS** OF GREAT BRITAIN AND IRELAND

The source of power which underlay the whole Industrial Revolution was coal – so much so that one economist has coined the phrase 'carboniferous capitalism' to describe it. In the 18th century coal had begun to transform the iron industry and had made possible the utilization of steam power. About 1800 coal-gas came into use for lighting, and later in the century for heating also. A membership certificate of the National Union of Gas Workers (*above*) gives an idea of gas production: on the left the coal arrives by sea, on the right the gas is extracted, and in the centre is stored in a gasometer. England was rich in coal deposits. There were seams in the north, in Nottinghamshire, in South Wales. *Left*: the Percy Colliery, Northumberland, in 1839.

Electricity, known but barely understood in the 18th century, was tamed and disciplined by scientists such as Faraday and Edison. By 1900, the Paris Exposition Universelle could include a 'Palais de l'Electricité' (*above*) triumphantly proclaiming its importance for the future. *Right*: the interior of an English power station in 1892, with steam turbines producing electricity for public supply. The dials at the back indicate the various areas being served.

Petroleum was discovered in Pennsylvania in 1859 and was rapidly exploited, Tarr Farm (*left*), near Titusville, being one of the earliest oil wells. The principal product was originally kerosene (paraffin), used for heating and lighting; only when the internal combustion engine was developed did the by-product gasolene become valuable.

'In what style shall we build?' was the dilemma of 19th-century architecture. Should it be a revival of a style of the past, or a new style for the new age? Did architecture itself belong to the past, to be superseded by engineering?

Revived styles. Italy and Central Europe favoured the Baroque, a style associated with some of the high points of their history. *Top*: the Victor Emmanuel Monument, Rome, begun in 1884. The Greek Revival, on the other hand, stood for high-minded humanism, particularly suitable for museums, as here (*above*) the Glyptothek in Munich by Leo van Klenze. English taste, led by Pugin, turned against these 'pagan' styles and promoted Gothic for both patriotic and religious reasons. One of its masterpieces is the Houses of Parliament in London, by Pugin and Barry, built during the 1840s and 50s.

A 'new' style could take many forms. In America the steel frame gave buildings a completely new scale, often clad – as on the Wainwright Building, St Louis, by Adler and Sullivan (*centre*) – with vegetal *Art Nouveau* ornament. In Spain, Gaudí was developing a strange 'organic' style at the Sagrada Familia, Barcelona (*opposite top*); while Eiffel, in Paris (*opposite bottom*) put his faith in the material that was already proving itself in railway stations and bridges: steel.

Russia differed from other European empires in simply expanding her own territory into Asia. It was nevertheless colonization in exactly the same sense as that of Britain or France. *Above left*: the double-headed eagle stretches her wings over a picturesque collection of races, while to the right lies India, a land as coveted by the Russians as it was prized by the British.

Germany had no colonies before 1884. Bismarck was 'not interested'. But between 1890 and 1914 she applied herself systematically to colonial administration and had all the makings of a leading imperialist power. *Left*: a cartoon from the periodical *Jugend* in 1896, making fun of German efficiency. A new officer arrives in the jungle to find everything in deplorable confusion, but before long the situation has been reduced to satisfactory order.

The fact of Empire may prove to be the 19th-century's most lasting contribution to world politics. For Europe and America, as we have seen, it was a century of 'revolution and improvement'. For the rest of the world, it was the century of European domination. Imperialism, however, was not just a sinister conspiracy. It was the natural consequence of material wealth, technical expertise and mutual competition.

Britain was the winner in the race for overseas possessions. British administration, normally just and efficient, did not discourage a sense of racial superiority, even in India. *Left*: a party of British guests in front of an ancient temple during the last years of the century.

France began her career of colonizer with the ideals of the Revolution still powerful. Her subject peoples were to be assimilated, to be Europeanized, to be made, as far as possible, French. By the end of Napoleon III's reign this policy had failed but the ambition was never relinquished. This montage picture (*below*) of France's colonial family – from Tahiti to Guiana and from Mozambique to Morocco – appeared after the turn of the century.

Classicism and Romanticism are the two main currents of 19th-century art. Once conceived as opposites, they now seem rather to spring ultimately from the same source.

Pauline Borghese – Napoleon's sister – was carved by Canova in the pose of a reclining classical goddess (*above*).

The Dream of Ossian by Ingres (*above right*) alludes to the hugely popular, but spurious, northern epic. It is a strange mixture of classical conventions and Romantic feeling. The blind poet rests his head on his lyre. Around him appear the spirits of the dead, including a stern helmeted warrior with a shield who was actually added later by a pupil.

Landscape as a symbol: the German Romantic painter Caspar David Friedrich made nature symbolize the crises of man's condition. In *The Wreck of the 'Hope'* (*right*) implacable sheets of ice are grinding the frail wooden ship to splinters.

Balzac, the giant, a literary genius on a superhuman scale, wrote over 100 books in 30 years, dying exhausted in 1850 at the age of fifty-one. Rodin, at the end of the century, made him the supreme symbol (*opposite*) of Romantic realism.

Iron was being used for a wide variety of purposes in the first quarter of the century. Brunel's iron ship, the *Great Eastern* (*left*), was a bold experiment which only partially succeeded. This photograph shows her under construction in 1857. Unprecendended in size, in construction (she had a 'double-skin' iron hull) and in method of propulsion (propellor and paddle-wheels combined) she was launched in 1858 but failed to pay her way as a passenger liner.

Steel took the place of iron in engineering when Henry Bessemer discovered how it could be manufactured on a commercial scale. By the 1870s the Krupp works at Essen contained some of the most powerful machinery in the world, such as the steam-hammer 'Fritz' (*left*), an English invention of the 1830s. Steel in tension revolutionized bridge-building, making possible the suspension bridge hung from a continuous wire cable. J. A. Roeblin's Brooklyn Bridge (*above*), designed in 1869, used a new method of cable-spinning which is essentially the same as that today. The span is 1,535 feet; at the time of its completion in 1883 it was the largest single-span structure of any kind in the world.

Old and new art clashed on several battlefronts – at exhibitions, in the press and in the theatres. The first night of Victor Hugo's *Hernani* (*far left above*), in February 1830, was one such confrontation. The play was a deliberate break with tradition in plot, construction and language. The conservatives filled the expensive seats, determined to drive it from the stage, but Hugo's friends, in the foreground wearing his cherry-red waistcoat, outclapped their opponents and won the day for Romanticism.

The rebels in painting, after the death of Géricault, were led by Eugène Delacroix, an artist whose revolutionary technique matched his subject-matter. His early *Dante and Virgil in Hell* (*far left below*) gives us Dante through the eyes of Rubens. Delacroix was a typically Romantic figure, reacting to literature, exotic cultures and music – this painting he called 'a symphony in green with a red key signature'.

Liszt plays to a musical and literary gathering (*above*). From left to right: the elder Dumas, Hugo, George Sand, Paganini and Rossini. At Liszt's feet, his mistress, Marie d'Agoult. On the wall, a portrait of Byron. On the piano, a bust of Beethoven.

Hector Berlioz (*left*) has much in common with Delacroix. Almost all his work was inspired by literature – from Virgil and Shakespeare to Goethe, Byron and Gautier. Shakespeare, indeed, was a 19th-century revelation to France and Germany.

Science gathered momentum throughout the century. Already by 1840 the laboratory of Justus von Liebig (*above*) was producing far-reaching results in organic and inorganic chemistry, including the extract of beef known as Oxo.

Physics: the Englishman Michael Faraday, seen here in his laboratory, typifies the 19th century's tireless experimentation. He made notable contributions to chemical research, but his main achievement was to show the relation between electricity and magnetism and to make the first dynamo.

Biology: during the 19th century interest advanced from the structure to the processes of living organisms. Claude Bernard, the greatest physiologist of his day (*below*, dissecting a rabbit), discovered the vasomotor system and was the first to describe adequately the roles of the pancreas and the liver.

Astronomy was able to make progress by the building of larger and larger telescopes. That of the Lick Observatory, California (*right*), completed in 1888, was a refracting instrument with a 36-inch 'objective' lens. Although an immense body of facts was built up, cosmological theory remained Newtonian throughout the century.

X-rays, were discovered by W. K. Röntgen in 1895. *Below*: the same hand taken by an earlier technique and by Röntgen.

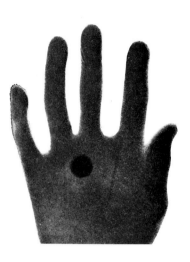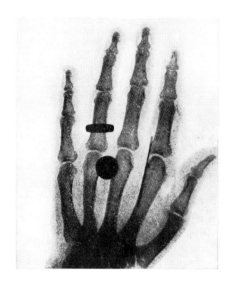

New dimensions to the universe opened out in all directions. *Below*: a lecture by the traditionalist geologist William Buckland, who saw fossils as evidence for the Flood. *Below right*: James Dewar's demonstration of liquid hydrogen. Such experiments led to the laws of thermodynamics.

Society rested upon the family in the view of most 19th-century moralists and to preserve the family inviolate a strict system of sanctions operated. *Left*: *Breaking Home Ties* (1890), an American scene which must have been common enough in rural districts throughout the world. The young son sets off to make his fortune in the big city.

'Many Happy Returns of the Day' (*below*). It is the little girl's birthday – in 1856 – and three generations of the family gather for her party. The painting is by W. P. Frith. Note the grandmother on the left, the paintings, and the gas chandelier.

Changing values in art and society

ASA BRIGGS

TALLEYRAND (1754–1838) once remarked that only those who had lived in France before the Revolution of 1789 had really experienced *la douceur de vivre*. Certainly the French Revolution and the European wars which followed in its wake represented a great divide in human history. What had existed before 1789 could never be restored. Thereafter there might be bustle, excitement, exploration, challenge, an unprecedented awareness both of opportunities and of problems, above all a sense of almost unremitting movement. Yet there were too many disturbances of traditional order and *tempo* for there to be any secure balance. There were also too many manifest and acknowledged contrasts and contradictions of expectation and of circumstance to permit either the privileged or the unprivileged, the powerful or the powerless to acquiesce easily in life as it was or as it seemed to be becoming. '*Oh triste dix-neuvième siècle!*' the French novelist Stendhal (1783–1842) was wont to exclaim. Although relatively large numbers of people made money out of change and enjoyed standards of comfort never before attained in human history, critical voices were never stilled. Every innovation, not least the railway, perhaps the most exciting of all the innovations, a symbol as well as a fact of progress, produced its rhetoric, for and against. Where for reasons of social structure there was little change in an age of change, there was little satisfaction. The characters in the plays of Anton Chekhov (1860–1904) live in a world of decay caused by 'inertia' and 'ignorance': in *The Cherry Orchard* (1904) one of them exclaims prophetically 'before we can live in the present, we must first redeem the past and have done with it'.

An age of movement

Because of the complexities of change and the variety of responses to it, the 19th century is a difficult century to 'place' in human history or to assess as a whole. If there was *tristesse*, there was also wonder. *The Wonderful Century* was the title of a book by A. R. Wallace, the biologist, published in 1898. Wallace was himself a critic of his age, yet he did not hesitate to conclude that 'not only is our century superior to any that have gone before it, but . . . it may be best compared with the whole preceding historical period. It must therefore be held to constitute the beginning of a new era of human progress.' Wallace pointed also to the pride as well as to the wonder. 'We men of the Nineteenth Century have not been slow to praise it. The wise and the foolish, the learned and the unlearned, the poet and the pressman, the rich and the poor, alike swell the chorus of admiration for the marvellous inventions and discoveries of our own age, and especially for those innumerable applications of science which now form part of our daily life, and which remind us every hour of our immense superiority over our comparatively ignorant forefathers.'

Wallace (1823–1913) was sophisticated enough to provide a balance sheet in his book and to devote one long section to 'failures' having catalogued 'successes'. Yet there were many less sophisticated people who were content with the 'facts' of progress, particularly the 'hard' facts which could be measured quantitatively, the facts of population growth, of urbanization, of industrial production, of literacy, of the franchise, or, at a lower but more meaningful level, of individual businesses, cities or countries. Many of these basic facts are set out in this book. So, too, are the details of the attempts to explain them in the 19th century in terms of 'laws' or of '*isms*'. Yet the historian must be even more sophisticated than Wallace. There were many 'facts' which did not fit easily into the picture of progress—facts of poverty, for example, and of exploitation, and there was seldom universal agreement about the 'laws'. The *isms* were matters of violent conflict as well as of intellectual debate. No previous century expressed itself in such a wide spectrum of diversities. During the last decades of the century, indeed, much that had been taken for granted earlier, even when the clashes had been fiercest, was openly challenged. The assumptions were questioned and overturned. There was, therefore, no 19th-century resting place.

Some of the changes of mood and of self-evaluation are discussed in this book, and later in this chapter contemporary evidence is examined in detail to illustrate and to explain just how complex were some of the contrasting ways in which different generations and different people within each generation related their own experience to that of the past and what they thought or felt would be the experience of the future. It is useful to begin, however, with the recognition that throughout the whole of the century notions of authority and forms of power were in flux, even though there were attempts to establish balances or compromises in almost every decade, particularly during the middle years of the century. 'The age of revolution,' wrote the Swiss historian Jacob Burckhardt (1818–97) in 1871, 'is particularly most *instructive*, in contrast to everything older and earlier, on account of the mutability of things, the multiformity of modern life as compared to earlier life, the strong change in the pulse beat, and through the great notoriety of everything connected with it.'

Burckhardt's label 'the age of revolution' has been widely used ever since. He saw, indeed, in 1871, as we can now see clearly in the 20th century, that the divide between the 18th and 19th centuries can be explained only if the French Revolution is considered alongside what began to be called during the 19th century itself 'the industrial revolution'. Both revolutions were unfinished. Both had universal implications. To explain the origins of each of them it is necessary to go back in time to long-term forces in European history. To perceive their consequences it is necessary to relate the 19th to the 20th centuries. They affected ways of feeling as well as of thinking, what may be called without exaggeration the whole 'human condition'. The intricate interaction between them set the terms of movement.

Revolutions

The French Revolution is discussed at length in Chapter II of this book. The events of 1789 acquired significance in the light of what came afterwards. Revolutionaries might disagree both about objectives and tactics, but throughout the 19th century the revolutionary impulse was never stilled. The Revolution itself was subject to continuous reinterpretation not only in France but in other countries. Yet it was recognized alike by revolutionaries and their adversaries that there had been a fundamental switch in history as a result of it. If the initial significance of the Revolution was that it occurred in the most typical and the most powerful of the traditionalist absolute monarchies of Europe, very quickly it was the universal appeal of the Revolution which mattered most.

The men who drafted the *Declaration of the Rights of Man and of Citizens* in 1789 appealed to universal and eternal principles because the established order rested on law and custom. Yet the simplicity of their language—'men are born and live free and equal under the laws'—opened the way to arguments which were to continue throughout the 19th century. Already by 1795 it was clear that different individuals and different social groups would not agree voluntarily for long on a common revolutionary formula or agenda. It was also clear that in any revolutionary sequence some of the most violent conflicts would not be between revolutionaries and their opponents but between revolutionaries themselves. The interplay in France between different groups of revolutionaries and different elements of resistance was to be repeated time and time again within different contexts throughout the 19th century: it constituted what has been called vividly by Eric Hobsbawm 'a dramatic dialectical dance'.

The problem of how to interpret the assertion of 1789 that the essence of the democratic ideal is the 'sovereignty of the people' haunted Frenchmen throughout what was to prove a politically restless 19th century, a century when there was always in the background the possibility of a recourse to the barricades. Attempts to reconcile aspects of the 'revolutionary tradition' with monarchy during the reign of Louis XVIII (1815–24) and, more deliberately, during the reign of Louis Philippe (1830–48) which followed a further, halted Revolution in 1830, proved impossible. The result was a further revolutionary sequence in 1848 itself during which the divisions between social classes became the decisive element in the story. The June Days in Paris saw a short, sharp, violent conflict between the propertied and the propertyless which revealed a new dimension both of revolution and of resistance. Thereafter the red flag was to be more prominent than the tricolour in all demands for a further instalment of revolution. In the meantime, France had once again revealed the pattern. As J. L. Talmon has written, 'In February 1848 Paris gave the sign to begin the Revolution; in June it provided an example of the way to liquidate it.'

To understand what happened to the 'revolutionary tradition' in France itself later in the 19th century it is necessary to take account not only of the revolutionary tradition itself or the resistances it created, not least among the peasants who had played a leading part in the aftermath of 1789, but of the Napoleonic legacy. Napoleon (1769–1821) had risen to power through the experience of revolution which offered him opportunities which he would never otherwise have enjoyed. He carried with him throughout Europe during the wars to which he gave his name many of the principles of the Revolution. Yet in France itself he codified and institutionalized, offering not further revolution but increased stability, a new Napoleonic order. Because he was so successful as a ruler inside France, Frenchmen turned back to him, sometimes through legend rather than through fact, between 1815 and 1848. When the revolutionary sequence in France had run its course by the summer of 1848 it was to a 'little Napoleon' that Frenchmen turned, Louis Napoleon (1808–73), who after a coup d'état (a very different phenomenon from a revolution) became Emperor of France, Napoleon III, in 1852.

The Second Empire, like the monarchy of Louis Philippe, was to last for eighteen years. Yet it never satisfied most of the protagonists of the principles of 1789. When it collapsed ignominiously in 1870, the creation of the Paris Commune revealed the continuing leftward impetus of an unfinished revolution, and when the Commune collapsed in its turn, the less extremist inheritors of the principles of 1789 sought to enshrine those principles in a new republic. Bonapartism did not disappear immediately as a political force, but the republic, accepted at first with caution, even resentment, lasted deep into the 20th century. There were many crises in its history, some on old issues—militarism, clericalism, authoritarianism—some on new social issues; and one of them, the Dreyfus case (which began in 1894) was to expose every facet and every flaw of French society. The Republic was not only nick-named *Marianne* but *la République des Professeurs*, even *la République des Complices*. Yet it survived and was consolidated without ever settling in France itself the continuing conflict between liberty and equality as ideals, a conflict which went back to the 1790s, or fully reconciling democracy and efficient government, a reconciliation which Napoleon himself had failed to achieve.

The democratic revolution was entangled in a mesh of complications of this order wherever it inspired revolutionaries during the 19th century. France had its own unique experience and its own ways of formulating it or of seeking to extend it, and in other countries also it is impossible to separate the history of revolutionary movements from national history as a whole. There was much in common in this pattern and in the 'dialectical dance', but 'nationalism' in the name of the sovereignty of the people was a strong enough force to guide, even to dictate, the course of particular revolutionary movements. The French revolutionaries of 1789 had launched the national principle along with the rights of man: they set out to 'liberate' other nations as they themselves had liberated the people of France. And they won allies abroad even after Napoleon had assumed power. Increasingly, however, the story became complicated, as is explained in Chapter VI of this book. Countries which mobilized their resources against Napoleon's armies kindled their own resistance by appealing to the pride of their peoples. After 1815 fraternity could often rouse greater support as an ideal than either liberty or equality. Revolutionaries continued to look to Paris in 1830 and in 1848, but as the year 1848 unfolded it was demonstrated first that France would not discharge a universal revolutionary mission, second that other countries conceived of their own revolutionary mission in nationalistic terms. Poland, 'the Christ among the nations', saw revolution as the means to nationalism rather than to individualism and freedom: such freedom did not extend to Ukrainians under Polish rule. In Hungary Louis Kossuth (1802–94), a nationalist hero, was interested in freedom for Hungary, not for Slovakia or Serbia. In Germany, where the drive towards nationalism had been particularly strong and the philosophies of nationalism particularly heady and assertive, revolutionaries found it difficult to sympathize with the aspirations of non-Germans. As one German liberal speaker remarked of Western Poland during the debates within the all-German Frankfurt Parliament (1848–49), 'our right is that of the stronger, the right of conquest'. Parallel to the Frankfurt debates, which began in March 1848 under a nationalist flag of black, gold and red stripes, a Slav conference, precursor of many to follow, opened in Prague in June.

The failure of the 1848 revolutions, 'the springtime of liberty', led directly to a period of tougher, more deliberately organized and sometimes more consciously manipulated nationalism which retained its power throughout the rest of the century. If 'romanticism and nationalism' had been a revolutionary theme between 1815 and 1848, 'realism and nationalism' was the main theme in the history of statecraft between 1848 and the 1870s. The great German historian Leopold von Ranke (1795–1886) told the King of Bavaria in 1854 that 'the fundamental tendency of our time' was 'the conflict between monarchic and popular sovereignty, with which all other conflicts are connected', yet it was possible for realistic politicians—Bismarck (1815–98) in Germany and Cavour (1810–61) in Italy—to achieve their objects without worrying too much about popular sovereignty or the claims of people in other countries. 'I have always heard the word "Europe",' Bismarck said in 1876, 'in the mouth of someone who wanted something from another which he dared not ask on his own account.' There were still international revolutionaries in the middle and late years of the 19th century—most of them in exile from their own countries—but they were operating in a world where the increasing power of the national state limited not only their own freedom to manoeuvre but the objects which they set for themselves. What advances were made towards political or social democracy during the last fifty years of the 19th century were made within circumscribed national contexts.

Iron, coal and steam: a second revolution

It is impossible to take such an analysis further without introducing the second of the two revolutions which transformed thinking and feeling during the 19th century. If political revolution was associated for much of the century with France, industrial revolution was associated for the first part of the century mainly with Britain. Just as the French Revolution of 1789 provided an ideal and a model even when the ideal was tarnished and the model misleading, so the British industrial revolution was treated both as a precursor and as a 'classic' case history in its own right. Many deductions about social history as well as economic history were derived from it, and it was mainly with British history in mind that Karl Marx (1818–83) set out to discover the 'laws of motion of capitalist society'—a quest which he himself compared with the attempt of Charles Darwin (1809–82) to discover the laws of evolution in the natural world—and reached his general conclusions about the role of economics in relation to historical change. 'The sum total of the relations of production constitutes the economic structure of society—the real foundation on which rise legal and political superstructures and to which definite forms of social consciousness correspond.'

It would certainly be impossible to discuss 19th-century 'social consciousness' without introducing, as Marx did, the steam engine. Steam power, a new source of power which broke the centuries-long domination of wind and water, was first developed and used industrially in Britain. Moreover, Britain developed the first sizeable factory industry, the cotton industry, which was soon exporting its products throughout the world, inside and outside Europe. The cotton factory with its new machines was a visible expression of progress. Yet it was also a centre of new social problems. The 'labour force' which manned the factories—women and children were, in fact, used more than men—had to learn a new discipline: at the same time, it was more than a 'labour force' employed by manufacturers, many of them 'new men'. It developed its own consciousness and ultimately its own institutions as a 'working class'. The term was as new as the phenomenon. So, too, was the use of the word 'industry' itself to describe not a human attribute but a sector of the economy.

The social structure of Britain favoured, if it did not 'cause', the rise of a factory-based textiles industry. There was a greater level and diffusion of technical skill and a greater interest in useful machines than in any other country in Europe. The pressures and incentives to change ways of production were strong, and they did not depend on the intervention of the state. The expansion of markets and the ploughing back of capital continued. So, too, did technological invention. Each new invention in spinning and weaving encouraged further invention in a sequence of challenge and response as interesting to follow through in detail as the revolutionary sequences in France which we have already noted. Moreover, there were generous supplies of coal in Britain, a raw material well described by David Landes as 'the bread of industry'. By 1800 Britain was using up 11 million tons a year, by 1830 more than 20 million, by 1845 45 million, and by 1870 100 million. Iron, too, was in ample supply, given further technical innovations in a sequence of challenge and response not dissimilar from that in the textiles industry. Iron was the master material of the early industrial revolution, and in 1830 British iron output, 680,000 tons, was greater than that of France, Germany and America combined: output had quadrupled in thirty years.

Iron and coal were the twin bases of what Lewis Mumford has called 'carboniferous capitalism', the capitalism which reached its technical climax in the invention of the railway, the application of steam power to transportation, 'the iron road'. Contemporaries were dazzled or horrified not only by the sight of the new steam locomotives but by the social phenomena which were associated with railway projection, construction and operation—the growth of a new and highly speculative property market; battles about land rights and urban terminals; fierce competition between different lines; unprecedented mobility; precise time-tables. 'We who lived before railways and survive out of the ancient world,' wrote W. M. Thackeray (1811–63), the British novelist, 'are like Father Noah and his family out of the Ark.'

By the time that the railways were built across Britain, there had already been a great transformation in the human environment, a transformation as great, perhaps, as that of the people who inhabited it. Huge industrial cities had emerged, provincial cities far from London, each with a distinct life of its own. In 1800 there were no cities in Britain, except London, with a population of over 100,000. By 1837, when Queen Victoria (1819–1901) came to the throne, there were five: by 1891 twenty-three. Urbanization is the main theme of Chapter IV of this book: within its intricate processes the early experience of Britain was unique. Cities, like railways, filled people with pride or fear, as ancient urban-rural dichotomies or rivalries acquired a new dimension. Outside or between the cities there were sometimes alarming tracts of 'black country', with slag heaps and derelict land: above the cities— London was no exception—there was a thick pall of smoke. Rivers were polluted, trees torn down. Britain passed through a 'bleak age' even when she was advancing to greater general prosperity. It was not merely the concentration of people in factories or in towns which generated problems—of health, of order, of social relations. The human imagination was being affected also. Contemporaries went to Manchester during the 1840s to try to read their times and to comprehend the significance of 'the type of a new power in the earth'. 'The age of ruins is past,' one of the characters remarks in the widely read novel *Coningsby* (1844) by Benjamin Disraeli (1804–81). 'Have you seen Manchester?' Coningsby himself came to the conclusion, having visited Manchester, that 'it is the philosopher alone who can conceive the grandeur of Manchester and the immensity of its future'.

Yet it was Manchester which Friedrich Engels (1820–95), with an equally strong sense of history and of prophecy, singled out as the 'classic type of modern industrial town' and identified as a centre of potential revolution. A new factory proletariat had come into existence. Bonds of 'personal devotion', 'chains of connection' had snapped. For the time being the new factory owners, themselves proud of their class and of its exciting achievements, might be dominant, but history was not on their side. Already the members of the proletariat were 'becoming more and more aware of their power and pressing more and more strongly for their share of the social advantages of their era'. Engels looked to a revolutionary future with hope; others with dread. Alexis de Tocqueville (1805–59), like Sismondi (1773–1842) before him and Hippolyte Taine (1828–93) after him, was deeply troubled when he contemplated the human costs of industrialization in its early British phase.'Here civilization works its miracles, and civilized man is turned back almost into a savage.'

Engels was wrong in believing that there would be revolution in 19th-century Manchester. Britain as a whole, indeed, was immune from political revolution throughout the whole century. There were many reasons why in Britain 'improvement' rather than 'revolution' was the *leitmotiv* of the period: some of them are set out in Chapter II. At the same time, it is not fanciful to treat the social consequences of industrialization universally as one element in a 'long revolution' which affected the texture of life even in countries where there were no coups d'état, no barricades and no violent social transformations. Socialism, revolutionary or non-revolutionary, was the link between the democratic revolution and the industrial revolution. So, indeed, during the first phases of the industrial revolution, was the articulation of 'middle-class' or bourgeois ideologies, ideologies like liberalism which marked a sharp break with the feudal past. New approaches to citizenship were evolved within a changing economic framework even when there was no *Declaration of the Rights of Man and of Citizens*. Cumulative market forces, influencing the volume and the distribution of wealth, must be set alongside political forces in any full account of the rise of democracy. During the first half of the 19th century the social contradictions of competitive, carboniferous capitalism were exposed, particularly in the years of financial and economic crisis which were always years of social tension. Understandably, indeed, a debate began—and it has never been concluded—as to whether the new working classes as a whole benefited materially from the vast increase in production. During the second half of the century, as industrialization became more general and as industrial organization tended throughout the whole Western world to become more impersonal and complex, social inequalities, expressed also in biological differences of physique, expectations of life and chances of death, were just as obvious. Nonetheless, there was no doubt about advances in both living standards and aspirations for the

The Machinery Court at the Great Exhibition, London, 1851. In the foreground is Fairbairn's crane, at the back the famous hydraulic press used in raising the tubular sections of Stephenson's Britannia Bridge.

future. Much of the social history of the last years of the century is concerned with shops and schools. The growth of the retail trade, encompassing as it did the growth of big department stores and of consumer co-operative movements, made life both easier and richer. The spread of education, related at several levels to the developing needs of industry, at the same time served wider social purposes, purposes of emancipation as well as of training. The whole scenery of society changed. Trade unions established themselves in many countries. In Britain and the United States, in particular, large numbers of voluntary bodies came into existence to organize 'charity' along with commercial agencies to dispense insurance. There was great variety of approach, even more so of philosophy. And in such a context political arguments about democracy were bound to be different in content and in tone from the debates of the late 18th century.

The political parties which developed their own organizational strength during the second half of the 19th century had to pay increasing attention to social issues—justice as much as liberty—even when such issues did not figure prominently in the minds of all their leaders and even in those cases when party members feared rather than hoped that the extension of the franchise would be the prelude to economic and social reforms. Although women did not get the vote in any European country during the 19th century, the extended franchise was the basis of late 19th-century

politics, the timing of extension varying from country to country, and even in those countries where there was little or no extension—a disparate group, including Denmark and Sweden as well as Portugal and Roumania—the interests of non-electors could not be overlooked by governments. In such circumstances 'liberalism' was in need of regular redefinition. So, too, was the most basic of all the inherited political terms 'the state'.

The powers of the state varied from country to country. 'The state,' it was enunciated in the preamble to the first of Bismarck's measures to promote national insurance, 'is not merely a necessary but a beneficent institution.' 'The more the state does for the citizen,' maintained the first Minister of Labour in New Zealand (one of the century's new countries, as different from Bismarck's Germany as any country could be) 'the more it fulfils its purpose. . . . The functions of the state should be extended as much as possible. . . . True democracy consists in the extension of state activity.' In Britain—with no standing army and with a long tradition of local decentralization—the word 'state' did not belong to most people's working vocabulary. Yet in Britain, too, which was often thought of by foreigners and by some Englishmen themselves as the citadel of *laissez-faire,* there was an overlap from the 1830s onwards between the discarding of old forms of traditional protectionism and the introduction of new modes of intervention. Thus, the corn laws, which protected landlords and farmers, disappeared in 1846, while a Ten Hours Bill regulating hours of labour in factories was carried in 1847 and a Public Health Act in 1848. By the end of the 19th century throughout Europe there were ample signs that the state could not exist simply as a 'night-watchman' guarding private property, but that it would be expected (with the help of experts and a more expensive administrative apparatus) to concern itself directly with the welfare of its citizens. In such circumstances, the role of the family, the basic 19th-century social institution, would be bound to change also. With the rise of industrialization it had already been changing in a factory district such as Lancashire, in which bread-winning economic roles were segregated from other family roles. Now in mature industrial society it was to begin to lose some of its welfare functions, although the process of loss was to be gradual rather than catastrophic.

The spread of industrialization

Cumulative changes were associated at almost every point with the rise and diffusion of industrialization: they are far from easy to date precisely. Already, however, in 1848, a year when the chart of political revolution can be meticulously plotted week by week, John Stuart Mill (1806–73), the British philosopher and economist, wrote perceptively that 'whatever may be the other changes which the economy of society is destined to undergo, there is one actually in progress, concerning which there can be no dispute. In the leading countries in the world, and in all others as they come within the influence of these leading countries, there is at least one progressive movement which continues with little interruption from year to year and from generation to generation: a progress in wealth, an advancement of what is called material prosperity. All the nations which we are accustomed to call civilized increase gradually in production and in population; and there is no reason to doubt that . . . most of the other nations of the world, including some not yet founded, will successively enter upon the same career.'

Three years after Mill, a supremely British writer brought up as a strict utilitarian, had surveyed current and future world-wide trends, British industrialists were given an unprecedented opportunity to display their leadership in industrialization at the Great Exhibition of 1851. The Crystal Palace, constructed of iron and glass, was a symbol both of the practical skill and the romance of industrialization. The Exhibition was deliberately planned to be international, to display 'the Works of Industry of all Nations'. As Alfred Tennyson (1809–92), the poet of modernity and one of the many poets to write verses about 1851, exclaimed proudly:

> *. . . lo! the giant aisles*
> *Rich in model and design;*
> *Harvest-tool and husbandry,*

Loom and wheel and enginery,
Secrets of the sullen mine,
Steel and gold, and coal and wine,
Fabric rough or fairy-fine . . .
And shapes and hues of Art divine!
All of beauty, all of use,
That one fair planet can produce.

Within the planet Britain was undoubtedly the main workshop, the centre of innovation, the hive of industry, the country which had *not* undergone political revolution in 1848.

Yet such a state of affairs could not last. By 1900 Britain was certainly no longer the workshop of the world, although she was still the world's main exporter, customer and financier. It is just as essential, therefore, in describing the shape of the 19th century to explain the difference in Britain's position during the first and second halves of the century as it is to explain the differences in France's place in relation to revolutionary political movements before and after 1848. 1848 and 1851 are useful vantage points, provided that it is borne in mind first that the revolutions of 1848 were followed by the repressions of 1849 and second that within three years of 1851, when the gospel of peace was proclaimed at the Crystal Palace along with the gospel of work, Britain and France alongside the Ottoman Empire were at war with Russia in the distant Crimea (1854–6). The rhetoric was more effective than the conduct of military operations, as is shown in Chapter VII of this book. 'We are not now engaged in the Eastern Question,' one British politician claimed, 'but in the battle of civilization against barbarism, for the independence of Europe.'

It was during the middle years of the century that Europe profited from Britain's example and emulated many of the British triumphs of industrialization. This was the period, indeed, when all the developments of the early years of industrialization reached their climax. Fifty thousand new miles of railway were laid in Europe between 1850 and 1870 to augment and link the 15,000 miles already there in 1850. Coal production rose sharply, particularly in the Ruhr area, continental Europe's first great industrial zone (1850: 1,640,000 tons; 1870 nearly 12 million tons). So, too, did the production of iron ore. In consequence, there were changes in the European balance. Slow to industrialize, France was less able to profit from carboniferous capitalism than Germany. The Paris of Napoleon III glittered and there was an ostentatious display of new wealth, most of it derived from finance and construction, but France was never again in the 19th century to enjoy the real power advantages which she had exploited during the rule of Napoleon I. If Britain led the way industrially during the first half of the century, Germany, after the unification of 1870, followed with its own industrial revolution during the second half of the century. This was to pose problems not only for France but for Britain. Between 1870 and 1900 world industrial production is said to have increased four times. Yet while real income per head continued to rise in Britain at a rate of between 17 and 25 per cent a decade, the British economy was neither as resilient nor as adaptable as it had been during the early stages of the industrial revolution. The owners or managers of old industries were cautious in their investment programmes and less adventurous in their marketing policies: new science-based industries were slow to emerge. There was already talk of Britain's lead having turned into a handicap: a more recent description is Britain's 'climacteric'.

During the late 19th-century phases of industrialization, when several countries, notably Germany, the United States and—a new portent—Japan, underwent 'industrial revolutions' of their own, there were three new aspects of industrialization which were transforming the picture yet again. First, science was coming to count for more and 'empiricism' for less in the technology, organization and development of industry. Some of the implications of this theme are treated more fully in the last chapter of this book. Second, iron gave way to steel—steel and its alloys—within the technological complex. Steel, a more sophisticated product than iron, harder, more tensile and stronger, had been in scarce supply in 1850. Output increased eight times between 1850

and 1870, and by 1900 both Germany and the United States were producing more steel than Britain. Third, new forms of power were being developed. The technological possibilities of the steam engine had been almost fully exploited before the last three decades of the century, and the future lay with the turbine—Charles Parsons produced the first steam turbine in 1884—the internal combustion motor, and electricity. The first public electric power station was opened in Britain in 1881, but Britain was to benefit less from the progress of electrification than many other countries. Already by 1900, carboniferous capitalism was giving way to new forms of organization, bigger in scale, more complex in structure, dependent on new and still rapidly changing technologies.

The place of Germany in the European economy during the last decades of the 19th century deserves as much attention as her place in the international political system. During the first half of the 19th century Germany, still disunited, had been renowned above all for its scholars, thinkers, poets and musicians. Romanticism, another of the *isms* of the period, which will be discussed at many points in this book and more fully below, was inextricably associated in Germany with nationalism. 'History is the self-consciousness of a nation,' A. W. von Schlegel (1767–1845) proclaimed, looking back, as many Germans did, to an ancient inheritance. Yet with the unification of Germany, achieved as a result of Bismarck's political realism, Germany looked forward to an ambitious future. Coal and iron played as big a part in the shaping of that future as blood and iron had done in the achievement of national unification. So, too, did the application of science to industry, in which Germany was more advanced than Britain. German capital equipment, smaller in scale and less efficient than British equipment in 1850, grew remarkably both in size and in performance, outstripping that of Britain during the last decades of the century. There was more capital and less waste, and there was a far more efficient educational system. At the same time, Germany began to emerge after 1870 as Britain's most formidable competitor in international markets. From 1875 to 1895, while the value of British exports stood still—volume rose substantially—the value of German exports rose by 30 per cent and volume correspondingly more. Britain retained her position as the world's greatest commercial power throughout the century, but the industries on which she had most depended earlier in the century—notably textiles—were more and more vulnerable. British coal production remained higher throughout the century than that of Germany or of the United States, but fears had long been expressed about British dependence, particularly in the export trade, on a diminishing natural asset. Coal, indeed, seemed in the long run to have more of the qualities of blood than of bread. 'A nation which exports coal,' wrote one journalist, 'is not really selling anything: it is draining itself of its life blood.'

The German industrial revolution differed significantly from the British in two other respects. First, the banking system played a more active part in industrial growth, setting the pace and helping to determine the structure. Second, the state itself was directly involved, a participant rather than a spectator. 'It was clearly those governments,' wrote Gustav Schmoller (1838–1917), Professor of Economics at Berlin in 1884, 'which understood how to put the weight of their fleets and their admiralties, the apparatus of customs, laws and navigation laws, with rapidity, boldness and clear purpose at the service of the economic interests of the nation and the state which obtained thereby the lead in the struggle and the riches of industrial prosperity.' In Japan, also, the first Asian country to industrialize, the same philosophy held. The Japanese government, keen to modernize during the 1880s and 1890s, made up for the lack of a sizeable entrepreneurial class by performing many of the functions of such a class and by facilitating the accomplishment of the remaining functions by the employment of deliberately planned monetary, fiscal and educational policies. Industrialization, therefore, was carried out within different frameworks from that of the 'classical' British industrial revolution. There was to be not one model of growth but several, one of the most important of them, that of communism, to be reserved for the 20th century.

'*Railway mania*' *reached its peak in England in the 1840s. Each scheme had to be submitted to a Parliamentary committee and rights were then granted to a specially formed company. A successful railway could mean a fortune for those who had invested in it. This German cartoon shows English promoters desperately bringing their schemes on the final day for presentation.*

What happened in 19th-century Russia and the United States, where there was a complete transformation of economic life after the Civil War (1861–65), is described more fully in Chapter VIII and IX. Even in the briefest preliminary survey, however, both countries must be fitted in. Russia, where the serfs were not emancipated until 1861, was already advancing towards industrialization during the last two decades of the 19th century, building railways faster than any other country—the Trans-Siberian railway, started in 1891, was completed in 1905—and opening up, with the full encouragement of the state, not only coal mines and iron foundries but oil wells. Two-and-a-half million workers were employed in industry and transport by 1900. Industrial output had trebled within fifteen years. There was even more spectacular growth in the United States. Vast natural resources began to be exploited actively as the great transcontinental railways were built. Steel output surpassed that of Britain by 1886, coal by 1900. There was a far more rapid rate of technological change than in Britain, more willingness to increase the amount of capital per man, more eagerness to scrap obsolescent equipment. Consumer industries were quick to grow also, although the key figures in the growth of the economy were vigorous, often ruthless, businessmen, tycoons, even 'robber barons', many of whom had made their fortunes out of railway building.

By 1900, British businessmen fitted comfortably into a society where tradition and enterprise had been reconciled: many of them had bought land and acquired titles. In the United States, where a new and distinctive 'achieving society' was emerging, a society in which government had to fight hard if it was to check, let alone control, business set the terms, often harshly, of both economic and social development. Businessmen were the leading men of the country. The system, for all its drive never, of course, lacked its critics. 'What I object to,' says one of the characters in W. D. Howells' *A Hazard of New Fortunes* (1889), 'is this economic chance-world in which we live. . . . It ought to be law as inflexible in human affairs as the order of day and night in the physical world, that if a man will work he shall both rest and eat, and shall not be harassed with any question as to how his repose and provision

shall come.' For all the advance in industrialization and the rise of real income in an 'economy of abundance', little had been done among the 'people of plenty', as the Americans had now established themselves, to provide minimum social security.

Population and prices

The development of the United States is explicable only in terms of immigration as well as of industrialization or of urbanization. In Europe and in the United States, indeed, some of the hardest of all 19th-century facts, difficult though they were to explain, were the population statistics. European population grew from 187 millions in 1800 to 274 millions in 1850 and 400 millions in 1900. Different countries grew at different rates—France, in particular, very slowly —but all grew. Between 1800 and 1850 Britain led the way, as she led the way in industrialization; between 1850 and 1900 Germany. Russia, which was as late in collecting population statistics as she was in industrializing, grew rapidly throughout the century. The economic and political implications of these hard demographic facts pose almost as many difficulties as their explanation. Yet there was no doubt of their fascination to contemporaries from T. R. Malthus (1766–1834) and his predecessors onwards. 'The fall of the Roman Empire, what was that?' a character in Disraeli's novel *Sybil* (1845) demands. 'Every now and then there came two or three thousand strangers out of the forests and crossed the mountains and rivers. They come to us in every year, and in greater numbers. What are your invasions of the barbarous nations, your Goths and your Visigoths, your Lombards and Huns to our population returns?'

At the beginning of the 19th century, Malthus in one of the most influential books of the period, the *Essay on Population* (first edition, 1798), which cast its shadow over subsequent history, had argued that population must inevitably outgrow subsistence. His *Essay*, designed to refute the optimistic or even utopian assumptions about the future of mankind which were common in the thinking of the Enlightenment, was used in a new industrial society to provide moralizing arguments for keeping down the size of poor families and keeping benevolence out of the poor laws. The poor were doomed to linger on the brink of starvation. Yet as population grew, the gloomy prophecies of Malthus were not fulfilled. In Britain itself, where commentators on agriculture had noted in the late 18th century ample signs of what Arthur Young, the most prolific of the commentators, called 'consumption, activity and animation', output kept pace with population growth until the 1880s when cheap imports of food and materials began to pour in from overseas. The increase in agricultural output in 1880 had been achieved by roughly the same labour force as in 1800 (1·7 millions), although as a proportion of the total national labour force those working in agriculture had fallen from 35·9 to 12·6 per cent and agricultural output, which had provided 40 per cent of the national product in 1800, now provided only 10 per cent.

Such a response in Britain must be set alongside the varying responses in other countries to population growth and to the rise of industry—a theme of Chapter V of this book—and it must be related also to the even more dramatic story of modern scientific agriculture and the mass production of food for international markets. The United States led the way in this bigger 'agricultural revolution'. The virgin lands of the Middle West offered unprecedented opportunities for mechanized agriculture. The opportunities were taken by hard-working and resourceful farmers, some of whose large-scale farms might be as big as one of Europe's smaller states. What was happening in the United States during the last decades of the 19th century was happening in other parts of the world also. On the immense plains of the Argentine, cattle were reared for meat in immense numbers; and, given good facilities for refrigeration (available from the late 1870s and 1880s), meat could be exported at competitive low prices across the Atlantic to the markets of Europe. Meat was also produced in Australia and New Zealand: indeed, in the year 1900 New Zealand alone exported four million frozen lamb and sheep carcases to Britain, along with enough dairy products to stock booming retail stores in every large English town. Agricultural 'mass production' had begun with wheat. Already by 1900, however, it had spread to a wide range of agricultural products, most of them grown in highly specialized areas where climatic or soil conditions seemed especially favourable—sugar, tea, cocoa, coffee, fruit. There was a migration of plants as well as of people. Moreover, many articles which had been on display as exotic oddities or as expensive luxuries at exhibitions held earlier in the century were now readily obtainable in markets and shops.

The effect of this 'consumption, activity and animation' on a world scale was the achievement of a remarkable degree of economic interdependence, through transport, communications in general, finance, investment and marketing. The invention of the steamship was not the least of the triumphs of steam. The first steamships crossed the Atlantic in 1838; and while in 1851 there were still only 185,000 tons of steam shipping registered in Britain, again the technical pioneer, as against 3·66 million tons of wooden ships under sail, by the end of the century 75 per cent of British ships (which together accounted for nearly half the world's total shipping tonnage) were driven by steam. The telegraph, first used in conjunction with railways, pointed to a new international technology, and telegraphic communication across the Atlantic, first established in 1858, became a matter of routine after the laying of a new cable in 1865. The opening of the Suez Canal in 1869 and the complex arguments about the building of a Panama Canal (not officially opened to traffic until 1914) revealed that new routes were being created as well as new rhythms of speedy communication:

> *Speak the word and think the thought,*
> *Quick 'tis as with lightning caught—*
> *Over, under, lands or seas*
> *To the far Antipodes.*

Yet even as it was encircled, the world remained divided: just as social communication was never fully established between class and class or nation and nation, so the 'contacts' between one part of the world and another were often superficial. There was an assumption throughout the last years of the century (no more fully explored, perhaps, than most of the assumptions about class and nation) that the world, like Europe itself, was divided by inexorable market forces or by Providence or by both into manufacturing and agricultural or primary product zones, the 'black' and the 'green'. The split between western and eastern Europe, described in more detail in Chapter V, was wide enough for one French writer to talk of 'Europe A' and 'Europe B', each with its own identity. The split outside Europe was even more obvious. Sometimes, it was thought of as the split between 'centre' and 'periphery' or 'rim': sometimes more profoundly as a contrast between different levels of development, psychological as well as economic or social. The export of capital (for railways, mines, ports and plantations) was an indispensable lever of unparalleled world economic growth, yet it entailed patterns of dependence as well as networks of interdependence not only in the formal empires which were painted in European colours on the maps but in Latin America and Asia. Interdependence as it was conceived of by people in countries with a manufacturing surplus might be viewed differently by people in primary producing countries where wages were low, living standards were inadequate, even in bare subsistence terms, and where because of international specialization, dictated from outside, there was a high degree of vulnerability to plant disease, harvest failure, exhaustion of materials or financial and economic crisis. The world was growing richer, but the paradoxes of poverty in the midst of plenty were known to late 19th-century critics, even if their full social and political implications were to emerge only in the 20th century.

In the meantime, while the effects of population pressure were not felt in most tropical countries, population increased in the new areas of overseas settlement even more dramatically than it increased in Europe itself. Overseas migration from Europe was at its height during the last thirty years of the 19th century, when 21 million people left Europe, half of them bound for the United States, half for Latin America, Canada, South Africa, Australia and New Zealand. Some of the emigrants returned: others helped to create new cities and to populate new countrysides. The United

Overpopulation: George Cruikshank's gloomy view of the future etched in 1851.

States, in particular and unlike Australia and New Zealand, attracted immigrants from almost every kind of old-world society. Germany, Britain and Ireland still provided the main source of supply when the Civil War ended. But during the 1880s and 1890s there was a huge influx from southern, eastern and central Europe. Italians, Slavs and East European Jews made their distinctive contributions to a pattern of American life which was still in flux. 'In the heart of the continent,' Daniel Boorstin has written, 'arose a new *homo Americanus* more easily identified by his mobility than by his habitat.' The new men included natural 'transients' and the politically 'uprooted'. Alongside Disraeli's comment about the European population returns of the 1840s or 20th-century comment about the populations of India and Indonesia should be set the lines engraved on the base of the Statue of Liberty in 1886:

> *Give me your tired, your poor,*
> *Your huddled masses yearning to breathe free,*
> *The wretched refuse of your teeming shore.*

The United States was often described as a 'melting pot': to most of its immigrants, however, it was a land of opportunity and hope.

It claimed to be dedicated to the making of 'better men': 'it is good to be shifty in a new country'. Although there were critics in America itself who complained that the free flow of immigrants served mainly to produce a docile labour force or political fodder for unscrupulous 'city bosses', the raw material for exploitation, corruption and crime, there was continuing pride (as well as alarm) in the process. 'The American people . . . diffuses itself, its energy and its capital, over a whole continent.' Characteristic of the times was the comment of a writer in the 1890s that 'only two cities in the German Empire, Berlin and Hamburg, have a greater German population than Chicago; only two in Sweden, Stockholm and Göteborg, have more Swedes; and only two in Norway, Christiania and Bergen, more Norwegians.' Not surprisingly, Chicago was the home of urban sociology. It was as much the 'shock city' of the 1890s as Manchester had been of the 1840s.

The facts of city life are set out more fully in Chapter IV of this book, but there is one other set of facts which provided a framework for 19th-century experience: movements in prices. Given the immense upsurge in production and in population and the increasing interdependence of world trade, there were complex and still controversial 'mechanisms'—though this is obviously an inadequate word—linking them together. Exported capital, the basis of the development of new lands, had its gestation period, dependent on its use and its location, which meant that decisions taken in one part of the century might take a considerable length of time to generate their full effects. Domestic industrialization, as we have seen, also produced long-term gains as well as immediate strains and stresses. In general, the 19th century was a period of falling prices, although there was a sharp rise in prices during the Revolutionary and Napoleonic Wars and a shorter price rise during the middle years of the century. There had been no period before with quite the same record. It was the gain in industrial productivity which lay behind the price fall, a fall which took place in a period of relative peace in Europe as well as of population growth. Costs fell both in industry and in agriculture. Prices as a whole were 40 per cent lower in the early 1890s than in the early 1870s, 'the convulsion of prosperity', when prices reached their 19th-century heights. The price of steel rails, for example, fell by 60 per cent in Europe between 1872 and 1881, and the price of wheat in Britain fell by a half between 1871 and 1895.

It is necessary, of course, to relate price movements to movements in interest rates and in profits and money wages if the economic history of the period is to be fully understood, but in relation to what may be called the general history of the period, the broad movement as a whole was what mattered. During the last decades of the century, as profit margins fell in a period of increasing international competition, farmers often suffered severely but consumers benefited. There was severe unemployment in particular years and a sense of 'depression' among businessmen, but new inventions were being introduced which looked forward to our own century and enabled further cost reductions to be made in a later period. The fall in international commodity prices during the period from the late 1870s to the mid-1890s certainly meant that the real wages of the employed workingman rose. During hard times, when unemployment was high, there was severe strain on the least well-off sections of the community, but such times were probably never quite as hard as the years of social tension earlier in the century when food prices reached their peaks and large numbers of workers were out of jobs. It had been an axiom earlier in the century, half-true though the axiom may have been, that 'you can never agitate a man on a full stomach'. During the last part of the century trade-union agitation, in particular, was often associated with good times, when labour's bargaining power was great, and more highly developed and persistent political organization made for greater continuity between good and bad times and fewer of the feverish, if sporadic, bursts of 'agitation' which had characterized the first decades of the century.

Europe and the world

Before examining more carefully the main contours of the 19th century, political as well as economic, and considering different aspects of change in relation to each other, it is essential to emphasize European ascendancy. The main lever of the ascendancy was economic, the pull of profit, but the desire to explore, the urge to Christianize or to 'civilize' and even the will to dominate played their part also. The deliberate quest for empire was less significant. For much of the 19th century there was little or limited interest in colonization as such; and even when formal empires grew rapidly, as they did, during the period between 1883 and the outbreak of the First World War, fourteen years after the end of the century, 'informal' empire, as we have seen, continued to grow with them. Mastery of the seas, knowledge of more advanced and still advancing technology, assumptions of social (even biological) superiority and in the last resort fire power (see Chapter VII) made possible unprecedented exploration and expansion.

For the Europeans, who fashioned a new geography, this was an age of discovery. The lure of Africa, the 'unknown' or 'dark' continent, was strong enough in the middle and late decades of the century to stir almost every section of European opinion from academic and philanthropic societies to avid readers of novels of romance, adventure and escape, from businessmen working in dingy city offices to civil servants and politicians preparing papers for cabinets. The stirring might be superficial and the anxiety to avoid embroilments as great as the drive to acquire new materials or territories. Yet it was difficult during the last forty years of the 19th century to ignore Africa, image or reality. America, which had ended the 18th and begun the 19th century with assertions of independence, was caught up also in the world network as seen from Europe: the North, which had risen to world significance as part of an Atlantic economy, which still survived in new forms, provided increasingly severe competition: the South, divided as it was into states of unequal power and resources, provided what economists would call 'complementarity'—raw materials on which Europe depended (particularly chemicals), food, markets and outlets for lucrative, if often highly speculative, investment. Asia, a continent where ancient religions and cultures were never eradicated, provided resistance, at least intermittently, but it was resistance on very unequal terms, as the British showed in the brief Chinese Wars (1839–42; 1857) and in their suppression of the Indian 'mutiny' (the term itself was indicative of the relationships) in 1857. British rule in India might be described by Macaulay as 'the strangest of all political anomalies', a military empire which was established in an unimperial age, a commitment 'dubiously balanced', as Eric Stokes has put it, 'by its actual commercial value to English industry'. Yet its existence had a profound effect on Victorian Britain and helped to set the terms of British relations with Russia, the great land power of the 19th century, a power which pursued throughout the century its own course of expansion across plains, mountains and lakes into Asia. By the end of the century the geopolitical element in 19th-century geography was apparent even for the general public to discern.

The making of empire is for us perhaps the most contentious of 19th-century issues. Indeed, the idea of empire always had its enemies as well as its friends in Europe. Yet the bare 'facts' by themselves were part of the 19th-century battery of facts, however protracted the arguments about empire might be. Whereas at the end of the 18th century the old colonial empires were in retreat, and commercial monopoly, the theoretical foundation of mercantilist empire, was out of fashion, at the end of the 19th century in an age of competition and economic rivalry the new tropical empires were in full advance. While the beginning of a new century was being celebrated in 1900 and 1901, Britain, the greatest imperial power, was engaged in a war in South Africa, where the main issues centred on the 'white inheritance'. Between 1800 and 1878 Europe added around 6,500,000 square miles to the territories painted in European colours on the maps. Between then and 1914 in an almost unbroken sequence of conquest a further 8,600,000 square miles were added. In 1800 Europe and its old colonies of settlement covered about 55 per cent of the land surface of the world; in 1878, 67 per cent; and in 1914 nearly 85 per cent. Sometimes—most often, indeed—the pressures to expand came from the 'periphery': sometimes—mainly, indeed, after 1883, when Bismarck made a 'bid for colonies'—the pressures came from inside Europe itself, a Europe at peace, if an uneasy peace, with

itself. The 'partition' of Africa depended on 'equilibrium' in
Europe. New claims were staked when it was difficult to stake new
claims in Europe or to challenge the power decisions which had
been taken inside Europe between 1850 and 1880.

The psychology of 'the lords of creation' has recently been re-
assessed in the light of 20th-century world history. Behind the
self-assurance there was occasionally uneasiness, even guilt. Yet
there were dreamers as well as practical men amongst them,
dreamers like Cecil Rhodes (1853–1902), who conceived of a
corridor of British-controlled territories across Africa and judged
every local crisis in Southern Africa in terms of bigger and wilder
schemes of expansion, economically lucrative and psychologically
satisfying. There were also 'pro-consuls' who treated imperial
possessions as laboratories for experiments in political and social
organization. Little-mindedness and big-mindedness could go together: imagination was deployed as well as, if less frequently than,
interest or calculation. In retrospect, it was the interim quality of
what was achieved which stands out, even in relation to the French
control of Algeria—Algiers had been taken in 1830 when France,
checked in Europe by the Vienna settlement, thrust south from
growing Marseilles out across the Mediterranean—or the short-
lived German interest in the Pacific or control of parts of Africa.
The word 'control' itself begged most of the questions. Wherever
Europeans went, they carried ideas and techniques as well as trade
and colonial institutions. There were complex 'culture contacts'
which were to produce unanticipated consequences. Only the
Russian land advance into Central Asia was to be fully consolidated,
but this advance, unlike the rest, except in the United States, was
through contiguous territories not through a scattered jumble of
disparate 'possessions'.

In the story of expansion, the images as well as the facts were
significant. The image of Africa, as has been pointed out convin-
cingly by Philip Curtin, was far more European than African.
Europeans for the most part did not ask 'What is Africa like, and
what manner of men live there?' but 'How does Africa, and how do
the Africans, fit into what we already know about the world?'
Richard Burton (1821–90), the explorer-anthropologist-writer,
liked the Arabs, about whom it was never difficult to have a
mystique, but generalized freely about the 'eternal restless suspicion' of Africans, their 'savage conservatism' and their dishonesty:
his *Lake Regions of Central Africa* (1860) is in this sense a characteristic, if an outstanding and outspoken, book of the century.
As far as Asia was concerned, there were always men and women
who were drawn to the ancient Asian religions and ways of life—
their numbers grew during the late 19th century—but there were
far more who propounded what to them was an unpalatable
myth of the 'unchanging East'. G. W. F. Hegel, the philosopher
(1770–1831), discerned in India 'the charm of the Flower-life', 'a
Garden of Love', but concluded that 'the more attractive the first
sight of it had been, so much the more unworthy shall we ultimately find it in every respect'; Marx pointed to 'Oriental
despotism' restraining the human mind within the smallest
possible compass in an 'undignified, stagnatory and vegetative
life' broken only by 'wild, aimless, unbounded forces of destruction'; the sociologist, Max Weber (1864–1920), turning to China,
dwelt on the 'extraordinary and unusual horror of all unknown and
not immediately apparent things which finds expression in in-
eradicable distrust'.

Within this context of thinking and feeling as much as in the
context of events, the non-European world was not allowed to
exist confidently in its own right or to figure as an area of autonomous change. Yet there were changes taking place in all the
continents which were not usually fully discerned at the time.
In Latin America, where the early dreams of independent unity
which followed emancipation were very quickly shattered—
Bolivar (1783–1830), the 'Great Liberator', was as much of a
dreamer as Rhodes—Brazil, which completed the achievement of
its independence in 1823, remained a unified monarchy, almost
equal to the United States in area, until 1889. During the 1880s its
population increased five times, slavery was abandoned as an
economic and social system, the monarchy was transformed into
a republic, and attempts were made to industrialize. The new flag

*The meeting of Stanley and Livingstone in Central Africa on November 10th,
1871, was an episode that caught public imagination. Here the two men receive
Arabs outside their house. African exploration had many of the qualities of a
Romantic quest: remoteness, exoticism, the lure of the unknown. The complete
reality, as Stanley's own books make clear, was more sordid and more disturbing.*

of the Republic bore the motto of Auguste Comte (1798–1857),
the French Positivist and pioneer of sociology, 'Order and Progress'. Across the Pacific Japan went through a more publicized
transformation. The transfer of power in 1868 and 1869 from the
Tokugawa family of *shoguns* (feudal rulers) to a group of new men
who looked to the boy-Emperor Meiji was the culmination of
complex historical processes. Its consequences were dramatic.
Japan was opened up to the West by the Japanese themselves, but
they took from the West what they themselves wanted—techniques, institutions, codes of law, fiscal and economic ideas,
education, communications. Germany, France, Britain and the
United States all provided models. Industrial growth was more
rapid than that of any other state in Asia. Silk and cotton textiles
provided 22 per cent of exports in 1900, but plans were moving
ahead for the opening of a government-financed large-scale iron
works. Already more than 30 per cent of ships entering Japanese
ports were Japanese-owned. Large family trusts, like the Mitsuis,
an old family, or the Mitsubishis, a new one, carved out economic
empires, modern in their organization and drive, feudal in their
flavour, involving banking, transport, manufacture and distribution. The Japanese had many admirers in the West, and they grew
in numbers after the Japanese defeated the Chinese in the War of
1894–95 (the Mitsubishis not only provided the ships but had
established strong interests in Korea and China before the War
started) and signed an alliance with the British in 1902. Parallels
were being drawn, indeed, between the positions of the British in
their islands off the mainland of Europe and the Japanese with an
expanding sphere of interest.

Throughout the 19th century the oldest of the empires, China,
played little part in the processes of change, except as a centre of
resistance, while the Ottoman Empire, now 'the sick man of
Europe', if not finally partitioned, as some Western statesmen
hoped, lost in territory, influence and prestige. The opening up of
the Chinese ports to Western trade did not mean the opening up of
China. Rebellions, murders, massacres (notably that at Tientsin in
1870) and succession crises accompanied the rise to power and the
ascendancy which followed of the Dowager Empress Tz'u Hsi
(1834–1908). The century ended in confusion. A brief period of
reform, urgently necessary reform after the defeat by Japan and
relentless pressure from Western countries to secure new concessions, ended abruptly with the restoration of the power of
Tz'u Hsi in 1898; and during the last two years of the century
disturbances associated with the 'Boxer' movement, a militant sect,
imperilled all Western interests in China. Foreign legations in
Peking summoned troops to their assistance in May 1900. In

June the Boxers, with many allies at the imperial court, entered Peking in force and burned down churches and molested foreigners, and after foreign naval parties had captured Chinese forts at Tientsin, which the Boxers had cut off from Peking, China declared war on the Western powers. Throughout July there was little clarification of the position. The Empress vacillated and veered, the Southern viceroys of the Empire refused to associate themselves with the war, and rumours of every kind spread. In August foreign forces entered Peking, and Tz'u Hsi, disguised as a Chinese peasant, accompanied by other members of the imperial family, fled in carts from the royal palace. Negotiations continued in 1901. No 19th-century novelist in the great age of the novel could have concocted a more colourful or more lurid plot with which to bring the 'wonderful century' to a close. Yet this was not the whole of the Chinese story. While millions of European emigrants (with some Chinese amongst them) were flocking across the Atlantic during the last decades of the century, Chinese migrants were firmly establishing themselves as indispensable merchants and middlemen throughout South-East Asia, forming in the process self-contained communities with growing wealth and sophisticated culture. Within the heart of the Western empires, therefore, in such countries as the Malay Settlements, the land of rubber and tin, or the far-flung islands of the Dutch East Indies, the Chinese had their place in the 19th-century pattern, as the Indians did in Fiji. In Trinidad there was the most remarkable mixture of peoples— African, European, Indian and Chinese.

Universal and national patterns: old and new styles

Similar intermeshing can be traced both in the design of objects— they are recorded in the catalogues of successive international exhibitions and of business firms—and in architectural styles. The exhibitions from 1851 onwards were usually deliberately international, designed as 'great occasions' to impress through their catalogues and through their coverage in newspapers and periodicals even those people who could not visit them. New York built its own Crystal Palace in 1853; Paris held great exhibitions in 1855, 1862, 1867, 1889 (the Eiffel Tower remained as an imposing permanent legacy) and 1900 (when there were 30 million visitors); Vienna tried to outbid everyone else in 1873; distant but booming Melbourne challenged 'provincialism' at its exhibitions of 1880 and 1888; Philadelphia was the centre of a great exhibition in 1876 to celebrate the centenary of the American Declaration of Independence; and Chicago went one better in 1893 when its huge World's Columbian Exposition near the shore of Lake Michigan paid homage not only to the triumphs of the century but also to Christopher Columbus.

Exhibition architecture was usually less interesting than Exhibition bric-à-brac. It was certainly less interesting than Exhibition engineering, and Smiles was right and characteristic of his times in picking out engineers, particularly the civil engineers who seemed to be imposing their sense of order on a developing world, as heroes of 19th-century society. Yet the history of architectural styles in the 19th century also must be studied in its world context. The Greek-versus-Gothic skirmish, with its 18th-century background, was fought in many countries, with the Greeks winning handsomely in North America and in Russia, while, long before the skirmishes were over, what A. W. N. Pugin (1812–52), the formidable and dedicated English spokesman of one single style, the Gothic, called 'the carnival of architecture' was already on universal display.

The relevant exhibits may still be compared—for example Cologne's Gothic cathedral, completed under the auspices of the *Domverein*, founded in 1840, and Budapest's Gothic Parliament House (1885–1902); Scotland's 'new Balmoral' (1853 onwards), Prince Albert's '*Schloss*', and Portugal's 19th-century rooms in the Palace of Pena outside Cintra—not to speak of Montenegro's royal palace at Cettinje; the neo-Baroque Paris Opera House, begun in 1861; the Monument of Victor Emmanuel in Rome (1884) and the Reichstag in Berlin (also 1884); 'Renaissance' derivatives, many of them 'freely treated', like Paris's Town Hall (begun in 1836), the castle at Schwerin in Germany (1844) or even the Law Courts at Birmingham (1887–91).

The carnival never closed. Indeed, a recent book by Paolo Portoghesi—*L'Eclettismo a Roma, 1876–1922* (1968)—traces the procession through the streets of 'the eternal city' far into the 20th century. There were, however, occasional attempts during the 19th century to assert the need for a specifically *new* style. 'In what style shall we build?' Heinrich Hübsch asked in 1834, and even during the 1850s Sir George Gilbert Scott (1811–78) was forced to ask whether or not it was 'morally' possible to invent a 'spick-and-span' new style. (Both the adverb and the adjective are as significant as the favourite expression 'freely treated' when applied to Renaissance architecture.) 'We cannot have one,' Scott concluded, because 'the particular characteristic of the present day is that we are acquainted with the history of art.' Eclecticism was thus very directly related to historicism, just as the 'architecture' of the engineers was directly related to the use of new materials. Twelve years before Gilbert Scott's comments, another English writer had anticipated the kind of answer Scott was to give while expressing it differently. 'Our age,' he exclaimed, 'has a very notable style of its own, and a very novel one, the style of this miscellaneous connoisseurship of ours, of instinct superseded by learning.'

The young Emperor of Japan, Meiji, took a leading part in encouraging the exchange of ideas with the West which helped foster Japan's rapid industrial growth. Here Europeans demonstrate their work before him at the foundry of the arsenal at Yokosuka.

Certainly in no previous century, in so many different countries, had there been such a relentless collecting, ransacking even, of most of the styles of the past, almost all of which acquired, nonetheless, an unmistakable 19th-century flavour in the process. 'It may well be doubted,' the writer of the official British report on the Vienna Exhibition of 1873 put it, 'whether the practical and the picturesque, the modern and the medieval, the East and the West will ever again mingle in one harmonious whole, with such equal aid from art and nature, as on the Prater of 1873, in the Buildings in the Park.' It was the mixing of styles even more than the reaction against 18th-century 'symmetry' or the preoccupation with elaborate decoration which accounted for the flavour. The element of carnival was almost always a matter of pride. The 18th century was rejected as 'uninteresting': the 'olden time' or the 'busy' present were quite deliberately preferred.

The ransacking encompassed things as well as styles—with archaeologists rushing to the ancient sites—one of them, Heinrich Schliemann (1822–90), amassing enough money in business to search after 1863 for the remains of Troy—and with Munich holding lavish international art shows in 1886 and 1888 which provided a model for other cities to copy. On the other side of the Atlantic, the newly founded Metropolitan Museum in New York hailed itself enthusiastically in 1870 as 'the greatest treasure house in the Western hemisphere'. It took the Americans far longer to appreciate the full significance of some of their own pioneering architecture, an architecture which owed little to foreign models, than it did to produce 'stately homes' bedecked with 'strange and costly toys of every era of civilization'. The proud citizens of late 19th-century Chicago would certainly have been surprised to read in a modern study of *The Rise of the Skyscraper* (1952) of 'the poison of the World's Fair' ruining its architect-impresario Daniel Hudson Burnham (1846–1912). Yet as John William Root (1850–91), one of the leading American pioneers, was already stating at the time, 'a new spirit of beauty is being developed and perfected. . . . Compare the best of our recent architecture . . . with the most pretentious buildings recently erected in Europe. In the American works we find strength and fitness and a certain spontaneity and freshness as of stately music, or a song in the green woods.' An earlier American pioneer, Henry Hobson Richardson (1838–86), has been hailed by Lewis Mumford as 'the first architect of distinction to face the totality of modern life', while Louis Sullivan (1856–1924), 'the Whitman of American architecture', tried to warn his contemporaries that 'a modern building could no more wear the dress of the classic than an architect could wear a peruke and a sword'.

Pedigrees

One particular late 19th-century cluster of styles influenced both objects and buildings. Just as the taste for the Gothic had expressed itself in the late 18th and early 19th centuries not only in restored castles and cathedrals but in novels, essays, pictures and furniture, so *Art Nouveau*, designed to break with mid-19th-century *pastiche*, spread from the graphic arts to other arts as it moved through Europe. With origins in the Britain of the 1880s, *Art Nouveau* was known variously as *Jugendstil* (the name of a magazine) in Germany, 'modern style' in France, *stile Liberty* (after London's store) in Italy, *Sezession* in Austria, where it arrived very late, and *Modernista* in Spain, where it was expressed in the magnificently original buildings of Antoni Gaudí (1852–1926). The undulating forms of *Art Nouveau* did not derive directly from any conception of structural necessity and were essentially decorative ideas imposed, often with a strong sense of fantasy, on a wide variety of materials. Yet because they broke with 'period imitation' and allowed for great originality, they looked to the 20th century.

In 'placing' the *Art Nouveau* movement in the history of taste, it is necessary to set alongside Gaudí's Cathedral of the Holy Family at Barcelona or the entrance arches to the Paris Metro system by the architect Hector Guimard (1867–1934) the 'simplified' chairs of Richard Riemerschmid (1868–1957), the glass and metal work of the American Louis C. Tiffany (1848–1933) and the furniture—and cutlery—of Charles Rennie Mackintosh (1868–1928).

There was no single literary influence on *Art Nouveau* com-

The main requirements of Victorian exhibition bric-à-brac were apparent ingenuity and 'prettiness'. This ornate 'furniture for a steamship on a new and condensed form'—shown in 1851—was lined with cork and, according to the makers, was 'immediately convertible into a floating life preserver . . . in the case of danger at sea'.

parable to the pervasive early 19th-century influence of the novels of Sir Walter Scott (1771–1832) which were rightly picked out by Charles Lock Eastlake in his *History of the Gothic Revival* (1872) as major influences on taste (including, for a time, costumes) throughout Europe. On the whole, it was the appearance of books rather than their contents which fascinated the devotees of *Art Nouveau*. (Oscar Wilde's Dorian Gray had nine copies of his favourite book bound in different colours and styles to suit his passing moods.) *Art Nouveau* posters, including the striking posters by Henri de Toulouse-Lautrec (1864–1901), carried very simple messages. By contrast, Eastlake, youngest member of a family devoted to 'taste making' (his book *Hints on Household Taste* (1869) was as popular in the United States as in Britain), dwelt rather on the appeal to the public of the involved details of Scott's plots. 'The fortunes of the Disinherited Knight, the ill-requited case of poor Rebecca, the very jokes of Wamba and the ditties of the Barefooted Friar did more for the Gothic Revival than all the labours of Carter and Rickman.' There was, nonetheless, a multiplicity of international influences, difficult to disentangle, on the making of *Art Nouveau*, influences which worked through words as well as images; and the early musical theory of Claude Debussy (1862–1918), with its conception of melody as 'arabesque', has been considered by Debussy's most perceptive biographer to be a 'reflection of the theories of the *Art Nouveau* movement'.

Part of the interest in tracing the history of 19th-century styles and tastes lies in comparing the different chronologies of development in different countries and in tracing the links between development in one place and in another. The great English artist J. M. W. Turner (1775–1851) was generally appreciated in France only in the late 19th century. Smiles was going out of fashion in Britain when he was most popular in Japan. By the time that *Art Nouveau* had established itself in continental Europe there was already a turn away from it in England. The outstanding 19th-century Russian novelists, including Feodor Dostoyevsky (1821–81), born in the same year as the great French novelist, Gustave Flaubert (1821–80), were not widely known in Britain until the 20th century. Exceptions were Ivan Turgenev (1818–83), whose *Fathers and Sons* (1862) could be quickly appreciated in all European countries, and Leo Tolstoy (1828–1910), whose life of withdrawal from the world after 1876 interested late 19th-century readers as much as his great prose epic *War and Peace* (1865–69). Dostoyevsky's *Crime and Punishment* first appeared in 1866 and *The Brothers Karamazov* in 1879–80, yet it was not until Mrs Constance Garnett translated them decades later that both readers and writers in the English-speaking world felt their tremendous impact.

Translation and travel both have their place, therefore, in the network of chronological connections. The seventeen volumes of Shakespeare's plays translated into German by A. W. Schlegel, the devoted disciple of Goethe, ensured that Shakespeare would stand out as a central figure in the German Romantic movement: the *Rubaiyat of Omar Khayyam*, translated from the Persian by Edward Fitzgerald (1809–83) and published in the same

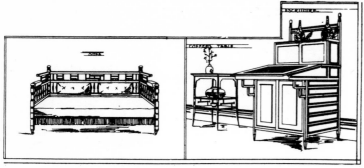

One of the influences which helped to purify design from the excesses of mid-Victorian ornament was that of Japan, known in Europe mainly from illustrations and exhibitions. This furniture, by Whistler's friend Edward Godwin dates from 1877.

year as *Self-Help*—1859—was hailed as a 'poetic transfusion from one language to another ... perfectly adapted to the new conditions of time, place, custom and habit of mind'. While the term 'transfusion' suggests a more direct process than experience usually warranted, there were certainly many cross references, many of them self-conscious. To take a quite different example, no history of 19th-century European 'tastes' would be complete without some consideration of the influence of Japan which was openly acknowledged, though it took different forms, not only by designers of *Art Nouveau* but by painters like Edgar Degas (1834–1917), Vincent van Gogh (1853–90) and James Whistler (1834–1903). Whistler's house in Chelsea, built and decorated in 1878 by his friend Edward Godwin (1833–86), with its sparse furnishings and its plain white and yellow walls, challenged established 19th-century tastes as much as any new American skyscraper.

Although few artists or writers actually visited Japan or travelled, like Paul Gauguin (1848–1903), to exotic places like Martinique and Tahiti, travel inside Europe by *trains rapides* or across the Atlantic by ocean steamboats influenced alike both artists and writers and their clients and readers. John Ruskin, it has been said, was more wedded to Venice than he was to his wife. The fate of the centre of Florence, where the claims of sanitary reform, a major 19th-century preoccupation, threatened the integrity of the historic core of the city during the 1880s, interested Englishmen at least as much as it interested the Florentines themselves. Thomas Cook (1808–92), the inventor of the 'business of travel' planned his first Continental tour in 1864. Where Englishmen led, others followed. Henry James (1843–1916) was not the only American to make an annual journey to what he called 'pluperfect Italy'. Of the Germans, it was written in 1887, 'with their newly-acquired wealth, their skill and general enterprise, [they] are ... almost the rivals in travel of the English. They spend nearly as much, they are almost as numerous ... and they are far more really accomplished travellers.' The Palazzo dell' Esposizione, opened in Venice for the first Biennale in 1895, was a contribution to tourism as well as to the arts.

Increasing travel did not always encourage genuine 'intercommunion of ideas'. Nor, of course, did translation or journalism: 'We *hear* about our neighbours far more than ever,' Frederic Harrison (1831–1923) complained in 1896. 'We have less *sympathy* with foreign thought, we have far less of the cosmopolitan genius than was common in the most fertile epochs of the human mind.' There sometimes seemed to be a marked contrast in this connection between 'the age of Enlightenment' and 'the age of nationalism', although in literature, at least, there was a carry-over between the two 'ages' both in styles and in objectives, even in the encyclopaedic casts of mind of writers like—if there ever was anyone quite like—Victor Hugo (1802–85). There were always men in the 19th century who claimed with the American Ralph Waldo Emerson that they could 'find Greece, Asia, Italy, Spain and the Islands—the genius and creative principle of each and all eras—in my own mind'. The Romantic poets during the first decades of the century, conscious of the limitations as well as of the opportunities of their own times, had dwelt on the power of poetry to

transcend all limitations of time and place, 'creating anew the universe' through what Percy Bysshe Shelley (1792–1822) called 'that imperial faculty, whose throne is contained within the invisible nature of man'; and the same message was proclaimed in the final movement of the Ninth Symphony (1824) by Ludwig van Beethoven (1770–1827) with its inspiring choral setting of the ode *An die Freude* by the poet Friedrich von Schiller (1759–1805).

At the same time, the whole theme of national cultural distinctiveness (which is discussed in its political context below) had been announced in 1800 in the influential *De la littérature considérée dans ses rapports avec les institutions sociales* by Madame de Staël (1766–1817). Apart from the artistic qualities of individual works of art, Madame de Staël suggested, whole national literatures might be said to have a common spirit or character. The same point was made more fully in Sismondi's *De la littérature du midi de l'Europe* (1813) by one of the first writers to appreciate the significance for the future of 'industrialism'.

By the end of the 19th century such conceptions of national cultural distinctiveness were commonplace. There is particular interest in the 19th century, therefore, in exploring variety within general patterns of thought and feeling—in distinguishing, for example, between French and German 'Romanticism', between French and British moral codes in the 'high noon' years of the mid-century, and between the Scandinavian and South European versions of 'innovation' and 'revolt' between 1870 and 1900. In one of the major universal arts, music, perhaps the most successful art of the century, national idiom came to be prized for itself. This was particularly true in a subject country such as Bohemia, where Bedrich Smetana (1824–84), who early in his career had been attacked by his fellow-countrymen as a 'neo-German', ended by writing six symphonic poems, *Ma Vlast*, which by their nature achieve their full effect only inside his own country. Already during the 1820s, when the first collection of Czech folk songs was published and the first Czech opera was performed on the stage, Frédéric Chopin (1810–49) had conceived of his Romantic music not only as an expression of his changing private moods but as a proud and defiant public expression of the spirit of Poland.

Time, place and immediacy

A necessary prelude to reading about the 19th century, a period of rich creative diversity, is to examine what survives both in the form of music and as a visual legacy. Yet there have been so many reactions and counter-reactions of tastes since the century ended (not to speak of hangovers and nostalgic revivals) that it is not easy to recapture what at the time were always co-existing, conflicting and changing 19th-century attitudes to tastes and styles. Labels like 'Romanticism', 'Victorianism', 'Aestheticism', 'Impressionism' or 'Modernism', all of which were being attached at some time during the century, do not always help either in the recovery of immediacy or in the task of discrimination, difficult though it is to do without them.

Even the sense of 'period' itself may be misleading. While it may be convenient to begin by dividing the century into three —'early' (pre-1848 or pre-Great Exhibition of 1851), 'middle' (1850s, 1860s and 1870s) and 'late' (on into the 20th century)— there were both 'breaks' and 'lags' which do not fit easily into such a scheme. The fall of Napoleon's Empire did not see the end of 'Empire' furniture or of 'Empire' costume. Romantic fashions were already going out when Queen Victoria came in. 1859, an *annus mirabilis* in literature which saw the publication not only of *Self-Help* and the *Rubaiyat* but of Victor Hugo's *La Légende des Siècles*, Mill's essay *On Liberty* and Charles Darwin's *Origin of Species*, has often been thought of as a 'break' within the middle period, the beginnings of a crisis of consciousness. The crinoline was established by 1856 and had at last disappeared before the fall of Napoleon III—and of Eugénie. It had an 'age' all of its own, and there were almost as many commentators on it as there were commentators on politics.

As for the 'lags', they are clearly traceable in the history of every 19th-century *ism*. Thus, for example, the germ of 'Impressionism' was present in Charles Nodier's travel reminiscences published in 1822, one year after he had visited a London Royal

Academy Exhibition at which *The Haywain*, the landscape painting by John Constable (1776–1837), was on display: 'Seen from close at hand,' Nodier wrote, 'it really consists of broad daubings of ill-laid colours which offend the touch as well as the sight . . . But seen from a distance of a few steps it becomes a picturesque piece of country, a rustic dwelling, a shallow river where little waves foam over the pebbles, a cart crossing a pond.' Nodier's praise encouraged an Anglo-French art dealer to transport *The Haywain* and two of Constable's other paintings to Paris and so excited the great French Romantic painter Eugène Delacroix (1798–1863) that under Constable's influence he repainted his picture *The Massacre at Chios*. It nevertheless took another half century for the techniques of 'Impressionism' to develop—there were many other influences on it, including developments in the science of light and of colour, and the invention of the camera—and for the name to be used (originally as a term of reproach). The first Impressionist exhibition of 1874 was bitterly ridiculed both by artists—including J. B. C. Corot (1796–1875), who himself played a part in the formulation of Impressionism—and by the public, and even by the time that the eighth Impressionist exhibition was held, this time with great success, in 1886, 'Impressionism', which never relied on manifestos, was still attracting only a minority of artists. Nineteenth-century anecdotal painting, moral in intent as it was so often, continued to appeal to a bigger public. At the first Venice Biennale, for example, the very titles of some of the pictures spoke for themselves—*Torturing Suspense (during the Operation of a dear Person), A Halt on the March of Banished Convicts in Siberia*, or, more simply, the picture which was most reproduced at the time, *The Duel*.

'Every picture tells a story'—and the story could be parable or puzzle—survived Impressionism and *Art Nouveau*. And if much of what is usually thought of as 'quintessentially' 19th-century belongs to the middle period of the century which had its own distinctive—though often compromised and always eclectic—curvaceous, often bulging, modes of expression, these modes must be related—through fashion and through advertising as well as through structural changes in society and culture—to what had happened before and what came later in art, architecture, literature and music. The long-term changes are obvious enough: the shift from aristocratic patronage (though it was not an eclipse, for aristocracies continued to set standards of taste in more than one country and in several arts, notably jewellery, retained much of their traditional influence); the great increase in the numbers of *parvenu* people with money to dispose of but with no education and with no inherited standards of taste—'You can't get high aesthetic tastes, like trousers ready made,' sung a character in *Patience* (1881) by W. S. Gilbert (1836–1911) and Arthur Sullivan (1842–1900); the growing use of 'brokers' and 'middle-men'—dealers, publishers, promoters, guides to tastes and manners, not to speak of food or 'household economy'; the belief in 'diffusion' (thought of as being almost as important as 'creation'). In 1845, Henry Cole (1808–82), a panegyrist of the new attitudes (he was also the main spokesman of the philosophy of the Great Exhibition of 1851 and the inventor of the Christmas card) coined the phrase 'Art Manufactures', and six years later another British writer professed that there were signs of a 'progress in the arts' similar to that in manners. Whereas art in the past had gratified the tastes of the few, now it served the wants of the many.

The multiplication of 19th-century objects in a more affluent society can be illustrated profusely, for there were almost as many categories of 19th-century things as there were different ways of designing, decorating, disguising or transposing the same thing. The period from 1840 to 1870 has rightly been described as 'the golden age of the fashion plate' with France leading the way and Britain, Germany and Italy copying. In Britain the prints of George Baxter (1804–67), reproduced by his process, patented in 1835, were extolled as 'equal to the finest productions of the old masters' with the additional merit of 'comparative cheapness'. What Baxter did for printing on paper Jesse Austen (1801–79) did for earthenware lids. Thomas Stevens (1828–88), among others, created elaborate machine-woven pictures. British 'Staffordshire' figures made their way around the world decorating the mantelpieces, often very

'*The English Milord upon the Rhine. How happy he looks!*' *says the original caption.* '*He dislikes the hum of men and sits all day shut up in his carriage reading the literature of his country.*' *More travel did not necessarily lead to a better understanding between peoples.*

imposing mantelpieces indeed, not only of Canadians and Australians but of Italians (Garibaldi was a favourite figure) and even Turks. Louis Antoine Jullien (1812–60), son of a French headmaster, opened shops in New York, Paris, Leipzig, Madrid, St Petersburg, Bonn and Vienna as well as London to sell music sheets with elaborate pictorial frontispieces. In the United States, Currier and Ives sold large numbers of cheap hand-coloured lithographs, and John Rogers, a 'sculptor' who specialized in 'groups', disposed of 100,000 of them between 1860 and 1890.

The Currier and Ives catalogue provides a glimpse of the range of mid-19th-century 'wants'. It included sixteen categories—Domestic, Love Scenes, Kittens and Puppies, Ladies' Heads, Catholic Religious, Patriotic, Landscapes, Vessels, Comic, School Rewards and Drawing Studies, Flowers and Fruits, Motto Cards, Horses, Family Registers, Memory Pieces and 'Miscellaneous in great variety'. The last of these categories included two of their most popular lines—burning buildings and temperance prints. All 19th-century creative movements in art must obviously be seen in this kind of context and related to the values of the middle period of the century when there was greater middle-class assurance than at any other time. The desire to discover a moral in everything was expressed, indeed, in relation to 'high art' as well as to the world of bric-à-brac. It was doubtless a sign of the times that the catalogue of the Karlsruhe art collection stated in 1852 that the works on display were shown 'to promote the good conduct of life' and that the pictures were meant to be 'looked at not only as a source of pleasure but as a source of instruction'. Yet the origins of these attitudes which were so influential during the 1850s and 1860s can be traced back long before 1852. There was 'Victorianism' in Britain before Victoria came to the throne in 1837 just as there was 'Victorianism' in countries over which Queen Victoria did not rule. The ten volumes of Thomas Bowdler's *The Family Shakespeare, In which Nothing is added to the Text; but those Words and Expressions are omitted which cannot with Propriety be read aloud in a Family* was first published in 1818: they had reached a sixth edition by 1831.

Aestheticism

Aestheticism—a revolt against such ideas and a direct assault on such restraints—has an even more complex pedigree than Impressionism, and the pursuit of the pedigree leads the historian through many mazes of 19th-century culture. The *Punch* cartoons by George Du Maurier (1834–96), with their languid and long-haired 'aesthetes' wearing velveteen jackets and knickerbockers and surrounded by admiring ladies in green, belong to the late 1870s and the early 1880s: *Patience* with its superb libretto, was first produced in 1881. Yet the phrase 'art for art's sake', which was in such wide currency throughout Europe during the 1880s and the 'decadent' 1890s was coined as early as 1835 by Théophile Gautier in the preface to what at the time was regarded as a 'scandalous' French novel,

Mademoiselle de Maupin. Four years earlier in Britain Arthur Hallam (1811-33), reviewing a volume of youthful poems by his friend Alfred Tennyson, had claimed generally—and it was a necessary presupposition of any theory of 'art for art's sake'—that 'wherever the mind of the artist suffers itself to be occupied . . . by any other preoccupation than the desire of beauty, the result is false art'.

The claim, not new even in 1835 or in 1831, that the writer and the artist inhabited and directed or should inhabit and direct an autonomous world, was never abandoned throughout the rest of the 19th century. In its more elaborate manifestations it was bizarre enough to amuse as well as to shock. Nevertheless, in its simplest forms, it seemed to avoid ambiguities. It appeared, indeed, to have its sanctions not in fashion, but in human experience as recorded in history. As Gautier himself put it in his poem '*L'Art*' (1857), the sculptor's creations survived the rise and fall of civilizations:

> *Tout passe—L'art robuste*
> *Seul a l'éternité;*
> *Le buste*
> *Survit à la cité.*

(*All fades away. Art alone is eternal. The statue outlasts the city.*) By the end of the century the claim was incorporated in all the many fashionable theories of 'decadence' which appealed to the literary and artistic avant gardes, those writers and artists who were not content simply to count the numbers of their clients or their readers, and who objected strongly to drawing 'morals' out of their own or other people's art. 'To notice only the picturesque effect of a beggar's rags, like Gautier,' Richard Le Gallienne (1866-1947), a spokesman of 'decadence', put it in 1892 in a comment on some recent illustrations of a volume of poems by Tennyson—and it was the 'only' which mattered—or 'to consider one's mother merely prismatically, like Mr Whistler—these are examples of the decadent attitude.'

The art alone was what counted, yet the difficulty always was that as a slogan 'art for art's sake' could be interpreted in radically different ways. Neither art nor beauty was easy to define, and not all the 'aesthetes', philosophical or fashionable, even during the 1890s, could disentangle themselves from moral issues. Some, indeed, got near to implying, if not propounding, a counter-morality to that of what they called the bourgeois or the Puritan world, the world which was consolidated in the middle years of the 19th century but had its origins long before. Some turned back, as critics of contemporary life often turned back throughout the 19th century, to the beliefs and rituals of the Catholic past. Walter Pater (1839-94), writing from the heart of Victorian Oxford, refused to define 'beauty', yet, while pointing to concrete manifestations of beauty in particular art forms—all art, he believed, should aspire to the condition of music—, he seldom lost the sense that there were 'ideals' which were capable of inspiring. The sustenance of art lay in its power to lift horizons, 'to set the spirit free for a moment'. The artist, he believed, had to 'grasp at any exquisite passion or contribution to knowledge . . . any stirring of the senses, strange dyes, strange colours and curious odours, or work of the artist's hands, or the face of one's friends'.

The double use of the word 'strange' in Pater's peroration to *The Renaissance* (1873), as much a Victorian peroration as the last paragraphs of Darwin's *Origin of Species*, indicates not only Pater's own peculiar sensibilities but the need, shared by many of his 19th-century predecessors and contemporaries, to break away from the accepted norms of Victorian behaviour. This sense of need was strong, indeed, among artists and writers who did not believe in the slogan of 'art for art's sake'. The English Pre-Raphaelites, who had formed a Brotherhood in 1848, and whose subsequent history had gone through many new phases and many unanticipated vicissitudes before they merged, not only in Du Maurier's mind, with the 'aesthetes' of the 1870s—had also tried earlier to escape from the busy world of the 19th century. In their case, they had looked back, like the Nazarenes in Germany before them, not to the world of the Renaissance, which Pater chose, but to the world of the Middle Ages, a world where legend and religion intertwined. At first, their sense of beauty—seeing things, it has been aptly said, as if without eyelids and going on to paint with the most meticulous technique—was so much at odds with that of their more conven-

tional contemporaries that, to take one well-known early example, the painting *The Carpenter's Shop* by J. E. Millais (1829-96) was sharply criticized on the sweeping grounds that it defied not only 'the recognized axioms of taste' but 'the principles of beauty'.

Yet Millais was to become immensely successful, and in 1885, when he stood out as the first British artist to be created a baronet (Tennyson was the first poet to be created a peer), he was earning £30,000 a year. His painting *Bubbles* (1886), published as a presentation plate with the Christmas number of the *Illustrated London News* in 1887, was soon turned into an advertisement for Pears' soap. Another far earlier painting by a Pre-Raphaelite, *The Light of the World* (1852-54) by Holman Hunt (1827-1910), who set out to edify and instruct, also belongs to 'popular' 19th- and 20th-century art. It is significant that John Ruskin, for whom art had a distinctive moral and religious function, admired the work of the Pre-Raphaelites both in itself and for its critique of utilitarian, industrialized society. For Ruskin 'art for art's sake' was always anathema. 'The beginning of art,' he wrote, 'is in getting our country clean, and our people beautiful'; and for all his youthful passion for Turner's paintings, he was involved in 1878 in a law case with Whistler, whose aestheticism he deplored and whom he described as an impudent coxcomb 'asking two hundred guineas for flinging a pot of paint in the public's face'.

In France, where 'Aestheticism' was even more complex in its pedigree than it was in England, Leconte de Lisle (1818-94) and the French Parnassian poets extolled a cult of beauty not for the many but for the élite: following Gautier, they found formal perfection in marble statues:

> *Sculpteur, cherche avec soin, en attendant l'extase,*
> *Un marbre sans défaut pour en faire un beau vase.*

(*Sculptor, search carefully, waiting for inspiration, for a faultless marble to make a beautiful vase.*) Yet there was a particularly dark as well as a particularly strange side to the quest for beauty in 19th-century France, where the artist's autonomous world was thought of not simply as a world of escape but as a 'Bohemia'. *La Bohème*, the opera by Giacomo Puccini (1858-1924), was a popular new opera in 1896, but long before, when popularity was not an issue, the little-known writer of *Scènes de la vie de bohème* (1849), Henri Murger, had defined Bohemia as '*bornée au nord par l'espérance, le travail et la gaieté, au sud par la nécessité et le courage; à l'ouest et à l'est par la calomnie et l'Hôtel-Dieu*' (bounded on the north by hope, work and gaiety, on the south by necessity and courage, on the east and west by calumny and the hospital). For Charles Baudelaire (1821-67), who dedicated his poems *Les Fleurs du Mal* (1857) to Gautier, beauty was to be sought and found in odd and sinister places and in subjects and in feelings which most people—Pater's Renaissance men as much as Smiles's heroes of self-help or French radical or Bonapartist politicians—would have found repellant. '*Viens-tu du ciel profond ou sors-tu de l'abîme, O Beauté?*' (*Do you come from the deep sky or from the abyss, O Beauty?*) Baudelaire asked, lingering more on the shades than on the skies:

> *Tu marches sur les morts, Beauté, dont tu te moques;*
> *De tes bijoux l'Horreur n'est pas le moins charmant,*
> *Et le Meurtre, parmi tes plus chères breloques,*
> *Sur ton ventre orgueilleux danse amoureusement.*

(*You walk over the dead, Beauty, whom you scorn; among your jewels Horror is not the least charming; and one of your dearest trinkets, Murder, dances amorously on your proud belly.*) It is easy to understand why democrats do not like cats,' Baudelaire wrote astringently in his private diaries: '*Le chat est beau.*'

Baudelaire was sufficiently at home in his century to describe 'a comparison of the nations and their respective products' at the Paris Exhibition of 1855 (of which Delacroix was a Commissioner) as one of the most remarkably interesting, attractive and revealing occupations for 'a dreamer whose mind is given to generalization as well as to the study of details—or, to put it even better, to the idea of universal order and hierarchy'. Yet Baudelaire did more than any other writer to identify the *mal du siècle*. The artist in his view could never accept the liberal or optimistic view of the world which found pleasure and pride in progress and which exalted the 'active' 19th-century man above all his forebears. Baudelaire has often been hailed as 'the first poet we recognize as being truly "modern"'. Yet he was, like other 19th-century writers, above all, a poet of his age who looked both before and after. It is difficult to avoid using the word 'Romantic' to describe him, and he certainly provided a link between on the one side Gautier and on the other the French 'symbolists' who thought of him as their 'ancestor'—Stéphane Mallarmé (1842–98), who conceived his poetry as music—Debussy was to produce Mallarmé's music without Mallarmé's words in *L'Après-midi d'un Faune* (1894); Paul Verlaine (1844–96), whose sense of sin, it has been said, 'appeared to be a refinement of aesthetic pleasure'; and Arthur Rimbaud (1854–91) who published his first volume of poems while he was still a schoolboy and who wrote nothing of importance after the age of nineteen.

For Rimbaud, ordinary expression meant little. 'The poet makes himself a *seer* by a long, prodigious, and rational *disordering of all the senses,*' Rimbaud exclaimed in a letter to a friend in 1871. 'He consumes all the poisons in him, and keeps only their quintessences. This is an unspeakable torture during which he needs all his faith and superhuman strength, and during which he becomes the great patient, the great criminal, the great accursed—and the great learned one—among men. For he arrives at the *unknown*.' In England, A. C. Swinburne (1837–1909), an extravagant, if less gifted admirer both of Gautier and of Baudelaire, shared the same sense of torture and defiance. The aesthetic should never be confused with the religious, the philosophical or the moral: the everlasting danger was what Baudelaire had called 'the great didactic heresy', *'l'hérésie de l'enseignement'*.

Romanticism

'Let us ask the *poet* for the *new*—in ideas and forms,' Rimbaud concluded his letter. Earlier in the same letter, however, he too had looked back to the Romantics. 'Romanticism has never been properly judged. Who was there to judge it?' Romanticism remains the most difficult and hazardous of all the 19th-century *isms* to interpret—both for the historian and the critic—but it cannot be left out of any chronology or any analysis. 'It was in itself,' Professor Talmon has written, 'a symptom of a loosening of "fixities" and "definities", and in turn came to act as a most effective solvent.' The element of restlessness in the 19th century cannot be explained without an attempt to understand 'Romanticism'.

During the early years of the century, A. W. von Schlegel, following in the wake of his more erratic and inconsistent older brother Friedrich (1772–1829), set out perhaps more purposefully than any other writer before him to identify what 'Romanticism' really meant. Surveying the literature of the past, he distinguished between on the one hand the rules of the French 'classical' tradition and on the other the freshness of medieval romances and ballads: he went on to point to the curiosity about life and the creative vitality of non-French writers as different as Dante, Cervantes and, above all, Shakespeare. The term 'Romantic' as applied to history—his friend, Madame de Staël employed it also in her book *De l'Allemagne* which she completed in 1810 and which was suppressed by Napoleon's police—was soon given such a wide application in relation to current literature and culture that for some authors and critics it came to be synonymous with the word 'contemporary'. The tag of 'modernity' was already there.

Already, moreover, almost every aspect of 'Romanticism', complementary or contradictory, including the adjective 'Romantic' itself, could be traced in Europe long before 1810—rejection of rationalism; preoccupation with the self; the cultivation of feelings; fear of age; the flight from the artificial and the pursuit of the primitive and the simple, the reckless and the strange, the picturesque and the grotesque; the urge towards untrammelled individual freedom; tension between desire and achievement or circumstance; the longing for the unattainable; delight in genius, not least misunderstood genius, as a 'force of nature' and in nature as a source of solace and of inspiration; *ennui, Weltschmerz*, 'intimations of immortality', *'l'éternel amour'*. These different aspects, tangled and even incompatible, wild-flower or hot-house, acquired what unity they possessed not through the mind but through the heart or the soul, through inner correspondences.

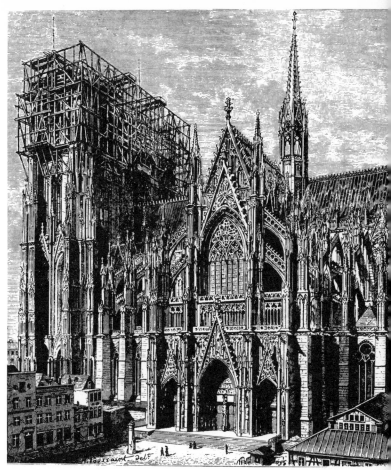

Cologne Cathedral had stood uncompleted since work ceased in 1560. In the 19th century the revival of interest in the Middle Ages provided a stimulus for its completion. The original designs for the façade were discovered in 1814 and 1816: building began in 1842, and finished in 1880—five years after this view was sketched.

The different themes of 'Romanticism' can be traced in different European countries as independent or linked versions of a universal upheaval of feelings and ideas. Some 'Romantic' writings or pictures or pieces of music acquired the status of general manifestos, sometimes for more than one generation. Thus, for example, Goethe's *The Sorrows of the young Werther* (1774), with its compelling portrait of the mind and soul of a misunderstood and tragic romantic hero, was translated into many different European languages and influenced artists and musicians (from Kreutzer in 1792 to Massenet in 1892) as much as writers. (Napoleon, also, took a copy of it with him on his Egyptian campaign.)

Yet the Romantic upheaval obviously did not spring simply from cultural diffusion. Independently of each other in different countries and during different periods of the 19th century Shelley could write 'our sweetest songs are those which tell of saddest thought' and Alfred de Musset (1810–57) could exclaim *'les plus désespérés sont les chants les plus beaux'*. Even minor writers or artists could act as important international links not only between different countries but between different arts. Thus, the English painter John Martin (1789–1854) fascinated the German poet Heinrich Heine (1797–1856) who believed that the French musician Hector Berlioz (1803–69) shared the same imaginative power and the same striving after 'physical immensity'. Thus, too, the American poet and writer of short stories, Edgar Allan Poe (1809–49), strongly influenced not only French poets like Baudelaire, who translated him, and the Symbolists, but the musician Debussy. When he began work on his opera *Pelléas et Mélisande* in 1893, Debussy was fascinated by Poe's *The Fall of the House of Usher*. So, also, was Maurice Maeterlinck (1862–1949), whose drama *Pelléas et Mélisande* was performed in Paris in the same year, five days after Wagner's *Die Walküre*. Maeterlinck could write fervently from Brussels, then the centre of the *Art Nouveau* movement, that his generation owed to Poe its 'sense of mystery' and its 'passion for the beyond'.

Because of the length and intricacies of the 'Romantic' pedigree and the complexities and ambiguities inherent in the word 'Romanticism' itself, as used over a long period of time, the term remains at best what Mario Praz has called an 'approximate label' and many attempts have been made to tabulate its varieties in neat synoptic tables. Other writers have suggested, without pointing to an alternative, that the term should be discarded. Yet during the period from 1815 to 1848 French and German 'Romanticisms', often in contrast with each other, dominated the European cultural landscape, influencing art, music, literature and politics. The great English Romantic poets were dead or had passed their prime by the late 1820s—indeed, the term 'Romanticism' was little used in England where there were few Romantic 'campaigns' like the campaign of the French Romantics to defeat 'classicism' or that of the German Romantics to create a national literature—and Lord Byron, who looked like and behaved like a Romantic hero, fled from England in 1816 when he was only twenty-eight years old and then and thereafter enjoyed more of a Continental than a British reputation. Yet, if there was no 'Romantic movement' in England, there was great Romantic writing, particularly lyric poetry; and in art, J. W. M. Turner—'the finest creator of mystery', as Debussy, echoing Ruskin, called him—carried his own subjective vision of the world far across the boundaries of 'representation' in some of the most beautiful expressions in water colour of what must be called the 'pure poetry' of Romanticism. 'All is without form and void,' William Hazlitt (1778–1830) churlishly complained, but no more churlishly than Turner's other critics and far less churlishly than Ruskin was to dismiss Whistler.

It was not Turner, but Eugène Delacroix, a reputed son of Talleyrand and a close friend of Chopin, who stood out at the time as the leading Romantic artist in Europe, providing what Baudelaire was later to call 'the volcanic crater hidden by bunches of flowers'. According to Delacroix, who turned for inspiration to the Bible, to history, to Morocco (after 1831) and to some of the great symbolic scenes in the Romantic history of the early 19th century—*Greece Expiring on the Ruins of Missolonghi* (1827), for example, or *Liberty Leading the People* (1830)—, 'the most beautiful works of art are those that express the pure imagination of the artist'. The theatrical or operatic element in his art paralleled a similar element both in French Romantic writing and in music. Indeed, Delacroix was an admirer both of Byron, 'an eternal inspiration', and of Berlioz, a Romantic in his life as much as in his art, who revelled in rich orchestration and in spectacular effects. Berlioz described in *Harold in Italy* (1834) the quest of Byron's hero for 'melancholy, happiness, joy', and married an Irish actress who, when she played Ophelia, introduced him 'unawares' to Shakespeare, whose genius, Berlioz wrote in his superb *Memoirs*, struck him 'like a thunderbolt'. At no point in the history of Romanticism can the different arts be studied in isolation from each other. 'Colours,' wrote Delacroix, 'are the music of the eyes . . . certain harmonies of colour produce sensations which music itself cannot achieve.'

That the term 'Romantic' was used to encompass not only pictorial artists as different as Turner and Delacroix but also John Constable and the German engravers Eugen Napoleon Neureuther (1806–82) and Adrian Ludwig Richter (1803–84) is as remarkable as the fact that it was also used to encompass not only Berlioz but the greatest of all musicians, Beethoven. A Romantic contemporary, E. T. A. Hoffmann (1776–1822), described, and thereby circumscribed him, as capable of setting in motion 'the lever of fear, of awe, of horror, of suffering' and of awakening 'just that infinite longing which is the essence of Romanticism'. The term 'Romantic' was also used more aptly in relation to Franz Schubert (1797–1828), who wrote the first of his six hundred *Lieder* (which broke with Italian *arias*) in 1814 (*Erlkönig* followed in 1815); to Karl Maria von Weber (1786–1826), who introduced the baying of wolves into his *Freischütz* (1821)—Berlioz introduced a real rooster into his *Benvenuto Cellini* (1838); to Schumann (1810–56), a devotee of Hoffmann, who could write the most quiet and intimate of Romantic music and at the same time rousing patriotic choruses (he interjected the themes of the *Marseillaise*, then forbidden in Vienna, into his *Faschingsschwenk aus Wien*): to Franz Liszt (1811–86), the greatest of all *virtuosi*, pianist and composer, in whose house the term 'The

Music of the Future' was coined; and above all, (as was shown in Chapter III) to his son-in-law Richard Wagner, whom he championed in youth with almost as much devotion as his daughter Cosima perpetuated the Wagner cult at Bayreuth after Wagner's death in 1883.

Music, 'the movements of our spirit disembodied' as Wilhelm Wackenroder (1773–98), another pioneer of Romanticism, put it, could be thought of as the supremely Romantic medium, capable both of intensifying the effect of words and of conveying without words the most intimate and the most subtle of feelings; and Romantic poets and painters alike sought to achieve in their own media the effects of music. Shelley wrote, for example, of 'a principle within the human being—which acts otherwise than in the lyre, and produces not melody alone, but harmony, by an internal adjustment of the sounds or motions thus excited to the impressions which excite them. . . . [to] give forth divinest melody when the breath of universal being sweeps over their frame'.

Yet just as Delacroix believed that in some respects the imaginative power of the visual artist could exceed that of the musician, so some of the most Romantic musicians, particularly Wagner, who might have been a painter and began by writing stories and plays, often tried to fuse music with other arts, believing that it was possible to create a new unity out of poetry and music. They set out, indeed, to promote an art which would appeal to all the senses at the same time (*Gesamtkunstwerk*). In Wagner's case, as his highly distinctive art developed, he acquired disciples, 'perfect Wagnerites', who looked up to him with awe. Early in his life when he saw Weber conduct *Der Freischütz*, Wagner had decided himself that he wanted to be 'not King or Kaiser, but to stand there and conduct' (Berlioz's symphonies, he also wrote, 'are the battles and victories of Bonaparte in Italy'): when in 1876 the famous Wagner Festival Theatre was built in Bayreuth, the little town became the centre of a cult.

Not all artists—and not all artists were Romantics—were so conscious of their power as Wagner, a power which, like all forms of power, tended to corrupt. Yet it is important to remember that 'corruption' did not start with Wagner. The same tensions, ambivalences and contradictions very quickly emerged in the political and social record of Romanticism as in the artistic. Napoleon, for example, had many of the attributes of a Romantic hero, a superhuman figure of 'genius', towering over his contemporaries, Hegel's 'world spirit on horseback', and poets, painters and musicians—not least Beethoven, who dedicated his *Eroica* (1804) to him—often served as willing myth-makers. At the same time, his spectacular successes depended both on propaganda (including the most heavy and uninspiring propagandist art) and on repression by force (including the repression of artists). After his exile to St Helena, he became a 'legend' and a 'cult' through the mediation of 'Romantic' writers and artists; and however much Romantic writers might criticize the Second Empire set up by his nephew in 1852, the connection between art and propaganda remained unbroken. It survived, moreover, not only in Wagner's Bayreuth but in the France of the Third Republic.

Throughout the century there were always 'Romantic' defenders both of 'revolution' and of 'order', of the claims of the nation and of the authority of the Church, and there were some who passed from a defence of the one to a defence of the other. William Wordsworth (1770–1850), who had welcomed the French Revolution of 1789, became one of Europe's most fervent conservatives, pinning his hope on Metternich; Victor Hugo, the most flamboyant and the most declamatory of the young French Romantics, began as a conservative—'*un royaliste voltairien*', as he described himself—and ended as a dedicated European spokesman—'trumpeter' or 'torchbearer' would be more appropriate terms—of freedom and progress. He was the most eloquent of the political enemies of Napoleon III, and after the fall of Napoleon III's Empire his public expression of pity for the defeated and persecuted Paris Communards in 1871 resulted in his violent expulsion from Belgium. It was Hugo, with his huge effort and output—as characteristic of most 19th-century writers, musicians and artists, as it was of 19th-century industrialists—who made the most eloquent, if often the most naïve and noisy claims for the Romantic poet as prophet. Drawing on legend, history, science and philosophy, he committed poetry to progress:

> *Comme une torche qu'il secoue,*
> *Faire flamboyer l'avenir.*

(*Make the future flare up like a brandished torch.*) Hugo was outstanding, not least for his long record of commitment, yet, particularly between the revolutions of 1830 and 1848, there were poets, artists and musicians everywhere who proclaimed the message of liberation—among them Chopin, Liszt and the young Giuseppe Verdi (1813–1901). Heinrich Heine, who had produced his *Buch der Lieder* in 1827 four years after Schubert's *Die schöne Müllerin*, was at the far left of the movement.

Between the two revolutions of 1830 and 1848 there were many other Romantic writers who followed different paths. Some, particularly in Germany, looked back to the Middle Ages, to forests and castles and knights, preferring, like the Nazarenes and the Pre-Raphaelites, the past to the present or, like the historian Jules Michelet (1798–1874) in France, finding inspiration in the past for the assertion of the claims of the people (Hugo himself presented a vast medieval tableau in *Notre Dame de Paris*, 1831). Others used the past to criticize the present (a tradition which in Britain ran through Carlyle, Ruskin and William Morris and ultimately became socialist) or, as in Germany, to reinforce the drive towards nationalism (as is shown in Chapter VI).

Yet the artist was by no means always a critic, and by the middle years of the century, despite the witness of Baudelaire or of Wagner, 'Romanticism' had frequently been tamed or assimilated so that it became an uninspiring affair of echoes and decorative renderings, an influence on style rather than an assertion of experience. Revived Gothic, Hugh Casson has written, began by being Romantic, next became Christian, and ended up respectable, the style as worn; and what was true of 'Gothic' was true of much else besides. There were, indeed, as many clichés in Romanticism as there were exaggerations, more that was derivative than there was that was creative. Lamartine had attributed to the 'Romantics' the achievement of substituting for the conventional lyre of Parnassus the strings of the human heart. The strings of the heart, however, could be plucked all too easily. In the cluster of qualities which were called 'Victorian', inside or outside Britain, sentimentality, as in the paintings of Sir Edwin Landseer (1802–73), not only had its own place but tended to colour the rest.

Each artist had his own particular relationship with his 'public'. Beethoven proudly followed his destiny; Schubert kept alive by entertaining; Gioacchino Rossini (1792–1868), not a Romantic musician, though he could write Romantic pieces, wanted above all else to please. The most popular Romantic composer in Britain was Felix Mendelssohn (1809–47), while in Vienna Johannes Brahms (1833–97) could always appeal to large audiences shocked by Wagner. Looking back to Beethoven, Brahms produced rich and moving Romantic music couched largely in classical forms, sometimes supercharged, as Percy Scholes has said of his work, with an 'extra-musical emotion'. In Italy, the long sequence of Verdi's glorious operas, glorious with an occasional touch of vulgarity, were understood by his enthusiastic public from 'his first to his last step' just as was the single Italian literary masterpiece by Alessandro Manzoni (1785–1873), *I Promessi Sposi*.

In literature, the growth of a new reading public, of an extended 'book trade', of a constellation of newspapers, journals and reviews and a new *genus* of critics set the terms of the world in which the writer had to move, even when he moved uneasily or rebelliously. In the world of the arts painters could sometimes wait—'We don't eat every day,' wrote Pierre Auguste Renoir (1841–1919) in 1869— but architects depended on custom. William Morris (1834–96), Pre-Raphaelite by origin and by conviction, socialist in his mature life, had to sell his wallpapers and furnishings to very rich men, most of whom he despised. Objecting, as he did, to 'art for the few' as strongly as he did to 'education for the few' or to 'freedom for the few', he nevertheless had to serve what he called the 'swinish luxury of the rich'.

From Romanticism to Modernism

Morris, in his poetry at least, was a late Romantic, and in the history

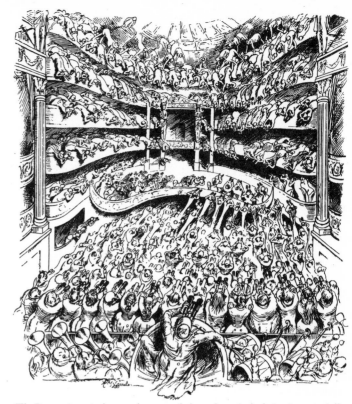

The Romantic artist became the centre of almost hysterical admiration, especially when, as in the case of Richard Wagner, he saw himself marked off from other men by his genius. This cartoon shows an opera performance 'in the presence of the Master'. (7)

of music 'Romanticism' continued to shape the sensibilities of musicians like Piotr Ilich Tchaikovsky (1840–93) and Anton Dvořak (1841–1904), whose work is still played to large and enthusiastic 20th-century audiences. Yet, during the last decades of the century, in literature, as in art and in scholarship, there were so many attempts to break with mid-19th-century 'compromises', so many efforts to challenge accepted assumptions, that new versions of 'modernism' were announced in the 1880s and 1890s. 'The modern spirit,' Cyril Connolly has written, 'was a combination of certain intellectual qualities inherited from the Enlightenment: lucidity, irony, scepticism, intellectual curiosity, combined with the passionate intensity and enhanced sensibility of the Romantics, their rebellion and sense of technical experiment, their awareness of living in a tragic age.' The combination is incomplete if it leaves out the desire for further, perhaps final, liberation from the tangles and traps of the preceding generation. For the German historian Egon Friedell, the chief hallmark of that generation was confinement: 'They lived perpetually in a wretched, padded, puffed-out world of cotton wool, cardboard and tissue-paper. In all their creations it is with the arts of adornment that imagination is concerned: with the art of the upholsterer, the confectioner, the stucco decorator.'

The term 'modernity' was far older than the emergence of the 'modern movement' in the 1880s and 1890s. It was not new, indeed, when the Goncourts—Edmond (1822–96) and Jules (1830–70)— authors of the most celebrated 19th-century Parisian literary *Journal*, used it in 1858. (The Goncourts also introduced Japanese art to France, and Edmond's last book was about Hokusai, the great Japanese artist.) It was from out of Paris, the Paris of Mallarmé, Verlaine, Rimbaud and Debussy, to which the German poet Stefan George (1868–1933) acknowledged his debt, that a new subjective and highly self-conscious sense of 'modernity' emerged. Defying not only bourgeois values but the favourite 19th-century belief in the claims of history, many of the 'moderns' stamped upon the passport of the Wisdom of the Ages, as Irving Howe has well put it, the bold red letters 'Not transferable'. Pre-history, indeed, seemed more interesting to many of the 'moderns' than history, the pre-history which was explicable only in terms of 'myth' and which rested on an understanding of primitive and magical forces. *The Golden Bough* (first edition 1890; second edition in 3 volumes 1900), which was read to Tennyson while his portrait was being painted by G. F. Watts (1817–1904), dealt with the 'solid layer of savagery beneath the surface of society'; and its author J. G. Frazer (1854–1941) concluded 'that we seem to move on a thin crust which may at any moment be rent by the subterranean forces slumbering below'. Sigmund Freud (1856–1939) insisted in the last year of the century that 'unconscious processes . . . are indestructible. In the unconscious nothing can be brought to an end, nothing is past and forgotten.'

'Liberation' against such a background obviously meant something different from 'intellectual liberation' which is above all else an affair of the mind. There was a reaction during the late 19th century, indeed, against what seemed to be superficial explanations of human thought and human behaviour. There was also an abandonment of the generally held mid-19th-century belief in the idea of linear historical development (as dear to Hegel and Marx as it was to Macaulay), and an increasing fascination both with a universal *condition humaine* and with the 'rhythm of eternal recurrence'. Henri Bergson (1859–1941) explored the subtleties of time and duration in an epoch-making essay of 1889. Creative artists, like W. B. Yeats, born in 1865, three years after Debussy, and Marcel Proust and Paul Valéry, born in 1871, were to push the explorations further. There were international implications at every point in the story. It was the German novelist Thomas Mann (born in 1875, the same year as Carl Gustav Jung) who talked of cultivating 'a sympathy for the abyss'. Some writers belonging to an older generation were influential in crystallizing new moods. Nietzsche (whose work is noted in Chapter III) reached the peak of his influence in 1889, the year he went mad. Arthur Schopenhauer (1788–1860), whose book *Die Welt als Wille und Vorstellung* had appeared as long ago as 1818, had a new impact throughout Europe.

It is not easy to summarize this intricate story, with the 18th-century Enlightenment at the beginning and 'contemporary' culture, still in flux, at the end, and many of the so-called chains of connection remain extremely dubious. Although 19th-century cultural historians, influenced by Hegel, believed that 'the art of every period is both the most complete and the most reliable expression of the national spirit', 'something like a hieroglyph . . . dark at first sight, but completely and unambiguously intelligible to those who can read the signs', their efforts to find underlying unities usually foundered at some critical point in the quest. All that it is possible to do in an essay is to explore cursorily the changing attitudes of the artist (backed or interpreted as they usually were by philosophers, historians, anthropologists or psychologists) towards what Matthew Arnold (1822–88) called 'this strange disease of modern life, with its sick hurry, its divided aims'. (Arnold had made his own attempt in 1857 to identify 'the modern element in modern literature', giving a 'pre-modern' answer in the sense that 'modern' has been used above, concentrating not on exploration at the fringes of experience or deep into the unconscious but on the 'free activity of the mind' and tolerance of divergent views.) An artist who lived, as Tennyson did, over a substantial part of a century of change could sometimes change both his own mind and his mood as dramatically as different generations within the century could react against each other. It is extremely rewarding, for example, to compare his *Locksley Hall*, published in 1842, with his *Locksley Hall Sixty Years After* published in 1886. In *Locksley Hall* Tennyson, like Hugo, put his faith in science:

Science moves but slowly slowly, creeping on from point to point.

While he did not seek to minimize the problems of a 'hungry people' —the great social topic of the 1830s and 1840s—he had confidence, also like Hugo, in the future:

For I doubt not thro' the ages one increasing purpose runs,
And the thoughts of men are widen'd with the process of the suns.

In *Locksley Hall Sixty Years After* the poet bewailed 'the rise of Demos', even the growth of Russian power, and found no comfort in evolution.

Gone the cry of 'Forward, Forward', lost within a growing gloom;
Lost, or only heard in silence from the silence of a tomb.

A noisy despair lurked behind his question:

Where was age so cramm'd with menace? madness? Written, spoken, lies?

Science and religion must be taken into account in tracing the movements both of the Romantic impulse and of the assertion of 'modernity' in the last decades of the century—science which worked miracles but encouraged doubts; religion which, even when it was orthodox, often carried with it the need for restatement both of language and of feeling. Grant Allen (1848–99), prolific writer and commentator of a new generation—he took Darwin and Smiles in his stride as well as Tennyson, and prepared the way for H. G. Wells—pointed out that the paintings of another Pre-Raphaelite, the late Sir Edward Burne-Jones (1833–98), were quite unlike those of painters before Raphael in that they had a unique 19th-century essence, 'deep-questioning, mystic, uncertain, rudderless: faith gone; humanity left: heaven lost; earth realized as man's [and what was man?], the home and sole hope for the future'. Four years earlier in 1887 Robert Browning (1812–89) had asked:

Which was it of the links
Snapt first, from out the chain which used to bind
Our earth to heaven?

By then there was far less confidence in the 'facts' of science than there had been in the brief mid-19th-century golden age of 'positivism' when Auguste Comte and his disciples were sure both of their statistics and of their sense of direction; and even the scientists of a new post-Darwinian generation—physicists as well as biologists —were becoming aware that flexibility and uncertainty lay beneath the mid-19th-century concepts of time, space, motion, matter, forms, even of 'law' itself. For the brilliant American historian Henry Adams (1838–1918), grandson and great grandson of American presidents, *The Grammar of Science* (1892) by Karl Pearson (1857–1936) 'shut out of science everything which the 19th century had brought into it. He told his scholars that they must put up with a fraction of the universe, and a very small fraction at that—the circle reached by the senses, where sequence could be taken for granted—much as the deep-sea fish takes for granted the circle of light which he generates.'

The 'doubting and questioning' of the 1880s and 1890s must be seen in 19th-century terms as the final stage in a running commentary on a century which was always a prominent feature of its intellectual life, with contemporaries divided, sometimes bitterly, about its 'constructive' and 'destructive' tendencies. 'We are living in an age of transition,' a mid-Victorian writer on the progress of physical science had put it in 1858. 'Mankind has outgrown old institutions and old doctrines, and has not yet acquired new ones,' John Stuart Mill had written in 1831, a year when Thomas Carlyle (1795–1881), making the same point, argued that 'the Old has passed away, but, alas, the New appears not in its stead; the Time is still in pangs of travail with the New'. In 1888 J. A. Froude (1818–94), the English historian, was arguing that 'the disintegration of opinion is so rapid that wise men and foolish are equally ignorant where the close of this waning century will find us'.

In writing his *History of European Thought in the Nineteenth Century (1804–82)* J. T. Merz took Goethe's *Faust* (1808)—for which Delacroix had prepared a set of lithographic illustrations—as 'the centre and beginning of our survey', singling it out as 'a comprehensive embodiment of 19th-century doubts and aspirations, leading us—if we try to understand it—now into the bewildering labyrinth of philosophy, now into the cheerful expanse of natural science, and again into the hidden depths of individual life, of religious faith with its mysteries of sin and redemption'. After the end of the century and long after Mill, he insisted that 'the thought of the century in its practical bearings is partly radical, partly reactionary—meaning by the former all those constructive attempts which try to go to the root of things and to build up on newly prepared ground; by the latter all those endeavours which, clinging to historical institutions and beliefs, aim at finding the truth and value which are in them, and the peculiar importance which they may have for the present day'.

Merz left out one crucial factor. Technology, so triumphantly displayed at the 19th-century exhibitions, always raised even more problems than did 'the cheerful expanse of natural science' at least until 'natural science' began to look a little less cheerful, if more 'open', during the last decades of the century. It was easy for John Vallance in his imaginary dictionary of 1924, published in 1824, to define 'impossible' in the best 18th-century perfectionist manner as 'a word formerly much in use even among persons of intelligence, but which is now considered to indicate paucity of information, limitation of intellect, and the absence of all grandeur of conception'. The Baconian dream of the conquest of the physical universe seemed in the middle years of the century to be turning into a reality when Auguste Comte was heralding a new age, the third stage in the evolution of humanity during which the laws of natural science were being supplemented by the laws of scientific sociology. Yet neither the vaunted triumphs of technology expressed by the last decade of the century, as we have seen, not only in more machines but in a cluster of new consumer goods, nor the growth of material comfort satisfied the critics. They were least satisfied, indeed, when they saw that many people really were satisfied. It was a source of bitter complaint to the Swiss historian Jacob Burckhardt, writing in 1870 before the advent of the 'modern movement', that 'large sections of society' would readily give up all their individual literatures and nationality, if it had to be so, 'for the sake of through sleeping-cars'. Nine years earlier Alexander Herzen (1812–70), a Russian exile in London, had asked 'on what principle are we to awake the sleeper?' 'In the name of what shall the flabby personality, magnetized by trifles, be inspired, be made discontented with its present life of railways, telegraphs, newspapers and cheap goods?'

Individualism and individuality

Herzen's reference to 'flabby personality' would have shocked most of the bourgeois men of the 19th century as much as literary and social critics were shocked by what they believed to be predatory and philistine elements in bourgeois achievement, particularly when these elements were coated over with smug self-satisfaction. To understand both 'Romanticism' and 'Modernity' it is necessary to emphasize that from the 18th century onwards there were two versions of individualism, each marking a break with the socially nuanced but aristocratically dominated societies of the older past. The first was the individualism of the *entrepreneur*, the second the individualism of the artist.

The first form of individualism–whether or not it was expressed in the styles of the Saint-Simonian technocrat, the hard-headed practical English businessman who distrusted theory and believed in work and more work, or the new American tycoons—was the most active force in early and mid-19th-century society. Nor did it ever lack its defenders, through to Herbert Spencer (1820–1903), the English philosopher-sociologist whose writings were more popular in the United States than in Britain. John Stuart Mill in his *Essay on Liberty* was at one with Smiles in urging that 'the initiation of all wise and noble things comes and must come from individuals, is generally at first from some one individual'. His dictum, that 'the only unfailing and permanent source of improvement is liberty, since by it there are so many possible independent centres of improvement as there are individuals', should be set alongside the opening sentence of *Self-Help*: ' "Heaven helps those who help themselves" is a well-tried maxim embodying in a small compass the results of vast human experience.' Smiles had a radical past when he wrote *Self-Help*, and it was characteristic of Mill, who was always preoccupied with his own individual development, that he quoted with approval the words of Wilhelm von Humboldt (1767–1835), a friend of Goethe and Schiller and the founder of the University of Berlin, that 'the end of man, or that which is prescribed by the eternal or immutable dictates of reason, and not suggested by vague and transient desires, is the highest and most harmonious development of his powers to a complete and consistent whole'. 'Individuality of power and development' was the chief object of human evolution.

There were at least as many complexities, however, in the pedigree of 'individualism'—particularly when it was expressed in terms of 'individuality' rather than of 'individualism'—as there were in the pedigree of 'art for art's sake'. First there was an obvious clash between the ideal of the artist creating his own world and that of the *entrepreneur* creating his. Different qualities were called for. Work,

thrift, perseverence and duty were deemed necessary to business success. The *entrepreneur* could not live in Bohemia even if he might sneak into it from time to time. The difference between the two 'ideals' spilled over into statesmanship. It comes out very clearly, for instance, in the contrast drawn by the English essayist Walter Bagehot (1826–77) between Sir Robert Peel and Byron, who were schoolboy contemporaries at Harrow. ('I was always in scrapes, Peel never,' Byron commented later.) Peel, descendant of two of the men who created industrial Lancashire and prime minister in what was perhaps the most outstanding of 19th-century British administrations, that from 1841 to 1846, had no belief in mystery or magic. Byron's mind was 'volcanic'—'the lava flood glows in *Childe Harold*'; all the thoughts are intense, flung forth, vivid'. Peel's opinions 'far more resembled the daily accumulating insensible deposits of a rich alluvial soil'. 'Sir Robert Peel was a statesman for forty years; under our constitution, Lord Byron, eminent as was his insight into men, and remarkable as was his power, at least for short periods, of dealing with them, would not have been a statesman for forty days.' The limiting phrase 'under our constitution' was not so limiting as it looks at first sight, for the French statesman Guizot was one of Peel's greatest admirers, and after the revolutions of 1848 wrote a eulogistic biography of him.

Second, the ideal of the *entrepreneur* carried with it, as Robert Owen (1771–1858) and the early socialists saw even before Marx, the fact of the exploitation of others. Not surprisingly, therefore, some Romantic critics pointed to the superior merits of 'association' or 'brotherhood' over unbridled economic individualism, while others developed theories of individual 'alienation'. Political economy, one of the most remarkable intellectual products of a new society in the making (Eric Hobsbawm has described *Principles of Political Economy* (1817) by David Ricardo as 'a masterpiece of deductive rigour') was studied carefully by Marx, but could be quickly dismissed by creative artists, traditionalist or revolutionary, not only as a 'dismal science' but as 'abstract', 'atomistic' and 'dehumanized'. They vied with each other in setting up their 'whole man' against 'economic man' and refused to turn deductive.

Nor was it simply political economy made flesh in 'industrialism' which generated such responses. There was a similar reaction to 'utilitarianism', the theory of the greatest happiness of the greatest number, and the aspiration to create a science of morals and legislation based on the pleasure-pain principle. Jeremy Bentham (1748–1832), the greatest and most original, if also the most idiosyncratic, of the English Utilitarians, was dealt with as summarily by Hazlitt as Hazlitt, as we saw, tried to dispose of the painter Turner. 'He has no great fondness for poetry and can hardly extract a moral out of Shakespeare. His house is warmed and lighted by steam. He is one of those who prefer the artificial to the natural in most things, and think the mind of man omnipotent. He has a great contempt for out-of-door prospects, for green fields and trees, and is for ever referring everything to Utility.' Bentham's conception of the free individual deliberately adapting means to ends, with a clear sense of his own self-interest, might satisfy many people who believed in 'improvement' and in industrialization as a way to improvement—it certainly produced practical results—but it did not seem to offer an adequate basis for the full flowering of 'individuality' in a complex society. John Stuart Mill who was methodically brought up as a Benthamite but who read with eagerness Goethe and Comte, was one of the first to recognize this.

The response of the critics was further hardened when they turned to the effects on individuals of the 'cash nexus' as Carlyle called it. Carlyle, indeed, could welcome 'captains of industry' while thundering against 'Mammon worship' and the 'Midas touch'. Honoré de Balzac (1799–1850), the great French novelist, dwelt on the implications of the rise of new men with new money, presenting a huge canvas of contemporary history in the making, private and public: his art was grounded in what Marx called 'a deep understanding of real conditions'. In Britain, Anthony Trollope (1815–82), another confident novelist who created the sense of a contemporary universe of his own, showed how there could be uneasiness about values even when there was neither open conflict nor unbridled drive for possession. Charles Dickens, too, (1812–70) was caught up in similar preoccupations. As Humphry House has written, 'Money is a main theme of nearly every book that Dickens wrote: getting, keeping, spending, owing, bequeathing provide the intricacies of his plots; character after character is constructed round an attitude to money. Social status without it is subordinate.'

Distaste for bourgeois man was just as apparent at every point in the great novels, neglected in their own time, of Stendhal, an heir of the Enlightenment who served as an officer in Napoleon's army, and of Gustave Flaubert (1821–80), whose first and best known novel *Madame Bovary* (1857) was the subject of an indictment for offences against public morals and religion. '*Un salon de provinciaux enrichis qui étalent de luxe est ma bête noire,*' Stendhal wrote in the unfinished autobiographical manuscript of *La Vie de Henri Brulard.* For Flaubert, writing was at times a means to 'not living', and in his books he struggled to create what he called 'a cleaner *milieu* than the modern world'. Flaubert did not exert the same spell on his successors as Baudelaire, but just as the Romantic poets had reached the heights of self-expression in the lyric poem, 'the chief glory of the Romantic movement', so Flaubert and the other great novelists of the middle years of the century (in England, France and Russia) ensured that the novel, which at the same time reflected and re-ordered the world, would be placed at the very centre of 19th-century culture, extending the curiosity and testing the critical power of its readers, disturbing and humanizing them at the same time. It is impossible to do justice to its history by talking simply of the themes of plots or the lives of novelists. The history of every art form should be examined in terms of its own 'technical history'—the transmission of notions of form and style from one writer to another and the unique qualities of particular writers. And more can usually be learned by exploring one novel on its own than by studying a catalogue.

Once again there were links with the other arts. The paintings of Gustave Courbet (1819–77), revealing the peasant 'impulse to grasp, thump, squeeze and eat', have been thought of as 'a bridge between the worlds of Balzac and Flaubert', while Stendhal's manner has been compared with that of Honoré Daumier (1808–79), the great French lithographer, cartoonist and painter. Both Stendhal and Daumier, employing the fewest of strokes, could unerringly pick out the bold lines and with supreme skill select the traits which counted. For Stendhal, hypocrisy was '*l'uniforme de mon siècle*', as Julien Sorel called it in *Le Rouge et le Noir* (1830). '*Le siècle si moral, si hypocrite, et par conséquent si ennuyeux*' is another of his unforgettable descriptions.

There was a strong note of irony not only in French literature or in Heine but in the English prose writings of Matthew Arnold and in the poems of his friend Arthur Hugh Clough (1819–61). Arnold, who was as keenly aware as Mill that he was living in an age of transition, ridiculed the enthusiasms of his bourgeois contemporaries, taunting them for their veneration of size, quantity and speed, condemning them for their 'Puritanism'. No other British writer in the cause of 'sweetness and light' ever made such fun of 'Mrs Gooch's Golden Rule'—'Ever remember, my dear Dan, that you should look forward to being some day manager of that concern.' Clough dwelt on the underlying hypocrisy: 'Honour thy parents; that is all, from whom advancement may befall.' In the same poem, *The Latest Decalogue*, he poured scorn on the mid-Victorian interpretation of the Ten Commandments:

> *Thou shalt not steal; an empty feat,*
> *When 'tis so lucrative to cheat . . .*
> *Thou shalt not covet, but tradition,*
> *Approves all forms of competition.*

Nineteenth-century 'realism' involved more than irony. Victor Hugo used the reports of Dr Parent-Duchatelet (1790–1836) and his journal *Annales d'hygiène publique et de médecine légale* in writing *Les Misérables* (1862), just as George Eliot turned back to English controversies about public health in the construction of *Middlemarch* (1871–72) and the painter Théodore Géricault (1791–1824) based his *Raft of the 'Medusa'* (1819) on observations in hospitals and lunatic asylums. Eugène Sue's *Mystères de Paris* (1842–43), a supremely Romantic work which inspired similar works in different parts of the world (Reynold's *Mysteries of London*, for instance, and J. W. Buel's *Metropolitan Life Unveiled or the Mysteries*

and Miseries of America's Great Cities) turned to the statistics of poverty, disease and crime as eagerly as the pioneering statistician Louis Villermé (1782–1863) in France or the Benthamite administrative reformer Edwin Chadwick (1800–90) in Britain. The main concern at this time was not with 'the working classes' but with '*les classes dangereuses*', the floating population of the great cities which ignored all the accepted 19th-century individual virtues. Both the 'romantic realists' and the statisticians are best thought of as explorers worthy to be set alongside the explorers of Africa, Asia and Australia. Certainly they both freely employed geographical metaphors, comparing the 'dark city' to the 'dark continent'. 'A hovel in one of the suburbs which they know least,' one writer on London put it, 'would be as strange to most Londoners as a village in the African forests.'

The later 'realism' of 'naturalist' writers, among whom Emile Zola (1840–1902) stood out prominently, drew less on a sense of adventure and more on positivist conceptions both of natural and of social science. For Zola, indeed, the enquiries of the novelist were akin to those of the scientist, and his series of novels *Les Rougon-Macquart* (1871–93) had as its sub-title '*une histoire naturelle et sociale d'une famille sous le Second Empire*'. There were optimistic and pessimistic streaks in Zola's highly controversial work—*La bête humaine* (1890) was an unresolved investigation of technical progress as indicated by the development of railways—but there was no free will. The individual was gripped in well documented, almost clinical situations where he could not choose: passive suffering was inevitable. The central problem in late 19th-century political economy—that of choice—played little part in Zola's quest for 'sociological truth'. And while there were 'poetic' or 'mythic' qualities in his work—along with what Lionel Trilling has called a 'fierce energy' —there was little of the sense of the depths of the individual personality which the 'modern' writers of the late 19th century were beginning to explore. Tennyson might write vituperatively in *Locksley Hall Sixty Years After* of 'the troughs of Zolaism', but he and Zola were at one in doubting whether the 19th century as it developed was achieving any of the hopes which had provided Hugo with his vision of the future.

Zola's name was involved in most of the literary and social controversies inside Europe during the last decades of the 19th century. So too was the name of Henrik Ibsen (1828–1906), 'the father of the modern theatre', who was one of the first writers of the century to write plays which were as gripping as novels. Ibsenism, indeed, became one of the new *isms* of the 19th century, and there were at least as many Ibsenites as there were Wagnerites. While it is not easy to do justice to Ibsen's work in simple sociological terms, it is plain that he did much to illuminate the relationship between individualism and individuality. In problem play after problem play, he exposed through a massing of images and the creation of a new mythology the limitations imposed on people as people by the pressure of dead institutions and the inhibitions of stifling social convention. He knew how difficult it was for fragmented people to liberate themselves: as the Provost argues in *Brand* (1866):

> *The surest way to destroy a man*
> *Is to turn him into an individual.*

Whereas Smiles anthologized success, Ibsen presented a gallery of failures: 'All that I have succeeded in doing, building, creating,' says Solness in *The Masterbuilder* (1892), 'all this I have to make up for, to pay for. And not with my own happiness only, but with other people's too.' Ibsen consistently refused to rest content with compromise. He abhorred the favourite compromises of the mid-century and questioned all its trust in frock-coated 'pillars of society'. 'The strongest man in the world is he who stands most alone.'

Ibsen put whatever general social trust he had not in material progress but in 'our women' and 'our workingmen'. 'The reshaping of social conditions,' he declared in a speech of 1885, 'which is now under way out there in Europe, is concerned chiefly with the future position of the workingman [Zola was perhaps most effective as a social observer in his working-class novels] and of woman. That it is which I hope for and wait for; and it is that that I will work for . . . for my whole life or far as I am able.'

The work and the hope represented almost the last turn in the 19th-century quest for individuality. Neither women nor workingmen (the former with their fashions, the latter with their segregated sub-cultures; the former scattered in their homes, the latter congregated in their workshops) were usually allowed to participate fully in the making of 19th-century history even in years of revolution; and during quieter times, for all the vaunted belief in the virtues of free discussion, as set out, for example, in Mill's *On Liberty*, neither women nor workingmen, as Mill himself was the first to point out, shared equally in that liberty. Society in the 19th century depended on inequality as much as on mobility. Many historians have found it possible to write comprehensively of 19th-century morals and manners while concentrating on male bourgeois standards and ideals and ignoring the subordinated position of women and the dependent position of workingmen. Yet much 19th-century cant billowed around these topics.

The way of self-help might be open to some workingmen, but it was never open to most workingmen; and the most articulate among them were aware that exhortation would neither assist them to find security nor allow them to realize their aspirations. They looked to 'union' rather than individualism for their salvation. Likewise, the 'womanly woman' was a doll not a full person, not least when she was placed on a pedestal. 'I was so demure and quiet in my talk about women always, and had kept myself so circumspectly, that my mother never had the leas suspicion of me,' wrote the remarkable author of the eleven-volume erotic English autobiography *My Secret Life*. Hypocrisy was the other side of 'earnestness', and there was always an 'other side' not only to the Victorians but also to their overseas counterparts. Prostitution, whether 'regulated' or 'free', was a necessary counterpart to the virtuous bourgeois home, and most of its practitioners, a very numerous group, not least in Britain, came from working-class families.

Nineteenth-century 'earnestness' covered over many of the fissures and most of the scabs in 19th-century society. Writers on Britain have often rested content with an explanation of it in terms of 'Evangelicalism', the Protestantism, established or sectarian, which encouraged stricter standards of individual morality, originally in the 18th century through 'vital religion', a religion of the heart, and finally, during the mid- and late 19th century, through what often came to be socially enforced codes of behaviour. During the early part of the century influential lay figures like William Wilberforce (1759–1833) and Hannah More (1745–1833), a 'Bishop in Petticoats', urged their contemporaries not to use the name of Jesus 'like the Allah of the Mahometans, a talisman or an amulet' but to have it 'engraved deeply on the heart'. They were involved in Christian 'causes' which always looked 'to a happiness beyond the reach of human vicissitudes'. Their successors shared their enthusiasms but tended to be selective in their choice of causes and to be willing, only too often, to separate faith and intellect. They were all too willing in addition to attribute Britain's national strength to its superior Protestant morality, and drew comforting contrasts between the English and the 'Continental' Sunday and between the 'good order' of British life and the slackness, corruption and superstition not only of 'heathens' but of European Catholics. Even Matthew Arnold condemned French moral attitudes: 'France takes the wishes of the flesh and of the current thoughts for a man's *rights*; and human happiness, and the perfection of society, she places in everybody's being enabled to gratify those wishes.' Everywhere in the Latin nations, indeed, Arnold wrote in 1874, 'you see the old indigenous type of city disappearing, and the type of modern Paris, the city of *l'homme sensuel moyen*, replacing it.' *La Bohème*, the ideal, free, pleasurable life of Paris,' he went on, 'is a kind of Paradise of Ishmaels.' Arnold thought it shameful that a Frenchman could call his children Lucifer, Satan and Vercingétorix, and attributed France's defeat in 1870 to a 'want of a serious conception of righteousness and the need of it'.

In fact, Evangelicalism is an inadequate explanation of what was happening in the 19th century. Essentially the same very limited kind of morality was propounded, even if it did not prevail, in countries where there are no exact equivalents of the British Sunday, of the Religious Tracts Society, of Exeter Hall, the great meeting centre of all the most noisy, if also the most humanitarian,

The Christian Mission in Whitechapel, founded by William Booth in 1864; it became the Salvation Army in 1878. Booth's mission was not only evangelical (he believed men had to be converted to be saved) but also practical and charitable—here the People's Soup and Coffee House, offering low-priced food for sale, stands next to the Mission Hall.

19th-century religious 'causes', or of evangelical aristocrats with eternally vigilant consciences like the seventh Earl of Shaftesbury (1801–85). The 'inner directed' man was not necessarily a Christian: he was certainly not necessarily an Englishman. The appeal of Smiles in countries outside Britain crossed all religious divides. When Smiles visited Italy in 1889—and his writings, as we have seen, were by then declining in influence in Britain itself—he was selected officially as 'an educator of the rising generation of Italians in honesty, courage and perseverance'. On a visit to Ireland in 1881 Smiles had felt that the priests ought to do more to enjoin upon their parishioners 'the virtues of self-reliance, prudence and foresight'. Yet even in Ireland Father Theobald Mathew (1790–1856) encouraged thousands of Irish people to sign the teetotal pledge.

The temperance movement, which influenced both middle-class and working-class people, had its origins not in Britain but in the United States. There were also 19th-century moralizing 'reform movements' in Islam and among Hindus in India. In France there would have been a far less vigorous attack by artists on bourgeois qualities like modesty, prudence, sobriety and thrift if these values had not been deeply embedded not only in Huguenot France but in provincial Catholic or even anti-clerical society. It was a German visitor to Vienna in 1859, F. T. Vischer (1807–87), who complained about smutty garrison jokes in a play by Johann Nestroy (1801–62), while admitting that most of the 'sins' of 'this buffooning capital' were innocent in character. And it was in Scandinavia, as we have seen, that bourgeois conventions seemed so stifling that Ibsen was driven to rebel and August Strindberg (1849–1912), a student of Zola and a correspondent of Nietzsche, scourged his contemporaries. Earlier in the century, Søren Kierkegaard (1813–55), whose Christian existentialism—like the superb poetry of the English Catholic priest, Gerard Manley Hopkins (1844–89)—has meant more to 20th-century readers than it would have done to those of the 19th century, had prophesied a new and 'frightful' reformation compared with which that of Luther would look to be no more than a 'jest'. The Norwegian painter Edvard Munch (1863–1944), who abandoned Impressionism during the 1890s to turn to haunting psychological themes of anxiety, fear and death, has been said to mediate both between Ibsen and Strindberg and between the 19th and 20th centuries.

If 19th-century bourgeois 'morality' is to be 'explained', therefore, it is necessary to examine more deeply the whole notion of 'the inner-directed man', to study more fully the personal relations between the sexes and the economic relations between 'masters' and 'men' in a post-feudal, industrializing, more mobile society. It was of the essence of this morality that it was thought to be relevant also to the aristocrat and to the artisan and that it had to be diffused through the agency not only of church or chapel but of voluntary movements and popular media of communication. (W. H. Smith (1825–91), the founder of Smith's railway bookstalls, was nicknamed 'Old Morality'.) The story of 19th-century morals has never yet been fully told, but key themes in it must be the power of property (the sense of property applied to people as well as to machines or to land and capital); the effort to make property permanent, not least in the universe of 'things'; 'home-centredness' (a German as much as a British ideal); the concern for greater cleanliness (sometimes coming before Godliness); the supporting role of domestic service in the bourgeois home (not so much a benign illustration of the 'gospel of work' as organized drudgery); the shift in emphasis towards 'modesty', 'gentility' and 'respectability' from the older aristocratic values of 'honour' and 'display'; the sense of 'struggle' necessarily entailed in the effort to reconcile more stringent codes of individual behaviour with what Humboldt had called 'vague and transient desires'. The British doctor William Acton (1813–75), who published a classic work on *Prostitution, considered in its Moral, Social and Sanitary Aspects* (1857) and who has been well described as 'the Samuel Smiles of continence', believed that much of what was happening in the 19th century could best be attributed to the cash nexus and to a more mobile society in transition: 'We are too apt in this utilitarian and self-seeking age to forget that incidental, as well as directed, duties attend the different social relationships.' In retrospect, it is perhaps simpler to relate continence to thrift and discipline to work, all the acceptable 19th-century qualities constituting one single psychological bundle.

Even a cursory study of Acton's writings explains why Freud's work was so profoundly to transform 20th-century ways of thinking and feeling. Yet awareness of the repressive character of 19th-century bourgeois morality preceded Freud, 'I believe,' wrote Samuel Butler (1835–1902) in his novel *The Way of All Flesh* which was not published until 1903, after his death, 'that more unhappiness comes from the source of the family than from any other. The mischief among the lower classes is not as great, but among the middle classes it is killing a large number daily.' *The New Spirit* (1890) by Havelock Ellis (1859–1939), Britain's most outspoken writer on sex, set out to justify a 'great wave of emancipation now sweeping across the world'. Ellis not only made much of the new role of women but pressed for a more complete 'social organization'. He included chapters on Ibsen, Tolstoy, who held that the first condition of happiness was that the link between man and nature should not be broken and that 'civilization' as its defenders described it was a huge humbug, and Walt Whitman (1819–92), the American poet and artist, who found deep delight both in nature and in the exercise of man's creative powers and refused to accept the 19th-century conception of duty on which so much of 19th-century morality rested:

> *I give nothing as duties,*
> *What others give as duties I give as living impulses,*
> *Shall I give the heart's action as a duty?*

Tolstoy and Whitman extolled the simple life: Oscar Wilde strained after the exotic. Yet Wilde, who defied at great cost the strictest moral conventions of his time—*The Importance of Being Earnest* (1895) was a skit on one of the favourite Victorian qualities —shared many of the same conclusions as the admirers of Tolstoy and Whitman and of Socialist writers like George Bernard Shaw (1856–1950). Wilde maintained that 'individuality' could only flourish under Socialism. 'Under the new conditions,' he wrote eloquently in *The Soul of Man under Socialism* (1891), 'Individualism will be far freer, far finer, and far more intensified than it is now. I am not talking of the great imaginatively realized Individualism of . . . poets . . . but of the great actual Individualism latent and potential in mankind generally. For the recognition of private property has really harmed Individualism, and obscured it, by confusing a man with what he possesses. It has led Individualism entirely astray. It has made gain, not growth, its aim.'

In his *Quintessence of Ibsenism* (1891), originally a Fabian lecture in a series which included one by William Morris on Gothic architecture, and another by a leading Fabian on Zola, Shaw went even further. 'There is no hope in Individualism for egotism. When at last a man is brought face to face with himself by a brave Individualism, he finds himself face to face not with an individual but with a species, and knows that to save himself, he must save the race. He can have no life except a share in the life of the community; and if that life is unhappy and squalid, nothing that he can do to paint and paper and upholster his little corner of it can really rescue him from it.'

The story of 'individualism', therefore, had an unusual 19th-century ending, but in fact it was only the ending of a chapter not of a book. The view of the 'rebels' did not prevail. The trial of Oscar Wilde in 1895 was followed by a reaction during which praise of the strident masculine virtues of the imperial adventurer—yet another kind of individualist—or of the sportsman (sports were everywhere coming into their own) drowned both the voices of the rebels and the survivors of mid-19th-century liberalism. The bourgeois *Yellow Press* counted for more than the avant garde *Yellow Book* (1894–97), and *Punch* caught the mood of its middle-class readers with sure instinct, as it had so often done since its first launching in 1841:

> *Reaction's the reverse of retrograde,*
> *If we recede from decadent excesses,*
> *And beat retreat from novelists who trade*
> *On 'sex', from artists whose chefs d'œuvres are messes.*
> *'Tis time indeed such minor plagues were stayed.*
>
> *Then here's for cricket in this year of Grace,*
> *Fair-play all round, straight hitting and straight dealing*
> *In letters, morals, art and commonplace*
> *Reversion into type in deed and feeling—*
> *A path of true Reaction to retrace.*

In some respects, the reaction was international. In the United States, where there was golf but no cricket, these were the years when 'social Darwinism'—linking economic and social dynamism to the idea of 'the survival of the fittest'—was at its height. 'It would be strange if the "captain of industry" did not sometimes manifest a militant spirit,' a university professor wrote in 1896, 'for he has risen from the ranks largely because he was a better fighter than most of us. Competitive commercial life is not a flowery bed of care but a battle.'

In France the Dreyfus case, which hit the headlines in 1898 and 1899, led to the widest and most bitter discussion of what military qualities really were and encouraged a new nationalism which combined an appeal to traditional values with demagogic fervour.

In the Germany of William II there was more ambivalence. The novels of Theodor Fontane (1819–98), like the stories of the Swiss writer Gottfried Keller (1819–90), were in a tradition which looked back to the literary renaissance in early 19th-century Germany. In very different vein, Wilhelm Busch (1832–1908) poked fun at all forms of bourgeois conventionality, while the *Wandervögel* movement gathered together groups of 'youth among itself' deliberately rejecting middle-class life. Yet the Empire depended on pomp and power, and however much the German middle classes might find poetry in the countryside while laughing at their own hypocrisy, they supported a regime which incorporated the most highly organized system of militarism in the world and which accepted without question that social prestige was bound up with military rank and honour. By the end of the 19th century there were other Germans, too, who were turning from the nation to the Volk, to Romantic notions of a new and more fundamental German revolution. Bourgeois ideals were to be under attack from a different direction. In the 20th century, as George L. Mosse has written, 'an ideology that was only vaguely relevant to the real problems confronting the German people ultimately became normative for the solutions to those problems'. And the ideology, alas, was already 'fully armed' by 1900.

II REVOLUTION AND IMPROVEMENT

Politics and society from 1789 to 1851

JOHN ROBERTS

'It was the best of times, it was the worst of times,

it was the age of wisdom, it was the age of foolishness,

it was the epoch of belief, it was the epoch of incredulity,

it was the season of Light, it was the season of Darkness,

it was the spring of hope, it was the winter of despair.'

CHARLES DICKENS, 'A Tale of Two Cities'

History creates myth

and myth in its turn can create history. Though some thought the French Revolution already over when the 19th century began, no event dominated that century so decisively; a hundred years later its ideals were still vigorously alive, its slogans still rallying cries. To call it an *event* at all is perhaps part of the myth. The confusions, conflicts and surprises of the revolutionary years were simplified and idealized. By 1847, when the print shown opposite was published, myth had largely taken the place of history. The Revolution had become a symbol.

The series begins with the Tennis Court Oath, when the Third Estate swore never to separate until a constitution had been granted, the Fall of the Bastille and the Fête de la Fédération, on the anniversary the following year. In the second row are the Proclamation of the Republic, the Siege of Toulon, at which

Bonaparte played a major part, and Bonaparte defending the Convention. The third shows the Battle of the Pyramids, Bonaparte establishing the Consulate and the Crossing of the St Bernard. At the bottom are the Coronation of Napoleon, the Return from Elba and his Farewell to his Troops at Fontainebleau.

It is notable that over half of the twelve pictures are devoted to Napoleon (events between 1804 and 1814 being conveniently forgotten). Whatever may have been felt during his lifetime and by unreconciled republicans, the belief that he had inherited and guaranteed, rather than betrayed, the ideals of 1789 had a wide popular currency. It was a belief which his nephew, Louis Napoleon, was trying to exploit just at the time when those woodcuts were printed. The proclamation of the Second Republic in 1848 was a conscious re-enactment of that of the First.

Serment du Jeu de Paume.
(20 juin 1789.)

Prise de la Bastille.
(14 juillet 1789.)

Fête de la Fédération au Champ de Mars.
(14 juillet 1790.)

Proclamation de la république française.
(1793.)

Siége de Toulon contre les anglais.
(1793.)

Bonaparte défendant la Convention.
(1793.)

Bataille des Pyramides.
(21 juillet 1799.)

Bonaparte dissout le Conseil des Cinq cents et établit le Consulat.
(18 brumaire. — 9 novembre 1799.)

Passage du Mont-Saint-Bernard.
(1800.)

Sacre de Napoléon et de Joséphine.
(2 décembre 1804.)

Retour de l'île d'Elbe.
(1814.)

Les Adieux de Fontainebleau.
(1815.)

The new age was marked by a host of symbolic acts and images designed to express the significance of what had occurred. *Right*: 'Man, finally satisfied that he has regained his rights, gives thanks to the Supreme Being' a print published in 1791. The tree of inherited privilege, with its escutcheons of noble families, has been felled, and divine lightning strikes the abandoned crown.

'La chute en masse' (*below*), the opposite of the *levée en masse*: a cartoon showing how the electric spark of liberty will overthrow the thrones of Europe. Electrical experiments were a contemporary craze.

To replace Christianity Robespierre evolved a deistic Rousseauesque religion centred upon the Supreme Being. In 1794, the painter David staged an elaborately symbolic ceremony in the Champ de Mars in which he played the foremost role (*bottom*).

The spirit of Revolution (*left*), one of the most striking of all revolutionary symbols, was carved for the Arc de Triomphe in 1833 by François Rude. *Above*: a counter-revolutionary family denounced. *Below*: Michel Gérard, a deputy, affected peasant costume.

'**We too know how to fight** and to conquer.' In the early days of the Revolution some enthusiasts undertook the cause of female rights. This print (*above*) of a young Amazon bearing her spear ('*Liberté ou la mort*') was published in 1789.

The Marseillaise is born: a patriotic picture of 1849 (*right*).

When the victors met at Vienna to restore Europe to its 'legitimate' rulers, they were not blindly trying to put back the clock to 1789. Neither the values of the Revolution nor Napoleon's reforms and rationalizations could be ignored. Stability was their main concern. They were afraid of radicalism, afraid of French aggression, afraid of change. These fears made for international peace but, in spite of their considerable success in avoiding large-scale wars, the history of the next thirty years was mainly to be one of struggle against the conservatism, social

and political, established at Vienna in 1815.

This Austrian caricature (*below*) shows most of the personalities who drew up the settlement: on the far side of the table are Francis I (1), Tsar Alexander I (2) and Frederick William III of Prussia (3). Wellington (4) is behind the globe. The other figures in the foreground, from left to right, are the Kings of Bavaria (6), of Denmark (5) and of Württemberg (7); and on the right of the table the Elector of Hesse (8), the Duke of Brunswick (9) and Talleyrand (10).

Louis XVIII, the brother of Louis XVI, returned to the throne of France in May 1814. His power was severely limited by a constitution, the terms of which he observed with a measure of prudence. This quality was lacking in his younger brother, Charles X, who succeeded him in 1824. The two brothers are seen here (*right*), Charles on the left, receiving troops at the Tuileries in 1823. But Europe longed for peace, and turned with relief to the private world of domesticity. The period after 1815 is that of 'Biedermeier', with its emphasis on security, middle-class values and the day to day pleasures of ordinary life. *Below right*: a German family in the 1820s.

Cracks in the new order came seriously in 1830. The Bourbons, it was said, 'had learned nothing and forgotten nothing'. In July Paris rose in revolt. Barricades were built (*left*: the rue Saint-Antoine) and the Hôtel de Ville seized. Moderate opinion favoured a constitutional monarchy and the throne was offered to the nephew of the last three Bourbons, Louis Philippe. *Below right*: he rides to the Hôtel de Ville preceded by the tricolour, unseen since 1815.

Eighteen years later, in 1848, another tidal wave of revolution hit Europe, with even more devastating effect. In Paris, Louis Philippe abdicated in February and a government of the republican left was formed, but this moved steadily towards the right, as middle-class opinion in the rest of France exerted its weight. A final popular outburst, the 'June Days', was suppressed by force.

Revolution spread. The Poles (*above*) set up a provisional government but were soon again suppressed by Russia. In Belgium (*below*) forcibly united with Holland, the 1830 Revolution was successful; a new independent nation was recognized under Leopold I.

All over Europe governments were shaken. In Vienna barricades were set up (*above left*) and revolutionary committees met in the cafés (*left*). For a while it seemed as though the whole Habsburg empire might fall apart, but eventually a compromise was reached and 'legitimacy' restored. Metternich and Ferdinand I stepped down; the young Francis-Joseph ascended the throne; and liberal reforms were initiated. A rising in Prague (*above*), inspired by Czech nationalism, was ruthlessly crushed; such hopes had to wait until 1919. In Italy, on the other hand, attempts to throw off the Austrian yoke (*below*: rebellion in Milan), though unsuccessful, looked forward to the national unity soon to be achieved.

Italian hopes, nourished on Mazzini's propaganda, the activity of the secret societies and the liberalization of the Papal States under Pius IX, culminated in the flight of the pope and proclamation of the Roman Republic (*right*) in February 1849. But Tuscany refused to rise; Piedmont was defeated at Novara; and after enduring a heroic siege under Mazzini and Garibaldi, Rome was forced into submission by French arms.

French gains were, on paper, the most substantial. The monarchy was abolished and the Second Republic joyfully inaugurated (*below*) under the leadership of a democratically elected president. Yet the people's choice was a man as devoted to personal rule as any Bourbon – Louis Napoleon.

Politics and society from 1789 to 1851

JOHN ROBERTS

IF A DATE has to be found for the beginning of modern history, July 14th, 1789, has more to be said for it than almost any other. The crucial act of that day was a Parisian riot which turned into an attack on a royal fortress, the famous Bastille, and the surrender of the governor after some hours of fighting. The real events concealed in these statements were ludicrously disproportionate to their subsequent idealization. The fortress was disused and half-armed; its guns were dismounted; it was defended only by a hundred or so pensioners and Swiss Guards. Its chief function was as a state prison, but its liberators found only a few miserable wretches in its cells. Human nature detracted further from the dignity of the proceedings; the commandant and some of his aged garrison were butchered after their surrender. Yet in later years to have been a *vainqueur de la Bastille* was to be assured of respect (and perhaps even of safety); many who had not been present on the day therefore appropriated to themselves the honour of membership of that ill-defined company.

Revolution: symbol, myth, fact

The storming of the Winter Palace, an act equally important in the history of another revolution, displays a similar disparity between legend and reality. The crucial importance of these comparatively trivial events lies not in what they were but in what they suggested. Their effective role was symbolic; they shaped other events by forcing men to recognize far-reaching implications. The fall of the Bastille gave confidence to resist a king to an elected assembly still unsure of itself and uncertain of the support on which it could draw. After July 14th the king would at least have to think twice before using armed force against the deputies, and would probably not use it at all. A minister who had just been discharged, against the wishes of the assembly, was recalled amid popular acclamation; this seemed to clinch the point. In a longer perspective, still more was implied. In the spring of 1789 nobles and commoners alike had asked in their electoral *cahiers* for the destruction of the Bastille. Oppression was now seen to be thwarted and despotism overturned; at the time it may have been royal despotism, but the event came in the end to stand for the overthrow of a whole order, whose crumbling, destruction and transformation were to take years of legislation and warfare. The fall of the Bastille remains properly the major symbol of the French Revolution because it was recognized at the time to be so.

It is, of course, a symbol which distorts and simplifies, but so does the myth implied in the phrase 'French Revolution'. At its simplest this phrase must connote a process stretching from the summoning of the States-General in the spring of 1789 to the final overthrow in 1815 of the Napoleonic Empire which had consolidated so many of the changes of the intervening years and done so much to diffuse the revolution outside France. Some would wish to go further back, beyond 1789, and some (as we shall see) to trace the French Revolution far beyond 1815. Besides this complication, there are other paradoxes and complexities. It was Chateaubriand (1768–1848), himself a Breton nobleman, who pointed out that the nobles began the revolution; and for all the real importance and bogus sentimentality which gathered around the counter-revolution and the emigration it must not be forgotten that something like nine-tenths of those of noble blood in France did *not* emigrate,

remaining there even during the worst of the Terror. Another important class, the majority of Frenchmen in 1789, is that of the peasants (however we define that misleadingly simple term); it is well-known that they burned the manor-houses and castles of their *seigneurs*, ransacking their archives and terrorizing their womenfolk. It is slightly less well-known that this was probably more important even than the storming of the Bastille in shaping the events of 1789, and it has been almost totally overlooked except by professional historians, that this peasantry was even at that moment in many places seeking not social and economic progress but reaction. The peasants were to prove the most tenacious source of conservative practice in France for the next half-century. A final example of the complexity of what we simply describe as *the* French Revolution is provided by the fate of the monarchy. The establishment of the Republic on September 22nd, 1792, was a great event and has been seen to embody the essence of the revolution. Yet when the States-General were summoned (which, in any case, had not been imposed on the Crown by the radicals), this had not been foreseen. The Republic, in fact, owed its establishment to the thwarting of the Crown's efforts to carry out many of those very reforms which revolutionary and Napoleonic governments subsequently drew from the pigeonholes of the *ancien régime* to put into practice in the name of the new order.

To begin a discussion of changing Europe between 1789 and 1851 with so rich and complicated a historical 'fact' is artificial, as any historical shorthand must be. Yet in one sense it can be justified; contemporaries recognized the beginning in 1789 of something new of outstanding importance. Even when, like Arthur Young (1741–1820), they then went wrong by thinking that it was all over by the end of June—'the whole business now seems over, and the revolution complete'—they were right to think the year decisive. We can now see this to be true, because the things that happened then in France released forces crucial for Europe as a whole. This was just because they took place in France. French culture and French ideas dominated the minds of thinking men as far east as the Urals. The monarchy of France, for all its weakness in the eyes of posterity and its struggles with privilege, stood at the head of a great state: it could deploy greater strength than any other monarchy west of Russia; France's population was the biggest of the western world and her rate of economic growth in the 18th century as rapid as that of her major colonial and commercial rival, Great Britain. Whatever the losses of the 18th-century wars, France was still the leading European power and, in consequence, what happened to France decided Europe's history as well as her own. 'The Revolution', the spectre of conservatives in the next century, frightened them just because they had seen it carried so far beyond France's borders after 1792, in the knapsacks of the armies formed by the thinking and training of the *ancien régime*, recruited by Lazare Carnot, 'the architect of victory' (1753–1823) and the Committee of Public Safety, and led by, among other old royal officers, Bonaparte. Yet even before this the European significance of what was happening had been quickly grasped. 'The French Revolution is one of those events which belong to the whole human race,' wrote Friedrich von Gentz (1764–1832) in 1794. With forty-odd years' perspective to help him, Thomas Carlyle (1795–1881) came to much the same conclusion in 1837:

The guillotine—symbol of the Terror—came into use in 1789. Previously it had been the privilege of the nobility to be executed by decapitation—now there was equality before the executioner. The guillotine was also swift and relatively painless.

'It appears to be, if not stated in words, yet tacitly felt and understood everywhere, that the event of these modern ages is the French Revolution. A huge explosion, bursting through all formulae and customs. . . .'

The 'terror of Terror'

As we read the letters and books of the men who experienced this 'huge explosion', it is difficult not to believe them at times deranged by the danger that they felt to threaten. Metternich is said to have used only eight metaphors to talk about society: volcano, plague, cancer, deluge, conflagration, powder magazines, influenza and cholera. True or not, this draws attention to the huge gap between an 18th-century, rationalizing mind such as that of Metternich (1773–1859) and the irrational, passionate turmoil of the French Revolution and its consequences. Yet a man like Edmund Burke (1729–97), whose imagination kindled more rapidly to a romantic glow and who found emotional comprehension easier, was just as violently repelled. The impact on the European mind was such that for a century men talked of *The* Revolution, and meant by it not just the chronologically defined events of any period, however generously its limits might be drawn, but an independent force, released by the events in France, and roaming up and down the public life of Europe like a beast of prey or, for a smaller but growing number of fanatics, like an avenging angel, for the myth of the Revolution was cherished on both sides of the barricades.

The word itself changed its meaning. In 1789, people still spoke of 'revolution' in a reassuringly restricted sense: it usually meant only a turn of the wheel of political fortune, a change in the hands which held power, or more general changes marking an epoch in a country's affairs, such as an invasion, or the arrival of a new dynasty. Even the British idolization of 'The Glorious Revolution', the centenary of which was enthusiastically celebrated in 1788, emphasized the limited and conservative nature of that

great deliverance: new occupants of the throne and the fiction that not only had there been no fundamental transformation, but that a threatened subversion of an old and healthy constitution had been averted. Events in France rapidly changed this usage. Clearly something much more fundamental was taking place when a nation consciously rebuilt its whole social and political system on the foundation of legal equality; when the property of the Church was secularized and a religious settlement imposed which was unacceptable to the majority of French clergy; when a king's head was cut off and thrown down as a challenge to other kings; when it was announced—and reiterated—that changes of equal scope were not only desirable but morally and logically necessary in all other countries, and that the Republic would promote them, if necessary by force of arms.

The image of Revolution as cataclysm which was created in France between 1789 and 1795 (and especially during the period of special emergency called 'Revolutionary Government', or, more widely, the Terror) was complex, but its most important elements are clear enough. Foremost came the idea of violence. The 18th century was certainly aware of the formal and informal role of violence in society. What was new was the institutionalizing of this violence in the service of political change. The crowds of *sans-culottes*, the street-fighting, the guillotine, the dictatorial and ruthless committee-men who nosed out suspects and enemies of the Republic were the face this process presented to the world. There was, of course, a great deal of exaggeration talked about the *buveurs de sang* and *septembriseurs*, but the mythical dimension of their activity was more important in forming a new idea of Revolution than the number of victims of the policy behind the machinery of Terror.

Another element in the image was the mob. Whatever the subsequent idealization of their contribution to working-class and revolutionary tradition, the participants in an 18th-century or early 19th-century mob were likely to be very unpleasant, callous, brutal, rapacious and dirty. Over the slum-dwellers of the towns and the half-barbaric peasants of the countryside there stretched only a thin sheet of order and civilization, fragile enough to be easily torn to shreds. This was the image which haunted the well-off. No doubt their alarm was exaggerated and over-dramatic; yet it was not to be corrected simply by pointing out the real social restraints implied by the existence of the better-off peasants or the small shopkeeper class. In any case, there was excuse for alarm because the image of *popular* revolution was assiduously fed by the revolutionaries themselves. Far from being common men themselves, the politically conscious artisans who made up the *sans-culottes* in Paris nevertheless applauded the oratory and reiterated the revolutionary cant which hammered home the lesson that Jacques was as good as his master, and they did so in an age when the image of social democracy in Europe was bound to be a terrifying one. The Revolution came quickly to connote mass violence and the tyranny of the poor. Even when this image was qualified (as it often was) by the conviction that it must end in military dictatorship, this was only an additional cause for alarm; the expectation of direct popular action remained terrifying.

Finally, the Revolution came to mean the extirpation of known landmarks, whether in principles, ideas or institutions. Political change was only a part of this. In France, primogeniture, nobility, tithes, chartered rights, monastic vows, battlements on manor-houses, family pews in churches and a hundred other familiar things were all swept away pell-mell; an almost universal anarchy seemed to be portended. The imposition of the language of Revolution—the *tutoyer* and *citoyen*—was another sign. There was talk of the *loi agraire* which would obliterate landed property itself (it has often been overlooked that the Convention ordained the death penalty for anyone proposing such a law). In the end, when tumult had passed and Napoleon had implicitly or explicitly defined what would and what would not survive of the old French society, many old landmarks turned out still to be there. But at the time it seemed that anarchy was only a step away and this impression haunted not only the statesmen of the Restoration but their successors as late as, for example, Bismarck.

Such visions as these explain what has been called the 'terror of

Terror'. Though understandable, it was superficial. Some men saw through it and assessed the French Revolution in a balanced enough way to dismiss the bug-a-boo of *The* Revolution. There was a great unwillingness to see the historical necessity of 1789; only Hegel and the Young Hegelians did so consistently. Most people looked for an explanation in the motives of wicked men. Only malevolence seemed a sufficient explanation for such meaningless destructiveness, and men worried over supposedly long-established conspiracies; the myth of the secret societies was another enduring creation of the revolutionary era. A thin plausibility was lent to their fears by the survival after 1815 of embittered revolutionaries whose devotion to *their* version of the myth of Revolution made them the first examples of a new breed: the professional revolutionary.

'Improvement'

This cataclysmic and dramatic view of what was happening obscured an equally important source of contemporary historical change. It can be expressed by the English word 'Improvement'. Indeed, the contrast between Revolution and Improvement reflects not only contrasting social processes but the national rivalry which was one of the continuing themes of European history in these years. Even when the French military monarchy was replaced, first by chartered legitimacy and then by constitutional monarchy, English statesmen distrusted France. They remembered the terrible power demonstrated in twenty years of warfare and were afraid that French governments, whatever their colour, could easily again be pushed on to the road of aggrandizement.

But here we are concerned not with this latent antagonism but with what a social scientist might call an alternative 'model' of change. It was presented in its most developed and concentrated form in English society. Usage is again an interesting guide. At a very early date, the word 'Improvement' had been used of agriculture. It described the process whose origins lay in Flanders during the late Middle Ages and which had spread to England during the 16th and 17th centuries; through it agriculture was continually stimulated by new and renovated techniques, scientific study and the intensive application of capital. By 1789 the result could be seen in the contrast between the English landscape and that of most of Europe, or in the beasts which grazed them. Better yields and fatter animals drew agricultural observers from all over Europe to English fairs and farmers; agricultural societies and the study of English agricultural authors were the evidence that European landlords found in England lessons that they would, if they could, apply at home.

This memorandum of the background of the idea of Improvement takes us at once to a consideration which was to lie at the heart of all subsequent history: the unprecedented increase of wealth—which was the essence of what had happened to English agriculture and, through it, to English society—could not be separated from concomitant social change. The early and special example of this came in agriculture itself; in all European countries except the Netherlands and, perhaps, Lombardy, agricultural improvement ran quickly into social obstacles. Seigneurial tenures, an unfree labour force, common lands, rights of turbary (cutting turf or peat for fuel) and grazing—in different parts of Europe these institutions and many others were tenaciously defended by men who felt their livelihood threatened by the innovators who demanded their removal. Within this context, Improvement was linked inextricably with social change and therefore with political and social struggle. By about 1800, the positive difference which agricultural improvement had made to continental Europe was still very small. But the changes which the next half-century were to bring were vast; by 1851 serfdom would have disappeared from Western Europe, though it had been widespread there in 1789.

Such implications are even more dramatic if the effects of 'Improvement' are examined in a yet wider context as a whole spectrum of change resulting from increasing wealth. Already in 18th-century England men had extended the idea of Improvement from the countryside to the towns; 'improvement schemes' were launched, and legislation set up Improvement Commissioners to supervise them. Capital and knowledge were thus applied to the betterment of environment as they had already been applied to agriculture. Soon the idea was extended to the moral life; the busy bee, it had been observed long before, by Isaac Watts (1674–1748) the dissenting minister and hymn writer, improved each shining hour, and manners could not only be Reformed but Improved by attention. Improving literature became conventional reading. There were so many other applications of the idea, also, that the English Whig historian, Thomas Babington Macaulay, could claim in a year of European revolutions, 1848, that 'the history of our country during the last hundred and sixty years is eminently the history of physical, or moral, and of intellectual improvement'.

Improvement is the theme which must accompany Revolution in any analysis of this period because it was the other great source of change. It both wrought change itself and was at the same time a symptom of change, deriving from a great material fact, the increase of wealth. This was the essence of the social process which had long been going on in England, which was to be seen at its most vigorous and intense in England in these years, and which was beginning to spread abroad. With the acceptance (however reluctantly and slowly in specific instances) of the implications of this extraordinary expansion of wealth, came a growing awareness of the need to adapt society peacefully in order to cope with them. We should not be confused by the clamour for *laissez-faire* (as has been shown in Chapter I): the establishment of *laissez-faire* was only the first of the social adaptations required.

When foreigners looked at England in the early and middle 19th century, they were often impressed; the spectacle of peaceful change was enhanced both by the enormous prestige attaching to the one country which had not faltered in its opposition to the revolutionary danger from France and by its startling increase of wealth. Yet they did not always find it easy to take its key ideas home with them. Guizot's '*Enrichissez-vous*' has been overquoted and was at once misrepresented, but it seemed to many Continentals to sum up a materialist, uninspiring creed. There was smugness

Ça me réchauffe, disait-il quelquefois. — PAGE 34.

'That warms my heart.' Monsieur Grandet, in Balzac's novel 'Eugénie Grandet', represents the narrow bourgeois materialism which to many writers and thinkers typified the age of Louis Philippe. The story revolves round M. Grandet's money, which his daughter inherits but which fails to win her the man she loves.

and complacency about the assumptions of peaceful change; Charles Dickens' Mr Podsnap is a convincing figure. And, it must be remembered also that Improvement often seemed on the brink of proving inadequate to grapple with the strains of a growing society, even in England, where men at times feared revolution and the clerks of the Bank of England stood to their arms to defend the national credit. Finally, doubt had been cast, before the century began, on the more general notion that progress was inevitable (an idea whose purest embodiment came in a French, not an English, book of 1793, Condorcet's *Esquisse d'un tableau historique des progrès de l'esprit humain*). The gloomy central argument of Thomas Malthus' *Essay on the Principle of Population* (first ed. 1798) that food supply could not expand at the same rate as population growth haunted even many of his opponents. What made most people able to ignore it during the next fifty years was the visible growth in European wealth which accompanied the growth in population.

Anciens Régimes, new principles

The big changes of this era, therefore, had peaceful as well as violent roots and took evolutionary as well as revolutionary forms. Before we turn to consider their nature we should try to be clear about what it was that was changed. Myths bred myths: fear of revolution and distaste for an emerging social order led to idealization of the society that was threatened; conversely, revolutionary enthusiasm often postulated a historic unity of corruption and immorality universally to be swept away. Of course such simple views were nonsense. Not only did they blur great complexities; they resolutely denied some of the great paradoxes of the age. Such cut-and-dried, red-and-black simplifications could hardly make sense of, for example, England's history in these years. In that country social change went fastest and furthest; most of what was later to be tenaciously defended elsewhere had by 1789 already disappeared in England where there existed even then institutions which revolutionaries in less happy lands were to fight for decades to establish. Yet this was also the country which was the most implacable and relentless enemy of the revolutionary danger embodied in France. Such complexities are, unfortunately, usually ignored by men driven by political passion and in search of release. From over-simplifications on each side there crystallized the idea of the *ancien régime*.

It was not a new phrase in 1789 and it was familiar enough not yet to be capitalized. It meant little more than 'under the rule of the last king'. By the time we find it in a letter (January 1792) of Queen Marie-Antoinette (1755–93) its bearing is still governmental but its application is a little wider; it seems to mean something like 'the previous state of affairs' or, even, 'the previous management'. Between then and the Restoration it turned into a phrase connoting, above all, social institutions and principles and (as we have said) a generous measure of moral approval or condemnation of them. The *Ancien Régime* (capitals were common by 1815) which was pilloried by the revolutionaries was static, irrational, immoral in principle and corrupt in practice, perversely pitting itself against the dynamic force of beneficial change. For the other side, it represented moral and practical order, the natural principles of society and the family, the authority of history and tradition, refinement and civilization.

The first important intellectual challenge to these myths was to come just after 1851, when Tocqueville published his great work, *L'Ancien Régime et la Révolution*, even if in the service of a political thesis he brilliantly substituted a new myth for the old. Most general historical arguments tend to take one of two forms: that things are more different than they seem, or that they are more alike; Tocqueville's argument was of the second sort. He illustrated the weakness of received ideas about the Revolution by showing how much of it had been anticipated before 1789 and how much of the past it carried forward in itself. There is much to be said for this; though we may now want to qualify Tocqueville's particular examples, his view can be given a European application. Above all, in other countries more than in France, the phenomenon we call 'Enlightened Despotism' anticipated much of the work of the revolutionary assemblies. The Austrian government's invasion of privilege in the Netherlands, culminating in the abolition of the

Estates of Brabant in June 1789, appeared to the Church and nobility of Belgium far more of a threat than what was going on in Paris; their resistance led to the complete collapse of Austrian rule by Christmas. The measures of Joseph II (1741–90) elsewhere, too, had been widely (and rightly) seen by his subjects to subvert the existing order; like many 18th-century reforming rulers, he was opposed by the privileged orders in almost all his dominions. The Civil Constitution of the Clergy would have made perfect sense to his civil servants. Such coincidences of aim, it should also be remembered, were favoured by the continuity of personnel in government and administration during this period. Revolution, even when imposed most blatantly and arbitrarily from above by French arms, could not make a clean sweep of the official classes, nor did it have to; it found plenty of men willing to work for it. The reforms of the Directory's satellites and the Napoleonic satrapies were often put through by bureaucrats recruited and trained by the *Ancien Régime*, like Lebrun, codifier of the Napoleonic Law, who had been secretary of the reforming minister Maupeou, or Zurro, Murat's minister of finance at Naples, who presided over the legal assault on the feudal system, which was a necessary preliminary to fiscal reforms he had sought under the Bourbons. They found the carrying-out of long-cherished projects congenial.

Another reservation must also be made if the *Ancien Régime* is not to be a misleading term. It was not a universally uniform, fixed state of affairs. Clemenceau once said that the Revolution was a *bloc*, to be taken or left as a whole; there is a danger of talking about the *Ancien Régime* in the same way. What people who talked about it were defending in different countries at different times were different things. There was no sharp break in the history of all institutions across Europe at a specific moment. Serfdom was abolished in France formally in 1789 and was already practically of little moment there; it still existed and was fundamental to the society in Russia in 1851. Another characteristic institution of the *Ancien Régime* was the corporatism expressed in most countries in (among other things) trade and industrial organizations, guilds, *jurandes* and the like. These were abolished (for the second time) in France in 1791; in spite of French occupation and a social structure in other ways very untypical of the *Ancien Régime*, Holland kept hers until 1818, and the atrophied relics of the British equivalents are still with us today.

Finally, we should remember the reference in the *Communist Manifesto* of 1848 to the division between town and country. In 1851, in spite of great changes since 1789, the *Ancien Régime* was still strikingly alive in the countryside, and the majority of Europeans were still country-dwellers. It was overwhelmingly the social order of a rural economy. Urbanization went hand in hand with enlightenment, sedition, and the destruction of old social ties; this, together with the threat to order arising from fear of the *classes dangereuses* was why conservatives deplored the growth of the towns and distrusted them. This was not to say that the countryside was quiet and orderly. The peasants were often a turbulent and dangerous force. Landlords lived in fear in bad years. But, except when peasants detonated political changes desired by others—as they did in France in 1789—they were almost always a reactionary and brutal influence. They tenaciously resisted agricultural improvement and capitalist exploitation of land, preferring communal usage and the morcellation of property. In France they were the only considerable force behind the counter-revolution. In Naples in 1799 they formed the Sanfedist army of Cardinal Ruffo and eagerly set about the lynching of progressive noblemen and middle-class jacobins. If the Habsburgs had been able to bring themselves to trust any popular force, it was in the Catholic peasantry of the Tyrol that they would have found their staunchest supporters. Peasants formed the armies that followed Napoleon out of Russia and beat him in Germany (and subsequently guaranteed Russia a military hegemony which was for thirty-five years the keystone of European reaction). In 1846 the peasants of Galicia turned on their Polish landlords and massacred fourteen hundred of them, thus nipping in the bud a Polish revolution and ensuring that the province remained quiet two years later when the rest of the Empire exploded. In Lombardy and Venetia they cheered the returning armies of Radetzky when the Piedmontese were beaten in 1849 and turned with pleasure on landlords who had supported the national cause and were now unprotected against them. The list could be almost endlessly lengthened. It is the face of the *Ancien Régime* that is usually forgotten.

Still, the term remains useful, even when these qualifications have been made. It stands for two things which are relatively clear. The first is a creed, a myth, a state of mind which first appeared in the emigration and counter-revolution. By 1815 there existed for the first time since the era of religious wars a broad agreement on principles between reactionaries of all countries. Far more noblemen in 1815 than in 1789 had some articulated ideas about social principles which they shared with their peers in all countries. The modern alternative to the progressive social ideal of the Enlightenment had 'crystallized. Traditional authority was respected in a new way, and so were historical and prescriptive rights.

The other sense of the term which is relatively clear is that which makes it stand for a number of institutions largely predominant in 1789 and no longer so in 1851. After all qualifications have been made, corporations and estates were no longer thought in 1851 to be an acceptable basis for political institutions in many countries; individual members of society, even when only qualified by wealth or education, increasingly were. The great dispute of the 19th century (as Stendhal called it), that between rank and merit, had been formally settled in favour of the latter in most countries. Social privilege might continue to exercise a real influence, yet 'the career open to the talents' proclaimed in 1789 was a reality by 1851. And though new nobilities proliferated as new states were created and regimes came and went, their very multiplication emphasized that the Europe of the aristocrats was passing. To these and similar changes we shall return when we have considered the actual story of the years from 1789 to 1851.

The role of France

France must come first in any account of the age of revolutions. Though the Belgians kicked off—they were the first to have a tricolour flag of red, yellow and black, the colours of Brabant—it was the game played in France which gripped the world's attention in 1789. In part because of this precedence and in part because of the mythology cultivated by revolutionary leaders, the rhythm of revolution elsewhere thereafter always responded to events in Paris (this qualification is important; European revolutionaries were not to be excited by an *émeute* in Amiens, or even in Lyons).

The first phase of the French Revolution was presided over by the Constituent Assembly. It gave France her first written constitution and laid the foundations of French public life down to our own day in equality before the law, a centralized administration working through the Departments, the sovereignty of the State and universal (though not at that time equal) suffrage. And it destroyed old France. It handed the country over to the Legislative Assembly in 1791, a body which plunged to disaster a year later, having taken France into war, and dragging down the monarchy with itself. One reason for its fall was that it could not dominate Paris. Two things were required to do so: secure food supplies and the confidence of the revolutionary and radical élite of the capital that reaction would not be allowed to repossess itself of power through the exploitation of constitutional freedoms and universal suffrage. The Legislative could achieve neither.

The revolutionary élite consisted of two elements, the radical faction in the clubs and among the politicians (they took their name from the most famous of the clubs, the Jacobins) and the *sans-culottes* who made up the National Guard battalions. These were the decisive force in the great 'days' of the Paris revolution. The two were to drift gradually apart under the Convention (elected in September 1792) which closed the first revolutionary era in France. The process was complicated and concealed by the self-deceiving cant of Robespierre (1758–94) who, somewhat unfairly, came to embody the principle of the Revolution for friends and foes alike. Before his fall, in the summer of 1794, he had helped to rebuild the structure of authority which the French state had lacked since 1789 and (with the exception of a final, half-hearted convulsion

Lamartine announcing the names of those forming the provisional government to the mob in front of the Hôtel de Ville on February 26th, 1848. He himself was appointed Minister of Foreign Affairs. But in the subsequent presidential elections of December 1848 he gained only seventeen thousand votes to Louis Napoleon's five and a half million.

in 1795) Parisian revolution came to an end for thirty-five years. With him disappeared the hope that the Revolution would bring about further social change.

Much that was irreversible had already happened, therefore, when France gave herself a new republican constitution in 1795. The Directory set up by it ruled for the next three and a half years, troubling alike those who feared reaction and those who feared fresh popular violence. It depended increasingly on force; generals loomed larger and larger in its affairs. One of the most glamorous of them, Bonaparte, accepted the role offered to him by some of the discontented. The coup d'état of Brumaire, year VIII (November 1799 in the old calendar) installed him in power as First Consul of the Republic and in five years his inauguration of the hereditary Empire crowned the transformation from revolution to personal dictatorship.

The changes of the Consulship and Empire—the Codes, the Concordat, the Prefectorial system and many another—were well-publicized and important. Through them Napoleon defined at last how much of the Revolution should be retained and how much should not. He built on its administrative foundations and went further by reconciling the Church, so that the Restoration of 1815 could not touch his achievement. Napoleon also reconciled laymen; he created his own nobility and caressed the old. In 1815, therefore, there was little obstacle to the reacceptance of traditional titles and to the reintegration of the old French ruling class. Finally, Napoleon's police harried liberals and old Jacobins (unless they served him as policemen or prefects, as many of them did); this helped to spread respect for the principles of 1789, and the chartered constitutional liberties of 1815 were to safeguard the individual. He was the greatest creative statesman of the era, not because of what he originated, but because of what he left established.

Not that the Restoration contented all Frenchmen. What it did was to give France fifteen years of peace, troubled though the years were by plots, assassination, and scuffles with rioting peasants or Luddite weavers. Then, in 1830, Paris again suddenly gave France a government. The July Days were watched with eagerness or alarm abroad, but at home the effervescence was quickly contained and Paris was not allowed to re-establish the dictatorship of '93. The dynasty was changed, but the electorate formed a smaller proportion of the French population than the unreformed electorate of England did of the English. Louis Philippe himself was a more reassuring figure than the alarming Lafayette (1757–1834), who had briefly again taken the stage; he soon began to behave in a reassuring way. The rule of the men of the *juste milieu* followed; those who wanted more were again driven to secret societies, plots and clandestine newspapers, unless they wanted to be shot down in the streets like the Lyonnais in 1834.

For eighteen years under the July Monarchy France was changing, but only very slowly. Still the greatest of western European powers, her population grew larger. But she was developing and growing richer at a slower rate than Great Britain or Belgium. It seems that the period in which the rural population of France was the largest in relation to the whole was in the last decade of Louis Philippe's rule. It is, therefore, hardly surprising that the next revolution, when it came in 1848, turned out to be the revolution of a pre-industrial society and not the one prophesied by those early socialists who searched the future for the meaning of industrialism.

Indeed, 1848 was the last occasion on which Paris conducted the European orchestra of revolution—the overture had anyway begun without her: in 1846 in Galicia, in 1847 in the Swiss civil war, and in Sicily in January 1848. Once under way, however, the year of revolutions again took its cues from Paris. This was very flattering for the Parisian makers of the February revolution of 1848. They exploited a collapse of confidence in the July Monarchy, symbolized by the disaffection of the National Guard. The groundswell of popular distress after two years of unemployment and a winter of near-famine carried them forward to create the Second Republic on February 24th. Long before its Constitution was ready, the incoherence of republican programmes, briefly masked by the rhetoric of the poet Lamartine (1790–1869), messages of sympathy to the oppressed Poles and ill-conceived public works schemes, stood revealed.

While other countries followed in France's wake—in a remarkable March Piedmont and the Papal States acquired new constitutions, Metternich fell from power, the Hungarian Diet carried important reforms, William II of Holland appointed a committee to revise the constitution, Venice proclaimed itself a republic and there was a revolution in Berlin—the confusion which reigned over the social policies of the French Second Republic were awakening the social fears which led to the barricades and the fighting of the June Days. The massacre of the Parisian workers which then took place showed how far the forces of Order had been strengthened since the days of the *sans-culottes*. The following weeks also showed the tenacity with which the great Revolution had now taken root; once it had crushed the Parisian worker, the Second Republic went on to enlist the countryside in its support. The Revolution had triumphed, and legitimists would have to forget dreams of another Restoration; yet they helped to give it its victory and to make it a conservative revolution. The Republic endured on this basis until captured in 1851 by Louis Napoleon Bonaparte who hastened to ratify his power before the tribunal of universal suffrage, the very touchstone of radicalism. The Revolution had triumphed indeed, but hardly in a way in which any of the giants of '89 or '93 would have approved.

European revolution and resistance

To go back to our starting-point, the Belgian revolt which begins the revolutionary story outside France in 1789 owed nothing to French example. But before long the contagion of French example and propaganda began to spread. All over Europe there appeared little groups of social and political dissenters, soon called 'jacobins', who are the first feeble beginnings of the phenomenon of the international Left. Their impact was negligible until the revolutionary wars carried the French armies into their neighbours' territory. When this happened the local jacobins collaborated with them and took part in the governments of the new satellite republics set up by *la Grande Nation*. By 1799 such satellites had appeared in Holland, Switzerland and most of Italy. Other areas—Belgium, the Rhineland, Piedmont, Savoy—had been at times ruled directly as parts of France. The result of this was the first great generalization of revolutionary institutions outside France. Constitutions in all the satellite republics stressed the Rights of Man and the Citizen and set up approximate equivalents of the French administrative and political machinery. Even the terminology of the Revolution was exported to the new daughters of the Republic; those local jacobins whose revolutionary sympathies proved too violent for French diplomacy or too troublesome to the French army were abused as '*Dantoniens*', '*anarchistes*' and, ludicrously, even as '*septembriseurs*'. From 1792, when Belgium had its first taste of French occupation, to the winter of 1799, when a French garrison in Genoa was alone left to represent the French presence once embodied in a chain of satellite republics, the French Revolution was a governmental and social actuality to millions of western Europeans.

The restorations of 1799 were rapid and complete, but brief. They were followed by the second great phase of the revolutionizing of Europe, the Napoleonic. As in the first phase, the movement of the French armies was decisive; where they went, conscription, the codes and the Prefects followed. Their conquests, too, changed the map, and did so far more ruthlessly than the armies of the Directory. In 1806 one of the most ancient of European institutions, the Holy Roman Empire, was swept away, and Germany began that evolution into consolidation and simplification which was to come to a climax in 1871. Even a wraithlike Poland emerged briefly from the shadows of the Partitions, the last of which had taken place in 1795. The Napoleonic era was the seed-time of the nations. The same setting of limits to Revolution which he showed at home was also shown in Napoleon's European schemes; his policy in effect restored the Papacy whose extinction

The 'Twelve Points' being declared in Pest, March 15th, 1848. Steered through the Diet by Kossuth and Ferencz Deák, these points, later to be known as the March Laws, were granted to Hungary by Austria as a result of the 1848 revolution. They guaranteed Hungarian home rule with a parliament at Buda-Pest elected on restricted suffrage; representation of towns in the parliament; equality before the law and for taxation; the right to hold public meetings; religious liberty and the abolition of serfdom.

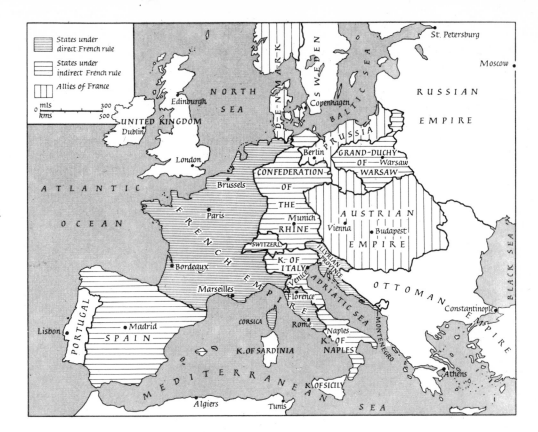

Napoleon's Empire at its greatest extent.

seemed near when the Roman Republic had been set up in 1798. He might later quarrel with Pius VI (1717–99) and carry him off to detention in France, but his own claim to stand in the heritage of Charlemagne was a tacit recognition of his fellow-monarch's power—the reality of which rested on the reversal by the Napoleonic Concordats of a century of church and state relations in Europe.

There was another dimension to Napoleon's revolutionary achievement in Europe which was scarcely foreshadowed by the Directory. War itself is a great revolutionary force. International competition (even when peaceful) is expensive and has always generated internal change. In order to resist the tyrant, the European monarchies had to adapt themselves. From this sprang the fact that by 1815 many of the changes which made modern Europe possible were irreversible.

Three ways in which this happened were of special importance: the attack on privilege, the adoption of revolutionary machinery and institutions, and the nationalization of social life. The first had begun, tentatively, under the Enlightened Despots; after 1789 the rationalization of the Holy Roman Empire was perhaps the most spectacular example, but there were many others. Some can be seen in a state where all these tendencies were at work, Prussia. The achievements of the Prussian reformers may have been exaggerated in the past, yet they began the destruction of Prussian feudalism, opened the army to the non-noble, set up national conscription to recruit their armies (they were highly conscious of the ability the Committee of Public Safety had shown to organize France for victory) and began to preach Prussian patriotism as something distinct from dynastic loyalty. An even more startling transformation came in Spain. There, nationalism joined hands with religious fervour to expel the invader and build the only great popular resistance movement to trouble Napoleon. Furthermore, the collapse of the Spanish monarchy created Spanish liberalism (a word Spain was to give to Europe). The Spanish constitution of 1812 was the fruit of a renewal of Spanish political life brought about by the need to resist. It was also to provide a shibboleth for European liberalism in the Restoration years and to give Spain herself an unhappy pre-eminence as the most turbulent of all European states of the 19th century.

Here, together with the aspirations of men who had enjoyed careers open to their talents and the experience of French administration and legal simplification, were realities which endured

the Restoration. On the surface, and in mood, the change of 1814 or 1815 might seem complete. But though the King of Sardinia re-entered his capital in the powdered wig of the *Ancien Régime* and restored immediately the order of precedence of his court which had existed at the moment of his departure, he ruled a new state. His civil servants had been trained by the French and his generals had learnt their soldiering from Napoleon. Even the boundaries of his kingdom were revolutionary, for they now included the ancient republic of Genoa; this was a symbol that the assertions of the rights of prescription and old institutions were not what really mattered in the Europe of 1815.

Authority restored, 1815–48

Nevertheless, both sides assiduously fed the myth of a sweeping Restoration, and after 1815 international opinion began to reflect the polarization which has existed ever since. The satisfied and fearful powers saw themselves everywhere threatened by national and social revolutionaries and by the danger of a resurgence of revolution in France. They co-operated as best they could to meet the threat. Metternich's persuasiveness did something to give reality to the shadowy 'Holy Alliance'—with which England's Tory government would have nothing to do. The first revolutionary wave—in Spain, Portugal, Italy and Wallachia—was weathered by 1821. But then the reactionary International began to find co-operation more difficult. The Greek War of Independence (1821–27) was the beginning of the trouble. Viewed abstractly, it was straightforward rebellion against the established rule of the Turks; Metternich would have liked to limit the question to this simple conservative proposition, but behind it there stretched a great chain of complicating circumstances. There was the Eastern Question in its 19th-century form: who was to rule at the Straits if the Turkish Empire crumbled away? There were the implications for other subject peoples in the Balkans, especially those nearer to Austrian borders. There was the practical difficulty presented by the curious phenomenon of phil-Hellenism, the force behind the wave of sympathy among the literate and educated classes which made the improbable figures of Albanian cut-throats and Aegean pirates the beneficiaries of the first of those high-minded orgies of international goodwill which were to be so potent a source of confusion and trouble in the future. In the end a new state appeared, the first since 1815 to be founded explicitly on the principle of nationality.

The importance of this was immense, but the July Revolution of 1830 rocked Europe far more. This was, of course, because it occurred in France and revived fears of a new revolutionary Republic. Its immediate practical significance was threefold: it acted as a detonator to revolt in Poland and even, in small measure, in Italy; it distracted attention from the Belgians' revolution against their incorporation in the Kingdom of the Netherlands (imposed in 1815) and so ensured the survival of the second national state to come into existence since Waterloo; finally, it set up a constitutional regime in France which was, for the next eighteen years, in spite of troubles and friction, to provide a partner for Great Britain in something like an International of liberal states. The formal embodiment of this, in so far as it existed, was the Quadruple Alliance which was formed to protect liberal regimes in Spain and Portugal in 1834. In eastern Europe, liberalism could do nothing and the Poles were crushed, but in Spain and Portugal the wicked uncles did not prevail; the later history of those two countries may well give rise to incomprehension that so optimistic a view could be taken of the future of liberalism in the Iberian peninsula in the 1830s, but that was how it looked at the time. Elsewhere, reaction redoubled its efforts and soon seemed unshaken in the saddle once more.

It was during these years that Russia began to shoulder the burden of being policeman to Europe which she so competently discharged in 1849. Her history reflects little of either Revolution or Improvement in these years; with Great Britain she was to be the only great power to escape revolution in 1848 and Russia's civil progress under Nicholas I (1796–1855) has often been summed up in the bitter phrase of Alexander Herzen (1812–70)—'the plague-zone of Russian history'. Russia's position as the great conservative power was based on two facts. The first was the ideological bent given to her government by the peculiar nature of Russian autocracy and the troubles which followed after Alexander I (1777–1825) had dabbled with liberal reform. In a great agrarian society like Russia, the virus of liberal, individual ideas might, within a framework of enlightened despotism (as in British India) have produced a healthy stimulus to peaceful change, but if left uncontrolled would probably lead to social disruption; under Nicholas I, conscious of his role, confident of the military simplicities of his thought, and alarmed by the revelations of the Decembrist conspiracy in 1825, the experiment of directed liberalism was not to be tried.

The other ground of Russia's office was sheer military strength. In 1815 this was at its peak, and it remained there so long as huge numbers of men moving on foot or horse were decisive in land warfare. The slowness of change in military technique in the early 19th century prolonged the Russian military supremacy which rested on sheer weight of numbers, and although the Crimean War was eventually to expose Russia's military weakness, Russian armies were, as the events of 1849 demonstrated, the ultimate argument of the Holy Alliance. In 1848 and 1849, Russia was the citadel of conservative principle in Europe. Secure at home, her rulers watched the revolutionary wave rising abroad.

Hard times in Europe began in 1845 with the potato blight which struck most alarmingly in Ireland, the Netherlands, Belgium and Germany. The following year similar disasters affected grain harvests. There was famine in some countries. Yet agricultural crisis was associated with a bigger financial crisis, a crisis of credit which led to a multiplication of commercial and industrial bankruptcies and to widespread unemployment. This complex economic upheaval 'revived every grievance', although the revolutions, when they came, occurred not at the height of the crisis but in the period of slow recovery which followed it. Meanwhile, the political preconditions of revolution had fallen into place. 1846 had brought what Metternich believed impossible, the election of a liberal pope. Pius IX (1792–1878) focused both liberal and national aspirations for many Italians. His election was a bad omen for Austria, within whose sphere of influence Italy was allowed to be; it would be difficult to be more papal than the Pope in defence of the order of 1815. Mounting troubles inside the Italian states began to push their rulers down the road of reform. The usual demand was for a constitution, a Civic Guard, a free newspaper; some assumed

that the removal of Austria would necessarily follow. The February revolution spurred on the Italian movement. Then came the most dramatic moment of the year, the March revolution in Vienna and the enforced resignation of Metternich.

If Russia was the citadel of conservatism, Metternich, more than any other man, was its personal embodiment. He had presided over conservative Europe from 1815 to 1848, or aspired to do so; his flight was the sign that Revolution had triumphed. This was an over-simplification. Just because so much odium attached to him, many Austrians—liberals and conservatives alike—felt they could go much more slowly than the radicals wanted down the road of civil rights and social reform. Everywhere, the national revolutionaries assumed too easily that there could now be no going back, since the arch-conservative was gone. This was wrong; his fall was only to reveal the difficulties of constructing a new order in central Europe and Germany.

In the Habsburg dominions, the Germans were suddenly confronted with the demands of the other nationalities. It had not seemed likely to them that their fellow-subjects would wish to be other than members of a Germanic state. Meanwhile, though the Vienna revolution had also released liberal and national revolutions all over Germany, where another step towards unification now seemed within reach, there appeared other unconsidered problems. How was a great multi-national state like Austria to be incorporated within the German national community? What was to be done with the Poles of Poznan? Their incorporation within a German state would mean their continued subordination; their liberation in a Polish state (at first favoured by some Germans) would mean the dismemberment of Prussia, probably that of Austria too, and the intervention of Russia. In the end, the German liberals at Frankfurt opted for the possibility of a Great Germany, incorporating all territories where Germans lived. This sealed the fate of German liberalism, for only the Prussian army could sustain such a dream.

1848 closed with the revolution on the defensive everywhere. A truce in Lombardy had given the Austrian army in Italy time to rebuild itself; it had already shown it could beat the Piedmontese—the only military force in Italy left to the Revolution after the defection of Naples and the Pope—and the Venetian revolution had been bottled up. The Slavs were disunited. The Czechs were crushed in June. The Magyars were the gravest threat to the Monarchy and were checked in October; this done, the Vienna revolution could be mastered, too. The Berlin radicals were swamped in the tide of nationalism which directed the German liberals' attention to their borderlands and away from the dangers of Prussian conservatism. The June Days had finished the disorders of Paris. The events of 1849 registered the consequences. A renewed war in Italy restored Austrian power completely and ended the reign of Carlo Alberto (1798–1849). The Russian army crushed the Hungarian revolutionaries and removed any chance that the Habsburg army could again be caught on the wrong foot by having too many revolts to deal with at once. The German revolution found itself impaled on the dilemma which was to last until 1866: *Kleindeutschland* and the acquiescence of the Prussian monarchy, or *Grossdeutschland* and radical revolutions everywhere against the German oppressors of other nationalities. The last flicker of the 'Springtime of the Nations' was a splutter of radical revolutions in a few German towns and the brief Roman Republic proclaimed by Giuseppe Mazzini (1805–72).

The ideologies that failed

What had been at stake? As the confusions which multiplied to confound the revolutionaries after the February revolution quickly showed, 1848 was a colossal disappointment above all because of the simple, clear, uncomplicated hopes people had had of it. It was also a great reassurance to rulers: their fears had been equally apocalyptic and were now overcome. It was the greatest of all demonstrations of the superficiality and stupidity of the red-and-black myth, progress versus reaction, Revolution versus Order. Revolution was not, after all, the crude, terrible bogy envisaged by so many Europeans since 1793, nor the pure, cauterizing and cleansing Evangel proclaimed by so many revolutionaries.

Europe according to the settlement of the Congress of Vienna.

Revolutionary politics turned out to be very much like other politics, a tangle of conflicting demands and interests, but with a much enlarged cast on the stage.

It had been fundamental to the myth that, basically, all revolutionaries wanted the same thing. Yet this was far from true, and even a quick glance at the variety of European society in the first half of the 19th century should have made this clear. The most striking example is the nature of the social demands of 1848. A social war had been feared; urban unrest had broken out in violence in all European countries in the 1830s and 1840s, and its leaders often talked the new language of 'socialism'. Yet its essence was often conservative; handloom weavers in England supported the Charter, workers in the manufacturing area of France broke machines, and Rhinelanders rioted against steamboats and free competition. Increasingly, such outbreaks were bound to seem alarming in the tense atmosphere of 1846–47, but they represented a poverty of political thinking to be exposed in 1848. In England and Belgium there existed a true industrial proletariat: no revolutions occurred. In Paris, there was a great wave of social protest, erupting finally in the June Days; driven by unemployment and distress, the discontented sought a remedy in a return to a state paternalism killed fifty years before. In Germany, the radical (but far from socialist) craftsmen of the Rhineland, Berlin and Saxony strove to keep alive a *sans-culotte* tradition of protest which briefly frightened their rulers in 1848, but were too divided and disorganized to do so. They, too, were hampered by seeing a remedy for their troubles in resisting industrialization and clinging to the past of the guilds. Luddism, not socialism and the destruction of

property, was the theme of the workers' revolutions in 1848. Public works were the main panacea, and it was a temporary one. This was, in the main, why they failed. The peasants of Germany and eastern Europe, being a half-century behind those of France in some cases, still had the future on their side. They therefore behaved like French peasants in 1789. Some won a great deal; the most important social change of 1848 was the abolition of compulsory labour services in east Germany and the Habsburg dominions.

'Liberalism', another bogy, was equally full of contradiction and division. In Paris and Italy people might seek the republic; in Germany and Slavic Europe leaders rarely hoped for more than the constitutional guarantees of the July Monarchy. A broad agreement about the Rights of Man was not enough to sustain a common revolutionary impetus. In so far as there was a generalized revolutionary principle in 1848, it was that of nationality—of all political principles the one most fertile in division and disruptiveness. Apart from the peasants, the nationalists were the men who salvaged most from the disappointments of that year.

Above all, political romanticism should have been exploded in 1848. The belief that all things would be made new either by a change in political arrangements or by the liberation of emotional and moral forces in the act of revolution was symbolized by the actions of Lamartine in 1848. Such gestures, myths and slogans had fifty years' history behind them and were to be shown up time and time again in the months that followed. Yet they were to prove of an incredible durability; they are with us still. Immediately, in the case of men like Mazzini, they were often confirmed and strengthened by experience in their belief that anything less than

Giuseppe Mazzini, the Italian patriot. An uncompromising republican who spent most of his life in exile, his main influence was through his journalism and his moral stature. The insurrections and secret societies that he organized were all ultimately failures, and the proclamation of the kingdom of Italy left him disappointed and disillusioned.

revolution was useless as an instrument of the total—perhaps totalitarian?—moral resurrection they desired; this conclusion was to be especially important for the subsequent history of the *Risorgimento* and Italian politics. But many other professional revolutionaries, too, learnt nothing from the failures of that year. Blanqui (1805–81) was not pushed off the revolutionary stage until 1871; Bakunin (1814–81), the Russian anarchist, was only beginning his career in 1849, when he attended his first revolution (in Dresden). If anything, the belief in the creative revolutionary minority was entrenched even more solidly by 1848–49 than by the example of 1789–94. It was enriched, too, by a new myth of astonishing durability, that of the directing social analyst whose insight enables him to seize the revolutionary moment. The idea, implicit in Saint-Simon (1760–1825), the pioneering French socialist, was to be reiterated in the vast body of literature of which the point of departure was the *Communist Manifesto.*

Patterns of change: economics and the new man

It is only when we stand back from the excitements and disappointments of the greatest revolutionary crisis in modern European history and consider the era from 1789 to 1851 as a whole that we can discern the pattern of revolutionary transformation. In the broadest terms this was 'the end of the Middle Ages'. More specifically we can point to the industrializing, the individualizing, the secularizing, and the politicalizing of European society.

All these terms are unsatisfactory, the first perhaps more than any of the others. It conjures up images of factories and steam engines and this, it is true, was the aspect of change which most quickly and forcibly struck contemporaries. Factories and steam engines dominated the new landscape of industrial England and Belgium and startled their visitors. Yet these were exceptional landscapes, and the progress of industrialization before 1848 in terms of coal and iron was slow. The change which 'industrializing' represented so dramatically was the culmination of a process involving a new ordering of the economy and there were signs of

this new ordering in countries with few factories and steam engines. It meant, always, a relative decline of the agricultural sector, the appearance of new institutions—banks for example, and stock exchanges, the rise of a commercial press, the formulation of commercial codes of law, a more rapid accumulation of capital, and a growing criticism of mercantilism and an advocacy of free trade. Such changes, which had been traceable in England since the 17th century, registered a move from status to market society. The idea that relations between men are more properly expressed by contractual obligations voluntarily undertaken than in any other way, received its extreme statement and development in economic life.

In the new economic order, men were offered a rapid expansion of the community's wealth in return for the abandonment of old ideas and institutions. Economic man, rationally self-directed towards the maximization of his welfare, replaced social man, tied by a multitude of inherited and historically determined usages to the obligations of that station to which God had been pleased to call him. Scientific capitalist farming replaced the collective working of divided fields and the ties of service and justice between landlord and peasant. Combination laws were passed to cut at the restrictive practices of ancient guilds as well as at the feeble shoots of early trade unionism. Government was expelled from the regulation of economic life in the name of economic rationality and abandoned together with 'mercantilism' a wide range of social and moral duties. Above all, property began to take on a new aspect. Its old collective, moral, quasi-tribal aspects dropped away as laws against entail, primogeniture, mortmain, or collective exploitation gradually spread across Europe. It is not always easy to see through the tangle of legal qualifications which surrounds what was going on, and English land law, above all, remained until the great Victorian reforms a jungle in which there lurked the survivals of an older view of property. Yet the essence of the process was that land was being turned into a commodity like any other.

The whole complex change sketched so far was deplored by critics who stood both on 'the Right' and on 'the Left', a point later often forgotten. The same was true of the second tendency of these years, the individualizing of society. This second tendency was indeed so closely linked with the first that the distinction between them can only be a formal one. Though the idea of the individual as an exploiter of himself, his capital, his skills and his opportunities is fundamental to the change in the economic organization of society, it also had other dimensions. The individual was endowed with a new dignity and significance. Women were not as yet fully involved in the process, but the advocacy of their rights as individuals had begun, often eloquently.

The legal and institutional expressions of such ideas are obvious, from the Declaration of the Rights of Man in 1789 onwards. But legal rights only defined a new sphere of action for the individual; what are harder to delineate are the assumptions which now came to govern his exploitation of it. As men were released from the restrictions (and protection) of family, Estates, *Stände*, and corporations which had defined their social relations under the *Ancien Régime*, ambition became more respectable, though at the same time, of course, denunciation of it mounted. The young man in a hurry made his appearance in European literature. In the 18th century he had no equivalent; the Adventurer was nothing like him. Now, merit and desert could be thought to justify untrammelled advancement. The Romanticism which reflected Rousseau's denunciation of the artifice and corruption of a society repressing the natural virtue of the good heart produced the archetypal literary hero of the next century, the young man at loggerheads with his environment. And the French Revolution and its wars provided scores of examples and precedents of what might be hoped for: Stendhal's Julien Sorel kept Bonaparte's picture under his mattress at the seminary.

The idealization of revolt and liberation and the cult of the young which began at about this time were to produce extraordinary paradoxes. The *Ancien Régime* had produced relatively few criticisms of itself from within its own ruling class; the 19th and 20th centuries were to prove time and time again that the most telling criticisms of the new order were to come from those who had enjoyed its privileges. The descendant of Louis XIV's Saint-Simon was the first great critic of the rationality of traditional government in industrial society. Marx, the son of wealth, was the living refutation of his own view that 'being' proceeded 'consciousness' and that ideology was determined by social class. Gladstone, reared in Toryism and the most romantic of all British prime ministers, was to enjoy his greatest hours as the liberator of the individual from the shackles of faith, tradition and history. In fiction, Stendhal again provides a touchstone of his age: Leuwen, the young hero, circulates exasperatedly in the world of French politics and finance, resenting the compromises it imposes upon him when, after all (and to his rage), it is only his father's fortune that makes his career possible.

Faith and freedom

The growing autonomy of the individual was reflected in a growing rejection of the formal restraints of religion. But in defining the secularizing process, the third tendency of the age, we have to be especially careful. The 18th century, after all, was and has remained the age *par excellence* of scepticism and moral laxity. This was, nevertheless, combined with the persistence, until the Josephine reforms, of traditional views of the relation between state-power and formal religion. The new international tendency after 1789 was a growing—though far from complete—acceptance that secular authority should not be deployed in the service of religious ends. The state was to become for religion, as for commerce, an umpire, no more. The history of this change in England, where practical toleration was already far advanced before 1799, was marked legally by the steady flow of statutes which whittled away the Protestant Constitution and the Anglican supremacy, and intellectually by the growth of rationalist printing and publication. England did not see the formal separation of Church and State, on the other hand, which came to some European countries and was embodied in Concordats. Everywhere the confessional state where it survived had to concede a measure of toleration. In Spain the Inquisition, for so long the judicial link connecting state and faith, was abolished, to the disapproval of the Duke of Wellington. Finally, and most important of all, churches lost much of their power of practical regulation of daily life, either in their courts, or through their laws enforced by lay courts. The great symbolic question was marriage; civil marriage was never to be extirpated from France after 1815. But there were other less dramatic changes of almost equal or greater significance. When, for example, the maintenance of the essential records of society was no longer the obligation only of the parish priest, much of his real influence and power was eroded.

In spite of the Concordats and ultramontanism of the Restoration, therefore, a Jansenist who survived from the pre-revolutionary century would have found much to applaud in the relations between religion and the state after 1815 (though his own views would have been out of fashion). Yet the hopes of the survivors of the Enlightenment and the *idéologues* would have been disappointed. In spite of the secularizations of ecclesiastical wealth, and the imposition of legal restraints which far outran the dreams of Enlightened Despots, the Church of the 19th century was visibly to grow richer and more powerful. The word 'anti-clericalism' had not been invented by 1851, but it was a reality long before that as critics of the Church pointed out new advantages which organized religion seemed often to enjoy even when its formal powers were more and more closely circumscribed.

The hopes of the 18th-century *philosophes* and civil servants were cut across by two important facts. One was the phenomenon we call, for want of a better name, Romanticism, which expressed itself among other ways in a new intensity of religious faith. The origins of it went back deep into the century before 1789, but it achieved its most spectacular ascendancy in the fifty years that followed. As it proceeded it owed something, there can be no doubt, to the second fact which helped to strengthen religion, the fear of revolution. In France, Italy, Spain and the Tyrol, the Roman Catholic Church proved the most effective mobilizer of mass forces against the revolution; even in the United Kingdom, the influence of the Irish bishops was thrown into the scale on the side of a

government which opposed Catholic Emancipation. It was also in the United Kingdom that the Evangelical revival and the new intensity of Methodist dissent were quickly seen to have a conservative influence emphasized by most of their leaders. In Protestant Germany the revival of pietism and the growth of sentimental religions was as early as the 1790s linked with political reaction.

The results of the religious revival were far-reaching and, no doubt, contained some unambiguously good elements, not least in practical philanthropy and in the desire for the abolition of slavery. Yet it is difficult to look at those features of it which were most conspicuous without a sense of regret. The sanctimoniousness of the new style (emphatically not confined to Protestantism), the obfuscation of philosophy, the cultivation of popular superstition, the aesthetic horrors of devotional art and the French architect-restorer Viollet-le-Duc (1814–79), the return of the Jesuits, English sabbatarianism and the cult of the Virgin—these were a heavy price to pay, and mark a retrogression of the European spirit. When J. H. Newman (1801–90) said 'Liberalism—there is the enemy', he was quite right; what he had in mind was lay appropriation of clerical revenues, but what he implied, as was recognized widely at the time, was opposition to the whole tendency of the age.

This reaction in the spirit explains why in 1851 the formal relations of Church and State were still not often cast in the liberal mould. Above all, the great question of the papacy itself and its temporal power had still to be settled after the false dawn of Pius IX. But organized religion had, within most states, already made a most important and significant concession. It had entered politics, accepting that its interests would have to battle with others for the goals it wished to achieve and to do so by using the new forms of social action created by the politicizing of society.

The new politics

Politicization—the word is ugly and cumbersome, but some such word is needed to sum up an elusive and complex process. What it indicated was first, a wider and wider acceptance of the assumption that society is a changing, not a static entity. To a society which saw itself as existing in a state of equilibrium, 'politics' was only marginally significant—at most, a matter of shifts in the composition of the ruling group. The regulators of such a society were usually not political but judicial forms; the problem of public power was to distribute its force in support of legal rights; the fundamental technique was one of assessing the correct relationship between the legal rights of interested parties. Even international affairs were strongly marked by this judicial emphasis. But acceptance, even reluctant, of the idea of change as a social norm required a new machinery for dealing with conflicting claims which could often no longer fit into juridical categories or which could only do so with anomalies and inappropriate distortions.

What came to be accepted more and more, as a result, was that bargaining and discussion ought to be fundamental determinants of the direction of public affairs and that a class of people, politicians, should undertake this. It also came to be held that certain groups in society (the definition of which varied widely, but the numbers of which tended always to enlarge, sometimes even to include all adult males) should identify these politicians by choosing representatives. Finally, it came to be accepted that when this had happened there was an authoritative form of procedure which would identify, in the end, those decisions to be supported and imposed by the state power. The outcome of politics was to be the unquestioned acceptance of the authority of collective action expressed as the law-making of the sovereign state.

This statement of what was happening is deliberately highly abstract and schematic; it has to be in order to take account of the variety of the change which it embraces. In some places one element stood out and others were not accepted; the idea of the sovereign state was acceptable, for example, in an Austrian empire where Josephinism continued to animate the action of government after 1815, while historic right and not abstract principle continued to be the basis of representation, in so far as it existed. Nonetheless men would certainly have agreed that two crucial contributions to the political education of Europe were made in

these years—English constitutionalism and the French revolutionary idea of popular sovereignty. Contrasted as, at times, they
seemed to be, their effect was, surprisingly, often convergent.

The word constitution was an anglicism imported into the French
language during the 18th century. A 'constitution' came to be
the crucial demand of early 19th-century liberals. By a constitution,
they meant defined rights for individuals and juridical guarantees
of them against the intrusion of power. In the early 1790s conservatives, too, could see advantages in constitutionalism as a
protection against unrestricted despotism. Later, the model most
frequently cited and demanded was that which Spain gave itself in
1812. It was imitated, for example, in the Piedmontese and Neapolitan revolutions of 1821. But the French Restoration *Charte*, a
conservative document, was a constitution, too, and all successful
revolutions between 1830 and 1849 resulted in the adoption of
constitutions. The Piedmontese *Statuto*, actually granted without a
revolution in 1848, was one of the longest-lasting written constitutions in modern history, surviving until Mussolini.

If the bias of constitutionalism was towards the restriction of
power, the bias of the doctrine of popular sovereignty was towards
its expansion. This was not necessarily reconcilable with constitutional liberalism; Tocqueville emphasized just this point. It
reinforced authority, where constitutionalism sought to guarantee
non-interference. Yet it was a great engine of liberation because of
the threat it presented to traditional authority and hierarchy. It
greatly reinforced the power of the state, and many people were
willing to acquiesce in this, since they believed that the working
of popular sovereignty might enable them to exercise power.
Above all, it provided the political theory for the institutionalizing
of nationalism.

In the arguments and struggles over constitutions and popular
sovereignty the basic pattern of modern political activity appeared. The best evidence of it is the emergence of a new political
vocabulary and of the simple division implicit in the terms 'Left'
and 'Right'. This division has obsessed our political thinking for a
century and a half and is only now beginning to give way. So
persuasive was it that attempts have even been made to present the
politics of non-European countries meaningfully in these terms.
The polarization which it indicated was to become even sharper
towards 1851 as more and more strenuous efforts were made to
comprehend on the same spectrum every shade of opinion. Yet by
then the extremes of socialism—anarchism and the idea of a
plebiscitary dictatorship—should already have made a red-and-
black, revolution-reaction dualism seem inadequate, to say nothing
of the difficulty of fitting English political experience into it. In
spite of this the distinction remained useful; it seemed to indicate
significant differences while not blurring the general division into
two camps.

On the political spectrum were dotted the other new political
ideas of the age. Here, although French political ideas were so
influential in these years, other countries also contributed. 'Conservative' had a French origin and it originally expressed a different
idea from the English translation. In 1831 in England, 'conservative'
was still a new cant word to Macaulay; it was chiefly important in
defining the new trend within Toryism away from old-fashioned
reaction. But it became, for Europe, one general term for the
Right. 'Liberal' had a Spanish origin; it quickly came to be
associated with the idea of constitutional liberties and generalized
public rights and equality before the law. 'Radical' was more
extreme and was the English contribution to Europe's new
political vocabulary; it had been used in a political context and in
its adjectival form in the 18th century; it now made its appearance
as a noun. Republicans, it was agreed, stood to the Left of radicals;
radicals might, but need not, be republicans.

Because of the prevalence of monarchy and all the associations
surrounding it, the notions of 'republic' and 'republicans' then had
dramatic connotations now unthinkable. When the first French
Republic appeared, in 1792, the only republics in Europe were
ossified antiquities like Genoa, Venice, the Imperial Cities and a
few smaller ones, or the United Provinces (with a quasi-monarchical
stadholderate), and the Swiss cantons. The example of America
was irrelevant. It was a long way away, and therefore not exposed

to the necessities of strong government which a European state
had to suffer; anyway, it looked as if it was likely to dissolve under
the natural burdens of faction and geography. By 1851, there were
still fewer republics in Europe. The new states which had survived
tended to be constitutional monarchies and some of the fossils had
gone. Experience of the previous half-century suggested (according to your view) either that they opened the way to anarchy and
licence (France, the satellite republics of the Directory and
Napoleon), or that they made possible a regeneration of the community unhindered by superstition and vested interest (France, the
satellite republics of the Directory and Napoleon). Republicans
recalled the virtues and practised the cult of antiquity; Brutus
(whom Dante had depicted in the depths of the *Inferno*) was
idealized and 'Senates', 'Tribunes', 'Consuls' and the *res publica*
consciously evoked the glories of republican Rome. Conservatives, on the other hand, recalled Cromwell and pointed out that
military dictatorship had, in fact, followed Robespierre's reign of
virtue.

The machinery of the modern state

The machinery as well as the concepts of modern politics also
began to make their appearance after the 1780s. Party had been a
parliamentary idea in 18th-century England; now it was carried
outside the representative assembly to denote an organized
opinion in the country. Political action adapted itself accordingly.
Oratory addressed itself to wider audiences, and more and more
successful demands were made for the removal of restraints on
publication and the right of assembly. The 18th-century movement
towards the spontaneous organization of societies for cultural,
philanthropic and social purposes was also politicized: 'club'
became a symptom of political disorder or an index of political
maturity according to your point of view. Yet the greatest change
in the 'structure of politics' was, everywhere, the transformation of
the state itself.

The fundamental change was simple: the State became stronger
than ever before. It began a henceforth almost uninterrupted
process of drawing power to itself. The governments of 1851 were,
therefore, and in spite of their misgivings, vastly more secure
than those of 1789. The material roots of this change comprised
the process of internal reform which has already been stressed
and which gave birth to new institutions such as conscription,
police forces, and centralized administration; the growing expertise of bureaucracies which began to be recruited and trained
on more objective lines and to work with better records and greater
knowledge; and, finally, the technical changes in warfare, transport and communication. When combined with the existence of
new devices such as Peel's metropolitan police forces, or the rural
gendarmeries of Europe, these solved, in most countries, the
problem of public order. Artillery could make rubble of the
barricades, if directed (by telegraph) and delivered (by rail) to
the right place at the right time. In England in 1848 this would
have been technically possible; it was to prove so elsewhere that
year. Moreover, new devices could also draw the sting of revolt
before it occurred, if governmental thinking allowed them to do
so; hunger was the great detonator of rural revolt, and the steamship and railway which made this particular problem of 18th-
century government soluble by regularizing food-supply were to
do as much for order as canister-shot and police barracks.

The other source of strength for the State was the new respect
which it began to enjoy. The Enlightened Despots had shown to
some discerning minds what could be done to generate power for
beneficial purposes if restraints on the operation of sovereignty
were removed. But this fundamental idea was accepted in legal
theory before 1789 only in England, and even there occasional
protests about the doctrine were heard and real conventional
restrictions on its operation existed. For many (though not all)
of those who desired change, the recognition of sovereignty was the
first step forward in 1789. The next step was the recognition of the
value of this idea of sovereignty in strengthening resistance to the
Revolution. Linked to the idea of nationality, it was capable of
generating a new power in the conservative states. It was Mirabeau
(1715–89) who pointed out to Louis XVI that Richelieu would

'*The champions of reform*': *from left to right, Lord Brougham, whose brilliant speech in the House of Lords was to some extent responsible for its passing the 1832 Reform Bill; Lord Russell, paymaster-general in Grey's ministry and the man chosen to explain the provisions of the Bill to the Commons; Lord Grey, the Whig prime minister who steered the Bill through parliament. Though it increased the electorate (by 217,000) and redistributed seats to give greater representation to the new industrial areas and disenfranchise the rotten boroughs, the Bill was not a radical measure. The qualification for voting rights was still property and there was no secret ballot.*

have given his right arm for the advantages presented to the Crown by the Constituent Assembly's abolition of privilege, and the lesson was soon learnt by intelligent conservatives. Such new thinking, or willingness to think, about the State was soon reinforced by the romantic idealization of historical realities and by idealist philosophy. If the 'General Will', as propounded by Jean-Jacques Rousseau (1712–78), a challenging idea, could nonetheless provide a device for making unjust societies moral, Hegel's development of the distinction between society and state gave the State—any State—an independent moral value above that of any subordinate association or individual. Man, selfish in society, could find in the State a moral cause to serve; above egoism, he was presented with a sphere for selfless, impersonal morality. The State could realize values no other group could realize; ethical purpose justified the law-giver's demands.

England apart

During the course of this survey, there have been references to England, examples drawn from her experience, indications of her influence. Something more than this is needed to understand not only her history but what she meant to Europe at this time. This is not only a matter of the diplomatic relations between states and the international role of England as a great power. The English domestic experience also had its influence, for in England Europeans felt that they could see the future and how it would work, whether or not they liked what they saw. There were ample signs of envy of England's wealth, of her enduring institutions and of her high level of general culture; the provocation of her commercial competition; the pontifications of her statesmen about illiberal regimes abroad; her export of capital and industrial skill; the ramifications of a worldwide commercial system, *Pax Britannica*, resting on the Royal Navy. Moreover, in the background were

the revolutionary wars. In them England had been the most continuous combatant, and they defined the shape of Europe— and therefore the extent of the Revolution—for the next fifty years.

These influences were in part due to England's own changing shape. She was, by 1851, a much bigger nation; her population was then nearly two-thirds that of France, while in 1789 it had only been about one-third. Her landscape had changed, registering the fact that more than any other nation she was an industrializing and urbanizing power. The towns and factories which appeared had combined with an enormous expansion of overseas trade to make her wealthier than ever. By 1851 there could be no doubt about the *per capita* measurement of this, and the worst social suffering of industrialization was past. Although agriculture, measured against individual manufacturing industries, was still the biggest single employer, the balance of social power was beginning to shift away from land. The old 18th-century antithesis of land versus trade had given way to the new one of land versus industry, even though the embodiment of this distinction in class differences was blurred and qualified by the growth of the professions, by the traditional readiness of the English landed classes to intermarry with business and allow their younger sons to go into it, and by the slow change in the social composition of the House of Commons.

Whatever the fear of revolution, England never had one. There were waves of alarm. In the early 1790s, in the years after Waterloo, and in the late 1830s and early 1840s when the Chartists were at their most militant, excitement combined with hard times to produce uneasiness among the ruling classes and hope among the would-be English Jacobins. Nevertheless, in 1851 Englishmen found themselves still with a structure of politics organically and naturally related to the one many of them had lived under in 1789. The monarchy, though sometimes threatened, was still there, and much the same oligarchy retained power and made up the governments of England as in 1789, though there had been an infusion of new peers and men of obscure birth under Pitt. Property still ruled England, even if it did not do so quite so mechanically or so 'traditionally' after the Reform Bill of 1832 as in the 18th-century electoral system. The electorate was still not a very large one and it voted by open ballot. The importance of 1832 was not what it changed, but the road it opened to change. It was a great precedent (Cromwell, the last great remodeller of the House of Commons, had been a dubious forerunner) and, sooner or later, a second instalment of parliamentary reform was inevitable on the same lines—franchise reform and redistribution—and on the same principle—parliamentary redefinition of the entitlement to a vote.

Given this structure and given the turbulent changes of the economic and social order, it is hardly surprising that English political life moved to rhythms very different from those of Europe in these years. The July revolution, it is true, was not without its electric effect in London. But 'Corn, Currency, Catholics'—the great issues of English politics before 1830—and Free Trade and government intervention to ameliorate the condition of Englishmen—the major issues afterwards—did not reflect European concerns. Nor did English politicians and parties fit easily into the Left-Right, Reaction-Progress stereotype. British politics had to wait for the disappearance of the Victorian Liberal party (not yet born in 1851) before it could be plausibly asserted to be a matter of class; the Chartists asked for nothing in principle incapable of realization. As the manufacturers pressed forwards towards the repeal of the corn laws, exhorted by the embittered rhetoric of the Dissenting pulpit and encouraged by the adhesion of the respectable working-man and of Sir Robert Peel (1788–1850), the prime minister, they found themselves opposed by high Tory landlords and Evangelical clergymen anxious to remedy social evils by legislating government inspectors into the factories and by such improbable associates as Lord Shaftesbury (1801–85), the Evangelical philanthropist, and the young Benjamin Disraeli. Chartists, Melbourne's Whigs, Peel's Conservatives, Liverpool's Tories, Pitt's Young Men, the friends of Charles James Fox—none of them fit easily into the Procrustean bed of Left and Right.

When so much was changing, it could not be expected that the confused, rich tapestry of latent assumption and prejudice which makes up a national outlook would go unchanged. Perhaps the most important change in outlook was that Englishmen in this period acquired a sense of themselves as top dogs which they were long to hold and slow to lose. It is not too much to say that it was the revolutionary and Napoleonic wars—significantly called by them the 'Great' War—which first made most Englishmen aware that England was a great power. There was an immense reinforcement of a patriotism already existing. After 1815 there was a widespread public assumption, which greatly benefited Continental liberalism, that the voice of England should be heard in European affairs. It grew stronger and stronger as the century proceeded and the interest in foreign affairs of the man on top of the Clapham omnibus was fanned by the flamboyance of Palmerston (1784–1865) and the xenophobia of sections of the press. Yet (and this may seem surprising in the 20th century) there was small place in this revaluation of national possibilities for domination over other races and what was later to be called imperialism. England was conservative about colonies; they might be interesting or even necessary, but unless their worth could be demonstrated as strategic, demographic or commercial goods, they were likely to prove a burden, a drain, and perhaps a disaster. Commercial, not political, supremacy was the idol of the early Victorian Englishman. What has been called the 'Imperialism of Free Trade' opened to him the markets in which he and his colleagues sold their wares, unconsciously arrogant in their assumption that their possession of twenty years' advantage over their European rivals was eternal.

The combination of swift and radical evolution with continuity of formal institutions is one explanation why the word 'democracy' remained a pejorative term in England throughout all these years. In 1851 the landed aristocracy seemed as securely in the saddle as in 1789. The Anglican church, even if its privileges were whittled away, still presided imperturbably over the great moments of the life of the rural Englishman and had at least begun to fight back against urbanism and industrialism. The monarchy was more firmly entrenched in unconscious acceptance than it was to be twenty years later, and less likely to be betrayed by the occupant of the throne than thirty years before. The electorate was growing by natural increase, but was still a small minority of the adult male population. The ruling class exercised its power through concessionary tactics and with a sense of responsibility that rarely faltered. The continuity of formal institutions was greater than in any European country and it even affected the nation's symbols; when Barry was to rebuild the Palace of Westminster he took as his starting point not the evocations of republican virtue and imperial rule with which Napoleon sought to impress Parisians, but the medieval world in which, it was believed, the Mother of Parliaments had from the start embodied the virtues and practices of Victorian constitutionalism. Even the Chartists respected parliament, and expected to carry out the transformations they desired by first gaining a majority in the House of Commons. Few Englishmen, indeed, stepped outside the assumptions of constitutional propriety; socialists were barely heard of, and republicanism had been irreparably damaged by the rise of Bonaparte and (what was regarded as) his betrayal of the Revolution.

Taken all in all, it was an astonishing achievement Europeans were right to admire. There was only one serious blot, Ireland. If Ireland was not quite, as Irish nationalists were later to assert, England's Poland, it was bad enough. The legal fiction of Union with England, proclaimed in 1800, was already proving inadequate during the 1830s because of social realities. The first step to dealing with the situation was Roman Catholic Emancipation (1829), but this only opened the door to further pressure for change. The famine of 1846, terrible as it was, paradoxically solved the problem for a time. It was later to emerge again. But

this was a cloud not easily discernible in 1851. In that year the Great Exhibition opened, the working class did not riot through its splendours, the revolutionary crisis, which had rocked Europe three years before, was over, and Britons took conscious pride in the solidity and continuity of their institutions. Virtue seemed rewarded; the blessings of Industry and Peace were at hand. Better was to come. In the 1850s, said Richard Cobden (1804–65) later, 'the great prosperity of the country made Tories of us all'.

Europe, 1851

The Great Exhibition is a fine symbol with which to close the story of Improvement. It embodied the abundance of industry; it was a monument to the new world of individualism; it proclaimed the universalism of the process. The cost of the new world was already being pointed out—by Owen, Carlyle, the French socialists, Marx and Proudhon—but even the hostile critics sometimes admitted that there was much to lay on the credit side of the balance-sheet. Marx's eulogy of the achievements of the bourgeoisie is often overlooked; thirty years before it, Saint-Simon had seen the material possibilities of a technologically conscious capitalism. The building of the Crystal Palace fits in neatly also in another way; we began with the destruction of a medieval prison, and we end with the erection of the world's largest glasshouse.

This juxtaposition is perhaps a little too neat; there was more to these sixty-two years than what was contained in the Crystal Palace. For a different way of pulling together the revolutionary threads in the age, we can turn not to a building but to an event. On December 2nd, 1851, the anniversary of Austerlitz, Louis Napoleon, president of the second republic, carried out a coup d'état, soon ratified by plebiscite, which left him with dictatorial powers. His act was rich with historical overtones. The reminiscence of the great Napoleon, his uncle, was obvious and, indeed, asserted; Louis Napoleon, too, posed as at once the restorer of order and the guarantor of the Revolution. He had a name which was a programme; he had also a revolutionary past, even to the extent of being believed to be a member of the subversive *Carbonari*. He had written about Napoleonic ideas, and also about the problems of poverty. He now inaugurated a regime in France (to be transformed into the Second Empire a year later) which was to be the most successful, in duration, since 1789, and which (unlike its nearest rival, the July Monarchy) was to succumb not to domestic revolution but only to defeat by a foreign enemy. Marx's furious sneers were, as so often, misplaced; Walter Bagehot, the English editor and commentator (1826–77), was a better judge: Bonapartism was what most Frenchmen wanted in 1851.

This was significant for Europe as well as for France. Bonaparte recognized and used two new realities created by the revolutionary age. One was the power of the State; its enormous increase meant that no government need fear the people so long as its servants and soldiers remained loyal. The other was that universal suffrage would legitimize an authoritarian regime. Bonaparte could, after all, truthfully say he had sought to defend the rights of the French voter under the constitution of the Second Republic against its politicians. His regime was an assertion of the sovereignty of the people claimed in 1789 against the claims of the *juste milieu* and the new notables. At a moment when the Holy Alliance was about to crumble, a new prospect opened and a new device was offered to those who wished to preserve the social order. Bismarck was to use universal suffrage to make Germany and preserve the Junkers; Cavour to unite Italy under the Sardinian monarchy. The era of plebiscitary authority had arrived. All this was announced by a vote by the French people, which fittingly closed, as another such vote had begun, the European age of Revolution.

III AUTHORITY AND PROTEST

Patterns of change from 1848 to 1900

JAMES JOLL

'Progress is not an accident but a necessity.
Surely must evil and immorality disappear; surely
must man become perfect.'

HERBERT SPENCER, 1851

'It is not by speeches and majority resolutions that the
great questions of our time are decided . . .
but by blood and iron.'

OTTO VON BISMARCK, 1862

After the turmoil of 1848

the autocratic regimes of Europe returned to power more than ever determined to retain their position and curb the forces of liberalism. Gradually the concessions granted in the year of revolution were eroded. In Austria, Metternich had gone, but the new ministers were in many respects at least as conservative as the old. In France the monarchy of Louis Philippe had been replaced, as we have seen in Chapter II, by a new republic, led by Louis Napoleon as President. But on December 2nd, 1852, he proclaimed himself Emperor.

Napoleon III's task was both easier and more difficult than that of his brother monarchs. Easier because he could make some show of being his people's choice, appealing to plebiscites and universal suffrage. More difficult because he lacked the security of a legitimate dynasty and had to rely upon the glamour of the Napoleonic legend, personal magnetism and continued success to keep his throne. Dazzling social occasions formed a major part of his programme. In 1855 Queen Victoria and Prince Albert visited Paris and were received at a series of splendid public ceremonies. Here the Emperor and Empress (the beautiful twenty-eight-year-old Eugénie, whom he had married two years before) greet the royal pair at the foot of the *escalier d'honneur* in the Tuileries. The courtyard has been covered in for the occasion and hung with a vast chandelier and national flags, including the tricolour and the Royal Standard.

The Catholic Church was under attack from two sides – from scientific rationalism and from evangelical fervour. It responded by closing its doors and adopting a posture of defence. Pius IX had begun with strong liberal sympathies, but the experience of 1848 made him change his mind. Henceforth the mask of Christ (as his opponents saw it, *above left*) was laid aside. In 1870 the first Vatican Council (*above right*) proclaimed Papal Infallibility, a provocatively extreme claim that drove many Catholics out of the Church.

Science undermined belief in the literal truth of the Bible. The writings of Huxley and Darwin (*right*), champions of the theory of evolution, aroused bitter controversy – Darwin being caricatured as an ape.

Intellectual barriers were giving way, just as social and political ones had done. Nothing could stop the expansion of scientific enquiry, the liberalization of education and the rise of a popular press. The result was a more broadly based culture than at any time in the past.

Education could no longer be confined to one social class, one sex, or one culture. Children learnt not only the old academic subjects, but increasingly the new sciences as well. Here a class of girls (*far left*) study botany in a New York school, about 1900.

Women demanded higher education and new colleges were founded to provide it. *Left*: students at Vassar, USA, scanning the stars.

A new power: the press. As literacy became widespread, newspapers began to be designed for the new mass audience. *Above right*: travellers at an English railway station eagerly snatching up the latest editions in 1875. *Right*: an early posed Daguerreotype, 1849, showing Parisian workers reading the papers.

The royal dynasties formed an interrelated group, divided, it is true, by national rivalries, but otherwise ready to support one another in the fight against liberalism. Personalities counted for much. Here the lone figure of Francis-Joseph stands on the staircase of Schönbrunn, June 15th, 1857. The occasion was the centenary of the Order of Maria Theresa, the members of which are about to sit down to an open-air feast. Francis-Joseph had succeeded to the throne in 1848 at the age of eighteen, and ruled for an unprecedented sixty-eight years, dying in 1916.

Intermarriage and state-visits cemented diplomatic relations, and the wives of monarchs could, if they chose, decisively influence events. Eugénie (*left*), the Empress of Napoleon III, certainly helped to keep her husband committed to a pro-papal policy. In 1867, the monarchs of Prussia and Russia visited Paris in order to see the Exhibition, and were entertained at a great banquet in the Tuileries (*right*). The situation was, in retrospect, heavy with irony, for within three years Prussian guns were to be at the gates of Paris.

The Prussian king, Frederick William IV. In 1858, the king became insane and his brother, the future Emperor William I, became regent. Nine years later war broke out with Austria, victory going to the rising power of Prussia.

Capitalism. In the newly industrialized countries, free circulation of money through investment and exchange was essential in order that supply should respond quickly to demand. Money bred money, but it was an unpredictable system that could easily get out of control. *Above left*: Wall Street, New York, during the bank crash of 1857. *Left*: the Consols Office of the Bank of England in 1894.

Socialism. How far should strikes be used for radical political ends, and how far for short term improvements? The London Dock Strike of 1889 (*right*) showed how powerful the working-class movement had become. Socialism in England inclined to persuasion, with an occasional whiff of anarchism, rather than to revolution. *Far right*: the Hammersmith Branch of the Socialist League, with William Morris seventh from the right with his hand on his chest.

Democracy. The poor looked to political action as a cure for economic ills. In England democracy functioned, on the whole, peacefully, through parliamentary representation and trade unions. *Above*: an election at Dover in 1863; the franchise was shortly to be further extended.

Communism: the first communist experiment was tried in Paris after France's defeat by Prussia in 1870. A revolutionary faction seized power and a second siege, this time by French troops, followed the first. *Top right*: the Napoleon column in the Place Vendôme, symbol of absolutism, is overthrown by a committee of citizens that included the painter Courbet. *Right*: government reprisals were ruthless and prolonged – this photograph is a posed reconstruction of one of the many executions, but was made immediately after the event and is as authentic as any engraving.

ASSOCIATED SHIPWRIGHT'S SOCIETY

WE ARE AS ONE

This is to Certify that_____

IS A MEMBER OF

THE ASSOCIATED SHIPWRIGHTS SOCIETY

Given under our hand this_____day of_____18__

_____Branch.

Alex Wilkie

BENEFITS.

BENEFITS.

Patterns of change from 1848 to 1900

JAMES JOLL

'WE MUST CONSIDER as *non avenu* everything that has occurred since 1848,' a leading Prussian conservative remarked with some satisfaction in 1851. Indeed, three years after the great wave of revolutions had swept over Europe—'What remains standing in Europe? Britain and Russia,' the Tsar had boasted to Queen Victoria at the outset of the year of revolutions—it looked as if all the hopes of constitutional progress and social change which had inspired the diverse revolutionary movements had been disappointed. Yet, behind the calm which the reactionary governments of the 1850s succeeded in imposing, forces for change were growing in strength, and within two decades the social and political face of Europe was to change radically.

Restored regimes

At first the restored regimes of the fifties looked exceptionally formidable to the disillusioned liberals who were confronted with them. In Austria the young Emperor Francis Joseph was relying on advisers every bit as conservative as Metternich, and in many ways more forceful. The national revolts in Hungary and in North Italy were fiercely suppressed. Lombardy was placed under military rule, and a uniform administrative system was imposed on the whole Monarchy in an attempt to obliterate national distinctions under a common German-speaking bureaucracy enforcing the rule of an absolute emperor. In Prussia the liberal constitution was rescinded and a new authoritarian one decreed by King Frederick William IV, and, in the other German states, as the hopes of achieving a united Germany faded, constitutions were revised so as, to a greater or lesser degree, to extinguish the liberal provisions introduced in 1848. The states of the German Confederation agreed in 1854 to set up an anti-liberal joint committee 'to remove the filth of the year of shame'; and even if the committee did not achieve much, and some individual states, such as Baden or Württemberg, were successful in keeping alive some sort of constitutional and parliamentary life, the existence of the anti-liberal committee was symbolic of the general attitude of the rulers of the German states, and in particular of the Prussian government.

The efficient Prussian civil service was running a state dominated by a narrow conservative ideology, whose main theorist, Friedrich Julius Stahl (1802–61), called for an end to parliamentary control and for the restoration of the power of a monarch personally responsible for all branches of government without any obligation to consult any representative assembly unless he chose to do so. At the same time, however, Stahl opposed any idea that the monarch might rule solely according to his whims, and he believed that the king had the duty to uphold the rule of law, the *Rechtsstaat*, in which every citizen knew where he stood under a system of

---

'**We Are As One**': the membership certificate of the Associated Shipwrights' Society shows a new found pride in the dignity of labour, as well as an awareness of the material benefits that unity can bring, illustrated in the six small pictures at the bottom. State insurance schemes started in the 1880s and here again it was Bismarck who was the pioneer.

---

impartially enforced laws, and could expect from the monarch the stern but incorruptible efficiency which had become traditionally embodied in the Prussian civil service.

The revival of conservatism in the German states forced many Germans to emigrate, some temporarily, others permanently. Among them were Carl Schurz, a leading liberal who rose to cabinet office in the United States, and Karl Marx, who settled in London to devote the rest of his life to the analysis of contemporary society and to the elaboration of a new theory of historical development and of inevitable revolution. For those liberals who stayed in Germany, the problem of achieving constitutional reform and German unification was necessarily seen in a new light after the failures of 1848. Many of them realized that it was lack of executive, and, above all, of military power which had led to that failure, and began to look for solutions to the German problem of a more realistic kind. (It is significant that the term *Realpolitik* was first used in the 1850s.) This involved both the organization of effective political groupings across the borders of the German states and the eventual acceptance of the fact that German unification could only be achieved under the leadership of one or other of the major powers in Germany, Prussia or Austria. Thus, even in the apparently stagnant conservatism of the restored German Confederation of the 1850s, there were already political forces and political ideas at work making for change; and there were also, as we shall see, powerful economic developments moving German society in the same direction.

In France, too, a strong authoritarian government emerged out of the confusion of the Second Republic; but it was not a conventional legitimist monarchy such as had been restored in Austria and Prussia. Napoleon III, before and after the coup d'état of 1851, was able to appeal to an electorate which was both disillusioned with the pedestrian rule of Louis Philippe and alarmed by the disturbances of 1848; but above all, the power of the name Napoleon was what gave him mass support at the outset of his reign. In his own vague pronouncements of policy, he was able to appear both as the inheritor of the republican tradition, since his use of universal suffrage and of the plebiscite gave the impression of a man dedicated to the principle of the sovereignty of the people, and at the same time to retain the support of the conservative forces, and in particular of the Roman Catholic Church. 'For me,' he said in a characteristic phrase of 1850, 'order is the maintenance of what has been freely elected and agreed to by the people, it is the national will triumphant over all factions.' Thus Napoleon's regime was an authoritarian one, but not a legitimist one, so that, for example, the monarchs of Europe were at first reluctant to regard him as one of themselves, and the Tsar refused him the conventional salutation of *Monsieur mon Frère* and addressed him instead as *Mon Ami*.

Napoleon III's rule was essentially personal, and the Second Empire, which he inaugurated one year after his coup d'état, depended for its success on the emperor's ability to build up a personal following and to use the glamour of his name to preserve his own position and to establish his dynasty. Opposition was controlled or limited by an effective police force; elections to the legislature were carefully managed by the prefects who represented the central government in the provinces; industrial development and the expansion of the banking system were encouraged and the support of the manufacturing and financial classes thus assured. Paris was replanned on a grandiose scale by Baron Haussmann (1809–91); and the creation of the broad new boulevards not only enhanced the prestige of the regime which constructed them but also, it was believed, made easier the control of the mob in any future revolution by clearing a field of fire for the forces of order. Above all, Napoleon III depended for his throne on a successful foreign policy which would live up to the aspirations for national glory which his name inspired; and, in the long run, it was his lack of clear aims and effective execution in the conduct of foreign affairs which cost him his throne. Since the Second Empire was a system of personal rule, without the built-in institutional support available to the conservative monarchs of Austria, Russia or Prussia, everything depended on the personality of the Emperor, and, as his reign went on, so his indecisiveness and ambiguities became greater. By the time of his fall in 1870, he had lost the confidence of the large majority of Frenchmen as completely as he had won it twenty years earlier.

The Pope and the liberals

In one respect in particular, Napoleon III's attempts to win the support of incompatible groups among his subjects led him into continuous difficulties. This was his attitude to the Roman Catholic Church. He needed Catholic support and he was also under considerable pressure from some of his entourage, especially from the Empress, to uphold the Church's claims both at home and abroad. For this reason he maintained a French garrison in Rome to safeguard the temporal sovereignty of the Pope, and thus found his freedom to support the movement for Italian unification

Before 1848 there had been hopes of a free united Italy led by the pope. Pius IX's reaction to the events of that year had destroyed those illusions, but 'Roma capitale' was still the watchword of the nationalists. After 1860 it might again have been possible to realize Cavour's ideal of a free Church in a free State ('libera chiesa in libero stato'), and in this contemporary English cartoon Garibaldi is shown recommending the cap of Liberty as a cure for the papal headache. But Pius IX was committed to anti-liberalism. In 1860 he lost four-fifths of his territorial possessions; in 1870 the rest.

severely restricted, since to Italian nationalists the possession of Rome seemed as natural a culmination to their achievement of nationhood as the possession of Jerusalem seems to the Israelis a hundred years later. In France itself, by a law of 1850, the Roman Catholic Church was given the right to run its own secondary schools and to exercise considerable influence over the conduct of the state primary schools.

Few measures were more likely to arouse the suspicion and resentment of the liberals. For it is in this period, more than ever before, that the Roman Catholic Church seemed to embody all the obstacles to liberal progress and reform and to be the strongest ally of conservative authority. Pius IX had begun his pontificate, to the alarm of conservatives everywhere, by showing a certain sympathy with some aspects of the liberal movement. In 1847 he had relaxed some of the controls over the press in his Papal States in central Italy, had created an advisory council of laymen to assist in the government, and was regarded by many as sympathizing with the cause of Italian unification. There was even talk of creating an Italian confederation with Pius as its head. The revolutions of 1848 and the establishment of the short-lived Roman Republic under the leadership of Mazzini and Garibaldi put an end to all that. Once the Pope's rule had been restored with the assistance of French troops, Pius IX was determined to resist the encroachments of liberalism, whether political or intellectual. Although eventually obliged to give up his temporal possessions, where, in the eyes of the liberals of Europe, the misgovernment and repression had only been equalled by that of the Kingdom of Naples, he remained a vigilant enemy of any doctrines which might undermine the spiritual authority of the Church. For conservatives in the Catholic countries of Europe, the Church was an indispensable ally, giving the sanction of religious approval to the reactionary measures of their governments: it was significant for example that the Austrian government in 1855 signed a new Concordat with the Vatican, which gave the church a more powerful position in Austria than it had had at any time since the reforms of the Emperor Joseph II in the late 18th century.

In 1864 the Pope attacked practically all current liberal thought in an encyclical which was accompanied by a document known as the Syllabus of Errors. Pius IX had already condemned any attempts at liberalizing Catholic theology; and now he summed up his views and launched an all-out doctrinal attack on liberal ideas in general—rationalism, freedom of thought and the subordination of the Church to the State. Finally, at the Vatican Council of 1870, two months before he lost the last vestiges of his temporal power with the entry of the Italian troops into Rome, he issued a decree claiming the infallibility of official papal pronouncements on faith and morals.

Throughout the mid- and late 19th century, hostility between liberals and the Catholic Church was growing, and, as a result, anti-clericalism became an integral part of the political programme of the liberal parties in many countries, notably in France and in Italy. Lay education, the separation of Church and State, the removal of Catholic influence over the legal system in such matters as civil marriage and divorce were practical political issues which were raised alongside the fundamental criticisms of traditional Christian doctrine being made by natural scientists and materialist philosophers. Thus political events—the attempt by Bismarck, with liberal support, to curb the influence of the Roman Church in Germany in the 1870s, or the Dreyfus Case in France in the 1890s, for example—could be represented as a struggle between reason and obscurantism or alternatively as one to maintain the traditional order, faith and morals against cynical and subversive agitators. Thus, on many occasions political disputes acquired a new ideological overtone.

Economic change and demands for the vote

The attempts to assert authority in the mid-19th century were weakened, and the protests against them strengthened, by the economic developments in the period. In Britain, the adoption of the principle of free trade before and after the repeal of the corn laws in 1846 was followed by—and was widely believed to be the cause of—a marked growth of prosperity. The manufacturers who were making fortunes out of a growing export trade, and the

bankers and financiers who were growing rich as London became an ever increasingly important centre of financial and trading activity, were gaining political importance and influence, and the old English ruling class was being steadily broadened to admit them. The consequence was a growing demand for an extension of the franchise so as to give the vote to a wider section of the middle class and to carry a stage further the process begun by the great Reform Bill of 1832. Thus parliamentary reform was a recurrent issue in British politics and a recurrent theme of popular agitation, so that in 1867 and again in 1884 legislation was passed increasing the number of voters. As a result of the latter measure, the British House of Commons was elected on a broad basis of adult male suffrage, although about two out of five adult males were still denied access to the polling booths and it was not until the 20th century that, in any country of Europe, universal suffrage was held to include women as well as men.

Similar economic developments elsewhere were leading to similar demands, usually initiated by a growing middle class wanting an increasing say in government. In France, Napoleon III encouraged the activity of bankers and entrepreneurs, some of whom became members of his immediate circle of advisers. More important still, Napoleon III was, as we have seen, a determined advocate of the principle of universal suffrage. For him as for Bismarck, universal suffrage was a weapon which he hoped to be able to use in his own interest, and one which might be used against the urban liberals who opposed his reign. In a country which was still predominantly rural and agricultural in spite of the growth of commerce and of industry, there was always a hope that it would be possible to use a fundamentally conservative peasantry to out-number the votes of the middle-class reformers in the towns. This did not always work out as expected, as the growing parliamentary opposition to Napoleon III showed, and he was obliged to make unceasing exertions in order to get his official candidates elected. However, under the Second Empire the idea of universal suffrage had become established in France, just as the move towards it was under way in Britain at the same time. By the end of the 19th century the extension of the franchise had become a primary aim for liberals everywhere, and a demand to which even conservative governments like that of Austria-Hungary had to pay some attention.

In Germany, it was economic development again which broke the conservative calm of the 1850s. During this decade there was a rapid increase in the pace of industrialization in Germany, while the population growth, which was so notable a feature of the European economy in the first half of the century, was more rapid in Germany than almost anywhere else. In the 1850s, therefore, the bases were being laid for the immense economic development of Germany after 1870. The advance of industrialization further enhanced the power of Prussia at the expense of that of Austria, so that even before Prussia's military victory over Austria and the South German states in 1866, the other states of Germany were being drawn inexorably into the Prussian sphere. Thus the achievement of German unification under Prussian leadership had an economic as well as a political basis; and Bismarck, hostile as he personally was to liberal concepts of parliamentary rule and responsible government, was obliged to enlist the support of the growing class of industrialists and financiers, as well as of the liberal professional men—lawyers and doctors and journalists—in order to achieve his aim of uniting Germany without seriously upsetting the position of the old Prussian ruling class. In 1866, just before the outbreak of the war with Austria, he proposed the introduction of universal suffrage in elections to a central German legislative body; and although he hoped that the Prussian landlords would be able to control the votes of their submissive peasantry and outweigh the urban liberals, the proposal was one which naturally pleased the liberals, suspicious though they might be at first at this offer from a man they regarded as an arch-conservative. Accordingly, universal suffrage became the basis on which the parliaments both of the North German Confederation, founded after the victory of 1866, and of its successor, the German Empire, created after the victory over France in 1870, were elected. The introduction of universal suffrage was followed by other measures which bound most of the liberals firmly to Bismarck—free trade, a uniform currency system, a central bank, a centrally controlled railway network and, signifi-cantly, measures to limit the power of the Catholic Church (the campaign named the *Kulturkampf* by one of the liberal leaders). Bismarck's alliance with the German liberals did not last long: by 1880 he had fallen back on the support of his natural allies, the conservatives, and was seeking a measure of reconciliation with the Roman Catholic Centre Party. In the meantime he had divided the liberal party on a number of issues, especially that of a return to a protective tariff against competition from foreign goods, a measure which split the industrialists from the doctrinaire free traders and from some of the bankers who believed in the free flow of international commerce. At the same time, Bismarck persuaded a number of liberals to support his anti-socialist legisla-tion and thus compromise their principles of free speech and the right of free assembly. By the 1880s, it is not unfair to say that the German liberals who remained loyal to Bismarck had little else in their programme than support for him and a belief in the virtues of German nationalism.

The development of industry in Europe had important political as well as social effects, therefore, in that it helped to create a new middle class anxious for a share in political life. Industrial progress involved technological progress of all kinds. With the completion of the European railway network, the general use from the 1840s on of the electric telegraph and, by the end of the century, the first appearance of the telephone, invented in 1876, communications of all kinds were immensely speeded up and facilitated. At the same time, the standard of public health rose; cities were provided with sewage systems and new supplies of fresh water; streets and houses were better lit. This material progress, however, faced the old authorities with a twofold challenge. Technological advance and the scientific discoveries which accompanied it and on which it was based meant that many people were questioning the traditional religious explanations of the origin and workings of the natural world, and throwing doubt on the right of ecclesiastical and spiritual authorities to lay down the moral and legal codes on which men were expected to base their lives. Secondly, growing prosperity and rising standards of living (in some areas and among some classes) only served to emphasize the contrast between those who were benefiting from material progress and those who were its victims. Even where the condition of the poor was improving, the condition of the rich was improving faster still and the difference between them became all the more marked. The 'Social Question' which had been raised at the outset of the industrial revolution, when political thinkers and humanitarian philanthropists, such as Owen and Sismondi, had first drawn attention to the disruption of the old social order caused by industrialization, and had suggested measures to mitigate the terrible conditions under which the industrial proletariat lived and worked, now took on a new aspect. By the 1860s it was becoming one of the central issues in European politics.

Religion and the crisis of conscience

The conflict between science and religion caused one of the great crises of conscience in the second half of the 19th century. A number of ideas in the various branches of the natural sciences and in the study of history itself contributed to the creation of an atmosphere in which the hitherto unquestioned truths of revealed religion began to be doubted. Charles Darwin, whose *Origin of Species by Natural Selection* was published in 1859, was only one of the thinkers whose work seemed to challenge the truth of the Old Testament account of the creation; and many popular scientific works suggested that there was no need to seek an explanation of the natural world beyond that provided by its material basis and the observable laws governing its development. Thus, many intellectuals found themselves wondering whether there was any need for a supernatural or divine explanation for the creation and development of the world, and began to question whether a divine basis for morality was required, and whether the laws of ethics might not rather be deduced from ascertainable laws of social change. We have seen how the Roman Catholic Church officially condemned any attempt to apply the methods of rationalism to questions of faith, and, although individuals in the Church reacted against the growing dogmatism of the Vatican and others left the Church altogether, the discipline of the Catholic Church was strong enough to withstand these criticisms. Among Protestants, on the other hand, the emphasis of whose teaching had been on the responsibility of the individual for interpreting the teachings of Christ, the problems created by the new doctrines were even graver. This was the situation in England especially—where the dilemma of serious Christians faced by a 'loss of faith' is repeatedly reflected in the literature of the mid-Victorian period. In Germany, starting with the publication in 1835 of David Friedrich Strauss's *Life of Jesus*, in which he applied the criteria of rational scholarship to the evidence of the Gospels, the reaction of many Protestant thinkers was to come to terms with the new spirit and develop a rational theology that would attempt to bring the truths of religion and of science into harmony with each other.

An illustration from Darwin's 'The Descent of Man' (1871) which expanded the theories of the 'Origin of Species'. Darwin tried to show that those males most attractive to the female or most able to defeat other males of the same species have most offspring. Above: development of ornamental hair in a type of monkey. It was Darwin's scientific presentation of the evidence in support of his theories which made him so dangerous in the eyes of Christian fundamentalists.

The desire to apply the methods of the natural sciences to all aspects of life not only provided the grounds for a revolt against the authority of the churches; it also produced a new approach to the study of society. The development of sociology—associated particularly with the work of Auguste Comte (1798–1857) in France and that of Herbert Spencer (1820–1903) in England—led to a belief that the laws governing society and social change could be ascertained by observation and predictions based on them. At the same time, the importance of collecting detailed data about contemporary society was being stressed, in the belief that this would provide the basis for informed legislation to remedy some of the ills produced by the industrial revolution.

Comte himself spent the last years of his life in the elaboration of a somewhat fanciful Religion of Humanity, which was to be the positivist substitute for traditional religion, but the positivism which he had elaborated earlier in his career had considerable influence both in France and, through the work of Herbert Spencer, in England, the United States, Latin America and elsewhere. It suggested that the seemingly impartial and objective methods of the natural sciences could be applied not only to the study of society in general but also to the explanation of such subjects as literature and history, as in the work, for example, of the Frenchman Hippolyte Taine (1828–93). The meticulous gathering of facts as a basis for introducing social changes—a method already put into practice earlier in the century by some of the English administrative reformers—began to be increasingly adopted by the governments of Europe from the 1870s onwards when even conservative rulers came to realize that they must take positive steps to improve the condition of the working class if they themselves were to survive.

'The hangman stands at the door'

By the second half of the 19th century the scientific thought of the industrial age was challenging many accepted religious and social beliefs; and, in contrast to the 18th century, when subversive philosophical ideas were limited to comparatively few people, these ideas were more widely available than ever before. Newspapers increased in circulation, and, by the 1890s, were deliberately designed to interest a mass audience. Nearly all the governments of Europe thought it their duty to supply a state system of primary education: the Prussian educational system had already been the envy of reformers during the 1830s; in 1870 the Liberal government in England introduced a new system of primary schools, and ten years later attendance at these was made compulsory; in France, Jules Ferry provided in 1881 a state structure of universal lay primary education, which, it was said, set up the anti-clerical schoolmaster as a rival to the priest in every village of France.

However, the spread of industry and the growth of cities also produced a direct political threat to the governments of Europe, in the form of mass political parties of the working class. In Germany, Ferdinand Lassalle (1825–64) founded the General German Workers' Association in 1863. In France a group of followers of P. J. Proudhon (1809–65) put up working-class candidates for the legislative elections of 1863. In 1864 the International Working Men's Association was founded in London, and Karl Marx became its most important leader. The aims and the leading personalities of these various movements were very different; but in each case their formation marked the entry of a new force into politics which was to be a challenge not only to the conservatives, but also to the liberal middle classes who were themselves just beginning to make an impact on the old order. As Friedrich Engels had warned the new capitalist middle class in 1848, 'Fight on bravely, then, gentlemen of Capital! We need your help, we even need your rule on occasions. You must clear from our path the relics of the middle ages and absolute monarchy.... You must centralize, you must change all the more or less destitute classes into real proletarian recruits for us.... Your reward shall be a brief time of rule. You shall dictate laws, you shall bask in the sun of your own majesty, you shall banquet in the royal halls and woo the king's daughter, but remember, the hangman stands at the door!'

The rise of the socialist threat to the established order in Europe was one of the main issues in politics and society in the last quarter of the 19th century. It was closely linked not only with the growth of industry and of the cities of Europe, but also with the fact that the extension of the franchise in many countries made possible for the first time the creation of mass political parties. Thus the small socialist groups of the 1860s were within thirty years important political factors in Germany, France, Austria, Belgium and elsewhere. Moreover, they were aware of themselves as belonging to an international movement, and for this reason often aroused in the minds of the governments and police of Europe a sometimes exaggerated fear of their power and of the possibility of a successful revolution.

In fact, the European socialist movement was from the start in an ambiguous position. Its strength came from the industrial workers whose immediate interest was to secure short-term practical gains — shorter hours, more pay, better working conditions; and they were ready to give their votes to political parties which seemed to have a real prospect of winning these goals. Thus in Britain, where from the 1870s both the Liberal and Conservative parties were active in introducing practical social reforms, the creation of an independent socialist party came comparatively late, and it was not a serious political force till the early years of the 20th century.

However, if the day-to-day politics of the working class were largely directed towards short-term practical objectives, the intellectual leaders of the international socialist movement, and especially Karl Marx (1818–83) and Friedrich Engels (1820–95), taught that revolution, working-class revolution, was inevitable and that the proletariat must rely on its own strength and not be content with palliative measures offered by the ruling class. The role of the socialist parties in this view was to improve the organization and arouse the class-consciousness of the workers in order to prepare them for the moment when they would take over the state and create a new social order.

Thus, the development of socialist parties in Europe was conditioned by the need to serve two different and possibly incompatible purposes. In those countries with parliamentary institutions

A socialist parable. Under both absolute and constitutional monarchies the trough is reserved for the privileged few. Free competition leads back to the jungle. Only by democracy does every pig have his fair share.

The socialist menace. In this cartoon of 1850 the autocrats of Europe are shown frenziedly sweeping the socialist beast, which had terrified them so badly in 1848, into the cellar. One waves a Constitution to drive it away. On the right a throne is being prepared for Louis-Napoleon, soon to become Napoleon III.

Far right: Friedrich Engels, Marx's devoted friend and co-founder of his 'scientific socialism'. At Marx's funeral Engels claimed that 'just as Darwin discovered the law of evolution in human organic nature, so Marx discovered the law of evolution in human history.'

and constitutional conditions in which mass political parties could emerge and flourish, the socialists had become by the end of the century a substantial political force with considerable bargaining power. In countries where such conditions did not exist, they were an underground force, entangled in a web of opposition movements. In both situations there were innumerable arguments about socialist tactics and about the aims of the socialist movement, so that in almost every socialist party there were rifts and divisions even at the moment when numerically the socialists seemed to be on the point of achieving dramatic success.

Inevitably, the nature of the socialist parties varied with the general political, social and economic conditions in each country. In France, where the revolutionary tradition was strong and, indeed, had been given new strength by the brief period of revolutionary rule in Paris under the Commune in the spring of 1871, industry was still widely dispersed and mostly small in scale. The socialist groups which began to be formed in the 1880s, when the amnesty for those who had taken part in the Commune made such action possible again, tended therefore to be decentralized and somewhat undisciplined. The doctrines of Proudhon, with their emphasis on local organization and on the direct control of the means of production by the workers in each factory, tended to seem more appropriate than those of Marx, which stressed the need for discipline and the centralized organization of economic life prior to the nationalization of all the means of production and exchange when the revolution came. During the last twenty years of the century, therefore, French socialists adopted many different attitudes, some calling for direct action to seize power and others advocating the mildest measures of practical social reform. In 1900 there were several rival socialist groups in existence in France, and it was not until 1905 that they were finally united into a single party—and even this left considerable latitude to the actions of its constituent local confederations.

Socialism in Germany

In Germany, on the other hand, the Social Democratic Party which had been formed by the union of the followers of Marx with those of Lassalle in 1875, was notable for its centralized discipline and the practical efficiency of its organization. The rapid industrialization of Germany, the growth of large scale enterprises and the massive expansion of the cities all created a large urban proletariat to which the Marxist analysis of capitalist society and of the future revolution, with its emphasis on centralization of the economy and on a disciplined, well-organized, class-conscious socialist political party, seemed appropriate. From 1878 to 1890, Bismarck had tried to limit the spread of socialism by placing legal difficulties in the way of the functioning of the Social Democratic Party: its papers were forbidden; its meetings were banned and its active militants were liable to expulsion from their homes. However, these measures did not prevent the rapid growth of the party, and indeed only served to increase the determination and dedication of its members. When, after Bismarck's fall in 1890, the anti-socialist legislation was allowed to lapse, the Social Democratic Party had 35 deputies in the Reichstag and a voting strength of a million and a half, which was to increase to some three million with 81 deputies by 1903.

However, for all its strength, good organization and disciplined

following, the effectiveness of the German Social Democratic Party was limited by the constitutional conditions which Bismarck had given to the German Empire. Although the socialists might win a number of seats in parliament, the powers of parliament itself were limited. The Chancellor was responsible to the Kaiser alone and not to the Reichstag; and although the budget had to be passed by parliament, the army estimates were voted for seven years at a stretch, thus largely removing the army from control by the imperial legislature. At the same time, the federal structure of the Empire meant that many important aspects of day-to-day life—education, the police, public meetings, for example—were dealt with not by the Imperial Parliament, but rather by the Diets of the individual states. The most important of these was, of course, Prussia; and here the old social and political structure had been left intact when the Imperial constitution was introduced in 1871. The landowners in the areas east of the Elbe still controlled the local government; and the industrial areas were under-represented in the Prussian Diet. More important still, although the Reichstag was elected on the basis of universal suffrage, the Prussian Diet (and that of certain other German states), was elected on a very restricted franchise which left power firmly in the hands of the richer classes and effectively prevented the Social Democrats from exercising any parliamentary influence inside the state of Prussia.

Thus although the German Social Democratic Party was the largest and apparently most successful socialist party in Europe and served as a model and example for the socialist parties in many other countries, and in some cases even gave them some financial support, and although it provided the German working class with an organization which looked after their cultural and recreational needs as well as their political interests, its practical political power was strictly limited. The result of this was that many German socialists stressed the aspect of Marx's teaching which emphasized the historical inevitability of the proletarian revolution. Confident that history was on their side and aware of the growing numerical strength of their party, they were prepared to wait for the inevitable triumph of the revolution and the foredoomed collapse of the old order, without themselves taking any positive revolutionary action. It was this that led, at the very end of the century, to criticism that, on the one hand, the party was neither actively promoting the revolution, nor, on the other, was it facing the practical realities of political life in the German Empire and working for immediate social and constitutional reforms.

The dilemma of socialist parties in all the industrialized countries of western Europe was a similar one. It was more marked in the case of Germany both because it was to the German Social Democratic Party that other European socialists looked for a lead, and because of the habit of the German socialists of discussing their problems publicly and in theoretical terms. In other countries, France, for example, the same issues were raised by the question of socialist participation in governments which were not exclusively socialist, as at the time of the Dreyfus crisis, when a socialist joined a coalition government and was bitterly criticized by many of his socialist colleagues for doing so. In Germany the discussion centred less on the practical advantages or disadvantages of specific political actions than on a fundamental debate about the meaning of Marx's teaching. The predictions which Marx had made about the

development of capitalist society—and they were central to his view of what could or could not be achieved—were not being fulfilled: the working class was not becoming progressively impoverished, but rather, in spite of all the blatant inequalities of capitalist society, was gaining some share of the increasing economic prosperity; the middle class was not being obliterated; the peasants were not, generally, being turned into a landless rural proletariat. Consequently, some of the assumptions on which ordinary Marxist political practice was based were false, and the socialist parties had to adapt themselves either explicitly or implicitly to the changed conditions.

The beginnings of trade unionism

The strength of the socialist parties of Europe depended on the extent to which they could count on the mass support of an organized working class; and the incentive to organization was the immediate gains which might be obtained. Thus, in the last quarter of the century, the most important aspect of the working-class movement was the industrial struggle for better wages and conditions. This was carried on more by the trade unions in the factories and mines than by the socialist parties in parliament, and the relationship between the parties and the unions became all-important. During the 1880s, there was a great increase in trade union membership and organization almost everywhere in Europe. The unions, from having been mainly concerned with the maintenance of craft standards or traditions, began to organize the un-skilled workers, and the effectiveness of the new organizations was demonstrated in, for instance, the great strike in the London docks in 1889 or the strike in the Ruhr coal mines in the same year. Such industrial action was not of course new—the atmosphere of a strike in the coalfields of north-eastern France in the 1860s is, for instance, vividly re-created in one of the masterpieces of French realist fiction of the late 19th century, Zola's *Germinal*, published in 1885—but by 1890 the strength of the trade unions made the strike weapon a more effective and a more formidable one than it had been earlier.

This inevitably gave rise to discussion about what purposes strike action should serve. The majority of trade union leaders in Germany, where they worked in close agreement with the chiefs of the political party, or in Britain, where by the end of the century they had still not finally committed themselves to support of an independent labour party, believed that strikes should only be used for immediate short-term practical ends. They were totally opposed to the idea, gaining ground in France, Italy and elsewhere, that a political general strike might be the decisive revolutionary act in the seizure of power. Nevertheless, there were, even before the end of the century, some outstanding examples of strikes achieving a political purpose—notably in Belgium where a general strike in 1893 succeeded in winning a substantial widening of the franchise. In practice, the weaker a trade union movement, and the less effective in winning immediate concessions, the more militant it tended to be. The powerful unions that existed in Britain and Germany were content to husband their strength and to use it for effective industrial action. Elsewhere, especially in France, where the strength of the unions was much less, partly as as a result of the geographical dispersal of French industry and the

comparative lack of large heavily industrialized areas and partly because of the number of small concerns employing only a few workers, the weakness of the trade union movement led to a policy of all or nothing, of revolutionary direct action which would encourage the rest of the working class to follow the example of a few active militants.

During the 1890s, therefore, in France, and, a few years afterwards, in Spain and Italy, a new theory and practice of industrial action was developing (known as syndicalism—from *syndicat*, the French word for a trade union). This was based on the assumption that political action was useless and that socialist politicians were no better than bourgeois ones. The only way to make a revolution, it was maintained, was by direct action to seize the means of production, thus bringing the factories under the direct control of the workers. The distrust of politicians and the faith in direct revolutionary action linked the syndicalist movement to earlier anarchist traditions of revolution, and in many cases syndicalist leaders in France, and still more in Spain, had strong links with the anarchist movement. For many anarchists, too, the possibility of direct industrial action seemed to offer a new and more promising tactical method of making the revolution, in contrast to the isolated acts of terrorism—assassination of prominent personalities, indiscriminate bomb-throwing in cafés, theatres and other places which seemed to symbolize the hated bourgeois world—which had been the typical, and futile, gestures of anarchist protest in the 1880s and 1890s. The syndicalist movement, like its socialist counterpart, included many different shades of opinion, united by the common belief in direct action as the only effective means of imposing changes on existing society, whether these were limited gains within the existing capitalist framework or a completely revolutionary new order.

Michael Bakunin (1814–76), the great protagonist of anarchist ideas in the First International, had, in his controversy with Marx, stressed the need to make the revolutionary movement itself resemble the society which it was hoped to create after the revolution. An authoritarian, centralized socialist party would, he maintained, produce an authoritarian centralized system after the revolution; a libertarian, decentralized, spontaneous revolutionary movement would produce a free society. Many of the French and Spanish syndicalists took up this idea, and stressed, for example, the necessity of education and self-improvement in the workers' movement, while retaining considerable distrust of intellectuals who were not themselves workers and who wanted to tell the workers how to behave. Bakunin had also taught that the people who made revolutions were the people with nothing to lose. His ideas, therefore, were most eagerly welcomed in those countries like Spain or Russia in which large numbers of people, including especially workers on the land, led lives of such precariousness and desperation that no normal political process seemed to offer any hope of improvement. By the end of the 19th century, there was established therefore in some parts of Europe an alternative tradition of direct revolutionary action in contrast to the belief in orderly mass political organization which the Social Democrats advocated. And, if the anarchists were never finally successful, their ideas were, in the early 20th century, to influence the theory and practice of industrial action even in countries like France where, it might be thought, the ordinary political and constitutional processes offered a better hope of improvement than direct revolutionary action.

The end of 'laissez-faire'

With the growth of working-class movements of protest and revolt, the governments and authorities of Europe themselves began to take more positive action to deal with the 'Social Question'. The view, widely held among liberals earlier in the century, that the state should not concern itself with the conditions of life of its citizens, but rather leave these to be regulated by the free play of economic forces—all that was suggested in the slogan *laissez faire*—began to be questioned. By the 1870s the idea of the role of the state was changing. Some statesmen, such as Bismarck, saw that the state must take positive measures to remedy the worst social evils if its authority was to survive. Consequently Bismarck accompanied his anti-socialist measures with an ambitious and pioneering programme of social insurance, financed in part by the money raised by the new protective duties on imports. At the same time, numbers of English liberals felt that inherited political and economic doctrines had to be re-examined in the interest of social justice and proposed new measures aimed at redistributing wealth and improving the lot of the poorest classes. The principle of using taxation as a means of taking money from the rich in order to give to the poor in the form of social benefits began to be adopted, even if as yet somewhat hesitantly, by the British Liberal Party in the 1890s.

The Churches, too, moved in part by genuine Christian charity, and in part by concern for the future stability of the social order, began to preach the necessity of a positive social policy. A movement, started in Germany by the Roman Catholic Bishop of Mainz, Wilhelm, Freiherr von Ketteler (1811–77), spread to Austria, where the Christian Social Party won considerable mass support and combined ideas of Catholic social reform with a strong element of anti-semitism. In France, similar ideas were developed by Count Albert de Mun (1841–1914), who also took the lead in a short-lived attempt to reconcile French Catholics to the republican government. This new spirit of social reform was recognized by the Vatican, when Pope Leo XIII, who reigned from 1878 to 1903, published in 1891 his encyclical *Rerum Novarum* in which he outlined a Catholic social doctrine and stressed the duties owed by the state to the poor and helpless. Under the pressure of movements of protest against the social conditions of industrial society, both liberals and conservatives had been forced to change their conception of the role of the state, and to accept a degree of government interference in social and economic life that would have been unthinkable fifty years earlier. 'We are all socialists now,' an English liberal statesman remarked light-heartedly towards the end of the century; and it was true that the *laissez-faire* state envisaged by the most extreme or the most *simpliste* of the classical liberal economists and political theorists was vanishing as fast as it was being created.

The irrationalist challenge

Movements of protest in one generation often turn into the orthodoxy of authority in the next. At a moment when the liberals of Europe seemed to be triumphant, with their ideas about constitutional government and universal suffrage becoming increasingly widely accepted, their faith in progress being widely shared and their confidence that all problems had solutions becoming the basis of an accepted ideology, these basic assumptions were already meeting increasing criticism. In the face of a working-class movement demanding radical reforms and of conservatives ready to sponsor active government policies for social improvement, liberal politicians and political theorists had by the end of the century abandoned many of their old beliefs about the nature of the state and the virtues of free competition and free trade. But liberal ideology was faced with more far-reaching criticisms and some of its most fundamental assumptions were being challenged in the last two decades of the 19th century. Just as the various socialist movements asserted that the liberal state, whatever palliatives it might offer, was incapable of producing true social and economic

justice and was inevitably bound to the selfish interests of the ruling class, so too some thinkers were offering a radical criticism of the rationalist and scientific philosophy on which liberal principles were based. The positivist philosophers and the natural scientists had challenged the authority of religion in the mid-century; by the 1890s they themselves were facing an irrationalist challenge.

During that decade, the works of Friedrich Nietzsche (1844–1900), written over the previous thirty years, at last began to be widely read. His untidy, inconsistent but powerful and poetic writings have not yet lost their explosive force today, and in the Europe of the 1890s his attack on the shams and hypocrisy of contemporary society and his insistence on the need for a new morality, the *Umwertung aller Werte*, a complete reassessment of all our values, and for a new élite of supermen who would transcend the limits of conventional ethical and political codes, struck the younger generation with extraordinary force and made them question all the assumptions of their predecessors. In a more conventionally academic way, the French philosopher Henri Bergson (1859–1941) stressed, in a series of works starting with the *Essai sur les Données Immédiates de la Conscience* in 1889, that reality could not be broken up and dissected and treated as a series of separate hard facts, but rather that it must be regarded as a continuous process which would not lend itself to the cut-and-dried analysis of positivist science. The young Italian thinker Benedetto Croce (1866–1952) published in 1893 his essay on *History subsumed under the Concept of Art* in which he criticized the scientific view of history put forward by the positivists and called for an intuitive and imaginative reconstruction of the past. The certainties of dogmatic positivism and the assumptions of optimistic and rational liberal beliefs were being widely questioned, and philosophers and artists, often in alliance, were stressing more and more the complexity of reality and the danger of over-simple explanations and solutions. The outline of this story is pursued further in Chapter I.

The technological advances of the industrial age were also being thought of more critically. As the factories spread and the cities grew, many people reacted against the ugliness of the industrial landscape and the dirty crowded towns. Machines were seen not as beneficent purveyors of progress but as monsters that were perverting men and alienating them from their true environment. In England, William Morris (1834–96) tried to revive the craftsmanship and sense of design which he believed to have existed in a vanished medieval tradition, and linked to the socialist ideas with which he sympathized, the vision of a purer, simpler pre-industrial world. At the very end of the century Ebenezer Howard (1850–1928) outlined his plans for 'Garden Cities' which would give the suburban city dweller some taste of the pleasures of the countryside—an idea which had already been suggested by the anarchist philosopher Prince Peter Kropotkin (1842–1921). In Germany, Austria and France young architects, such as August Endell (1871–1925), Otto Wagner (1841–1918) and François Hennebique (1842–1921), were reacting against the historicist styles which a previous generation had found appropriate to the municipal buildings of the cities and even for the factories themselves.

The same trend in favour of more simplicity and more open air also led to the founding in Germany at the turn of the century of youth movements dedicated to what was thought to be a more spontaneous way of life than was possible in the industrial cities or in the over-elaborate cluttered houses of the newly enriched bourgeoisie. The *fin-de-siècle* may have been an age of decadence in which artists and writers like J. K. Huysmans (1848–1907), Aubrey Beardsley (1872–98) and the young Maurice Barrès (1862–1923) were advocating what Barrès, in the title he gave to a group of his early novels, called *le Culte du Moi*, an extreme individualist aestheticism in which refined, exotic and elaborate experiences were cultivated for their own sake (the poet Charles Baudelaire (1821–67) provides a link with earlier generations). But it was also a period in which new styles of life and new standards of design which were to transform the physical appearance of many European cities in the first half of the 20th century were already being developed.

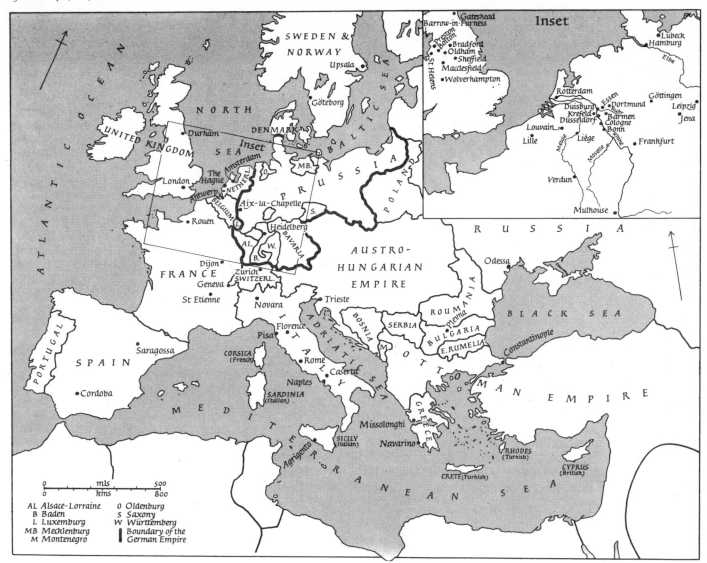

Europe after the Congress of Berlin in 1878.

Art as protest

The 19th century was an age in which to many people the artist seemed to embody the gesture of protest against authority. One of the products of the Romantic movement had been the concept of the independent artist, not beholden to anyone, pursuing his own vision whether or not it brought him material success and ready to starve in a garret if need be rather than compromise with conventional materialist values. The concept was retained as the context changed, for throughout the century many artists, musicians and writers did their best to live up to this picture of themselves and plunged into 'Bohemian life'. (Henri Murger's *Scenes of Bohemian Life* published in 1848 and used as a basis for the libretto of Giacomo Puccini's opera *La Bohème* (1896) was one of the most famous of the many literary evocations of this milieu.)

But some artists also thought of themselves as critics of society in a more explicit way, as well as living in a manner which was itself an implicit criticism of existing middle-class values. In painting, Gustave Courbet (1819–77) or in literature Emile Zola (1840–1902), for example, used a new realism of expression to reveal the sufferings of the poor and to attack the harshness and hypocrisy of a society which made such things possible. Courbet ended his life in financial difficulties because he had put his beliefs into practice sufficiently to become a member of the Paris Commune and to be involved in the decision to demolish the column in the Place Vendôme erected to commemorate Napoleon's victories, and thus to the revolutionaries a symbol of despotism and militarism. Although many of the artists whose work was artistically revolutionary were by no means actively involved in revolutionary politics, nevertheless, throughout the second half of the century, some of them were attracted to advanced political movements:

in the generation after Courbet, for instance, Camille Pissarro was a sufficiently active supporter of the anarchists to design covers for their pamphlets. The theatre, too, became a medium in which society could be attacked either explicitly or by implication. Dramatists such as Henrik Ibsen (1828–1906) or Frank Wedekind (1864–1918) used their plays to dissect bourgeois society and to expose the violent and unhealthy passions, the sordid motives, which often lay behind the smug and prosperous exterior of 19th-century middle-class society. Indeed, Ibsen, together with Nietzsche, became one of the great liberating forces for the younger generation at the end of the century, opening up forbidden topics and suggesting a whole range of new social and psychological ideas for eager discussion among the young in revolt against the values of their parents.

Form as well as content could symbolize revolt in the arts. The catcalls with which Wagner's *Tannhäuser* was received in Paris in 1861 or the derision which greeted the first Impressionist exhibition there thirteen years later showed how technical innovations in the arts could shock and startle the public. Wagner's art was revolutionary, not just because of the technical innovations in his music—the extension of the harmonic language, the building up of whole operas out of short recurrent motifs or the new richness and variety of his orchestration—but also because of the claims he made for it. Each of his vast music dramas was conceived as a *Gesamtkunstwerk*, an integral work of art, a world in itself, combining the resources of poetry, music, the theatre and the visual arts, and made exceptional demands on performers, directors and audience alike. By the time of Wagner's death in 1883, his work was the object of violent controversy, but he had disciples and admirers all over Europe. (A *Revue Wagnérienne* was founded in Paris in

1885 to study Wagner as 'poet, thinker and creator of a new art form'. George Bernard Shaw wrote *The Perfect Wagnerite* in 1898.) Wagner's work and teachings seemed, rightly or wrongly, to offer a totally new concept of what a work of art should be. Moreover, during his lifetime, Wagner had been a truly revolutionary artist in that he demanded a revolution in society in order to produce the conditions under which his works could be adequately performed. He had fought on the barricades in Dresden, alongside the anarchist Michael Bakunin, in the last desperate attempt in 1849 to save some of the revolutionary political achievements of the revolution of the previous year, which Wagner had hoped would provide the basis for a new revolutionary national theatre; and he lost his job as conductor of the Dresden Opera as a result. Subsequently, in his search for an ideal patron—since it was clear that his hopes of a revolutionary state which would promote his works were bound to be disappointed—he fixed on the young King of Bavaria, Ludwig II, a passionate admirer of Wagner both as man and artist. Wagner published a number of pamphlets abusing those—among whom the Jews were prominently included —who opposed his conception of a new music drama, derided the 'music of the future', and denied him the conditions for the performance of his works. Although he succeeded in persuading King Ludwig II to back his grandiose plans, and finally built his own festival theatre at Bayreuth, this was largely at the expense of Ludwig's personal fortune and produced repeated difficulties with the Bavarian government. Wagner, in fact, was typical of those who thought of the artist as being above and beyond the ordinary conventions, ruthlessly subjecting others to his own needs and standards, acting out in practice some of the traits attributed by his close friend (and later bitter critic), Friedrich Nietzsche, to the *Übermensch*. At least in Wagner's case the scale and originality of his work and the profound influence which it had on the development of European music went far to justify his claims.

The revolution in European painting brought about by the Impressionists was a revolt in terms of art itself; and its implications were aesthetic rather than social. (The name was derived from the title of a picture by Claude Monet (1840–1926), *Impression, Sunrise*, painted in 1872.) The break with the conventions of the academic painting of the day which so shocked the public was the result less of a deliberate attempt to revolutionize painting than of following through a new conception of depicting the light, colour and movement of nature, based, in part at least, on new scientific theories about light and colour (see below, Chapter I). Just as, early in the 19th century, the concept of the role of the artist in society had changed as a result of the romantic conception of the independent artist, beholden to no one and living outside the canons of conventional social behaviour, so, in the last quarter of the century, the attitude of the artist towards the natural world was also changing, first by challenging the conventions for the depiction of that world, and then, by the early 20th century, by questioning the value of depicting the world in a naturalistic way; and finally by denying, in abstract painting, the value of depicting the natural world at all. These revolutions were, to a considerable extent, the result of the influence of, and reaction to, technological change.

In the 1830s photography had begun to be used for the recording of people and places—a task which had hitherto been that of the artist. The effect on artists was twofold: first, photography set

a new standard of realism, and many artists looked at photographs as a means of obtaining new naturalistic effects in their painting. (It was characteristic for example, that Courbet's critics attacked the paintings in which he was aiming at a realistic, unembellished and unidealized depiction of peasant life or of landscape, for being like photographs.) But if, by the middle of the century, photography had contributed to a new realism in painting, by the end of it artists began to feel that there was no need for them to do what photography—continuously improving its techniques for making, for instance, an instantaneous record—could do as well or better. A painter such as Edgar Degas (1834–1917) was able to use the instantaneous images of photography to give a new vividness and tension to his pictures of race horses or ballet dancers, but in the process was moving away from the realism conventionally regarded as photographic. By the 1880s and 1890s, it was the established painters of the academies and salons whose work became more and more like conventional and lifeless photographs; and the post-Impressionist painters began to go further than ever before in their revolt against an exact realism. Gauguin (1848–1903), Van Gogh (1853–90) or Cézanne (1839–1906) seemed to be searching behind the surface images which photographers could record for some inner formal structure or emotional meaning in the objects or landscapes or figures which they painted. In the next generation, the trend was to go further still. In the words of the manifesto of a German group, *Die Brücke*, in 1905: 'Today photography takes over exact representation. Thus painting, relieved from this task, gains its former freedom of action.' Within a decade the first abstract paintings had been produced and the whole concept of the artist and his relation to the real world radically changed. By 1914 European art had undergone one of the most fundamental revolutions it had ever experienced.

Rhythms of change

An attempt to analyze the history of Europe in the second half of the 19th century in terms of Authority and Protest suggests that at no stage did the rule of Authority last long. Movements of protest in one generation could easily become the new established authority in the next. While in many countries the new liberalism of the middle classes had successfully challenged the conservatism of the old aristocracy, liberalism itself was already being challenged by the socialist movement and by new concepts of the role and function of government. The belief in the rational methods of the natural sciences which had questioned the validity of traditional religious authority was itself by the end of the century being questioned by a new irrationalism. The canons of realism which writers and artists had tried to establish in the face of conventional ideas of propriety and good taste in the middle of the century were by 1900 being abandoned as a result of new aesthetic doctrines and a new vision. The industrial and technical progress of the 19th century produced a protest against the values and the way of life of industrial society. Behind the solidity, material prosperity and optimistic belief in progress characteristic of most of European society in the late 19th century, the forces which were to overthrow that society were already massing. Yet the result of these constant changes and challenges had been to produce a civilization of enormous richness and variety whose achievements can stand up to comparison with those of any other age of European history.

By the end of the century Romanticism had acquired a sophisticated and self-consciously 'aesthetic' flavour. Aubrey Beardsley's 'Return of Tannhäuser to the Venusberg' (1895) shows how the interpretation of a medieval legend had changed since Wagner's more robust treatment of 1845.

IV CITIES

Population and the urban explosion

F. BÉDARIDA

'Our age is pre-eminently the age of great cities.'

ROBERT VAUGHAN, 1843

Too many people

crowded into the bursting and ill-equipped cities of the 19th century. It was a new and unforeseen phenomenon. The old capitals of Europe trebled or quadrupled their populations. New industrial towns in areas like the Ruhr, northern France and the Black Country of England spread outwards until they touched each other. In America, huge cities grew from nothing in a few decades.

The pace was too fast for all its implications to be grasped. Plans and regulations followed in the wake of problems which it was already too late to solve. Streets of terrace houses and tenements, often without sewerage or water, were thrown up as cheaply and quickly as possible. Increases in public services had to be heaped upon systems never designed to bear them. Coal fires belched out smoke and soot from thousands of chimneys, polluting the atmosphere with yellow fog. Poverty, no longer a matter of small groups scattered in the countryside but of vast masses, assumed a new dimension of horror. Epidemic diseases, such as typhoid or cholera, were difficult to control. The evils bred by hunger and despair—crime, violence, prostitution—multiplied. Yet at the same time the traditional pleasures and amenities of urban civilization— wealth, elegant living, commerce and the arts—were flourishing with a brilliance that had hardly been matched before. The social

split between rich and poor in cities epitomized the social problem of the whole century.

In all these respects London constituted the object-lesson of Europe. Englishmen were acutely alive to the questions that it posed. The journalist Henry Mayhew, who left the most detailed record of the London poor, began his book: 'I enter upon this subject with a deep sense of the misery, the vice, the ignorance and the want that encompass us on every side.' General Booth, the founder of the Salvation Army, could write in 1890: 'The lot of the negress in the Equatorial Forest is not, perhaps, a very happy one, but is it so much worse than that of many a pretty orphan girl in our Christian capital?' Foreign observers told the same story: J. F. Hogan, an Australian, called it 'this modern Babylon'. Hippolyte Taine, from France, noted how one had to drive for a whole morning before reaching the outskirts of London. Most vividly of all, another Frenchman, Gustave Doré, appalled and fascinated to equal degrees, brought Victorian London to life in his engravings of the 1870s. His picture of London traffic (opposite) might be an illustration of the passage of Dickens' *Nicholas Nickleby* where he speaks of 'vehicles of all shapes and makes', mingling 'in one moving mass like running water'.

Cities are too varied for any generalization to be meaningful. Few were totally new creations in the 19th century, and each was conditioned by its past as well as its present. **Naples** (*right*), until 1860 the capital of the Two Sicilies, suffered no sudden industrial transformation. In the centre its buildings were modernized peicemeal, but became surrounded by dense slums supporting a population who lived largely on the streets. **Sheffield** (*far right*) had been a manufacturing centre before the 19th century. Its industry was revolutionized in the 1850s by the introduction of electro-plating.

Barcelona, Spain's second city, spread outwards from its medieval centre – right foreground in this view. Beyond are the 19th century suburbs and factories, and to the left the port, modernized in the 1870s, and the new railway station.

New York (*centre*) was growing more rapidly than almost any city of the Old World. Skyscrapers, which began in Chicago, were transforming its skyline by the 1880s.

Rotterdam (*right*), one of Europe's busiest ports, renewed itself progressively as trade and traffic increased. It was the meeting place for shipping from central Europe via the Rhine and from the rest of the world via the New Waterway, built between 1869 and 1890.

New Paris was largely the creation of Napoleon III and his Prefect of the Seine, Baron Haussmann (*far right*: a caricature showing money falling through his sieve). During the 17th and 18th centuries wide straight streets had been opened inside and beyond the medieval town walls (*boulevards* orginally meant 'bulwarks'). Haussmann's plan extended this feature by a system of radiating avenues linking important squares and public buildings. The bird's eye view (*below*) depicts the city as it was before Haussmann; the inset plan shows the new boulevards super-imposed in heavy black. The result was a city of greater dignity and ease of communication.

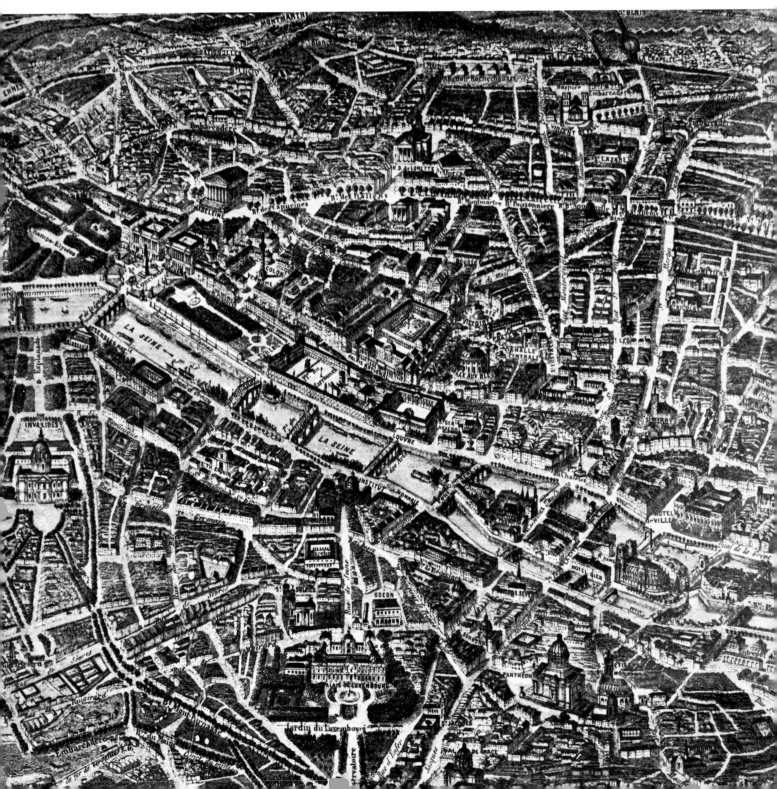

Old Paris fell before Haussmann's pick-axes, so that by 1870 few traces of the medieval city survived. *Above left*: demolition for the new Rue des Écoles. *Above centre*: work goes on by floodlight on a part of the Rue de Rivoli, a street already planned by the first Napoleon. As the city expanded former villages were engulfed to become suburbs.

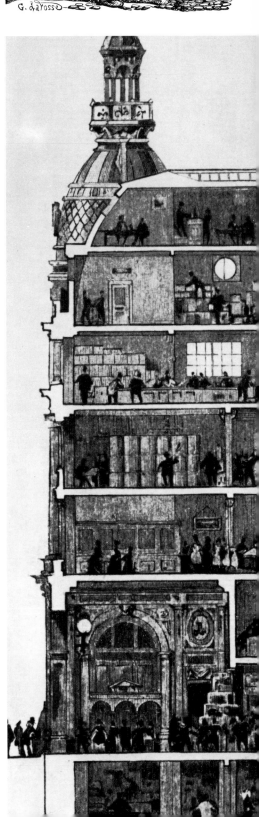

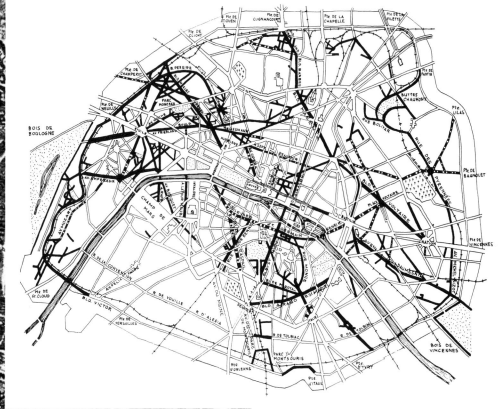

Palatial shops selling every conceivable item of necessity or luxury spring up along the new boulevards. This section (*right*) shows part of 'Les Grands Magasins du Printemps' on the Rue du Havre, built in an exuberant Neo-Baroque style in the 1880s.

Fashions in shopping: the Constantinople bazaar (*below*) served a way of life that went back to Byzantine times. In Western Europe, the glass-roofed shopping arcades that became so popular in the 19th century were a variant of the bazaar, enlarged to a grandiose scale – that of Milan (*above*), designed in 1865, being the largest.

After nightfall the 19th-century city acquired a strange, artificial beauty. Gas lighting and, later, electricity prolonged the day in a way that had been unthinkable hitherto. The idea of the city's 'night life' was born. Even a wet evening in Liverpool (*above*) had a magic to which the Age of Romanticism could not help responding.

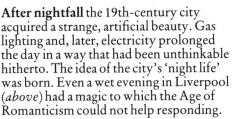

England had suffered some of the worst effects of non-planning, but by the end of the century was evolving a new answer: the 'garden suburb', an area of irregular streets and moderate sized houses picturesquely landscaped amid grass and trees. The prototype was Bedford Park (*left*), on the western edge of London, laid out in 1876. The 'Queen Anne' style houses, built by fashionable architects, notably Norman Shaw, became favourite places of residence for intellectuals and artists who wanted a semi-rural existence while remaining in touch with the city. Suburbs like this were to cluster round large towns during the next fifty years, mainly in northern Europe and America.

Urban poverty was the greatest single problem confronting 19th-century civic authorities. Doré's engraving called 'Devil's Acre, Westminster' (*above right*) is a vivid image of how the poor lived. Relief measures came slowly, and largely as a result of efforts by individuals like Shaftesbury and Booth. *Above*: a 'night refuge' for the London poor in 1859. In the background the names of new inmates are registered; sinks for washing are on the right; the room is heated by the stove in the centre, while all around the men lie on low beds that are almost like coffins.

Public transport within the city had been almost unknown before the 19th century: now it became a pressing necessity. New solutions proliferated – above the streets, on the streets, under the streets. *Above left*: inside a crowded horse-drawn omnibus in London in 1859. London was the first city to build an underground railway. The first section opened in 1863; Baker Street Station (*left centre*) was built in 1868. The use of steam locomotives limited the growth of underground railways but with the advent of electricity around 1900 they were adopted in Paris, Vienna, Berlin, New York and Philadelphia. In New York, the Elevated Railway, known as the 'El' (*below left*), proved efficient, but never became popular in Europe.

Sewers in the first half of the century were totally inadequate for the size of the new cities. Poor districts often had none at all. London's sewers were enlarged in the 1840s (*right centre*: laying pipes in 1845) but until the 60s still discharged into the Thames, producing outbreaks of cholera. The Paris sewers (*bottom*) were largely the work of Haussmann and follow the lines of the boulevards.

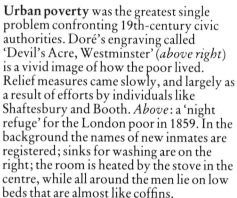

Vienna's plan reflected not only the stages of the city's growth but the social strata into which it was divided. The old ramparts had been pulled down in 1857, to be replaced by a broad and handsome boulevard, the Ringstrasse, clearly visible in this panoramic view. Within the Ring lay the old city, clustered round the cathedral of St Stephen. The Ring itself was lined with public buildings. Starting on

the left, the Neo-Gothic
Votivkirche, the Renaissance
University, the two Museums and
the Neo-Baroque Opera (on the

inner side). Outside the Ring,
previously isolated buildings like
the Karlskirche, the Schwarzenberg
Palace and the Lower Belvedere

(seen, left to right, in the
foreground) were now surrounded
by middle-class streets and
houses.

107

In the new world of Australia and America cities could be built with some awareness of the problems likely to arise. Melbourne (*left*), named after Queen Victoria's first prime minister, grew from nothing to a city of half a million people in sixty-five years. From the beginning it was planned on a grid system, with the main streets 99 feet wide. Such a plan is infinitely expandable but infinitely monotonous. Oklahoma City (*below*) mushroomed even more rapidly: founded on the morning of April 22nd 1889, when the state of Oklahoma, previously Indian territory, was opened for settlement, it had *by the next day* a population of 10,000, mostly in tents. This drawing shows it ten months later, in February 1890.

OKLAHOMA CITY

INDIAN TERRITORY.

Population and the urban explosion

F. BÉDARIDA

THE RICHNESS and variety of 19th-century civilization rested in part, at least, on the great expansion of cities. It was in the cities also that most of the movements of protest became articulate and organized. Cities, indeed, were increasingly thought of as 'problem centres'—and there were protracted debates about their ways of life and their contribution to social change. Moreover, during the early years of photography and the revolution of the Impressionists, they began to be looked at in a new way, at least by an *avant-garde* generation of artists and writers. For Baudelaire (1821–67), who wrote of the 'active and fertile' poet's need to make 'multitude and solitude' equal and interchangeable terms, there was a special excitement in 'bathing in the crowd'. The same excitement infected many of the aesthetes who saw in the city the indispensable agent of what Walter Pater (1839–94) called 'the quickened, miltiplied consciousness'. The very feverishness of the city, condemned by writers who dwelt on the peace and order of the countryside, was an aspect of its not infrequently fatal attraction.

Such a reaction was highly sophisticated, and it should be compared with earlier 19th-century reactions, when pastoral myths from older centuries were newly clothed in romantic language and when traditional fear of the 'complexity' of the city was heightened by the growth of industrial cities and by the sense that they included within them 'two nations' segregated from each other. William Wordsworth (1770–1850) at the dawn of the century foresaw with concern the great growth of the 19th-century city:

> *At social Industry's command,*
> *How quick, how vast an increase! From the germ*
> *Of some poor hamlet, rapidly produced*
> *Here a huge town, continuous and compact,*
> *Hiding the face of the earth for leagues—and there,*
> *Where not an habitation stood before,*
> *Abodes of men irregularly massed*
> *Like trees in forests—spread through spacious tracts,*
> *O'er which the smoke of unremitting fires*
> *Hangs permanent, and plentiful as wreaths*
> *Of vapour glittering in the morning sun.*

At the end of the century the *fin-de-siècle* writers, anticipating some of the moods of the 20th century, believed that cities came to life not in the morning sun but in artificial light. Richard Le Gallienne (1866–1947) reflected the view that the great capital cities of the world were 'modern Babylons' and when he wrote of London he was not thinking of Westminster Bridge in the early morning but of Piccadilly at night:

> *London, London, our delight,*
> *Great flower that opens but at night,*
> *Great city of the midnight sun,*
> *Whose day begins when day is done.*

Reactions to urban growth were not only contrasting but contradictory. They expressed themselves in a welter of images, and they revealed consciously held or unconscious attitudes and values. Cities both attracted and repelled; they served both as places of fear and as scenes of pride. Rousseau at the end of the 18th century had seen cities as 'abysses of the human race', places of perdition where, as Wordsworth also believed, country people

would be lost and degraded. Herder (1744–1803) on the other hand hailed them as 'entrenched camps of civilization', while according to Hegel only the great modern city allowed the mind to stretch to its fullest dimensions. Industrial cities were as fascinating and as disturbing as the great capitals. 'The inconceivably immense towns' born of the industrial revolution were described in 1832 by the *Manchester Guardian*, itself a product of a new society, as 'without previous parallel in the history of the world'. And W. Cooke Taylor, the historian and statistician (1800–49), claimed that the modern industrial community introduced 'a system of life constructed on a wholly new principle'. Evoking the awakening of Manchester on a Monday morning Thomas Carlyle (1795–1881) hailed 'the rushing off of its thousand mills, like the boom of an Atlantic tide, ten thousand times ten thousand spools and spindles all set humming' and judged this 'spectacle of man's power surpassing that of nature' as 'sublime as a Niagara or more so'.

'How vast an increase'

There was no doubt about the facts of urbanization. The 'eternal order of the fields' was giving way to a new world of stone and brick, of cement and metal, of factories and shops, of wealthy houses and of slums. Railways, streets and boulevards endlessly crossed and recrossed. Suburbs followed suburbs, each in turn swallowed up and surpassed by the next.

Statistics spoke for themselves. In a little more than a century, the population of London and Paris multiplied by four, Vienna by five, Berlin by nine, New York by eighty. Those were only the capital cities. But Lancashire, the Black Country, the Ruhr, Northern France, not to speak of parts of the United States and of Japan, were transformed into vast agglomerations of towns all touching one another. The fact of conurbation existed long before the word was invented. Manchester, a quiet market-town, had 75,000 inhabitants in 1800, jumped to 400,000 in 1850 and reached 720,000 in 1910. Stockholm, slumbering with only 6,000 inhabitants in 1800, had 350,000 by 1914. The population of Düsseldorf rose from 10,000 in 1800 to 360,000 in 1910, that of Essen from 6,000 in 1850 to 300,000 in 1900. The case of a comparatively new place like Odessa, which swelled from 6,000 to 480,000 inhabitants between 1800 and 1914, is similar to that of small but very old urban centres like Oslo, which went from 10,000 to 250,000 in the same period, or Budapest (from 50,000 to 900,000). The destiny of ancient towns followed the same curve. Between 1800 and 1910 Lyons rose from 110,000 to more than 500,000, Rotterdam from 50,000 to 400,000, Antwerp from 60,000 to 300,000 and Hamburg from 150,000 to more than a million.

More spectacular still was urban growth in the New World. Chicago, which until 1830 consisted of 'a dozen of log cabins, one store, two taverns and one fort, settled on a site of mosquito-ridden bog of soft mud,' took off on its rise in 1833. The boom was rapid: 4,000 inhabitants in 1836, 180,000 in 1865, 360,000 in 1872, 1,800,000 in 1900, 2,200,000 in 1910. An 'old' town like Philadelphia, which had 40,000 inhabitants in 1800, reached a million and a half by the end of the century. Among the hundreds of other mushroom-towns, Oklahoma City was founded in a unique way as the result of a frantic dash by hundreds of settlers on horseback or in carts on April 22nd, 1889, at noon when a gunshot signalled the opening of an old Indian territory; within a few months a new town had been created with streets in orderly lines, dwelling houses, shops, offices and public buildings.

Everywhere, from Australia to Siberia, from the prairie to the pampas, towns were springing up, often destined for lightning growth; coffee made São Paulo as gold made Johannesburg. And the old colonial posts also experienced an equally rapid development; Buenos Aires, for instance, which had fewer than 40,000 inhabitants at the beginning of the century, had reached 175,000 by 1870 and in 1910 the figure had jumped to 1,300,000.

The Age of Great Cities was the title of a work on the urban revolution published in 1843 by a professor of history at the University of London who was also a close observer of social life. The author, Robert Vaughan (1795–1868), was right. While it was true that small towns were affected by the strength of the movement, that numerous country villages were transformed into little urban centres and that middle-sized towns were multiplying, it was the formation of enormous concentrations that was to be most significant. *Metropolis* or *Grossstädte*, the settlement in very large cities, was reaching a scale never before known.

On the chart below are shown, by country and by continent except for Asia and Africa, the number and the total population of towns of more than 100,000 inhabitants.

	1800		1850		1913	
EUROPE	*No. of Towns*	*Total Population (in thousands)*	*No. of Towns*	*Total Population (in thousands)*	*No. of Towns*	*Total Population (in thousands)*
United Kingdom	2	1,120	12	5,250	50	16,000
France	3	770	5	1,660	15	5,800
Belgium	–	–	2	350	5	1,450
Netherlands	1	200	1	230	4	1,400
Germany	2	320	4	780	47	13,800
Austria-Hungary	1	250	3	730	9	4,300
Switzerland	–	–	–	–	3	450
Italy	5	1,150	7	1,500	13	4,120
Spain	3	370	4	680	5	1,600
Portugal	1	200	1	240	2	530
Balkan States	1	600	2	720	7	2,100
Scandinavia	1	100	1	160	4	1,250
Russia	2	470	3	1,100	20	8,000
Total: EUROPE	22	5,550	45	13,400	184	60,800
NORTH AMERICA	–	–	6	1,400	53	20,000
LATIN AMERICA	–	–	2	400	8	3,900
AUSTRALIA	–	–	–	–	2	1,200

The growth of cities. The left-hand column, under each of the three dates, gives the number of towns in each country with a population exceeding 100,000; the right-hand column, the combined population figures of those towns.

Pattern and pace

At the threshold of the 19th century, Europe's preponderance had seemed overwhelming and it was only toward the end of the century that the emergence of America, Asia and Australia began to affect statistics. In 1800, indeed, the distribution of European cities was more a reflection of the past than a forecast of the future. They were of contrasting types; on the one hand, modern cities of the European north-west—capital cities, trade and administrative centres, great Atlantic or Baltic ports, such as London, Paris, Amsterdam, Dublin, Hamburg and Copenhagen; on the other hand, cities that had inherited the Mediterranean civilization, living still on a prosperity that had been built up between classical antiquity and the Renaissance. Thus Italy led from the standpoint of number of cities and their size, with Naples, Rome, Genoa, Milan, Palermo, followed by the Iberian peninsula (Lisbon first, then Madrid, Barcelona and Valencia). While two modern, dynamic centres—London and Paris—ranked first and third in Europe, two other powerful agglomerations recalling a glorious

past—Constantinople and Naples—came second and fourth, both of them ports and trading centres, melting pots, cities alive alike with activity and poverty, both guardians of a culture more than two thousand years old.

In Asia, although the census is rudimentary and far from precise, great human throngs were packed into the cities. At the beginning of the 19th century China had several large cities that were centuries old: Peking, Shanghai, Canton, Hankow, Tientsin each numbered several hundreds of thousands. In Japan Tokyo counted half a million inhabitants, Osaka and Kyoto around 400,000 each. In India, such swarming centres as Calcutta and Madras had perhaps attained similar size followed by Delhi and Hyderabad, Bombay and Benares each of which had between 100,000 and 200,000. Urbanization in Africa was far more restricted; there was only one great city, Cairo, which must have counted a quarter of a million. In the Asian and African worlds, the century did not bring the same urban development except in places influenced by trade which brought modernization with it. That was especially true of Japan, where Tokyo exceeded the figure of two millions in the early years of the 20th century.

Tokyo represented another feature of 19th-century urbanization—the appearance of the 'million-man' city. There were none in 1800, but by 1900 there were twelve. They were significant not only on account of their new dimensions, but because of the transformation of their social structures and of the relationships between man and the city. Around 1900, London was still the largest city in the world with more than six and a half million inhabitants (there were as many Londoners as Belgians). Paris came next, with nearly four millions, then Berlin. Other European cities with more than a million inhabitants were also capitals: Vienna (1,500,000), St Petersburg and Constantinople (1,200,000 each). Moscow had a million. Outside Europe, three were in the United States (New York, with its three and a half millions ranking third in the world, Chicago and Philadelphia, the three being the largest economic centres in North America) and two were in Asia, again capitals: Tokyo and Peking.

This development of very large cities, linked with the power of concentrated capital and made possible by technical progress in construction, distribution, provision of services like sewerage and lighting and, above all, transport, created a new kind of civilization for city-dwellers. The growth of small and middle-sized cities did not necessarily change the social patterns of their inhabitants nor their daily routines. Furthermore, such centres had always existed. But the birth of giant cities, to which nothing in past history could be compared, confronted man with a new destiny. Vaughan wrote of these 'vast experiments', the great cities, as a challenge and stimulant on the road to progress. Others, however, like the Belgian poet Emile Verhaeren (1855–1916), did not conceal their distress as they contemplated 'inexorable growth'; who would ever be able to stop the thrust of the *villes tentaculaires*?

In spite of its expansive thrust, the process of urbanization was contained within certain limits. Unduly emphasizing the urban aspects of the new mechanical civilization would risk falsifying its proportions. The whole world did not become 'citified'. In the first place, the rhythm of growth was far from consistent throughout the century, and there was a sharp contrast between the situation before and after 1850. Until about 1850, only certain countries, even certain regions were affected by the rush to urbanize. It was England's privilege to be in the vanguard of the process under the pressure of the industrial revolution. Old towns and new ones developed there with lightning rapidity. Liverpool, Manchester, Birmingham, Leeds, Newcastle bore witness to this growth (note however that at the same time spas and pleasure centres like Brighton and Cheltenham were developing equally fast). Other pilot zones, the industrial regions of Belgium, France and Germany, were experiencing the birth or rapid growth of textile centres like Mulhouse, Lille, Krefeld, mining towns, ports and railway centres.

Elsewhere the movement toward urbanization went along at a fairly moderate pace. There traditional, even archaic attitudes continued; protected by their walls old towns led a sleepy slow-motion existence observing their ancestral customs without the shade of a

Lyons was France's first industrial city, specializing in silk-weaving, chemicals and tanning, as well as being a centre of banking and trade. Heavy industry came *later after the introduction of the railways in the forties. Soon Lyons was discovering all the horrors that the English Industrial Revolution had already experienced.*

single factory chimney or a wisp of smoke, at least until the railways reached them. In the Netherlands up to 1850 and in France to 1830, the rural population was growing at a faster pace than the urban. Many large towns were still barely industrialized; their craftsmen worked in shops and tiny *ateliers* and a floating population of manual labourers, domestic servants and semi-vagabonds were there to fill the requirements of the wealthy or to earn a living in transport and services. In 1840 Milan had only two steam engines. Lyons was then the only large industrial city on the European continent. Other industrial towns fell within the category of towns with 20,000, 50,000 or 80,000 inhabitants; even in England, that was the average size of the 'new towns'.

From 1850 to 1860 however, the pace was stepped up. Throughout Europe and even more noticeably in America there was an enormous urban thrust. In the *Communist Manifesto*, Marx wrote in 1848, 'The bourgeoisie has subordinated the country to the town, creating immense cities.' In fact, from the plains and the mountains, the rural exodus drained off great throngs of country dwellers to the urban centres. Their concentration in the larger places was immediate; in 1815 only 2% of Europeans lived in towns of more than 100,000 population whereas in 1910 15% of them lived there. In 1851, only 28% of Manchester's adult population had been born there. At Munich in 1895 37% of the inhabitants were native born; and in Russian centres swelled by the *moujiks* the percentage was even lower. Towns of considerable size became immense cities: masses of houses, of railways, warehouses, factories and mills where the newcomers looked with amazement at the grey smoke overhanging everything by day and the light illuminating the sky by night. Ceaselessly and inexorably the urban landscape spread into the countryside.

Buda and Pest, on opposite sides of the Danube, were united into a single municipality in 1872. As the centre of Magyar aspirations, its most flourishing period was *the last quarter of the century when a series of splendid public buildings was erected.*

Here, however, a second qualification must be introduced. Without doubt it was the towns which provided the thrust and served as poles of attraction; towards them gravitated new power. Yet the extent of this rapid increase must not be overestimated. Even while diminishing, the country areas mostly remained predominant; not only in regions of archaic economy but also in advanced countries where capitalist industry and commerce were highly developed. In the United States the urban population which had accounted for 6% of the people in 1800 was still only 20% in 1860, 28% in 1880 and 40% in 1900; and it was only after 1920 that it began to outnumber the rural population. In 1910, in the four Scandinavian nations—Sweden, Norway, Denmark and Finland—country-dwellers numbered 10 millions out of a total of 13 millions, a proportion of nearly three-quarters. In Italy, in the Iberian peninsula, in the Balkans, country people held the majority in overwhelming numbers. In Austria, they represented four-fifths in 1843, two-thirds in 1890.

Even in the most highly industrialized countries, it was not until the end of the century that the balance swung in favour of the towns—in Germany in 1890, in Belgium in 1900 (where at mid-century the urban centres had accounted for just one-third of the population). Only England was different, ahead of the other nations; in fact speeded-up urbanization had begun there in the last third of the 18th century, and at the beginning of the 19th a third of the English were already city dwellers. The 1851 census showed an equal number of city and country dwellers. In 1880 towns accounted for two-thirds of the population and in 1900, for more than three-quarters. France was far behind, with 20% in the towns in 1801, 25% in 1851, 41% in 1901. Even in countries where the growth was very rapid, such as Russia where the urban population tripled between 1861 and 1914, percentage growth was less marked because of the very great increase in the total population; between 1880 and 1914, only 20% of Russians were living in towns.

The conclusion is clear. Even at the end of the 19th century, only a minority of mankind were town dwellers. In the larger part of Europe and America, and *a fortiori* in Asia and Africa, the majority continued to live in the country. Many of them realized, however, that it was the large city, even though it was 'in the minority', which constituted the driving force in the new industrial and technical civilization that was being formed. In spite of resistance, the modern city was influencing and shaping the rest; the small town imitated it, the country fed it. To everyone it seemed to hold the key to the future.

The industrial town pre-eminent

Because of its diversity, urban development requires classification. It is fitting to place the industrial town at the head of any list. Because of its novelty (note the use of the term 'new towns') and because of its hectic work pace, it symbolized the mechanical and manufacturing 19th century. Basing its prosperity on an ever-increasing industrial concentration, it arose sometimes from a simple hamlet, sometimes from an old market-town, or sometimes from a small ancient city. Very quickly new buildings smothered most traces of the past. Instead of growing up around the cathedral, the castle or the market square, the town was built around factories, workshops, blast-furnaces, coke-ovens, lime-kilns, warehouses, wharfs. Everything, including the monuments and public buildings, belonged to the 19th century. First to expand at the beginning of the century, the textile centres advanced fast through their spinning and weaving of cotton; there echoed the steady rumbling sound of the looms, there were the processions of women and children who made up most of the labouring force. In the iron and steel towns and those devoted to chemical industries, of lightning growth, the landmarks were the factory smokestacks, the railroads, the canals with their black, brackish water, and their workers' dwellings were lined up drearily in the greyness. Everywhere in these ugly, closed-in towns (Charles Dickens' 'Coke-

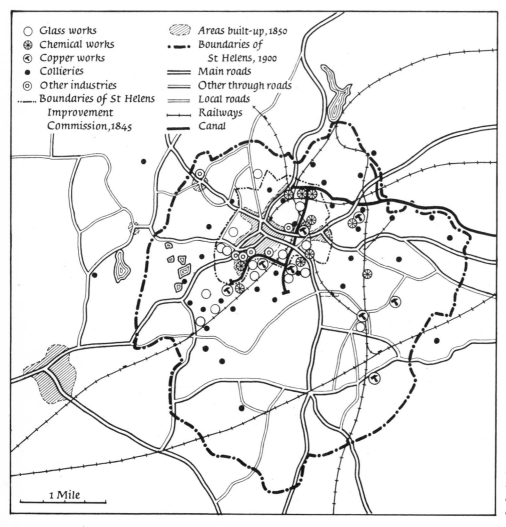

St Helens, Lancashire, in the 19th century, showing how the concentration of glass and chemical works contributed to the town's expansion.

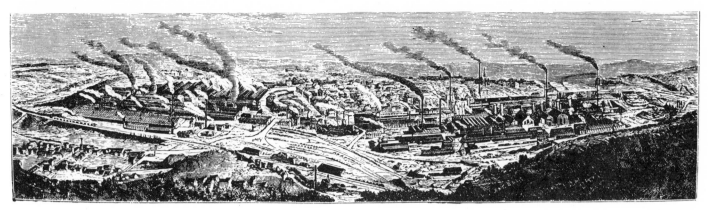

Le Creusot, south-west of Dijon, owed its prosperity to the huge Schneider ironworks and arms factory, established in 1836. Coal was mined locally.

town') the industrial proletariat was predominant, confined in a depressing atmosphere: 'not the refuge of a civilization,' as J. L. and B. Hammond have put it, 'but the barracks of an industry'.

England led the way. Very quickly the prototype multiplied. The new agglomerations sometimes had the aspect of large centres of animation and attraction for an entire region: Manchester, Sheffield, Leeds, Bradford, all centres of distribution and servicing as well as of industry. But most often, the industrial town remained a middle-sized place with from 25,000 to 200,000 inhabitants, such as Bolton and Oldham, Gateshead and Wolverhampton, Preston and Macclesfield. The perfect example of the new manufacturing town, Middlesbrough, with 150 inhabitants in 1831, 5,000 in 1841, 40,000 in 1871, 90,000 in 1901, developed in three successive economic stages: first as an outlet and exporting centre for the Durham coalmines, then as a centre for the iron industry and finally at the end of the century as a steel town. The same industrial setting prevailed at St Helens, except that there it was glass and chemical products that predominated; the thick acrid smoke from the alkali works blackened the countryside round about and attacked the greenness of trees and hedges; an 1846 account described 'irregular masses of brick houses, two or three churches with square towers, tall chimneys vomiting smoke, and conical glass houses giving out occasional flashes of flames'. The visitor was said to hear everywhere 'the clank of hammers ringing against iron' and to breathe everywhere 'a strange compound of smells'. 'The streets have been apparently laid out without any plan, as chance or interest might direct.' The result was that in rainy weather certain areas became seas of mud, filthy bearers of germs. And the *Chambers Edinburgh Journal* concluded, 'Like many other manufacturing places, St Helens seems to have been built in a hurry,' the promoters having as primary concern the erection of factories with scarcely a thought for housing the people.

In Belgium along the Sambre and the Meuse, and in France in the Nord and Pas-de-Calais, there were similar scenes all through the *pays noir* even though there as elsewhere the mining villages kept their semi-rural character. In Alsace, Mulhouse, where cotton was king dominating European markets from the time of the Continental Blockade, during the Napoleonic Wars, onward, pulled down its ancient ramparts and put up spinning and weaving works and machine-building shops, took over new land in the direction of the station and the canal, built workers' suburbs and became one of France's first basically manufacturing cities. Saint-Etienne, centre of gravity for a large industrial valley with a string of small mining and metallurgical towns, spread its blackened houses and congested neighbourhoods on either side of a straight, five-mile-long street. In the Ruhr, the countryside with its gentle green valleys, its clumps of trees and villages nestling in the hollows, gave way after 1850 to a black and smoky urban complex, where little was left but mines and factories, blast-furnaces and rolling-mills; an endless string of towns all touching one another, workers' suburbs stretching out interminably from Duisburg to Dortmund, Düsseldorf to Barmen-Elberfeld. Perhaps this last-mentioned centre, with its rival twin cities teeming with chemical and textile works, provides the best example of 19th-century urban

life in the Ruhr. Cloth-making, haberdashery and embroideries gave it its first prosperity (Engels's father was a manufacturing proprietor in Barmen); later, chemicals and machine-making took over. The Wupper river, its waters polluted by the dye-works, separated the two towns; the oldest factories and warehouses dipped their feet into it. Suspended sixty or eighty feet above the water and the streets for a dozen miles there now ran an electric railway, the *Schwebebahn*, which by night looked like a fantastic illuminated torpedo among the old black houses. Leaving the centre and going up the slopes above the river one could see the new 19th-century buildings, the lavish villas of the bosses and the more modest houses of the foremen. Farther north, Essen typified the company town; everything there belonged to the flourishing Krupp family, from the factories to the workers' quarters and the municipal libraries, just as on a smaller scale Le Creusot depended on Schneider or Barrow-in-Furness on Vickers.

The ancient city transformed

Yet the industrial town as just described was not the most usual type of 19th-century town. Most urban centres developed from active old towns in favourable situations; the traditional activities centering around the market-place or port, while administrative functions or old artisan skills, as the case might be, were gradually supplemented by new industrial and commercial activities. Alongside the ancient neighbourhoods, the historic heart of the city, were built new quarters around the stock exchange, the station and the factories. Secondary and tertiary activities were evenly balanced; often the tertiary predominated.

This composite pattern, where the present was rooted in the past, where manufacturing and trade had equal footing with cultural and religious functions, prevailed in most European towns. In this way Marseilles and Milan developed, as did Antwerp and Leipzig, Prague and Geneva. The last of these cities, an old Huguenot centre situated at a natural crossroads, specialized in business and luxury goods and flourished through a union of capital and skill. Zurich's progress was more suddenly achieved, during the second half of the century, through a combination of banking, textile and metallurgical industries and education, stimulated by foreigners (a fifth of its population in 1900 consisted of Germans and Italians); the old part of town with its narrow, twisting streets on the banks of the Limmat and the Lake, was already jostled by fashionable neighbourhoods that rose in terraces to the east and by industrial or working-class areas toward the north-west.

The ancient capital city of Hanover had a double image in 1900 as a result of rapid growth (20,000 inhabitants in 1800, 50,000 by mid-century and 300,000 by the century's close). On the one hand, there was the old Guelph town, with its tall houses with tiny windows and painted beams, ancient towers, wooden bridges, Renaissance buildings, the old Gothic town hall, the royal castle modelled on Versailles. On the other hand, there was the modern business town with its wide avenues, fashionable shops, a monumental station, public gardens, a swarm of costly, substantial villas in green surroundings. There were also industrial suburbs given over to weaving, dyeing, refining, the manufacture of carriages, machinery and rubber. Another capital, Munich, followed the destiny of its princes, the Bavarian kings. Along the old salt road, a residential city grew up, ornamented with monuments, palaces, theatres, museums, the Academy—buildings made banal by too close and servile imitation of Greek or Byzantine originals. Yet in addition to serving as a centre of artistic activities, Munich developed its commerce and consumer industries (clothing, food, furniture) and easily triumphed during the 19th century over its former rivals Augsburg and Ratisbon.

Old stagnating towns might reawaken brusquely. At Dijon, a tranquil, provincial bourgeois town, where the well-to-do drew handsome profits from their properties in the rich wine-growing district all around, the stroke of fate came in 1849 with the creation of the railway, the 'P.L.M.'; immediately around the station with its workshops and locomotive-sheds there sprang up new mechanical trades; fairs and markets extended their business; mustard, gingerbread and liqueurs were exported throughout France and across Europe. Rheims, an old cloth-making town, began its transformation as a manufacturing centre in the 18th century but it was the introduction of merinos in 1804 that gave the woollen industry its impetus, splitting it up into flannels, velvet, muslins and lightweight fabrics; to absorb a population that quadrupled in a century the old city packed around the cathedral was surrounded with workers' suburbs.

On either side of the Alps two big cities, Milan and Lyons, resembled each other in many ways. Both were crossroads cities, strategic highway and railway centres, one in the heart of the Po basin, the other in the Rhône valley, both busy and prosperous places based on the silk industry and on banking. During the 19th century they both became powerful poles of regional development, while in their vast proletarian neighbourhoods working classes fed on revolutionary teachings and hopes. Dickens had a bad impression of Lyons, seeing there 'houses high and vast, dirty to excess, rotten as old cheese and as thickly peopled'. The evils of all manufacturing towns were there 'melted into one'. Poverty was alarming; wretched children like insects 'were lolling out of windows, and drying their ragged clothes on poles, and crawling in and out at the doors, and coming out among huge piles and bales of fusty, musty, stifling goods; and living, or rather not dying, till their time should come, in an exhausted receiver'.

'Queen of the Bosporus', Constantinople, 'urban monster' touching two continents, symbolized the city of history; *Istanbul*, its Turkish name, has the same meaning as *Polis*. Its heritage was drawn from the most brilliant civilizations; the exceptional advantages of its geographical site and of its port ensured that even in an age of declining Ottoman power it would continue to grow as an immense urban complex. Many parts of the city, indeed, are still unmistakably of the 19th century. Stretching along on both sides of the Bosporus, the city brutally revealed the contrasts between the luxury of the rich and the poverty of the masses, the filthy little streets of the shanty towns and the glittering elegance of the wealthy homes. The city's activities centred around two poles, the bazaar and the palace, since its principal resources were trade and power. In the great bazaar were crammed all sorts of goods, luxury fabrics, weapons, glassware, everything the city created, produced, imported or consumed. More or less legally the 'very honorable corporation of slave traders' continued to make substantial profits from the sale of negresses, Circassians and black or white eunuchs. A mosaic of races, religions and languages, the merchant city was a mixture of populations: Anatolian and Egyptian, Greek and Armenian, Serb and Jew, Valdaque and Syrian, as well as gypsies, Persians, Italian merchants and of course English and French—recently arrived or descendants of old families. Muslims represented only half the total population. The apparently changeless past was present everywhere, not only in the superb vistas of the Golden Horn but in the white walls of the seraglio with its wooded surroundings rising above the blue Sea of Marmara, in the vast domes of Santa Sophia and the multitude of mosques with their small cupolas and their elegant minarets. Above the port, spreading over the gentle slopes of seven hills, in the direction of the suburbs of Galata and Pera or on the Asiatic side toward Scutari were marble palaces and rose-coloured houses

and gardens. But the magic city which dazzled visitors when seen from a graceful caique among the sailboats at anchor or from one of the modern steamboats, was also a pile of wretched houses and of dirty, overcrowded slums. In the twisting, filthy alleys there were stray dogs and pigs. Abject poverty and disorder marked the labyrinth of hovels which were periodically ravaged by fire—thousands of houses were made of wood—or by epidemics fostered by malarial conditions and filth. Such was the double image of the City-Paradise of the Orient in a century of progress.

On the banks of another famous bay, which rivals the Golden Horn for its beauty and renown, Naples (called by Stendhal Italy's only capital) spread out in a vast conurbation, noisy and picturesque, between the port and the Castello Sant'Elmo and little by little encroached on the Pausilippe or the industrial seaboard in the direction of the Castellamare dockyards and the coral works of Herculaneum. Capital of the Bourbon kingdom, the city experienced many changes of leadership; fought over at the beginning of the century by the French under Murat and by the English, then turned over to the Bourbons, it passed through a period of recession after the unification of Italy, sharing the neglect and under-development of the South to the advantage of the busy North. Lacking capital and industrialization, the port made painful headway and local production remained that of craftsmen working by hand, following old-fashioned methods. The unique fact about life in Naples, which was at the same time a royal, upper-class city and a working-class centre, was the extraordinary mingling of activities and of classes in the same neighbourhoods. At the gates of magnificent residences, Baroque palaces with enormous columns flanking huge doorways, in the heart of elegant quarters, either old or new, hundreds of people were packed in their slums, cramped and dark, smelly and smoke-filled. Just as at Constantinople, the animals—goats, chickens, donkeys, sheep—lived with the people. In the midst of this swarming mass, many of the poor preferred the open and actually lived in the streets. The city's size was swollen by reason of the existence of the port and the immigration of *cafoni* from Campania, Calabria and all parts of the South. The result was a floating population which worked only occasionally or was chronically unemployed, and was continually searching for means of survival; idle men easily turned into petty criminals who begged, stole and gambled, at *lotto* especially; the more venturesome emigrated. Throughout the year numerous traditional festivals of a religious or non-religious nature enlivened daily life as did popular theatre productions and songs and dances associated with the various neighbourhoods. Superstition was entrenched, illegitimacy also. Girls from Naples and from rural areas, often turning to prostitution at a very early age, were omnipresent *donne di piacere*, proving the frank statement made by an Italian jurist in a book on urban crime, 'large cities are arenas where life is feverish and passions without limit'. In spite of public authorities and the police, the powerful and solidly entrenched secret society, the *Camorra*, continued to exert its influence over all social life and everyone, fiacre-driver, fishmonger or keeper of gambling houses, took orders from it and scrupulously paid his dues. Enveloped in the Mediterranean social structure, the urban life of Naples like that of Constantinople still seemed virtually unchanged at the beginning of the 20th century.

There are many other examples of traditional cities in the 19th century, often of a more modest size, since very large agglomerations remained the exception. For example, certain university towns were spared industrialization and followed scholarly pursuits in tranquillity. Taine, visiting Oxford, Matthew Arnold's dream city, had the impression of plunging several centuries into the past, into a completely medieval setting. Upsala, Louvain, Aix-en-Provence with their libraries and fine hotels maintained the same calm existence. In Germany, this was equally true of Heidelberg, Bonn and Jena; at Göttingen, a peaceful city of ancient houses clustered between the station and the town hall, students in flat caps and with scarred faces walked like masters in the main street.

In the Balkans, Sarajevo represented the large market town grown into a supply centre for the region and capital of Bosnia; the bazaar where craftsmen worked with metal, the white minarets

Like other American colonial cities which had grown up in the 18th century, Philadelphia (until the middle of the century, the second largest city in the Union) was increasingly transformed by America's prosperity. This street scene of 1888

brings together many characteristic figures: the lady posting a letter, the street musicians and the orator. Note too the telegraph wires, the horse-drawn bus and the paving-slabs waiting to be laid.

and the Mohammedan and Jewish costumes gave it an oriental atmosphere, yet in close juxtaposition were new administrative and industrial communities built under the Austrian regime. In the midst of the Hungarian *Puszta*, towns of 50,000 inhabitants, like Debrecen or Hódmezövásárhely were little more than overgrown villages with low houses surrounded by gardens, where there lived a population of peasants farming the adjacent land—a situation similar to that of Calabrian or Sicilian towns like Agrigento or Enna. Bucharest at the beginning of the century was only a collection of villages bristling with towers and domes, with dusty or muddy streets. Little by little the efforts of the Roumanians transformed the place into a European capital with clean modern avenues bordered with hotels and parks.

Russian cities, except for St Petersburg and Moscow, also gave visitors from the West the impression of being only villages in disguise; the Frenchman Custine in 1839 and the Englishman Mackenzie Wallace in 1875 described the great width of the streets, the open spaces, the scattered public buildings, the little wooden houses with their grey boarding, the bazaars where merchants awaited their customers; in certain cases, as at Nijni-Novgorod, they noted the fortress, the kremlin with its towers, steeples and walls. But Russian towns were changing also; towards the end of the century workers flowed into them, some to remain, some on a seasonal basis, and within a generation the sons of *moujiks* were to become true city dwellers.

New cities for new worlds

In the new countries, another type of town flourished mightily, the town created *ex nihilo*. It developed rapidly according to a strictly modern pattern. Even in the case of old settlements like Boston, Quebec or Philadelphia, the traces of the past were in-

creasingly submerged by the 19th-century urban mass. New York in 1800 was only a small but busy port; where Washington Square now stands there were gallows, and Greenwich Village was founded in 1822 by families who moved there in search of pure country air. But starting in 1830–40 there was a lightning development; property bought in 1833 for $55,000 was sold two years later for more than $200,000. The whole of Manhattan was gradually occupied. By 1897 the neighbouring towns of Brooklyn, Queens, the Bronx and Richmond had been taken in, to form the City of New York, occupying a huge area of 210,000 acres. During the last twenty years of the century there began to go up tall buildings of more than ten storeys—modest skyscrapers, in imitation of those in Chicago, and immediately termed 'outrageous' and 'monstrous', or 'eyesores'. While the poet Walt Whitman (1819–92) admired this extraordinary vertical city embraced by the arms of the sea, another poet, Rudyard Kipling (1865–1936) had only scorn for a city 'corrupt, lawless, shapeless': 'a long, narrow pig-trough'.

American towns grew along the same pattern, building in the same way, following a grid-plan with streets intersecting at right angles, with houses from five to twenty storeys high, with intense traffic of tramways and lorries, huge signs and billboards, and new buildings going up everywhere and with perpetual excavation and demolition in order to put up something even larger and more modern. In such a way Baltimore and Detroit grew, as did St Louis and New Orleans. Los Angeles began its expansion in 1900, Seattle a little earlier. On the Pacific coast Tacoma typified the usual development of a new town; site of a 'sawmill village', the location was chosen in 1873 by the Northern Pacific Railroad Company as a terminus on Puget Sound at the foot of Mount Rainier. There was an immediate boom; within a few years there were real estate developments, offices, hotels and apartment buildings, and Kipling visiting the city in the midst of the work in 1880 wrote, 'On the rude, crude streets men were babbling of money, town lots and again money . . . and round the corner in a creaking boarded hall the red-jerseyed Salvationists were calling upon mankind to renounce all and follow their noisy God.' Wherever the choice of site proved favourable, the new towns were destined to grow and progress; such was the case of Denver and Colorado City. Yet if the location was badly chosen, the towns died along with the special interests that had brought them into existence. Thus, for example, numerous railroad towns like Cheyenne City, quickly passed into history. The same fate met Carson City when the silver mines were exhausted in the desert wasteland, and such was the fate of Dawson City, Alaska, which had known the Klondike gold rush at the end of the century.

Another category of new towns consisted of those colonial settlements where new, European-type towns were placed alongside ancient towns which maintained their traditions and ways of life. In North Africa at Algiers, Tunis, Tlemcen, beside the confused mass of Arab towns with their *kasbahs* and native markets and their labyrinths of alleys, the French built virtually independent cities on rectilinear lines with spacious squares and avenues. In India, British towns, green and flowering, were built alongside ancient native cities. At Madras and Lahore there stretched out over huge areas the bungalows and gardens of the small British colony, occupying four-fifths of the ground space while beside them the vast Indian population was crammed into the overcrowded houses and narrow streets of the old city. It was not until 1911, however, that New Delhi was created as a model capital constructed according to a strict plan.

More unusual examples of development are provided in Latin America, where the old Spanish colonial settlements experienced a sudden impulse to growth when Uruguay and Argentina came into their own. Tucuman, Cordoba and Buenos Aires retained some traces of the past—mud or brick houses with green *patios* and grilled windows, and promenades along the *Corso*—but the new areas built on a grid-plan were crushing these relics of the past more and more. Buenos Aires with its blocks of new buildings stretching out for miles in rectilinear uniformity, and with its business district and busy wide avenues in the centre of the city, recalled Paris, London and New York. In the outlying districts, shanty-towns received the newly-arrived immigrants, the Indians, the half-breeds, the homeless, in multi-coloured encampments which retreated before the encroachment of real estate developments and new constructions.

Social geography

Whether their success could be traceable to their economic role as great business centres (as in the case of London, Copenhagen or Lisbon) or to their political functions (as in the case of Paris, Berlin and St Petersburg), capital cities grew rapidly during the 19th century. Such concentrations of people, by creating enormous consumer markets, stimulated local production; sometimes in the 'metropolitan industries' of clothing and fashion, building, furniture and jewelry; sometimes in activities associated with big modern business enterprise, usually located in the suburbs. But, however advanced industry became, it was a third sector that almost always came to predominate, that of 'service' activities, ranging from domestic service to retailing and to entertainment. The 'attractions' of the city were most obvious in this third context—opportunity, display, excitement. If capital cities were often 'Babylons', they were also 'Meccas', and much social investment, particularly during the last decades of the century made its way into the provision of services from hotels to taxicabs.

From these brief reflections upon the many types of 19th-century city, there emerges the sense of a social geography of the city, in which the salient factor is the immense chasm between the urban classes. Everything separated them. From the standpoint of housing, income, living standards, means of existence, culture, the old upper classes or the new middle classes felt that they were besieged and threatened by the proletarian masses of newcomers. Confronted with new city-dwellers—rootless, often rough and

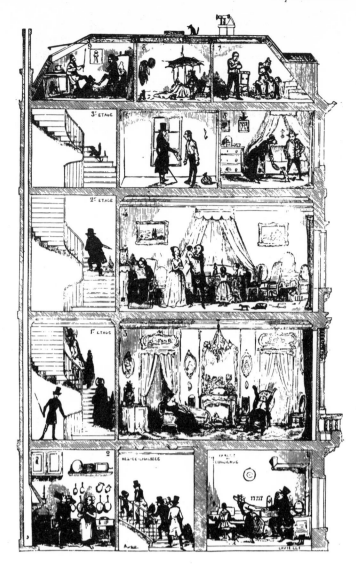

'*Social geography*' could work vertically as well as horizontally. In this section of a Paris apartment house, the ground floor contains the kitchen (where the cook gives free soup to her relatives) and the room of the concierge, dancing to her daughter's piano. The first floor is the best; in an elegant drawing room Monsieur yawns and Madame sleeps. The second floor houses a more bourgeois family; the third a young bachelor who cannot pay his rent and an old retired clerk who keeps a dog and a mistress. In the attic, at the very top, live those with no money at all—an artist, a philosopher and an unemployed workman with wife and children.

brutal, condemned to poverty and insecurity—those inhabitants of the city with property to defend often complained of an invasion, and the old cry often rang out, 'The barbarians are among us!'

Of these social contrasts and the nature of the class structure in capitalist urban society, there is more than enough evidence. In the Paris of 1860, according to Haussmann, more than a million persons out of the city's 1,700,000 lived in poverty or need. The population of Roubaix which tripled between 1850 and 1870 had a third of its total made up of tramps or of Belgian immigrants. In London at the same period the ruling classes (aristocracy and middle class) formed less than 5% of the population; more than four-fifths were manual workers, skilled craftsmen or labourers. Research carried out by Charles Booth (1840–1916) at the end of the century gave British opinion a rude shock when it revealed that 30% of Londoners lived in poverty. Another philanthropist-cum-sociologist, Seebohm Rowntree (1871–1954), in a study of York in 1899 (a middle-sized ancient town, relatively little affected by industrialization but typical of many provincial places), disclosed that 20,000 persons, or 28% of the population, were living 'below the poverty line'.

In traditional towns these social contrasts had been accepted without shame; rich and poor mingled in the same neighbourhoods, yet with the downfall of the old urban society with its *nuances* of social structure, and with the articulation of new social hopes and fears, segregation became increasingly prevalent. Bourgeois and working-class neighbourhoods were isolated from each other. The expressions 'West End' and 'East End' may have originated in London but the reality existed everywhere. In Paris, when Haussmann's great rebuilding projects in the reign of Napoleon III emptied old neighbourhoods and uprooted thousands of workers who found shelter in the east, the north or other outlying districts, we can trace the beginning of the *'ceinture rouge'*, the red belt. Natural factors of topography, wind and sunshine, also played a role, manipulated by the ruling classes to guarantee their comfort. A guide to Leeds at the beginning of the century noted that because of prevailing winds from the west, columns of smoke from the many factories drifted to the east where the workers' dwellings were located, and that these, moreover, were situated on low flat land that retained the smoke and impurities. In Marseilles the famous main street, the Cannebière, cuts the town in two; to the west rises the elegant bourgeois city, to the east the workingmen's district. Railways provided a new divide, 'the two sides of the track'.

Nowhere was a city's geography so clearly set forth and so expressive of social division as in Vienna. Three different towns were very distinctly set in three concentric zones. At the centre, inside the Ring, was the aristocratic quarter with its ancient houses, elegant hotels in Baroque or Classic style, its streets and squares enlivened by small crafts around the cathedral of St Stephen. Spreading out from the Ring, the ramparts of which were demolished in 1857 and replaced by a series of imposing public buildings, were the residential quarters of the bourgeoisie, the liberal professions and the world of business; wide, comfortable avenues, apartment buildings several storeys high, constructed without imagination, but substantial and respectable. The outlying area of working-class suburbs constituted the poor and dreary third zone; 'home' for a proletariat gathered from all parts of the Habsburg Empire 'settled' on the two banks of the Danube among the factory smokestacks. New proletarian suburbs stretched on endlessly, so it seemed, especially on the left bank of the Danube which was flat and grey. Beyond, the countryside began; and on the calm green slopes of the Wienerwald there were pretty villages with vines and open-air cafés where the bourgeois Viennese and the better paid artisans enjoyed pleasant Sunday outings.

If segregation roused in some people a feeling of social guilt (particularly towards the end of the century, when it became fashionable for London and Paris aristocrats to pay visits to Whitechapel or Ménilmontant and ease their consciences by setting up soup-kitchens), in the majority of cases it only reinforced the fears and anxieties of the upper classes. As for the workers, it plunged them into solitude and convinced them of the wretchedness of their lot. 'Every large city,' Engels taunted, 'has one or several "bad neighbourhoods"—where the working class is concentrated. In general it is assigned to a remote area where, hidden from the sight of the more fortunate classes, it must make out alone as best it can.'

Naturally, when the poor succeeded in shaking off the degradation resulting from their poverty and became conscious of the injustice of their condition, the ferment began. The hope of a better world aroused an idea of social strife. The city throbbed with confused dreams while waiting to be shaken by revolutionary jolts. The historian Georges Duveau has written of Paris under the Second Empire, 'Paris is neither a great iron works nor is it a vast wallpaper factory; it is a dream factory.' This could be said in varying measure of all large cities where revolutionary ideas were fostered. That was what struck terror into the supporters of order. It was no longer a question simply of correcting pauperism or of helping the 'submerged tenth'—the city was felt to be the very crux of the 'social question'. It became the crucible for the great social movements of the century.

The anxiety of the 'haves' was two-fold. On the one hand, individual outbreaks of crime were feared, and the increase in such outbreaks was directly attributed to the malicious influence of large cities. Was there not risk of anarchy when the laws of estab-lished society are broken by uncontrolled violence on the part of the 'dangerous classes' (the term was used in Paris, London and New York)? Disorder, theft, murder, alcoholism, illegitimacy, prostitution—all these social evils abundantly described in 19th-century philanthropic reports and in literature—would they not drag society back to the savage state in spite of the police and the courts? On the other hand, the fear was political. For the 'haves', the city promoted the revolutionary cause. By concentrating people in large masses it gave them new power; why should they not be tempted to use it? Lord Shaftesbury, crossing the English Midlands in 1830, admitted to the secret worry that shook him in front of these crowds of workers—'the mass of mankind whom nothing retains but force or habit'—and he concluded that the absence of revolution had to be considered as 'a standing miracle'. More brutally, Saint-Marc Girardin wrote in the *Journal des Débats* in 1831 concerning the domestic strife going on between the 'haves' and the 'have-nots': 'Our commercial and industrial society has its sore spot as all other societies do; this sore is the workers. . . . Each factory boss exists in his factory as the colonial planters did among their slaves, one against a hundred. . . . The savages who threaten society are not in the Caucasus nor in the steppes of Tartary, they are in the suburbs of our manufacturing towns.' These lines, which were written just after a workers' insurrection had been crushed in Lyons, were equally applicable to the Peterloo 'massacre' in Manchester a dozen years earlier.

Insurrections, riots, urban confrontations punctuate the century; Parisian barricades in 1848 and 1871; Chartist agitation in England; long marches of the unemployed in Hyde Park and Trafalgar Square; street battles in Vienna, Milan, Prague, Barcelona; Black Sunday in London; 'Bloody' Sunday in St Petersburg when the cavalry charged with bared sabres into a crowd of demonstrators on Nevsky Prospect. Each city in turn was enriched with libertarian tradition and revolutionary legend. That is what Proudhon meant when he contrasted the Paris of oppression and tyranny symbolized by the authority of Napoleon III and the broad new boulevards of Haussmann with the 'Paris of the old days whose ghost appeared in the light of the stars, with whispered cries: *Vive la liberté!*'

Was the nineteenth-century city 'sick'?

According to a pessimistic theory which has had many advocates, from John Ruskin (1819–1900) to J. L. and Barbara Hammond, from Patrick Geddes to Lewis Mumford, the 19th-century city was the victim of serious degeneration. In contrast with the harmonious city of the Middle Ages, it condemned the city dweller to an unhealthy, unbalanced and inhuman existence. The urban organism was 'sick'. The symptoms of its illness are easy to enumerate: unhealthiness, overcrowding, ugliness, anarchy given free rein for the benefit of private interests, and dehumanization through the lack of social communication.

A similar indictment has been drawn up against cities a thousand times. And arguments to support it were not lacking throughout the century. All reports of administrators, public health officers and philanthropists constantly repeated the charge of unhealthiness. Witness the great epidemics; cholera twice ravaged Europe, in 1832 sweeping the continent from Marseilles to St Petersburg and again in 1848–49 claiming hundreds of thousands of victims, even reaching England. The explanation for this was simple; because of the inadequacy of sewers, the water-borne germ was spread by polluted rivers or more often seeped into wells and springs, contaminating them. Many other epidemics, typhus, scarlet fever, smallpox, added to the cemeteries at regular intervals. As late as 1897–98 in Middlesbrough 1,500 cases of smallpox were recorded, with 200 dead. Filth was exposed in the very centre of cities. Poor neighbourhoods were without sewage-drains; at Rouen, Blanqui noted, along the passages separating the houses there ran 'a fetid stream carrying greasy water and filth of all sorts which rain down from all floors and lie stagnant in pestilential pools'. In England in the slum areas, vividly described in the great reports of Edwin Chadwick (1800–1890), the majority of the houses were served by privy middens only; many others were equipped with pan closets; these were emptied into carts and the contents sold to farmers for manure or deposited in the sea.

Another evil of urban life, overcrowding, was prominent everywhere but most drastically in the large cities. Around 1890 statistics comparing the choked conditions in European capitals showed that in Paris 14% of the people lived in overcrowded buildings (that is, more than two to a room); in Berlin and Vienna the proportion was 28% and in St Petersburg, 46%. In London an inquiry made by the Registrar General in four working-class neighbourhoods revealed an average of 1·6 persons to a room (the proportion was 2·5 in Moscow and 1·5 in Vienna for the entire city). Everywhere the map showing overcrowded areas coincides exactly with the mortality map. To meet rental costs, families in Great Britain took in lodgers; in Germany and Austria, in addition to subletting they practised the system of *Schlafleute*, the literal renting of a bed, without too much concern about promiscuity. Taine, returning from a visit to the poor quarters of Liverpool, wrote: 'What a sight . . . there are ten to twenty streets where on every stairway droves of children swarm, five or six on each step; drawing nearer, one sees in the half-light of the corridor the mother or an elder sister squatting, half-dressed. The smell is that of a storeroom of rotten rags.'

As for ugliness, the list drawn up by the detractors of the cities is equally accessible and equally long, in the novels of Charles Dickens, for example, or in the denunciations of William Morris. There was neither colour nor form but only monotony and uniformity in the alignment of houses and streets. Barracks or prisons were suggested by the huge façades of factories, hospitals and blocks of flats. As for the monumental style of public buildings, it was confined to a clumsy imitation of everything from Classical to Baroque, Gothic to Byzantine, without leaving anything out. Criticizing this loss of taste in the industrial era, Raymond Unwin, the pioneering town-planner (1863–1940) remarked: 'Men today are so accustomed to living in a milieu where beauty has little place that they cannot comprehend what a uniquely astonishing thing is the ugliness with which they are surrounded.'

Those who hated the 19th-century city added to these criticisms others of a sociological nature. In their opinion, a city given over to the confusion of private interests and to the law of profit, without plan or imagination, lost its social significance; it symbolized man's rupture with his fellow-men. Personal relationships were reduced to a minimum; the individual was isolated in the throng. The large city bred anonymity, the sense of a 'lonely crowd'. At the same time, in an era of liberalism triumphant, private property was held to be sacred and became untouchable; non-intervention had become the rule. There followed the refusal to place the welfare of the group above the rights of the individual and the disappearance of the sense of urban *ensemble* which had so strongly distinguished the Renaissance and the Classical era. The victim of this unbalanced, dehumanized society was the city-slave, prisoner of the barracks-city. Nothing was left for him but to share the fate of millions of other city dwellers, 'the life of men who toil without hope, and yet with the hunger of an unsatisfied desire', as George Gissing (1857–1903), the English novelist, put it.

Without denying all these morbid symptoms, defenders of the 19th-century city, then and more recently, have advanced arguments in support of their attitude. In the first place, they have said, such a one-sided picture, painted completely black, must be balanced by recognizing the positive achievements of the new centres on both technical and social levels. Admittedly imperfect, the cities were centres of progress. 'Black spots' in one particular place or at one particular time were often obliterated; evils which had been accepted for centuries as the will of Fate were attacked even if they were not obliterated; there was a process of increasing social control, of challenge and response. Furthermore, the defenders of the city have pointed out, if urban life was so depressing and repugnant, how can we explain the continual influx of rural people tempted by an existence which in their eyes shone with a thousand marvels?

Among the positive contributions of 19th-century urban civilization must be included the establishment of great public services, frequently controlled by the municipalities themselves, often with great civic pride. After an early period during which cities grew so fast that their social investment could not keep pace with the rate of growth—a time when expert knowledge of engineering and medicine was inadequate, when their inhabitants were most deprived and criticisms sharpest—the infrastructure began to take shape: road systems involving the paving or asphalting of streets and the making of sidewalks; impressive networks of sewers (in Paris before Haussmann there were only 100 kilometers of sewers, mostly of very small capacity; Haussmann brought the figure up to 560 kilometers); water distribution services, water sometimes being brought not only in pipes but in aqueducts over great distances, with the result that consumption tripled or quadrupled in a few decades; organization of household waste collection; creation of parks and public gardens, municipal baths and laundries. In short, the daily life of city dwellers was made more convenient and comfortable. Hygiene progressed. The chance of life became more equal.

Urban life was improved also thanks to the organization of a public transport system. No doubt throughout the century city-dwellers travelled mostly on foot, sometimes covering long distances, doing two or three miles daily to get to work. For the leisured classes there were private carriages with more or less elegant trappings, and cabs which dashed through the streets. But new means of public transport were being introduced. They eased the life of city people, linked the suburbs with the centre and made possible the indefinite extension of the urban mass. First it was the railway with special rates for workers (cheap workmen's trains), then the tramway, means of popular transport *par excellence* 'gondolas of the people'. (Horse-drawn trams were increasingly being replaced after 1870 by the mechanized and electrified lines.) More expensive, the omnibus, inaugurated in Paris in 1828, and from there introduced into London, was much less used. Urban transport of the future, no longer on the surface but underground, made its first appearance in London in 1863—the steam-powered underground. New York combined the elevated and the subway. At the turn of the century, metropolitan electrical railroad systems were developed simultaneously in the principal capitals: Paris and London in 1900, Vienna in 1901, Berlin in 1902, New York and Philadelphia. The systems have outlasted the appearance of the automobile.

The underground, like other urban technical achievements, struck wonder into the hearts of many; admiration for the city as a creator of riches where man gave proof of his energy and his capacities; civic price in municipal achievements; a consciousness of an extraordinary concentration of resources combining intelligence, spirit of enterprise and technical skill. Even before the coming of the underground, Heinrich Heine (1797–1856) recorded the fascination that seized him one morning in London when, standing on a street corner, he watched the crowd of workers arrive in the City: 'I saw one of the most remarkable sights the world can offer to the astonished gaze . . . the tumultuous surge of faces alive with varied passions, their alarming eagerness to love, to suffer, to hate; I am speaking of London.' A place of struggle, the city was also a place for exchange and fellowship. For the natural milieu it substituted an artificial environment, the technical milieu, by means of which it introduced a new cultural world, a world not only of new modes of life but of new choices. It is not surprising that many liberals hailed urbanization optimistically as a decisive factor in the material and ethical progress of mankind—'the very symbol of civilization', as *Chambers Edinburgh Journal* wrote proudly in 1858, 'foremost in the march of improvement, a grand incarnation of progress'.

V COUNTRYSIDES

The revolution in world agriculture

F. M. L. THOMPSON

'Even in the agricultural districts the labourer
does now occasionally indulge himself in
a meat dinner, or seasons his dry bread with a morsel
of cheese . . . It is reasonable to conclude
that the great mass of consumers, as their circumstances
improve, will follow the same rule.'

JAMES CAIRD, 1851

The revolution in the countrysides

during the 19th century was on the whole gradual and undramatic, a matter of more ears of corn and faster-growing animals— though it was not without its violent moments. But it was perhaps even more important than the revolutions which transformed Europe's towns, its social structure and its industry, since without more food the towns could not survive and industry could not grow. To meet the demand farmers and landowners experimented with new methods and new tools. Mechanization began slowly to make food cheaper and to enlarge the scale of cultivation. The railways and such processes as canning and refrigeration put market farming on a Europe-wide and then a world-wide basis. All these changes proceeded at different rates in different areas, but their effects were broadly the same. A way of life that had lasted since the Middle Ages was being swept away. In country after country, as the urban 'proletariat' came into existence, the rural 'peasantry' disappeared.

Those who were aware of these changes and could take a wide view of them—the educated classes, the thinkers, poets and artists—reacted ambivalently. 'Improvement', as we have seen in an earlier chapter, was an ideal to which nearly everyone sub-scribed, and it was clear to them that, both economically and socially, what was happening was an improvement. But as children of the Romantic generation, increasingly depressed by the aesthetic horrors that seemed to accompany progress, they could only regret it. By the end of the century 'byegones', folk museums and records of village life were already being assembled.

In the 1820s and 30s, however, a painter like Constable could accept the countryside as it was with pleasure and appreciation. He was himself a countryman. The farm implements that he sketched were not simply picturesque objects; he knew well how they were made and used. In *The Cornfield* (opposite), for instance, the plough by the gate is of the Norfolk type with high 'gallows' (i.e. the wheeled frame in front of the ploughshare). In other paintings he was to include canals as part of the rural scene. North-west Europe, and England especially, retained this combination of traditional beauty with modern prosperity for decades to come, but in the rest of the world new agricultural landscapes were being created, from the vast grain-fields of the United States to the sheep and cattle of South America, Australia and New Zealand.

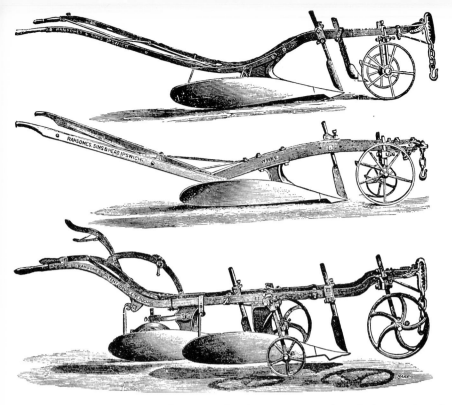

Improved design and mass production, even more than the harnessing of new sources of power, were responsible for increased farming efficiency. Three models of ploughs by Ransomes, a leading English manufacturer, are shown *above*. Top: the 'Newcastle' plough, invented in 1864; it was made in five sizes and could be fitted with different shares and coulters. Centre: the woodbeam plough, a more traditional design. Bottom: the double plough, pulled by three or four horses, ploughed two furrows at a time. *Below*: two applications of steam power to farming. In steam ploughing, the engines were too heavy actually to move across the fields. One solution was to pull the plough along a cable. The plough itself has eight shares, one set of four used in each direction. With steam threshing (*bottom*), the wheat was fed into the machine at the top, the grain falls into the row of sacks on the left, and the straw is carried mechanically to the top of a strawstack.

The seed-drill, an 18th-century invention, was improved in the 19th. Its advantages over broadcast sowing were that it could plant the seed deep, in straight rows, and cover it over with soil. Seed is fed into chutes at the back, each furrow being made by a coulter.

An experiment important in the evolution of reaping machines though not itself in common use was Bell's Reaper (*above left*) of 1827. The horses pushed instead of pulled. The corn is seized by the revolving slats in the front, cut by horizontal clippers a few inches from the ground, and laid flat alongside.

Mowing and threshing continued to be done by hand in the traditional way alongside more modern methods. *Left*: threshing rape, a grain used for cattle-cake, in Sweden, 1888. The two rows of threshers, wielding jointed flails and standing in an enclosed 'floor', beat alternately in time to the fiddle.

The mowing team (*below*) in Suffolk *c.* 1880, gives some idea of the number of men needed to do the work later taken over by a single machine. The scythe, which only came into general use in the 19th century, was itself an improvement on the sickle. *Bottom*: The culmination of developments in reaping and threshing was the combine harvester. Pulled by over thirty horses, it cuts the wheat on the left, threshes it in the middle, ejects the straw at the back and deposits the grain in sacks on the right.

Trade fairs, culminating in the great national and international exhibitions, meant that innovating ideas could spread rapidly. *Upper left*: a meeting of the English Royal Agricultural Society at Bristol in 1842. In the foreground, from left to right, are new models of plough, dibbling machine, turnip cutter, dynamometer, hoe, chain harrow and chaff-cutting machine.

The world came to London in 1851 to admire, among other things, the new agricultural machinery being produced (*above*). At the back are the latest steam-engines; in the foreground ploughs, farm carts, turnip-cutters (for cattle feed) and harrows. Ransome and Garrett, whose stalls appear prominently, are included in the painting above left: Garret is left foreground behind the dibbling-machine, Ransome further back to the right, wearing yellow trousers and holding a paper.

Railways and waterways brought supplier and customer closer together. *Left*: a train on the Liverpool and Manchester Railway of 1831, carrying sheep, cattle and pigs; and a section of the Rhine at Ruhrort, showing two of the steamboats that were turning the great rivers into transport arteries.

Vast markets, officially controlled, made trade more efficient and cleaner. *Right*: Les Halles, Paris, a project initiated by Napoleon, but not finished until 1862 under Haussmann. The twelve iron and glass pavilions were equipped with gaslight and water.

Pre-industrial cultivation went on in Russia and Poland, with their vast estates and backward methods. *Left*: a Russian peasant of 1880 using a primitive wooden plough, without even a mouldboard for turning the soil. *Centre left*: a Hungarian country town, with its thatched houses and informal market.

English enterprise in developing agricultural machinery did not immediately transform the countryside. These farm workers of the south Midlands (*below left*) were photographed in 1857. The large sieve behind them is a winnowing van.

Swedish prosperity could support a few luxuries, though life was hard. The family sleep in curtained wall-beds; round loaves hang from the rafters near the stove.

Nostalgia for a way of life that was dying led to the formation of museums of folk life, crafts and costumes. *Below*: the Nordiska Museet, Stockholm in the 1890s.

A rare survival of early farming was photographed (*below*) at Kila in Sweden in the early years of this century. In the middle distance are the grain strips growing rye, oats or barley and, enclosed by a fence, the cabbage beds of individual farmers.

Another countryside – that of the sportsman, the traveller and the connoisseur – co-existed alongside the countryside of the working farmer. Hunting had always been the country gentleman's favourite pastime, though increasingly it tended to interfere with agricultural operations. Here the prince de Wagram's hunt, in France, prepares for the chase, while a ploughman works the field alongside. Shooting holidays, a new amusement for the urban rich, grew up with improved travel.

The cult of nature sprang in part, paradoxically, from a union between Romanticism and the Industrial Revolution. The poets of the turn of the 18th century – Wordsworth, Byron, Goethe – had taught their readers to respond almost mystically to the grandeur of mountains and waterfalls, the stillness of lakes and the brooding melancholy of forests. The railways made it easy actually to reach such scenery. One of its early devotees in America was Asher B. Durand, whose *Kindred Spirits* (*above centre*) shows his friends Cole the painter and Bryant the poet communing with untamed nature.

The seaside, ignored by previous generations as a source of enjoyment, became even more popular than the country. Beginning in England, where sea-bathing was recommended for health and practised by the royal family, it was soon taken up all over Europe. William Powell Frith's *Ramsgate Sands* (detail *right*) shows the mingling of classes that might be encountered on the beach; whatever the pleasures they found there, it is clear that sunbathing was not yet one of them.

The tourist industry began to open up the delights of nature, both at home and abroad. Every social class except the very poor could now afford to see a little of the world. Picturesque areas, like the mountains of eastern France (*opposite below*), were eagerly explored. Guide books and hotels multiplied; special tourist clothes became fashionable; new leisure activities from mountaineering to swimming enlivened the social round. *Opposite above*: 'Cook's Excursion Gallop', a song of 1870 making fun of Cook's Tours. The party is happily scrambling up Vesuvius during an eruption.

The effects of a market economy were felt in almost every part of Europe, as regions began to specialize in particular commodities for the sake of greater efficiency. Denmark gave up grain for dairy products. *Above*: the old method of producing butter and cheese. On the floor stand skimming pans, where the cream gradually separates from the milk. *Above right*: the first mechanized co-operative dairy. The centrifuge on the right, powered by the steam engine, effects a rapid separation of the cream. *Right*: Cotswold sheep from Northleach went to improve the flocks of the United States about 1861.

Co-operative dairy farming was successfully tried in Denmark as one solution to the problem of peasant holdings too small to make individual profits. This photograph (*below*) taken about 1889, shows the members of such a co-operative established in an old rural deanery on the island of Møn.

Dutch cheese brought fame to towns like Gouda and Edam (*left*). Conditions in 1850 were still pre-industrial, with the cheese-makers sharing space in the stable and the milk still being brought in by a girl carrying buckets on a yoke. The finished red, round cheeses stand on shelves to the right.

A Friesian bull, brought to Lincolnshire in 1806, established a breed that was to remain in favour until today. Stock-breeding in the 19th century was chiefly a matter of consolidating the achievements of the 18th.

Model farms were established by aristocrats or royalty for experiment and teaching. Hohenheim (*below*), a royal foundation in Württemberg, attracted students from all over Europe. Its extensive grounds included sections devoted to almost every crop and farm animal. Fruit trees, barley, wheat and potatoes occupy the fields on the left, while the large expanse on the upper right is given over to research.

As the frontier moved west land owners in the middle of America settled down to a comfortable existence. This neat farm (*above*) in Wisconsin was painted by a local artist in the 80s, and shows many typical features of the region: the big fields, the wooden fences, the clapboard house, the red-painted outbuildings and barn raised on a stone base. Behind the barn a corncrib, a slatted structure used to store ears of maize for feeding cattle.

Shearing the rams on an Australian sheep station in 1890 (*below*). Trade in wool established itself here early, since it could be transported without deterioration. By the 1840s Australian wool was underselling European.

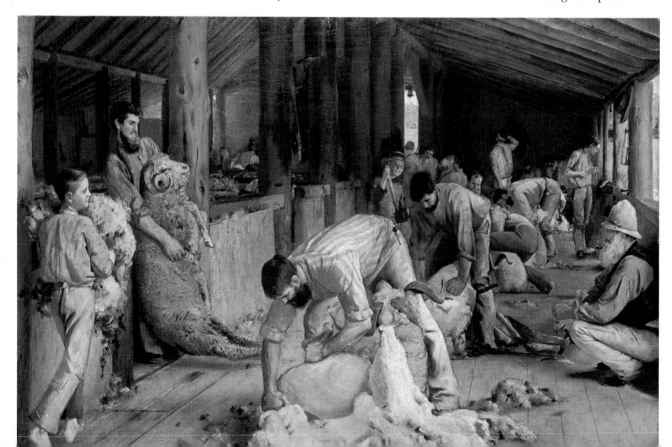

The revolution in world agriculture

F. M. L. THOMPSON

THE COUNTRYSIDE as a way of escape from the strains of urban civilization into an earlier, uncomplicated, more natural mode of existence is a concept which matured rapidly in the 19th century, in the face of the urban explosion and the ambivalent responses to the city and to city 'ways of life'. One task of this chapter is to show that although the existence may have been more natural, it was not more comfortable, except for those who did not have to earn their living from the soil. Nevertheless in Europe, as in the United States, there had always been rural as well as urban myths. The two, indeed, went together. The idea of the innocent, tranquil, pastoral countryside belonged to the 18th century and was carried forward into the 19th. And by the end of the 19th century there was ample evidence of nostalgia at the disappearance of peasant dress, plough teams and the 'organic' life of the village community. There were also signs of a new cult of 'outdoor life'. In Germany, in particular, 'Volkish' writers, drawing deep on romantic argument and images, dwelt lovingly on 'nature' and the 'rootedness' which they associated with it. 'A countryside,' wrote the novelist Otto Gmelin, 'becomes a landscape insofar as it is a coherent whole with its own characteristics. But this can happen only when it becomes the experience of the human soul, if the soul recognizes the rhythms of the countryside as its own rhythm.'

In fact, the rhythm of the countryside changed considerably in the 19th century, a century when much of mankind, particularly Western mankind, was liberated from its grip. In the process, which can be studied in depth in relation to every particular countryside, there were inevitably many casualties. Some of these, had there been different laws and institutions, might not have been inevitable: they were expressions of the inhumanity of man to man, of the oppression of class, of the exploitation of the weak by the strong. Others, including the destruction of traditional customs and forms of social organization, the transformation of traditional and picturesque landscapes, were quite unavoidable. For these traditional modes were incapable of constraining the prime motive force of the age, the pressure of population, and equally incapable of providing for the sustenance, let alone the improving sustenance, of the growing numbers. In some of the newly developing specialized agricultural regions of the world, like the mid-west of the United States and Australia, agriculture very quickly became an industry, dependent, like other sectors of industry, on the machine. Though rural-urban dichotomies existed there too—'hay seeds' or cowboys versus 'city slickers' and bankers: 'bush' versus city—they were only loosely related to the European tradition.

The need for more food

The grand strategy of countrysides everywhere was determined by demography. In a Euro-centred world it was the behaviour of Europe's population which mattered most, because this was the population which possessed the means, financial usually but physical sometimes, of making its wants effectively felt. Asia and Africa signified, but in a generally passive sense; in 1900 their own population explosions were by and large yet to come, and up to this point they had responded to outside pressures rather than generated their own internal forces of change. Between 1789 and 1900 Europe's population grew by something between two and two and a half times to reach a total of 400 millions. In the same

period some 50 million Europeans emigrated, and along with the small number of earlier 17th- and 18th-century emigrants provided the main force for the peopling of the Americas and Australasia. In certain regions, and for a limited time, this expansion could spend itself simply by occupying empty spaces, reproducing the farming methods and the social organization of the parent body and having no further effects, in much the same way as periods of medieval population growth often meant little more than the planting of new villages similar in type to the old ones. But in sum this expansion meant rural transformation on a world scale, drawing large parts of Europe itself into a market economy for the first time, and creating an international economy capable of satisfying Europe's demands for foodstuffs and industrial crops.

International trade in the basic agricultural products, aside from the tropical products, was negligible in 1789, and the small movements of grains between countries were far outweighed in bulk and value by the movements of luxuries like wine. By 1900 the annual trade in cereals and livestock products, and in the raw materials like cotton, wool and jute, was reckoned in millions of tons. In addition the domestic supply of domestic national markets had increased enormously. The producers of these goods, and the countrysides which yielded them, were all affected by this process, but some much more than others. To examine the detailed tactics of the changing countryside is to search for the factors which brought the full force of change to bear, or deflected it, studding the landscape of 1900 with a whole series of palimpsests.

The brown and the green

Outside England, where recent enclosures were considerable enough to have left a visible mark in the eastern and midland counties in new-grown hedges and the rectilinear lines of fields, and Denmark, where state-directed consolidation of holdings and enclosure was in full process of creating a landscape of small peasant-owned farms, the countryside of 1789 was a traditional one which bore few marks or scars of any recent changes. The scars were human and social, and they were the traditional lot of the great bulk of the European people, some 90% of whom lived in and off the country. They were the bent, gnarled, animal-like creature, whom Arthur Young discovered to be a French peasant woman working in the fields; they were the serfdom and labour services which had prevailed in much of Europe since the Middle Ages; they were the rough and sour rye-bread or the maize-meal gruel, that provided the staple food of much of the rural population. This countryside had three major dimensions, physical, economic, and social. These elements criss-crossed to produce a complicated pattern in which there were great variations in degrees of prosperity and wretchedness, yet the essence of each dimension was simple. Physically, Europe consisted of the land which lay in open fields, under a two- or three-field system, and that which did not. Economically, land was either devoted to subsistence farming or to farming for the market. Socially, there was the country of the serfs and large estates and the country of the free or near-free and small farms.

The open fields stretched right across Europe from France through to the black earth region of Russia until they merged into the almost uninhabited steppes of the Don Cossacks. They were cultivated in the medieval way under what Arthur Young called 'the common barbarous course' of fallow, winter wheat, spring corn, the generic system of the whole northern European arable plain and lowland area. This gave the entire area a certain uniformity of appearance, brown and gold, with the large bare tracts showing up particularly in the summer, perhaps covered in a ragged way with some naturally sown weeds and grasses which lack of energetic fallow cultivations had failed to suppress. It made up a landscape which the agricultural improvers viewed with withering contempt, a weedy, slovenly, neglected landscape. A discerning eye, however, might have detected a fairly steady eastward deterioration, from the comparative neatness of the French Champagne country tilled by its relatively advanced wheeled ploughs, to the disorderliness of the Russian central and southern cereal region, where an utterly primitive wooden ploughing stick without a ploughshare was the main implement, and where sparseness of population made for careless use of the abundant land.

This three-field landscape was not confined to the northern plain, but was to be found wherever extensive grain growing was carried on, in much of southern Italy and Sicily, and in the wheat-growing areas of northern and central Spain. Conversely not all the northern plain was in arable, and not all the arable cultivation was under the three-field regime. Leaving aside the great tracts of uncultivated heath and waste land, which were especially extensive in northern Germany and East Prussia, there was the highly developed pasture farming of the true Holland of the coastal provinces, where specialization in cheese production provided the classic dairy countryside of scattered farm houses, grazing dairy herds, meadows, milkmaids, and cow byres; the Dutch had long since come to rely on imported Baltic wheat for their breadstuffs. There was Flanders, the 16th- and 17th-century home of rotational systems in arable husbandry, intensively cultivated with the neatness of garden ground, producing grains, roots, vegetables, and artificial grasses, and with scarcely a speck of fallow to be seen. But among major arable regions it was only in Britain that there was clear visual evidence of departure from the ancient routines. Parts of the midlands, it is true, with their wheat-beans-fallow sequence, were not unlike much of the rest of Europe, though even there the widespread presence of grass leys made for a generally greener landscape. But in the corn-growing eastern counties, and in southern Scotland, the new husbandry had made sufficient advances to produce a distinctive landscape, of hedges and large herds of cattle or flocks of sheep penned within them, of fields of corn, turnips, and clover, sainfoin or lucerne, and precious little fallow; a countryside of country houses and parks, of individual farmhouses as well as compact villages.

Over the rest of Europe the main aspect of the countryside was fixed by physical features and geographical factors. The hill and mountain regions, of Pyrenees, Alps, and much of the Balkans, were naturally regions of pastoral farming, where climate and topography gave rise to distinctive agricultural practices and social systems. The forest and woodland areas, to be found over much of Europe, but especially in Scandinavia and northern Russia, had their own landscape of small cultivated clearings; in Russia, in particular, these might often be only temporary assarts, cultivated for a few years while the richness of the wood ash from the burnt trees lasted, and then abandoned to revert to natural birch forest while the people moved on to make a fresh clearing. Where the need for outdoor labour was seasonal, and thus particularly in pastoral regions, farming was often accompanied by small-scale industry. As a final major division there were the Mediterranean lands with their vines and olives, giving the impression of richness flowing from a parched, dusty landscape.

In visual terms there was no clear distinction between the areas of subsistence and those of commercial farming. To be sure, where there was really intensive cultivation and every available inch was cherished into yielding something useful, as in the Low Countries or the Po Valley, farming for the market predominated. Conversely the scenes of most primitive, wretched, and negligent farming portrayed by Arthur Young in western Europe or William Coxe in eastern Europe, were scenes from subsistence farming. But the great bulk of the countryside lay somewhere between these extremes, and in particular it was not possible to infer from the presence of the three-field system that no cash crops were being grown. Indeed one of the features of this system was the ability to provide for a certain level of non-agricultural demand, and furnish a modest surplus of the higher quality grains for sale while at the same time producing sufficient coarse grains like rye, maslin or buckwheat to feed the cultivators themselves. It might be that where the pull of the market was consistently felt it acted as a spur to greater efficiency within the generally unmodified technical structure, and provided some of the means to achieve this in the form of supplies of town-manure. But it could almost equally well be the case that the main effect of producing a regular saleable surplus was to reduce the level of subsistence left for the cultivators. In part this was determined by institutional differences, as relatively weak demand forces were ignored by free landowning peasants, and their full effects were felt by the unfree, the serfs, and those with precarious tenures. In a very broad sense the general configuration of an eastward fall in personal freedom and in the level of techniques conformed to such a pattern. The fundamental fact, however, was that everywhere outside England and the immediate vicinity of the few large European towns, the pull of the market was too feeble and diffuse to set up any great strains on the sources of supply or to pose any clear need for revolutionizing the techniques of production.

Social patterns

Many contemporaries, anxious to remedy the general backwardness of techniques, argued that the necessary precondition was a radical change in the social relations and institutions of the countryside, so that individual enterprise with individual rewards might replace the traditional structure. It was indeed in this sphere, especially in the sphere of legal rights, that change was to be most pronounced in the next fifty years. Change, however, was greatest precisely in those areas where the old feudal order was already most rickety and undermined before 1789. The second great frontier in the countryside of 1789, though not so immediately visible as the frontier which marked off the three-field region, the brown and gold country from the green, was of equal antiquity and possibly greater endurance. It lay along the river Elbe and a line from the Bohemian border to Trieste, and it marked the limit of the servile region of Europe. To the east of this frontier lay the area of vast landed estates—the enormous domains of the Junkers, and of the Polish, Habsburg, Magyar and Russian aristocracy—and the area of agrarian serfdom. With some exceptions, like the colonies of free German peasants who peppered the region up to the Volga, the cultivators were unfree peasants, owing regular forced labour on the lord's land for much of each week, bound to the land and sold with it. Many Polish and Russian serfs were virtually in a condition of chattel slavery, could be bought and sold separately from the land, and were valued according to their skills or accomplishments. Italy south of Tuscany, and much of Spain, had most of the same characteristics as this region of serfs and latifundia. The Balkans, though the peasantry were certainly unfree, did not share the same large estate system, with its considerable demeşne farming, as the rest of the region, and when it emerged from Turkish domination in the 19th century, it emerged as a region of peasant holdings.

Peasant holdings were more typical of Europe west of the Elbe. In western Europe serfdom as a working arrangement for the cultivation of the fields had long since decayed, and although many traces of the medieval order survived in the shape of personal obligations—which on the whole were petty and irksome liabilities to perform services for lords, or to use only the lord's mill for grinding corn, or to suffer the lord's exercise of sporting rights, rather than serious material burdens—the peasant, or more frequently the village community to which he belonged, was in control of his holding and the way in which it should be cultivated, and in legal terms was free to enjoy the fruits of his own labours. As serfdom had declined, so also had the system of exploitation which it had supported, and the large demesne farms managed by bailiffs or stewards on the lord's behalf which were so common in the east were almost unknown in the west. The western countryside still supported a social structure of peasant and lord, but although there were landlords and large estates these were concerned with the collection of rents and dues, not with the management of agricultural production. The unit of production left behind by the ebb of demesne farming was the individual peasant holding, its potential limited by its size and by dependence on family resources for labour and capital, and constrained by communal rights especially that of *vaine pâture,* the right of grazing on the stubble-fields, but on the whole able to survive as a viable unit in the demographic and market circumstances of the 18th century. Here and there, and particularly in the northern half of France and in the Low Countries, the process of subdivision had created many holdings too small to support their occupiers, who accordingly earned part of their living by working for other peasants; but the class of entirely landless agricultural workers was not yet considerable enough to impress itself on observers as a major component of the rural social structure. Such a class was readily identifiable only in Britain, where a whole complex of factors acting over the previous two to three centuries had thrown up a different unit of production, the commercial farm, which functioned with a landlord-tenant farmer-agricultural labourer structure, a structure which had long ago eliminated the Continental-style peasant from the scene. Farms of the English kind, run by tenants who paid a commercial rent to a landlord, employed wage labour, and lived by producing cash crops, were not unknown in western Europe, particularly in northern France, but they were still isolated islands, surrounded by a peasant sea.

Revolution and the peasants

In the summer of 1789 the peasant sea was whipped into a storm so violent that its effects determined the broad shape of events for the next fifty years. The French peasantry in 1789 undoubtedly had their grievances—they made great long lists of them in the *cahiers*—and their condition had deteriorated in the previous decade, culminating in the bad harvests of 1788 and 1789 whose high prices hit all except the largest peasants with regular saleable surplus crops, a minority who of course profited from the situation. But in relation to its consequences few peasant uprisings can have had such insubstantial and accidental causes. As the Bastille fell on July 14th—itself an urban *émeute*—rumour and panic swept the countryside, fear of counter-revolution, of foreign invasion, of brigands. Responding to the hysteria, all over the country bands of peasants set out to settle old scores, to burn châteaux and above all to destroy manorial records, which set down their obligations and dues. At the end of three weeks of this *Grande Peur*, as it was called, the fabric of French feudalism and the apparatus of royal government in the provinces lay in ruins. Seeking to reap some prestige from superior force before it was absolutely necessary to bow to it, the gentry and bourgeois deputies of the National Assembly, on the famous night of August 4th, went through the touching scenes of the 'voluntary' abolition of feudalism. It was the night of August 4th which shaped the rural image of the Revolution, and largely settled the changes which the Revolutionary and Napoleonic armies later brought to the rest of the European countryside which they conquered.

As befitted a revolution directed by property-owners, the law abolishing feudalism was reasonably tender towards property rights. Broadly, all the surviving marks of personal servitude, all the apparatus of seigneurial jurisdiction, and all obligations owing to the Church, were swept away without compensation; other rights, in particular perpetual rents and certain kinds of tithes, were not deemed to be so feudal, and were simply made redeemable for cash; yet others, the customary rules of cultivation which peasants applied to each other, were not thought of as being feudal at all and were not mentioned in the decree. Having taken the law into their own hands, the peasantry were not too inclined to observe the terms of the decree, and in the Jacobin phase of the Revolution the law was modified in 1793 to give up the pretence of redemption of dues. The essential effect, however, remained the same. Seigneurial and ecclesiastical dues were swept away, so that peasants who before the Revolution had been virtually the owners of their

Red Clover.

Artificial grasses, so called because they were deliberately sown in fallow fields, had the dual advantage of providing cattle with more nourishing pasture and of improving the soil when ploughed for subsequent crops. Two of the most common were sainfoin and red clover.

holdings, but not legally so since they paid small fixed quit-rents or *cens*, were converted into the legal proprietors. Conversely, estates which had consisted largely of bundles of rights to receive *cens* simply melted away, and all that survived for the landowner was such land as he might have had in hand or leased out at economic rents. Tenures which reflected commercial rather than juridical arrangements, however, were not touched; thus the peasant who was a tenant paying an economic rent, or a *métayer* with some form of crop-sharing agreement with the owner of the holding, found his condition unchanged. Thus a redistribution of titles to property, rather than a redistribution of actual possession of property, was the major consequence of the Revolution. It is true that in addition to these changes, a large amount of land did actually change hands between 1789 and 1815, land which was confiscated from the Crown, the Church, the monasteries, and the emigrés, and sold off or given away by the state. Some of the beneficiaries of this process were peasants, either starting up as landowners or enlarging their holdings; others were merchants or professional men, buying either for investment in status, or for speculation; many were the new court favourites, endowed with estates every bit as large as any of the *Ancien Régime*; and still more were the original emigré owners, buying back their property either directly or through agents. In this colossal merry-go-round of revolutionary land transactions, it has never been possible to decide whether there were any pronounced changes in the structure of ownership. It is more certain that the great mass of peasant proprietors in 19th-century France had not been created by the revolutionary land settlement so much as confirmed by it in possession of their holdings.

The impact of the Revolution on the countryside was thus at once radical and profoundly conservative. Radical in a lawyer's sense, because it tore up the roots of land law in status and obligation and converted those who had been legally tenants by service—however nominal the amount of service might have become—into individual freeholders. Conservative in a double sense, for not only were existing tenures that were commercially based left untouched, but also the traditionalist tendencies of the peasantry were reinforced by the legal transformation. The main resistance to 18th-century efforts to improve techniques through enclosure, consolidation of holdings, and the introduction of new crops, had come from the peasantry, anxious to stick to their familiar routines. The ability to preserve customary methods was considerably enhanced when a large fraction of this peasantry became proprietors and thus without any immediate superiors to cajole or induce them to adopt new farming techniques. Hence the Revolution did not establish the legal and tenurial conditions under which capitalist exploitation of the land could proceed, as it was proceeding in England. Rather it established conditions under which the individual peasant was as free to pursue a preference for traditional inefficiency as he was to pursue a preference for increasing his income.

The French armies, eagerly proclaiming the abolition of feudalism and tithes, carried this legal revolution with them across Europe. Acting sometimes by themselves, sometimes with the help of local liberals, and sometimes in continuation of the work of local enlightened despots, this revolutionary force saw the establishment of a free peasantry in the Low Countries, western Germany, Switzerland, Italy, the Illyrian coast, and Spain. In most of this region, except for Spain and southern Italy where the large estates survived the legal freeing of the peasants and remained the basis of agricultural organization, emancipation revealed or confirmed an essentially peasant agriculture, as in France itself. Matters were otherwise in Prussia, where the influence of the Revolution, because of its overwhelming military success, was decisive in impelling the regime to embark on the emancipation of the serfs after 1807. Here the process was influenced by the large landowners and firmly controlled by the civil servants, and care was taken to see that while the peasants were liberated from their servitude most of them were liberated from their land as well. The trick was worked through the compensation provisions, under which the peasant was obliged to surrender between one third and

one half of his former holding to his seigneur in return for his legal freedom, a proportion which was crippling for those whose servile holdings had been small. As the emancipation decrees were slowly applied over the next forty or fifty years, it became apparent that the surviving holdings of the small peasants were too small to be viable, and they were forced into the position of landless labourers, cultivating for wages the now swollen large farms of the former lords which they had previously cultivated as serfs. A minority of large peasants survived the emancipation and emerged to prosper as wealthy farmers of fair-sized holdings, employing some of the labour of their less fortunate fellows. But the main beneficiaries of Prussian emancipation were undoubtedly the Junkers, who found themselves converted from feudal seigneurs into large-scale capitalist farmers, provided with an adequate and cheap labour supply. Here, almost alone in Europe, the revolutionary impact on the countryside had produced conditions which directly encouraged the expansion of production for the market.

The old pattern persists: 1789–1848

Otherwise, as Europe digested the legal and institutional upheavals in the years between 1789 and 1848, their most noticeable effect seemed to have been to give explicit confirmation to the line of division which had already existed in practice before 1789. Central and eastern Europe remained the region of serfdom and of labour services—the *robot*—in the first half of the 19th century, while Europe west of the Elbe was the region of free peasants and peasant agriculture. Agriculturally the revolutionary period had produced only one real novelty in the countryside, the successful introduction of sugar-beet cultivation, with government subsidies and encouragement, when access to West Indian cane-sugar supplies was cut off by war. Once established, western European governments took care that it continued to get sufficient protection to survive and flourish, so that by 1900 both Germany and France were not far short of self-sufficiency in sugar. Apart from this, the most insistent impression of the countryside in the first half of the 19th century is of its traditionalism and conservatism, of expansion of gross output as trade in basic agricultural products expanded, but of expansion achieved largely by simple extension of already established methods. Contemporary observers were eager to pounce on any available evidence of agricultural progress, and reported many instances of new crop rotations, improved management of resources, and introduction of new implements. But even in England, the centre of mechanical innovation in agriculture, the elaborate and intriguing seed-drills, clod-crushers, or primitive reaping machines, which were reported from this period, were not in the least representative of typical farming operations; while the early trials of equipment for steam-powered cultivation, spectacular though they often were, related to engineers' dreams rather than to the farmer's world.

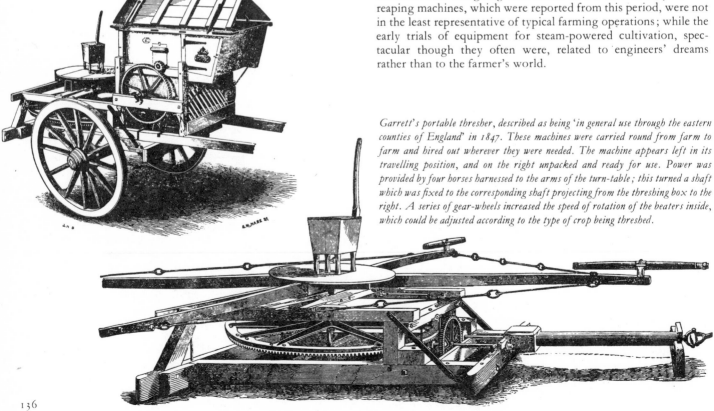

Garrett's portable thresher, described as being 'in general use through the eastern counties of England' in 1847. These machines were carried round from farm to farm and hired out wherever they were needed. The machine appears left in its travelling position, and on the right unpacked and ready for use. Power was provided by four horses harnessed to the arms of the turn-table; this turned a shaft which was fixed to the corresponding shaft projecting from the threshing box to the right. A series of gear-wheels increased the speed of rotation of the beaters inside, which could be adjusted according to the type of crop being threshed.

Hay-tedding meant separating and spreading the hay for it to dry, a laborious operation formerly carried out by men with forks. It could now be done quickly and easily by the mechanical tedder.

Before 1848 the world of the farmer and the peasant was a pre-railway world, and as such was essentially static, a world bound by seasonal rhythms and restricted not so much by lack of know-ledge as by lack of the means to procure more manure and fertilizer, the only way to break out of fixed and inefficient cropping patterns. It may have been that in the areas which now emerged as those of fully established peasant proprietorship the 'magic of private property' produced a landscape of more industrious, careful, and efficient management. This had been Arthur Young's theory, and it was shared by many later observers. The explanation of a neat, intensively-cultivated and prosperous-looking country-side as an area of owner-cultivators, and of an unkempt countryside as one of tenants or *métayers*, did not, however, always fit the facts. Sismondi plainly thought that this was the case when he con-trasted the garden-like appearance of the Tuscan plain with its intricate irrigation works, its neat poplar-lined fields, its careful husbanding of night soil, its intensive market-gardening and its lush vineyards, with the Genevan countryside from which he had come, where the rivers were allowed to run to waste and no efforts were made to obtain the maximum returns from the land. In the Tuscan case he saw peasants who were virtually landowners, in Geneva cultivation by tenants and labourers. Yet Flanders was every bit as garden-like as Tuscany, with immaculately kept small holdings, intensive cultivation by spade husbandry, and specializa-tion on vegetable growing. The Flemish were quite as assiduous as the Tuscans in collecting night soil and in buying supplies from neighbouring towns; the only difference seems to have been that the Flemish peasant distributed it through a pipe and sprinkler from a tank carried on his back, while the Tuscan spooned it out over his fields from a large wooden tub with a gigantic wooden ladle. But although the ownership of the land of Flanders was divided up among small proprietors, the actual cultivators were—by the middle of the century—rack-rented tenants and landless labourers. The peasant proprietors had become simple landlords, and the actual labourers and small farmers lived, according to Laveleye (1822–92), miserable lives among the splendid harvests, and were among the worst off in all western Europe. Laveleye made much the same point about Lombardy, where it was in the most intensively cultivated and bountiful region of the Po Valley, with its irrigation works, its rice fields, its mulberry trees and its vineyards, that the labourers had the most miserable conditions. He made this as a point against large farms, for the region was cultivated in farms of 250 to 750 acres, for the most part by tenant farmers who themselves were wealthy men. It was equally a point against the owner-occupier thesis.

The market revolution

If the appearance of the countryside was an unreliable guide to the agrarian structure which it supported, it was a much better signpost to the more critical factor of the proximity or absence of markets. Thus, Ireland, which was a country of peasant holdings, could be divided into the area of commercial farming of the south east, producing wheat, beef and butter for the English market and barley for the domestic brewing industry, and the rest of the country, devoted to potato patches and subsistence. The first area had middling-sized farms and reasonably substantial and comfort-able dwellings; the second experienced increasingly minute sub-division in the first half of the century, constant encroachment on the unrewarding bog-land as the margin of cultivation was re-lentlessly pressed outwards from the more fertile areas, and pro-liferation of the wretchedness embodied in the mud cabins, mere hovels without windows, chimneys, or furniture, which could not be matched for beastliness and degradation unless one travelled as far as Russia. Ulster was different again, a countryside of small if not minute holdings, but not a countryside of utter poverty; the cabins, miserable enough in comparison even with the cottages of English agricultural labourers let alone with the farmhouses of English tenants, at least usually boasted windows, and quite often were stone-built. The tenantry, besides their potatoes, would have a field or two of wheat or oats, and expected to keep a cow as well as a pig, and to have some butter to market. Many also were not pure farmers, but ran their holdings in harness with domestic work in the linen industry, and this helped to lift them above the level of the utter destitution of the peasantry of the west of Ireland. When the bitterness of the Irish agrarian situation—the religious differences, the antipathy to absentee landlords, the harshness of ruthless evictions, the resentment of extortionate rents—is stripped away, the abiding lesson of pre-Famine Ireland was that subsistence farming in a situation of rapidly growing population was a recipe for technical stagnation, immobility, and increasing misery leading to catastrophic starvation.

Ireland, or rather those parts of it which were remote from market influences, was perhaps an extreme case of increasing misery in the pre-1848 period. But similar, if not so fully developed, tendencies were visible elsewhere. In France, where population growth was not particularly vigorous, it was in the northern zone stretching from Normandy and the Pas de Calais across to the Rhine that technical changes were most noticeable, even though they proceeded slowly: a decline in the fallow area, the introduction of clover and other artificial grasses, an increase in livestock especially cattle, an improvement in implements of which the growing use of iron ploughs was the most important, and some increase in grain yields. This was precisely the area that was in touch with the markets of Paris, the northern towns, and those of Alsace. The population growth of the region was absorbed partly by those towns, and partly within the countryside by growth in the agricultural labouring class. Farming grew steadily more com-mercial, and the appearance of the countryside slowly changed as the great sweeps of land under identical crops of the three-field era were replaced by a patchwork of small strips and fields each under the crop which the individual farmer felt it most profitable to grow. It was in the centre and south-west of France that tech-niques remained unchanged, and it was of this area that Delisle's 1852 observation rang true 'that a thirteenth-century peasant would visit many of our farms without much astonishment'. It was the region without ready access to markets, and without ready outlets for any surplus population. As its population grew, it was not wage labour which increased, but the size of peasant holdings which diminished; it became the region with the highest proportion of peasant proprietors to total agricultural population, and the region nearest to the 'potato' standard of living.

In Germany the line of the Elbe still stood out as an agricultural frontier. To the east, growing population found a ready outlet in heath and waste land, which if uninviting and not very fertile was at least empty: the arable area in this East Prussian region was more than doubled between 1815 and 1849, an extension of the rye and wheat lands much assisted by the progress of emancipa-tion and the creation of a large supply of wage labour. The labourers lost in status, but at least did not suffer from increasing hardship. In the west, and perhaps to an even greater degree in the south where, as in Bavaria, the progress of emancipation was extremely dilatory before 1848, matters were different. Here there were no vast new areas to bring into cultivation, and population growth put rising pressure on the available land. Peasant holdings grew smaller, few opportunities for wage employment existed, by-employment in domestic industry began to be threatened by urban and foreign competition, and peasant indebtedness mounted. An explosive situation built up, with rural population pressing at the seams of available land, from which relief only came with the massive transatlantic emigration of the next two or three decades. Non-commercial peasant Germany was perhaps coming within sight of an Irish predicament just before 1848; the rapid extension of potato cultivation and its swift conquest of peasant diets was an ominous sign. As in Germany, so in Sweden; the adequate, if rude, livelihood of the Swedish peasant, symbolized by the year's supply of round ryebread loaves which he was accustomed to string from the rafters of his house, was being whittled away by a rising tide of population. Through much of Europe Samuel Laing (1780–1868), observing the state of the people in 1848 and 1849, saw 'the whole body of small proprietors reduced to the condition of a soldiery on leave', mainly as a result of rising numbers and techniques which were changing too slowly to cope with them.

The 1848 revolutions occurred, therefore, in an increasingly tense rural atmosphere, though they occurred largely for non-rural reasons except insofar as bread and potato riots in the towns were due to harvest failures and high food prices. The peasantry were not undisposed to join in, though their most significant activity was in France, where they offered the first massive demonstration of the essential conservatism to which their possession of the land impelled them. In most of Germany the peasants grumbled, but left the town liberals to fight—or fail to fight—their own battles. To the east, where serfdom and the *robot* persisted, there was still a potentially revolutionary countryside. In the dress rehearsal in Galicia in 1846 the Polish gentry had failed to enlist the Slav peasantry on their side against Vienna, and instead the Habsburg rulers had turned the serfs to hacking down their foreign, Polish, landlords in a bloody display of the power of pitchforks and scythes. In 1848 every side, the liberals and radicals of the towns, the Magyar nationalists in Hungary, and the defenders and restorers of the Habsburg power, tumbled over themselves to announce the abolition of the *robot* in order to prevent an empire-wide scything down of the directing and educated classes. The peasantry accepted this gift without noticeable gratitude, though they did forebear to carry out the widely-expected uprising. The abolition of serfdom in central Europe was the one enduring result of the 1848 revolutions in the countryside, almost its only enduring result.

Agriculture industrialized

If one is looking for an event which launched the countryside into a period of rapid change in the next quarter-century, however, it is not 1848 which signifies, but the opening of the British market in 1846 after the repeal of the corn laws. Again and again observers in the 1850s and 1860s remarked on the ramifications of free access to the British market, whether it was a question of explaining the mounting prosperity of the Dutch dairy-farmers and their new houses and creameries, all built from cheese, or a matter of marvelling at the transformation of the Hungarian plain from traditional torpor to bustling modern granary of Europe. Yet even the opening of the British ports was less an important event in its own right than a gesture of recognition that the days of British self-sufficiency were finally ended, and that Britain needed to look to the world at large for her supplies of food. The 'world' for the next thirty years effectively meant Europe, for the new territories overseas were in no position to challenge Europe agriculturally until, by the late 1870s, they had been opened up to production, and transport development in railways and shipping had reached the point where they could compete in price in the distant markets. And 'Europe' meant the areas which were in touch, by water transport or by railway, not only with the British market, but with the urban markets of the Continent itself. Above all, the years between 1846 and 1880 were the years when the railway opened up the European countryside—railway mileage increased more than four times between 1850 and 1870—and rescued it from the fate to which, in the first half of the century, it had seemed to be doomed.

It is arguable that until about 1850 the early stages of industrialization and urbanization had been made possible by an increasing surplus of materials, men and finance extracted from a fundamentally traditional and technically static agriculture, by means of a tightening squeeze on peasants and labourers and at the expense of a deterioration in their living standards, rather than by an agricultural surplus made available by technical improvements and increasing productivity. Exceptions to such a hypothesis could be found in most parts of Europe, mainly in the immediate surroundings of the larger towns, where agriculture tended to supply the urban food market not by a tightening of belts but by an expansion and specialization of production. And a major exception existed in England, where in spite of the fact that most polemicists insisted that there was a dichotomy between agriculture and industry and that the two sectors had opposing interests and inverse prosperity, mutual dependence had in practice operated to the advantage of both for many decades: the expansion of agricultural output and the prosperity of farmers had gone hand in hand with industrial expansion and prosperity, and full-time working and good wages in industry had produced brisk demand for food and high incomes for farmers.

But it was after mid-century that the emphasis shifted more generally across Europe, and the countryside both supported and responded to more rapid industrialization and urbanization by accelerated technical changes which raised output and increased productivity so that the material conditions of the rural population improved.

What happened was the extension of the market economy to most parts of the countryside, and the railway builders were the chief agents of this process. The social cost of the process lay partly in the departure of large numbers of people from the countryside, either to towns and factories in their own countries, or to strange lands across the oceans; and partly in the disruption of the traditional communities and practices of peasant Europe, with the loss of security and certainty that accompanied the rise of individualist farming and an individualist society. For those who wanted the rural world to stand still, this was the time for action; peasant customs, traditional costumes, crafts, festivals and houses, were changed and eroded as individual household production of things like clothing and furniture receded before the invasion of town-made and factory-made goods. Conscious efforts at preservation began to be made, and by the 1880s an 'olde-worlde' cult of folk art and costume had been launched in an effort to promote the idea of the tourist countryside. To find these things in their natural habitat it was now necessary to journey to the Balkans or to Russia. And it was precisely in Russia that the major exception to the transformation and amelioration process was to be found. Here the swelling export surplus, particularly of grains, was won not by improved methods of cultivation, but by the age-old device of turning the screw on the peasantry and obliging them to make do with a smaller slice of the cake.

The railways were the means by which the demand of the towns for food and of industry for raw materials like wool, leather, flax and hemp were conveyed to the countryside. As the main routes of the 1850s were provided with the branch and feeder lines of the 1860s and 1870s, this influence became ever more widespread. Through the railways the cultivators obtained higher incomes, and these could be spent on the means of improvement, on the seeds, livestock and implements which produced greater output. The railways brought back to the countryside not only consumer goods for the farmers, but also some of the supplies of manures, fertilizers and feeding stuffs that were needed for raising output. And they were channels of communication for ideas as well as for goods; the transmission of knowledge of agricultural techniques was greatly speeded up. Railways of course did not stand alone, though they were the most widespread form of transport development; especially in western Europe the network of canals and rivers was of great importance in the movement of agricultural produce. The virtual canalization of the Rhine and the intensity of the steam-drawn barge traffic on it made a deep impression on Laveleye in the 1880s.

Nor should the extent and completeness of the rural transformation be exaggerated. Many localities, even within well-railwayed countries like Germany and France, still remained unaffected and near-medieval. In Switzerland, where the lower-lying areas were well served with railways by 1870, the alpine communities still continued in their unhurried traditional ways, the herds of cattle making their annual spring departure for the alpine meadows. This was still a local occasion, a *fête*, as the village turned out to send off the caravan of cows, headed by two guide cows carrying the bells, their heads decked with flowers, followed by the rest of the cows, and the bull carrying a copper cheese-kettle between his horns, the whole column surrounded by an undisciplined rabble of goats, marshalled by two or three young cowherds sounding horns and yodelling, and the rear brought up by the headman leading the expedition's horse laden with the rest of the cheese-making equipment. They were off for a four months' stay in the Alps, in the most primitive conditions, in a hut without chimney or windows, using odd stones and rocks for furniture, and living on milk, maize flour gruel, and hard bread which was never less than six months old. Here was a pattern of life undisturbed by commercial influences. And it was only during the 1880s that the Habsburgs were planning their civilizing mission of driving a railway through the Balkans to link with the Turkish line, thus to achieve the climax of 19th-century European civilization, a through Pullman trip from Paris to Constantinople.

Nevertheless there were very considerable changes in the countryside in the high railway age. The most significant were the decline in the bare fallow area in arable Europe, at least up to the Russian frontier, and the closely associated release from the scarcity of manure which had held Europe in its grip for centuries. With supplies of manure limited by the head of livestock which could be kept, and the livestock limited by the amount of fodder which could be grown, cereal acreage or yields, and therefore cash crops, could not be increased unless the fodder could be increased. English farming, borrowing from the Low Countries, had broken through this barrier since the mid-17th century, and had evolved the sheep-and-corn husbandry based on new fodder crops and increased grains from the increased fertility derived from greater manure supplies. Now the elements of the system were re-exported to Europe, and root crops, artificial grasses, and increased numbers of livestock became common. The greater fertility which furnished increasing crop yields was aided by the spreading use of artificial manures—guano, superphosphate, nitrates, and potash—though outside the Low Countries and northern France, and much of Germany, where the use of potash in particular grew very rapidly after 1860, these were no more than marginal supplements to increased supplies of farmyard manure. Almost equally significant were improvements in the quality of livestock, the cattle breeds of the Continent, but above all the sheep and the pigs, being greatly improved in this period, very largely through the importation of English breeding stock. Less significant, perhaps, in terms of its

The improvement of cattle by selective breeding and feeding, begun in the 18th century, was intensified in the 19th. These four breeds were among the most popular. (a) The Charolais, accepted as the best of the French breeds—fast maturing, hard working and excellent for meat. (b) The Shorthorn, even faster to mature, reached enormous size—though to do so it required intensive high-capital farming including cow-sheds and especially rich food. Evolved in England, it had been introduced into France in 1825 and was officially sponsored in 1836 (the first French herd-book was set up in 1855). (c) The Hereford, heaviest of all English breeds. Like the shorthorn, it was introduced into France from England in the 1820s. (d) The Angus, which produced particularly high-quality meat. The breed originated in Scotland, became popular in England in the first half of the century and was first seen in France in 1856.

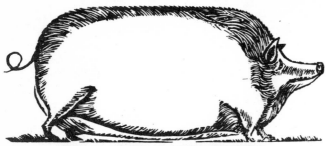

POSITIVELY THE LAST WEEK !!

J. MARSH,

HAS PURCHASED A

GREAT NOVELTY !!

Which may be SEEN ALIVE !!

AT THE

STAR YARD, OXFORD,

A WONDERFULLY

LARGE PIG,

Weighing 68 Score 12 lbs.,

From the Birmingham Cattle Show, Bred and Exhibited by W. B. WAISMAN, Esq., Yorkshire.

This is the Largest Pig ever seen and has gained 14 Prizes.

Admission, 2d., Children & Schools, 1d.

The PIG will be on her legs at 12, 2, 4, and 6 o'clock.

Hall and Son, Printers, New Road, Oxford.

This exhibition poster, dating from about 1840, shows not only the length to which selective breeding had been carried (the pig obviously found it almost impossible to stand on its legs) but also the element of showmanship which competition could engender.

contribution to total output, but more dramatic visually, was the transformation of the Danubian plain into one of Europe's chief granaries. Long-established as Vienna's chief source of wheat, the Hungarian plain was cultivated in traditional and low-yielding fashion until the mid-century. New means of access to more distant markets, especially the British, and the effects of emancipation which left a country of vast estates and large units of production, created the climate for rapid modernization in the third quarter of the 19th century. Hungary had become, by the 1870s, one of the main export markets for British steam ploughing and threshing gear, and its flatness and its vast fields lent themselves to successful adoption of steam-powered agriculture on a scale which dwarfed Britain, and was perhaps only rivalled by the American mid-west.

Work, sport and travel

The coming of the railway also gave a new dimension to the countryside of leisure, and practically created the tourist countryside. To the landowning classes the country had always been a place for sport, as much as a place which produced food or provided rents. For centuries large tracts had been set aside for the chase, and the presence of hunting forests and hunting lodges was indeed one of the traditional features which distinguished the countryside of the aristocrats and large estates from the countryside of the peasantry. While the encroachments of farming for the market somewhat curtailed the sprawling hunting areas of central and eastern Europe in the course of the century, more than enough remained to preserve the forests of Bohemia and Hungary, let alone Russia, as the scenes of hunting on a baronial scale of extravagance and arrogance. All that changed here was the greater ease of commuting between town house and hunting lodge, and the greater comfort and luxury of life in the forest. In the more intensively farmed regions pressure on space led to the development of new

forms of the sporting countryside, developments which reached their peak in the railway age as landowners and their retinues moved easily up and down the country, and as the urban rich were enabled to join in the fray, giving it a fashionable and cosmopolitan rather than a bucolic air. Typically, in Britain, the quarry—whether fox, pheasant or partridge—was carefully preserved and nursed in relatively small pockets of woods, copses or covers, while the sport itself, the fox-hunting or the shooting parties, fanned out over the neighbouring farmland, often leaving its mark in the shape of special hunting gates and fences and hedges kept safe and trim for jumping. This dual-purpose countryside created its conflicts between farmers anxious for their crops and gentry anxious for their game, and between poachers and gamekeepers; these undertones of rural tension were soothed by the participation of some of the tenantry in the hunting, and to some extent balanced by the way in which sport induced landowners to keep up an interest in their estates. For a countryside more wholeheartedly devoted to sport the gentry were driven to the open spaces of the north, above all of Scotland, where the grouse moors and deer forests were almost denuded of inhabitants and given over to the large-scale sheep grazing which was the only form of exploitation compatible with the game.

The sporting countryside and the tourist countryside overlapped at many points, both physically and in clientele, for whether in 1880 or in 1900 tourism outside short-distance journeys to the seaside was still very much confined to the well-to-do, and when it took place in country districts was still very much a form of outdoor physical exercise. Angling perhaps provided the greatest area of common ground, for it became in the course of the century a sport of the visitor from the towns while remaining a sport of the landed gentry also; and with the services of railways and steamships to hand it was the cause of much journeying to Scotland, Ireland, or Norway, where many rivers, lakes, lochs and fjords became part of a regular fishing countryside equipped with fisherman's inns and hotels and furnished with local specialists in suitable flies and tackle. Visiting the countryside for pleasures unconnected with the pursuit of animals, however, was a 19th-century, and a railway, development. Wealthy aristocrats had, of course, long been accustomed to taking prolonged tours as part of their education, relaxation or recuperation. The grand tours of the 18th century, however, had been largely a matter of visiting the centres of ancient urban civilization in Italy to view the architecture and art collections, or of expeditions to take the waters at the spas of Germany. The intervening countryside had been a regrettable nuisance to be

As land was farmed more intensively, the gentry went further afield for sport and relaxation. In central Europe the forests, and in Britain the rough country of northern Scotland became popular. Above: trout-fishing in a Highland stream.

negotiated as rapidly as possible, a possible source of peril from accidents or highwaymen and discomfort from dirty inns, rather than a source of pleasure. Attitudes were changing at the very end of the 18th century with the beginning of the Romantic Revival, the cult of folk ballads, and admiration for the naturalness of un-spoilt, unsophisticated, rural life. Scenery began to be appreciated simply as scenery, and some of the aristocracy began to make tours simply in order to admire lakes and mountains, woods and waterfalls, country views and scenes of country activities.

This kind of appreciation was fostered, and socially deepened, by easier, faster and cheaper travel from the middle of the century. The urban middle-class appetite for travel was catered for by the railway excursions and tours originated by Thomas Cook, building on his experience in organizing trips by special trains to London for the Great Exhibition in 1851; and it was provided with a literary diet by Baedeker, whose guides blossomed out to cover all the European countries during the third quarter of the century and had embraced the New World before its close. Neither could have flourished unless the growing tourism had continued to be attracted by the towns, the art galleries, the spas, and the seaside resorts; but both also had a large place for the holiday countryside. The muscular middle-class Englishmen opened up the Alps to mountaineering and rock-climbing in the 1860s, and a little later began turning the local methods of winter travel into the delights of winter sports. The Swiss hotel industry was fairly launched, and Switzerland's image as a tourist landscape was firmly shaped. For many the countryside had ceased to be a place where livings were earned by the toil of farming, and had become a place to be enjoyed because it was unspoilt, a place where exertion brought a sense of achievement, not financial rewards.

Challenge from overseas

For those who looked to the country for their living the financial rewards became harder to get in the last two decades of the century, for this was the period when the new countrysides of the Americas and Australasia came to economic fruition, and produced their first massive impact on Europe through vast supplies of cheap grains, meat and dairy products. Until railways were sufficiently developed to open up the interior, and steamships had sharply reduced ocean freights—developments which were not far advanced until the late 1870s—the agriculture of the rest of the world had been complementary to, rather than competitive with, European agriculture. There were exceptions: Australian wool was competitive, and became important from the 1840s, before railways had been built in Australia, and while sailing ships carried the wool, a trade which they long continued to dominate; and the United States, in the days of sail, built up a sizeable export trade to Britain in flour, preserved beef and pork, and in unmilled wheat. But the great American trade was in non-competitive articles, in cotton, maize, and tobacco. The typical pre-railway role of the rest of the world was to provide Europe with tropical and sub-tropical crops, with cotton, sugar, coffee and tea, more often than not the product of plantation economies and grown, in the Americas, by slave labour: this was the colonial countryside, surviving from the 18th century far into the next.

Direct North American agricultural competition with Europe was a matter of the settlement of the old mid-west, up to and just across the Mississippi, in the 1850s and 1860s, and above all a matter of the opening up of the prairies in the 1870s and 1880s. The railways, coming fast behind the frontiersmen, were important in this process, but farm mechanization was almost equally important in opening these territories to commercial production, and especially in making the Dakotas into the great wheat-growing areas of the late 19th century the development of special sod-breaking ploughs was of paramount importance. In the space of scarcely half a century the American farming countryside had its centre of gravity shifted from the New England states to the prairie wheatlands, and its techniques transformed from the hickory scratching-sticks of the early pioneers to the highly mechanized farming of the Dakotas. It had become, by the last quarter of the century, a countryside of isolated homesteads, grain silos by the railways, great gangs of up to sixteen ploughs drawn by steam traction

Canadian farming expanded rapidly in the second half of the century, until the country became one of the greatest grain-producing areas in the world. This pamphlet was issued in 1882 to attract settlers to Manitoba.

engines, and immense reaper-binders which might require a team of forty horses. In the interval, so rapid was change, the same countryside could have passed through the stages of open-range cattle raising, the true cowboy countryside, and of fenced ranching, before the homesteaders and arable farming had arrived. After a short time the US wheat prairies were followed by the opening of the Canadian west with its market at Winnipeg, in the last decade of the century. In South America, Argentina, long a source of hides and bones for Europe, became a source of beef with the development of refrigerated ships, and experienced its first great railway boom in the 1880s: the vast empty spaces of the grasslands awaited peopling and stocking with cattle. After crisis and setback, the Argentine was ready by 1900 for its next phase of frenzied development and its emergence as a major wheat as well as beef exporter. In Australia the sheep-station countryside pushed further and further into the outback in the 1870s and 1880s, its fortunes hanging on water supply from the wells which alone made sheep-raising possible in the dry country, and on the barbed wire which preserved the sparse grazing for the sheep, not the kangaroos; the rabbits, arrivals from the old world, were less easy to keep away. In New Zealand the pace of settlement was leisurely from the 1830s until refrigeration opened the British market to the produce of its pastoral economy. Then, from the 1880s, Canterbury lamb and New Zealand butter and cheese were exported to Britain in rapidly increasing quantities, and the green rolling grassland of the South Island, a country of independent owner-farmers with their neat houses and of a handful of giant land companies with their farm-factories, became a distant but integral part of the British agrarian economy.

Agriculture patterns in Europe: 1880–1900

Such overseas agricultural annexes did not entirely supplant agriculture at home, but they did force it to make violent changes. The new lands, as they were brought into cultivation or stocked with animals, bore a prosperous and productive look, though their farmers knew lean times in the decades after 1880 since there was a world-wide tendency to over-production and most agricultural prices fell steeply, to the benefit of the world's urban consumers but to the dismay of its food producers. In the old world the effect of the great price fall was much more serious, as farmers found the import competition overwhelming. In France and Germany governments put up the shutters, and protection kept out the American wheat and kept internal agricultural prices above world levels, though it could not stop some decline. The result was that farmers were encouraged to persevere with their existing crop systems, but at the same time found that their incomes were falling. Protection did not inhibit all changes, and indeed it was in these decades that significant portions of French agriculture began to wear a mechanized look for the first time as hay-mowers and reapers were introduced, and threshing machines at length almost banished the flail, in efforts to cut production costs. Such efforts did not succeed, however, in preventing a fall in the living standards of the peasantry in France and Germany, and of the agricultural labourers in east Germany; in Germany the rural exodus to the towns increased to the point at which farming, in the east, became heavily dependent for seasonal labour on migrant Polish workers, segregated and housed in rough barracks on the large estates.

In Britain, where by 1880 agriculture was already a minor part of the economy occupying barely 10% of the population, free trade was preserved, and agriculture was left to face the blasts of competition as best it could. The grain farming of the east and south suffered severely, and the finely-balanced intensive stock and corn husbandry which had been the technical masterpiece of high farming was put out of gear. Much cultivated land was abandoned and allowed to tumble down to natural grass, reintroducing to the downland areas a green countryside which survived until the plough returned, accompanied by bags of fertilizers, after 1940; and introducing to much eastern lowland a countryside of weed-ridden pasture and neglected buildings. Even more arable land was converted to grass, and in general the countryside became noticeably greener and less golden. Livestock farmers fared much better, and profited from the cheap imported grains and cakes which they needed for fodder. Even for them, however, the competition of imported meat could be severe, and there was a widespread switch into dairying and the supply of fresh milk to urban markets whose demand increased rapidly. The complete collapse of farming and the reversion to dog-and-stick farming in which one man in ranching fashion looked after an area which had formerly supported a dozen farmers and their workers was rare. But rural depopulation was widespread, and the inhabitants of the countryside thinned out in proportion to the growth in the number of cows. Some of this depopulation was the result of the displacement of labour by machinery. Indeed, by 1900 the gangs of scythers were becoming a rare sight. But more of it was the result of the general slackening of the intensity of farming, of a countryside falling to lower levels of production and therefore employment.

It was the agricultural exporting countries of Europe, however, which were faced with the greatest problems by the influx of overseas produce. Agricultural protection was of no use to them, since it was their export markets, not their own home markets, which they wished to preserve; and they could not afford to let their agricultural sectors run down, like Britain, for they had no great industries to support their economies. The small countries of western Europe adjusted successfully to the new situation. The Dutch abandoned what cereal growing they had, and concentrated entirely on their dairying; served by co-operative creameries and marketing organizations, Dutch cheese and butter held its own in export markets, and the peasant farmers prospered. The Danes carried through the biggest adjustment of all, for they went into the depression as mixed farmers, dependent on their grain growing as well as on their pork market in Germany. Tariffs soon lost them the pork market, and grains were given up as unprofitable. Instead they switched to intensive dairy farming with its associated pig- and poultry-keeping, supported by grass and roots grown at home and cheap imported grains, and serviced by a highly-developed system of co-operatives which provided some of the advantages of large-scale enterprise to a country of small peasant holdings. Switching their attention to Britain almost for the first time, by 1900 the Danes had established a firm hold on the egg and bacon market.

Where the small exporting countries showed ingenuity and flexibility, and preserved prosperous countrysides, the large grain exporting countries, Russia and the Danubian plain, reacted to the American wheat and corn by striving to remain in business in the same commodities produced by pre-American techniques. In Russia the emancipation of 1861 had at first been accompanied by some slight improvement in the lot of the peasants; but its compensation provisions, and its confirmation of the communal agrarian organization of the *mir* involving frequent repartition of peasant lands, had served to condemn agriculture on peasant holdings to traditional inefficiency. Mounting population aggravated pressure on peasant holdings, and made it easy for large estate owners to continue to run their farms with primitive labour-intensive methods. At the same time Russia had to maintain and increase her agricultural exports, the only exports she could hope to have, in order to pay for imports of capital goods for her rapid industrialization of the 1890s and to service her rapidly growing foreign debts. These several factors put a squeeze on the Russian countryside in which the only way to reduce costs in order to continue to compete in the world grain markets was to reduce the standard of living of the peasants. The countryside of 1900 had no more bitter example of the consequences of maintaining traditional techniques in the face of a world economy, no clearer instance of the wretchedness caused by the survival of traditional landownership structures and peasant communes into the modern world. Where population growth and transport developments had brought the countryside of 1900 under individualist control and commercial farming, there was, to be sure, hardship, instability and social fluidity to be found, but generally there was also more to eat and greater well-being than there had been in 1789. It was where profound change had been warded off or prevented that the countryside of 1900 was a potentially explosive landscape.

An early refrigerator, used in a cold-storage warehouse in Glasgow in 1891. It worked by a combination of compression and expansion cylinders powered by a steam-engine, and was capable of discharging 110,000 cubic feet of cold air per hour.

VI NATION BUILDING

The birth of the modern state

JOHN RÖHL

'Nationalism . . . mocks at treaties, tramples
on historic rights, puts diplomacy in disarray . . .
and tomorrow perhaps will unleash
accursed war.'

EMILE DE LAVELEYE, 1866

Revolutionary France

released the pent-up forces of European nationalism, becoming the acknowledged symbol of radical patriotism everywhere. It was a symbol that never lost an element of paradox. 'Liberty, equality and fraternity' stood for a new universalist ideology, yet France's conduct was governed, as before, by self-interest. When the Empire replaced the Republic the paradox deepened. Napoleon—rightly in many ways—saw himself as the liberator of Europe, sweeping away what was archaic and oppressive, improving administrations, reforming laws, destroying privileges. Yet this revolutionary was an emperor. Could the crown co-exist with the tricolour? As the century progressed the answer seemed to be clear. However necessary Napoleon may have been as the agent

of transformation, it was the tricolour alone that represented the aspirations of nationhood. The colours might change—black, yellow and red for Belgium; green, white and red for Italy—the pattern and the ideals remained the same. Everywhere the *state* had to work together with the *nation*, to create the *nation-state*: neither could exist without the other.

The splendidly decorated flag shown here is one of several made for Napoleon's last public ceremony, held in Paris in the summer of 1815. Against the tricolour background stand the symbols of empire—the crown, the eagle, the laurel-wreathed 'N' and the bees, taken over by Napoleon from what he thought was the heraldry of his Merovingian predecessors.

The First Consul saves France (*left*). Ignorance tries to pull her into the abyss, but Napoleon introduces her to Justice and Abundance, who carries the olive branch of peace.

Poland: the founding of the Duchy of Warsaw (*right*) in 1807 gave new hope to Poland after nearly forty years of partitions. But Spain was unconciliated. Nationalism here took its inspiration from resistance to Napoleon. *Far right*: Goya's *Shootings of May 3rd* commemorated the uprising against Joseph Bonaparte in 1808.

As long as Napoleon retained supreme power, he could not give the nations of Europe real freedom. His rise and fall (*above*), as seen by a German satirist in 1814, is indicative of his status among European liberals.

Germany: The Confederation of the Rhine was created in 1806 (*left*) on the ruins of the Holy Roman Empire.

Italy: in January 1802 Italian delegates were called to Lyons and the Italian Republic was proclaimed (*above*). Napoleon was 'elected' president. But it was all a mockery. In 1805 he went to Milan to be crowned King and the Carbonari was born, a revolutionary secret society pledged to independence and unity.

A united Italy had been the dream of Italian patriots since before the time of Dante. In 1848 revolution broke out in Milan against the Austrians, in Rome against the pope and in Palermo (*top*) against the Bourbons. In all three cases it was defeated. Only in Piedmont, already independent, was there secure gain – the granting of a constitution by King Victor Emmanuel. It was from the Piedmontese port of Genoa that 'The Thousand', Garibaldi's army of liberation, sailed on May 5th, 1860, arriving at Marsala in Sicily (*above*), on the 11th.

The German Empire was proclaimed at Versailles on January 18th 1871, after the surrender of Napoleon III and shortly before Paris capitulated. The creation of the Second Reich (the first was the Holy Roman Empire) crowned the ambitions of German nationalists, though Austria was excluded. Here, in the Galérie des Glaces, Bismarck, the nation-builder, stands with Moltke at the foot of the throne.

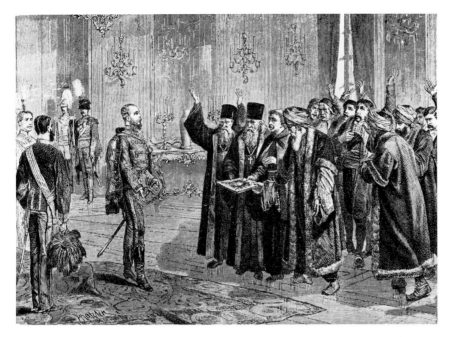

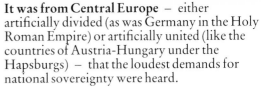

It was from Central Europe – either artificially divided (as was Germany in the Holy Roman Empire) or artificially united (like the countries of Austria-Hungary under the Hapsburgs) – that the loudest demands for national sovereignty were heard.

For Germans, the Wartburg became a national rallying point. In 1817 students held an '*auto-de-fé*' at which they burnt anti-patriotic books and such un-German articles as French corsets.

Hercegovinans (*top left*) swear allegiance to Francis-Joseph after their province had been transferred from Turkish to Austrian control in 1878.

Hungarians resented the hegemony of Vienna. In March 1848 they set up a virtually independent state. But in September an Austrian army under the Serbian general Jellačić (*left*) marched to Budapest and in August 1849 finally defeated the Hungarians at Temesvar.

Bulgaria, (*above right*) an almost forgotten name before the 19th century, recovered a sense of national awareness in hostility to the Turks. Semi-autonomy in 1879 was followed by unification under Alexander of Battenberg.

Czechs remained underprivileged in comparison with Hungarians, and felt themselves to be threatened by German elements. In 1897 the Austrian Prime Minister, Count Badeni, tried to introduce legislation to allow Czech as an official language in Bohemia, alongside German. The attempt was defeated after angry scenes in the Viennese Parliament (*opposite top right*).

Roumania, caught between Russia and Turkey, made her bid for independence after the Crimean War. Two *divans ad hoc* (*left*), together with European and Turkish representatives, voted for a united nation under Prince Alexander Cuza.

A settlement of the whole complex Balkan question was achieved in 1878 at the Congress of Berlin (*right*). The principal representatives are shown, left to right: Karolyi (Austria), Gorchakov (Russia), Disraeli (Great Britain), Andrássy (Hungary), Bismarck (Germany), Shuvalov (Russia) and – extreme right – Mehmet Ali (Turkey). Roumania, Bulgaria, Montenegro and Serbia were made independent, Bosnia and Hercegovina given to Austria, and parts of Asiatic Turkey to Russia.

Greece's struggle for freedom engaged the sympathy of the West more than any other cause, mainly because of its literary and romantic associations. Byron died trying to organize an army at Missolonghi in 1824, and when the town was eventually taken Delacroix painted his moving allegory *Greece expiring on the ruins of Missolonghi* (*right*). The sufferings of the Greeks, however, roused the Powers to intervene, and through the aid of England, France and Russia they were eventually (1832) guaranteed an autonomous state.

The new king, Otto of Wittelsbach, son of Ludwig I of Bavaria, enters Athens (*below*). This vast commemorative painting by a fellow Bavarian portrays the event with a certain idealization – the Theseion in the background standing for classical culture revived – but the experiment did not work out well. A revolution in 1862 brought about Otto's abdication and a change of dynasty, but Greek nationalism itself was never again questioned.

The birth of the modern state

JOHN RÖHL

NEITHER CITIES nor countrysides fully satisfied men's sense of belonging during the 19th century. Their loyalties were attached increasingly—and often with great fervour—to the 'nation'. 'The sentiment of nationality is not new,' wrote Professor Carlton J. H. Hayes, a well-known American historian, in 1926. 'The sentiment of patriotism is not new. But nationalism is new. Only since the 18th century has there been a conscious and purposeful attempt to redraw the political map of the whole world on national lines and to instil in the hearts and minds of all human beings a supreme loyalty to their respective nationalities and to their several nation states.'

Certainly, the nation-state, which finally emerged in Europe—later to spread round the world—in the period between the late 18th century and the early 20th, is by far the most important form of political organization in the world today. It emerged in three distinct ways. In the countries bordering on the Atlantic, from Spain to Scandinavia, much of the work of unification and con-solidation was accomplished by reforming and centralizing monarchs from the end of the middle ages onwards. In these regions, the nation-state came about primarily through internal revolution within the old historic frontiers. In Central Europe, in those areas we now know as Italy and Germany, the nation existed as a cultural and linguistic unit long before a state was created to encompass it, and the nation-state arose here by the unification of numerous small states into a larger whole, as well as by the 'clearing of the feudal undergrowth' as in the West. Finally, in Eastern Europe lay the great multi-national empires of Austria, Turkey and Russia, those 'monsters incapable of life', as Mancini called them in 1851. In these 'prisons of the nations' there could be no compromise between the people and the state nor any chance of using an existing state as a nucleus around which to build a nation-state; here, in the East, nation-states were born by seceding from the larger empires.

These three ways of achieving nation-statehood are also, by and large, chronologically distinct from one another. In the west, the formative period of the nation-state was the great 'Atlantic Re-volution' which occurred in the second half of the 18th century. In England the new, closer relationship between the state and society had been symbolized by, among other things, the composition of *Rule Britannia* in 1740 and *God save the King* in 1745. Later in the century the successful revolt of the American colonies and the emergence of a great new nation-state with a free constitution and a flag symbolizing national unity made a profound impression in the Old World, not least upon France. The French Revolution itself not only transformed that country into a modern state in the space of a few years but also made a deep impression upon those neighbouring countries—particularly Belgium, Holland, the Rhine-land, Switzerland and Italy—which were to fall under more or less direct French control in the ensuing wars. If the breakthrough of the nation-state principle must thus be dated in Western Europe and North America to the end of the 18th and the early part of the 19th century, that in Central Europe clearly took place in the dozen years between 1859 and 1871 when 'nationalism' had become a commanding ideology.

The third stage—the break-up of the three eastern empires—is less clearly defined, partly because the disintegration of Turkey,

the 'sick man of Europe', was a gradual process, beginning with the military reverses of the 17th century, and partly because the triumph of the nation-state in Russia's western regions during and after the First World War proved in some cases to be transient. It can be said, nevertheless, that the outstanding developments in this eastern area were the break-up of the Habsburg Empire in 1918 and the Peace Settlement of Versailles. It might be suggested that the time-lag of roughly half a century between the first and second stages and again between the second and third stages is related to a corresponding time-lag in economic and social developments. The sequence could be extended by a further half-century to include the disintegration of colonial empires that has happened in our own day.

Nothing better illustrates the growing refusal of educated opinion in Western Europe to accept the dynastic state than the outcry caused by the sale of Corsica by Genoa to France in 1768. The young Napoleon, who was born a Frenchman as a result of the transaction but suffered 'infinitely' at the French military academy on account of his foreign accent, wrote accusingly of the French: 'It is not enough that you have robbed us of what we love most, you have even destroyed our manners and customs.' Rousseau accepted the plea of the rebel dictator of Corsica, Pasquale Paoli, to draft a constitution for the island in 1765, but he did so only after demand-ing information on 'everything that serves to reveal the national character' of the Corsicans. In 1770, a year after the French military subjugation of the island, Rousseau boasted that he had been 'the first to see a nation capable of freedom and discipline, where the rest of Europe saw nothing but a mob of rebels and bandits'. Dr Johnson's friend James Boswell (1740–95) visited the island and caused a stir by appearing at the Shakespeare Jubilee in 1769 attired in the Corsican national costume. Boswell's *Journal of a Tour to Corsica* (1768) made such an impression on the British public that when the fugitive General Paoli (1725–1807) arrived in England in September 1769 he was received by the king and granted a life pension of £1,200 per annum. British sympathy for independence movements, particularly of small countries like Greece and Belgium, was to be of considerable importance throughout the 19th century.

The annexation in 1772 of large tracts of Poland by Prussia, Austria and Russia inspired Rousseau to utter his famous remark that there were no longer Frenchmen, Germans, Spaniards or Englishmen but only Europeans who felt everywhere at home 'provided they find money to steal and women to corrupt'. In his *Considérations sur le gouvernement de Pologne* (1772), Rousseau sug-gested a number of ways in which the Poles now under foreign rule might preserve their national identity. Education should be designed to 'give each human being a national form, and so direct his opinions and tastes, that he should be a patriot by inclination, by passion, by necessity. On first opening his eyes, a child must see his country, and until he dies, must see nothing else'. Poles should have a 'national physiognomy' which would distinguish them clearly from all other people. At the age of twenty 'a Pole must not be just another man; he must be a Pole'. National dress should be worn, a national militia formed, and gymnastic exercises under-taken with the ultimate aim of driving all foreign soldiers from Polish soil.

France: nationhood through revolution

It was, however, the events in France after 1789 which best exemplified the transformation of the 'segmentary state' of the *Ancien Régime* into a modern, centralized nation-state. The French nation was born when, at the suggestion of the Abbé Sieyès (1748–1836), the elected representatives to the Estates General turned themselves into a National Assembly. In the month of August 1789, aristocratic privilege, which Sieyès had likened to 'some horrible disease eating the living flesh on the body of some unfortunate man', was swept away together with all the provincial exemptions which had so restricted the effectiveness of the 'absolutist' monarchy. All Frenchmen, including Protestants and Jews, comedians and the public hangman, were given full civil—though not yet political—rights. The ancient provincial 'governments' were replaced by 83 *départements*, and in 1790 the greatest of all the corporations, the Catholic Church, was brought under state control, its vast lands confiscated for the nation, and its dioceses restructured along the new departmental lines.

In place of loyalty to the dynasty and the traditional religion, a new national mythology was deliberately fostered to encourage a sense of unity. When the Bastille was demolished, its stones were carried as souvenirs to all corners of the kingdom. 'Trees of Liberty' were planted in many towns and villages. A decree in June 1793 ordered the erection in all communities of 'an altar of the fatherland on which will be engraved the Declaration of Rights, with the inscription: the citizen is born, lives and dies for the fatherland'. The blue, white and red tricolour cockade which was popularly worn after the storming of the Bastille became compulsory during the Terror. Everyone had to carry a *certificat de civisme* which was, however, issued only on examination by public authorities of one's character and beliefs. By 1795 a whole string of new national festivals—to the Republic, to Youth, Husbands and Wives, Old Age, Agriculture, Liberty—had arisen alongside the most popular of them all, the great *Fête de la Fédération* to commemorate Bastille Day. At the first of these in 1790, Lafayette, the commander of the National Guard, swore an oath in the Champs de Mars in front of a crowd of some 300,000. At Robespierre's Festival of the Supreme Being in 1794, another huge crowd sang the *Marseillaise* accompanied by an orchestra numbering two hundred drummers alone. Article 12 of the 1791 Constitution declared the purpose of these festivals to be the attachment of the citizen 'to the constitution, to the fatherland and to the laws', and one member of the Convention thought they were 'gradually conducive to creating a need in men of seeking each other's company and mingling together'.

The French Revolution introduced the first comprehensive system of national education, and here, too, Rousseau's influence is apparent. Robespierre's friend Michel Le Peletier de Saint-Fargeau, whose assassination by royalists in 1793 became the subject of one of David's heroic canvasses, proposed that all boys and girls over the age of five be educated at public expense in national establishments away from their families, and that the curriculum include the singing of patriotic songs, the teaching of the more glorious events in French history, gymnastics, and work on the soil. In Brittany, Prieur de la Marne organized a youth movement whose members took an oath and underwent military training, and whose banner was inscribed with the words 'Hope of the Fatherland'.

For a brief moment, at the height of the crisis of 1794, it even looked as if the many non-French languages spoken in France would be forcibly extinguished. One member of the Committee of Public Safety complained that 'federalism and superstition speak Breton; emigration and hatred of the Republic speak German; counter-revolution speaks Italian, and fanaticism speaks Basque', and added menacingly: 'In a free people, language must be one and the same for all.' A decree of July 1794 forbade the use of any language but French in public transactions, but this was revoked in September, and Breton, Basque, Provençal and Alsatian German have survived to the present day. The emergence of the nation-state in France did, however, hasten the decline of *patois* and the growth of a common French language: service in a national army, attendance at schools and festivals, and the administrative centralization

begun by the Revolution and completed by Napoleon, all strongly contributed towards this trend. The greatest unifying force of all was hatred and fear of the enemy, which inspired the famous decree of August 23rd 1793 calling on all Frenchmen to lay down their lives in defence of liberty. 'The young men will go forth to battle; the married men will make arms and transport food; the women will make tents, uniforms and will serve in the hospitals; the children will prepare lint from old linen; the old men will gather in the public places to rouse the courage of the warriors, to excite hatred of kings and to preach the unity of the Republic.'

'The French people vote the liberty of the world'

In the 'glorious dawn' of 1789, few observers would have predicted that the French nation would soon find itself at war with the rest of Europe. On the contrary, the prevailing mood was one of international brotherhood and good will. In France, the tricolour was frequently flown alongside the flags of the United States, Britain and Poland. Baron de Cloots, a Prussian of Dutch origin, in 1790 marched to the National Assembly at the head of an 'embassy of the human race' composed of thirty-six foreign enthusiasts attired in national costume. In a letter to Mme de Beauharnais he wrote: 'The French flag cannot wave over London and Paris without soon being hoisted all round the globe . . . People will travel from Paris to Peking as they do from Bordeaux... The more I reflect, the more I conceive the possibility of a single nation, and the facility with which the Universal Assembly, sitting at Paris, will conduct the whole human race.' Four months after the war had begun, the Legislative Assembly granted French citizenship to Bentham, Wilberforce, Washington, Madison, Schiller, Klopstock, Kosciuszko and Pestalozzi. The final article of Saint-Just's 1793 constitution read, perhaps a little optimistically: 'The French people vote the liberty of the world.'

It was the refusal of the rest of the world to rise in the cause of liberty which confronted the revolutionaries with a dilemma. Belgium apart, only in Ireland and distant Poland was there a sympathetic response, in both cases with disastrous consequences. More and more it seemed as if the kings, their courts and other vested traditional interests were preventing the nations of Europe from attaining their liberty. In November 1791, Isnard exhorted the Assembly to inform the world that if the kings made war on the peoples, 'we shall engage the peoples in a war against the kings'. A year later the Convention promised that France would 'extend help and fraternity to all peoples wishing to recover their liberty'. Only seven deputies, amongst them Robespierre, opposed the declaration of war. Even Cloots shouted for war, partly to liberate the human race, but partly also to gain the 'natural frontiers' of the Rhine, the Alps and the Pyrenees for France.

Another new principle which was to be of great importance in the future was that of self-determination, and here too a significant change in the French attitude can be noticed. In November 1789, the Assembly declared the union of the Papal enclave of Avignon and Venaissin with France. The inhabitants of the fief protested and invoked the principle of self-determination. The Assembly agreed, and voted the union only after repeated plebiscites had demonstrated beyond doubt that that was the will of the people. By the time of the French invasion of Belgium in 1792, a less tolerant attitude prevailed. Property belonging to the 'accomplices of tyranny' was confiscated, and the failing French monetary system was imposed on the luckless inhabitants. General Dumouriez in vain tried to convince the Convention that the results of the plebiscite held under French military supervision bore little relation to the real desires of the Belgians. The French commissioners despatched to Belgium argued that the wish of an 'infantile and imbecile people' to retain the *constitution nationicide* of 1790 could not be respected. By 1795, Belgium had become a mere geographical expression, having been divided into nine new French *départements* and administered as an integral part of France. The Rhineland and north-western Italy were similarly treated without even the pretence of a plebiscite. The Dutch United Provinces, Switzerland, Lombardy and the Dalmatian coast were, on the other hand, permitted for the time being to retain a semblance of separate identity as the Batavian, Helvetian, Cisalpine and Illyrian Republics respectively. Under Napoleon, 'France' eventually came to stretch from Hamburg and Amsterdam in the north to Rome and Corfu in the south; French prefects administered in Florence and Turin, Antwerp and The Hague, Lübeck and Cologne, Barcelona and Saragossa. Beyond this vast empire an outer circle of vassal-states, often ruled by one of Napoleon's relatives, extended from Spain and Naples to the Grand Duchy of Warsaw.

Even allowing for the fact that many of the reforms introduced by the French in these areas were warmly welcomed, it is yet remarkable that there was so little popular resistance to the extension of French power. Where popular risings did occur, they were almost entirely inspired by traditional loyalties and old religious ties. The Tyrolese, for example, revolted in 1809 under Andreas Hofer (1767–1810) not against the French, but against their fellow-Germans from Bavaria who wanted to absorb them into their newly-enlarged and progressive kingdom. In the great Spanish revolt of 1808, the horror of which was recaptured in the paintings of Goya (1746–1828), the Catholic clergy took a leading part. In Russia, too, it was the peasants who rose against the invader, who was depicted as Anti-Christ, and resistance became especially violent when rumours spread that Napoleon had desecrated the churches of Moscow. In the Italian and German states, opposition to French rule, if it existed at all, was confined to a tiny minority of intellectuals.

Italy: power politics and idealism

At first, General Bonaparte's victories were actually welcomed by Italian patriots as a first step towards national regeneration. Later, when the hopes raised by his creation of a Lombard legion under the red, white and green tricolour were dashed, educated opinion turned against the French. Vittorio Alfieri's *Misogallo* (1790–96) provided one of the first signs of an awakening belief in Italian moral primacy. The growing francophobia was also reflected in the call for the purification of the Italian language of Gallicisms and the insistence of men like the Piedmontese Count di Cocconato that all public business be conducted in Italian. By 1807, members of the Carbonari movement were pledging themselves to revolution by signing their names in blood.

Nevertheless, when the Congress of Vienna again divided the peninsula into eight separate states in 1815, when French influence there was replaced so completely by Austrian that Italian statesmen were deprived of the opportunity of playing off one of the Great Powers against the other, the idea of efficient and independent government was kept alive by those Napoleonic officers and civil servants who had been discharged at the Restoration. It was they, together with a substantial class of dissatisfied lawyers whom Edmund Burke had recognized as the most dedicated opponents of traditional authority, who rebelled in 1821, 1831 and again in 1848, each time under the tricolour flag. Though particularism and municipalism was still so strong that in 1831 the rebel government of Bologna could arrest seven hundred 'foreigners' from Modena who were seeking protection from the Austrian army, a nationalist literary movement was by that time assuming substantial proportions. Silvio Pellico's little volume on his twelve years in Austrian prisons, *Le mie prigioni* (1832), had the effect of stamping Austria—not entirely justly—as the great oppressor. The work of the Abbé Gioberti (1801–52), *Del Primato morale e civile degli Italiani* (1843), advocated a federal solution under the Pope, though privately the author expressed grave misgivings about the Curia. If the neo-Guelph cause made a sudden leap forward with the election of a supposedly liberal Pope in 1846, that cause was lost as suddenly by Pius IX's suppression of Mazzini's and Garibaldi's Roman Republic with French armed help in 1849. Cesare Balbo, who published the newspaper *Il Risorgimento* jointly with Cavour, pressed for a federal union under the presidency of the King of Piedmont. To this solution too, however, there were many obstacles.

Even after the absorption in 1815 of Genoa, Mazzini's birthplace, Piedmont-Sardinia was small, containing only one-fifth of Italy's population, and many of these spoke French. Its government was as oppressive as any on the peninsula. The only advantage it possessed was its relative diplomatic independence, and its King,

Count Camillo di Cavour, the brilliant and devious prime minister of Victor Emmanuel, had come to politics via journalism. He advocated a moderately liberal constitutional monarchy for Piedmont, seeing her as the potential nucleus of a united Italy, and it was mainly his diplomatic skill which gave her such European importance. Realistic, anti-republican and none too scrupulous, he had little in common with the idealistic Mazzini. But he was able to make an ally of Garibaldi, for whom Italian unity was more important than any other consideration. Cavour died in 1861, just as the new state was coming into existence.

Charles Albert, was anxious to use this to gain further territory, initially at the expense of France and Switzerland. When these hopes were disappointed he turned his attention to the fertile plains of Austrian Lombardy. His double military intervention there in 1848–49 was motivated far more by territorial greed and fear of the Milanese revolutionaries than by a wish to further the cause of Italian unity. In the second campaign which ended so disastrously at Novara, the Lombards remained entirely passive, many of them preferring Austrian to Piedmontese rule. That Piedmont enjoyed a genuine popularity by the time of the next Lombard campaign, in 1859, was largely the work of her brilliant and cunning Prime Minister, Count Camillo di Cavour. His internal transformation of Piedmont in the years 1850–55 brought that country into line with western Europe and turned her not only into the most prosperous of Italian states but also into a haven for exiles from the rest of Italy. The money which Paris and London bankers now invested in Piedmontese enterprises gave them a not insignificant interest in her further advancement.

The expansion of Piedmont

The parallel between Cavour and Bismarck is as compelling as that between Piedmont and Prussia. Both men were *Realpolitiker* in the good and the bad senses of the word. If they believed that there were strict limits to what the politician could achieve, they did so because, not scrupling to use underhand methods, they were able to achieve far more than more honest and more optimistic statesmen could ever hope to do. Cavour's ready use of secret funds to bribe the press, of the civil service to secure the election of pro-government deputies, and of the beautiful Countess di Castiglione to seduce Napoleon III, not only began a dangerous tradition in Italian politics but necessarily brought him into open conflict with the austere revolutionary Mazzini. This believer in politics as the art of the impossible spent much of his life in exile in London, dressing always in black and sacrificing, as Denis Mack Smith has bitingly put it, 'personal comfort, the company of his family, and the lives of his friends'. He and Garibaldi were sentenced to death *in absentia* after the discovery in 1833 of the plans of his Young Italy movement to foment revolution; twelve Piedmontese were executed for their association with the plot. Cavour repeatedly expressed the opinion, in private, that the Mazzinian dream of a united Italy was 'a lot of nonsense'. He sent a contingent of Piedmontese troops to the Crimea not to draw the attention of Europe to the plight of Italy but because King Victor Emmanuel (1820–78), thirsting for glory, would otherwise have sacked him. He came to a secret arrangement with Manin and his fellow exiles in Paris not because he shared their views but to split the republican movement. Cavour's secret pact with Napoleon III at Plombières in 1858 was intended to secure the eastward expansion of Piedmont to the Adriatic, and by no means as the first step towards a united Italy. Indeed, he promised Napoleon handsome compensation for his military assistance against the Austrians in the shape of Nice and Savoy and a Central Italian kingdom possibly under the French emperor's cousin—a promise which did not deter him from sending his agents into the central duchies to prepare their annexation by Piedmont. Though the war of 1859 did not go exactly according to plan, Piedmont did double her size within a year to become the largest Italian state by the acquisition of Lombardy and the duchies, and Napoleon did get Nice and Savoy after his troops had marched in to 'arrange' the plebiscite.

The expansion of Piedmont would have halted there but for the miraculous achievements of the swashbuckling Garibaldi and his famous thousand Redshirts. Cavour knew that Napoleon III was already too suspicious of the power of Piedmont to assist in another Austrian war to annex Venetia, that conflict with the Pope might provoke foreign intervention, and that the great southern Kingdom of the Two Sicilies could only be acquired by revolution. Garibaldi's incredible successes first in Sicily and then on the mainland took Cavour completely by surprise and forced his hand. The devotion inspired by this uneducated and simple man, who washed his own shirt and slept in the hay even after occupying the splendid palace at Caserta, led not only the peasants to venerate him as a saint but Hungarian exiles and South American negroes, as well as the son of an English Cabinet minister, to join his band of guerrillas. Though an agnostic, he presided at high mass in Palermo cathedral, sitting on the royal throne dressed in his red shirt and unsheathing his sword when the Gospel was read. Cavour, realizing that the king 'could not accept the crown of Italy at the hands of Garibaldi', invaded the Papal States in defiance of a decree of excommunication and Garibaldi meekly surrendered the dictatorial powers he had assumed over the south to Victor Emmanuel II.

Even after the acquisition of Venetia after the Austro-Prussian war and of Rome during the Franco-Prussian war, the new Italy remained essentially an enlarged version of Piedmont. The word 'annexation' was deliberately used to emphasize the dependence of the south on the north; Victor Emmanuel retained his old dynastic numeral; the Piedmontese *statuto* of 1848 became the constitution of Italy; and the French departmental system of administration was introduced in an attempt to override particularism. This was certainly not the Italy for which Mazzini had been fighting. 'I had thought to evoke the soul of Italy,' he wrote, 'but all I find before me is its corpse.' He died in Pisa in 1872 still hiding from the police, though once he was dead the king unveiled a statue to him in Rome. Garibaldi was even more highly honoured—his bed and other furniture were carefully preserved as national relics—but he was hardly less disillusioned and only occasionally put in an appearance, dressed in his poncho, in parliament. The Catholics, too, were horrified by the loss of the Pope's temporal power, and refused to participate actively in politics until after the Great War. In the south, hatred of the new overlords was so strong that the peasants joined the landowners in a civil war which lasted for four years and cost more lives than the unification wars put together. D'Azeglio in vain urged that the independence of Naples should be restored. All these troubles, coupled with the trauma of the Fascist take-over of 1922, have led many historians to ask whether a federal solution might not have been preferable, or whether Cavour, had he not died prematurely in 1861, might have possessed the skill to solve Italy's problems. One can only say that the history of Germany, where a sort of federalism was tried and where the founder of the new state did survive to rule it for a further twenty years, provides a far from encouraging answer.

Germany: the impact of Napoleon

Napoleon I's impact on the German states was even greater than his impact on Italy. The entire left bank of the Rhine became an integral part of France. Austria and Prussia were allowed to survive, but after the war of 1805–06 they were both deprived of their western territories and forced into still greater dependence on Napoleon. The 'Holy Roman Empire of the German Nation', which Pufendorf had recognized as an 'almost monstrous political system' in the 17th century, collapsed at Napoleon's touch, and with it disappeared the Imperial cities and the Imperial knight-ships and abbeys. At their expense and that of the ecclesiastical principalities, a number of 'middle states' were created, the largest of which—Saxony, Hanover, Bavaria and Württemberg—became monarchies by the grace of the French emperor. These states were linked in a Rhenish Confederation which was totally under French control.

Far from being resented, Napoleon was widely welcomed and admired in Germany by men of such differing political opinions as Goethe, Metternich, Beethoven and Heine. Hegel, who caught a glimpse of the emperor while running through the streets of Jena with the manuscript of *Die Philosophie des Rechts* under his arm, immediately recognized him as the 'world spirit on horseback'. Napoleon had once demonstrated his admiration for Frederick the Great by placing his bust between those of Washington and Mirabeau. His rationalization of German frontiers, his emancipation of serfs and Jews, and his abolition of restrictions on commerce, all earned him firm support. As late as 1914, some Jewish families in southern Germany displayed portraits of the French emperor in their homes.

Even in Austria and Prussia, French reforming influence was inescapable. 'We must do from above what the French have done from below', Hardenberg (1750–1822), Prussian Chancellor, told Frederick William III, his king. Partly because the reforms did not go far enough, but largely because Germany was not yet ready for such thorough-going modernization, the hopes of Stein (1757–1831) of placing Prussia at the head of a German national regeneration did not materialize. The King himself was hardly a German nationalist, his famous edict of 1813 'To My People' still being addressed in the traditional style to 'Brandenburgers, Prussians, Silesians, Pomeranians, Lithuanians'. When General Gneisenau (1760–1831) presented his plans for a popular insurrection against the French, Frederick William remarked coldly, 'Good as poetry'. However, Gneisenau was himself not a nationalist. Twice in 1812 he suggested that England should annex large parts of northern Germany and that 'the peoples thus united with Britannia will feel extremely happy under a free constitution'. (By the same token, when fortunes were reversed, he demanded the annexation to Prussia of Alsace, Lorraine and the Franche Comté, and the extradition and execution of Napoleon.) The same non-nationalist attitude permitted all the German states, including Prussia and Austria, to send contingents to assist Napoleon in his march on Moscow: over half of the *Grande Armée* of 1812 was composed of non-Frenchmen. Even after Napoleon's retreat, the German people did not rise. The 'Battle of the Nations', to which so monstrous a monument was erected at Leipzig a century later, was in fact fought entirely by professional armies.

Romanticism and revolution

In the German intellectual world, however, the story was a different one. The romantic movement with its emphasis on Germany's cultural greatness originated—not entirely by accident—at a time when her political influence was at its lowest ebb. Like J. G. Herder (1744–1803) before him, Friedrich Schlegel (1772–1829) became aware of Germany's peculiar national character while visiting Paris. Friedrich Schiller (1759–1805), in his fragment on *German Greatness*, insisted that the 'German Reich and the German nation are two different things'. The *Nibelungenlied* was rediscovered before the French Revolution, in 1782, but it was during the French occupation of Germany that August Wilhelm Schlegel (1767–1845) prophesied that this ancient poem would become the German *Iliad*. Tieck's edition of the medieval *Minnelieder* appeared in 1803. Two years later Arnim and Brentano published their collection of folk songs under the title *Des Knaben Wunderhorn*. The greatest work of all, the *Kinder- und Hausmärchen* was published by the Grimm brothers (1785–1863; 1786–1859) in 1812–15, to be quickly followed by their edition of *Deutsche Sagen* (1816–18). That nationalism did not run deep even here, however, is shown by the fact that, when the tyrannical elector of Hesse-Cassel returned to his throne, the two Grimms ran alongside his coach cheering.

Few of the writings of the time advocated concrete solutions to Germany's problems. Hegel was perhaps the most realistic when in 1802 he called for a 'Theseus' to unite Germany by force, a sentiment echoed in the conviction of Karl von Clausewitz (1780–1831) that the only way to solve the question of German unity was for one of the states to subjugate all the others by the sword. Many writers were anxious, however, to turn their minds to the problem of how to inspire the German people with greater national fervour. Heinrich von Kleist's (1777–1811) 'Catechism for Germans, composed after the Spanish catechism for the use of children and old people' was written at about the same time as his play *Die Hermannsschlacht* (1808) in which he more or less openly advocated that the Germans should themselves commit atrocities with the aim of attributing them to the French.

The most extreme of all the early German nationalists was 'Father' (*Turnvater*) Friedrich Ludwig Jahn (1778–1852), who was also virtually the only one to try to put his ideas into practice by organizing youth movements of various kinds. Even Heinrich von Treitschke (1834–96) later referred to him as a 'crude peasant' and 'noisy barbarian'. Dressed in his 'true German costume' consisting of a gown of unbleached cloth, his hair and beard flowing, he accompanied the Prussian troops into Paris in 1814 and knocked the tuba from the mouth of the goddess of victory on the Arc de Triomphe. His plans for rousing the German people included the introduction of national festivals to commemorate the great events of Prussian history, the building of monuments on the sites of victorious battles, and, of course, the reform of education on nationalist lines. Jahn hoped to abolish the regular Prussian army and replace it with a national militia. This dream was realized, if only to a limited extent, in the setting up of Lützow's black-uniformed free corps which was ambushed and virtually annihilated in an encounter with German troops of the Rhenish Confederation led by a Württemberg general. In 1810, Jahn founded his first gymnastic society by leading the pupils of his Berlin school on to a heath and instructing them in drill and athletics; these *Turnvereine* soon spread throughout Germany. Jahn's project for reorganizing student life was rejected by Fichte, then rector of Berlin University, as 'un-German'. The first *Burschenschaft* was founded in June 1815 at Jena. On Jahn's suggestion this movement adopted the black, red and gold tricolour symbolizing the struggle out of the black night of servitude, through red blood to the golden day of liberty. It was one of Jahn's disciples, the student Karl Sand, who murdered an anti-nationalist writer with a primitive Germanic dagger in 1819, two years after the Wartburg Festival at which several of Jahn's opponents had been burned in effigy. Jahn even proposed that the future German state should include Switzerland, the Netherlands and Denmark, as well as Prussia and Austria. At the centre of this vast empire a new capital, called Teutonia, was to be built. A century later, Hitler planned to rebuild Berlin as a world capital with the name Germania.

The reinforcement of Prussia's position on the Rhine at the Congress of Vienna, coupled with Austria's failure to re-establish her position there, was the third sign—after the loss of Silesia and

During the first decade of the 19th century the German poets Brentano and Arnim published a collection of old ballads and folk poems under the title 'Des Knaben Wunderhorn' ('The Boy's Magic Horn'). Works such as these, idealizing the heroism and glory of Germany's past, fanned the flames of nationalist ideology.

the collapse of the Holy Roman Empire—that the German balance of power was slowly shifting against Austria and in favour of Prussia. Most of the 'middle states' created by Napoleon were permitted to survive, and set about winning over their new subjects by granting constitutions and ensuring enlightened government. In so far as they succeeded, they created new obstacles in the path of the German unification movement. Where they failed, the newly annexed areas became centres of nationalist feeling, as was the case in Protestant Franconia which had been ceded to Bavaria. The same dissolution of old loyalties and discovery of a new German identity occurred in the towns.

The Paris revolution of 1830 which sparked off a successful Belgian revolt against Dutch rule and a catastrophic Polish rising against Russian domination, also reverberated through Germany. At Hambach on the left bank of the Rhine, a mass meeting in 1832 demonstrated that Jahn's black, red and gold flag had become a truly popular symbol. Metternich's reactionary policies again triumphed, but not for long. The Paris revolution of February 1848 detonated revolutions in Vienna and many other cities. In Berlin, where the street fighting was at its most violent, King Frederick

William IV (1795–1861) was obliged to tour the streets draped in the national tricolour. The Prussian monarchy did not recover the prestige thus lost until 1866.

When the Frankfurt Parliament met in the Paulskirche in May 1848, the triumph of the popular movement seemed complete. But revolution had everywhere stopped at the foot of the throne, with fateful results not only for the cause of liberty but for that of unity as well. Only if the revolutions had swept aside all historic frontiers could a German nation-state based on Herder's concept of *Volk* have emerged. Once the historic frontiers remained in force, the problem of German unity posed itself in all its complexity. The frontiers of the German Confederation itself were of little help in determining the extent of the new state: not only would such obviously German areas as East Prussia have been excluded, but such obviously non-German areas as Czech Bohemia and the Italian Tyrol would have been included.

The German population of Prussia's three eastern provinces had participated in the elections to the Frankfurt Assembly, but what of the Poles living in that area? In 1815, when Prussia was confirmed in her possession of her Polish territories, the king had proclaimed that the Poles 'ought not to deny their nationality', and that to this end 'your language should be used beside German in all public transactions'. These rights had, however, been withdrawn after the Polish uprising of 1830. By 1848 it was clear that Polish nationalism was no longer confined to the landed gentry. If the Poles were still prepared to remain subjects of the King of Prussia, they were not prepared to be submerged in a German nation-state. Among the delegates at Frankfurt, opinion on the Polish question ranged all the way from those who wanted to undo the injustice of the Partitions to those who wished to prevent the emergence of an independent Polish state altogether. Initially, the pro-Polish faction predominated, but only because a war against Russia to liberate all the oppressed nationalities of Eastern Europe seemed imminent. Gradually, opinion shifted in support of the Berlin government's new hard line, partly because the moderates feared an alliance between the Poles and the German republicans, to counter which they would have to rely on Prussian military force. Finally when open fighting broke out between Poles and Germans in Posen, national self-interest triumphed completely over the cosmopolitanism which had been so in evidence in the early days of the revolution.

That the democratic faction which had taken the Polish side in this dispute was by no means indifferent to considerations of national greatness became apparent in the Schleswig-Holstein question. The invasion of Denmark by the Prussian army was greeted with delight in the Paulskirche, and when Prussia withdrew as a result of British and Russian pressure it was the Left which shouted most loudly about 'national honour' and the 'German military spirit'. It is no exaggeration to say that many of the speeches then made at Frankfurt anticipated the demagogic chauvinism of a later epoch in German history.

The most difficult problem of all was, however, that posed by the multi-national Habsburg empire. The inclusion of its German and Czech parts in the new German Reich would have left the eastern half of the Habsburg possessions on the other side of the Leitha either at the mercy of the Magyars or to break up into its component parts, so inviting Russian domination. Basically, the Austrian Germans had to choose between three courses. They could give up the empire in which they still played a leading role to become members of a new German nation-state; they could abandon the new German nation-state to Prussia which would leave them weaker both in Europe and in the Habsburg empire itself; or they could try to establish a firm grip on the Danube monarchy and seek to dominate Germany from Vienna, so creating a vast new state of seventy million people stretching from the Baltic to the Balkans. In the circumstances it was hardly surprising that the rulers in Vienna should opt for the last alternative and reject the Imperial German Crown being proffered by the National Assembly at Frankfurt. Nor was it surprising that the Prussian king should turn down the 'diadem composed of the filth and mud of revolution, of broken loyalty and high treason', for he saw it, not unreasonably, as a 'dog-chain with which they are trying to tie me to the revolution of 1848'. With Frederick William's

The three 'pillars of Austria', as seen by a French satirist after the nationalist risings of 1848: Jellačić, the Croat general commanding the forces that helped to crush the Magyars; Radetzky, who at the age of eighty-three defeated Piedmont at Novara in 1849; and Windischgrätz, who suppressed the revolt in Prague and aided Jellačić in Hungary.

refusal of the crown, the attempt to unite Germany by resolutions and majority decision had failed: there remained only the way of 'iron and blood'.

The Austro–Prussian see-saw

In the struggle for supremacy in Germany which dominated the history of the years between 1849 and 1866, Prussia seemed at first to have the upper hand. While Austria was still busy quelling the Magyars with Russian and Serbo-Croat help, the Prussian army under Prince William, later the German Kaiser (1797–1888), quickly restored order in those states which were eventually to make up the Reich of 1871. On the advice of Radowitz, a Catholic Rhinelander, Frederick William proposed the establishment of a 'German Reich' under Prussian leadership, with which Austria would be only loosely associated in a 'German Union'. Bavaria and Württemberg took fright and appealed to Austria who, with Russian backing, inflicted a humiliating retreat on Prussia.

Now it was Austria's turn to take the lead. Under her 'Iron Chancellor', Prince Schwarzenberg (1800–52), the successor of Metternich, the liberal concessions made in 1848 were withdrawn and a stifling centralization was imposed over the entire Danube monarchy. Using this power as his base, Schwarzenberg set about trying to solve the German problem to Vienna's advantage. To undermine the influence of Prussia, he sought to tighten Austria's hold on the South German middle states and to isolate Prussia diplomatically by retaining the good will of Russia. The 'most important instrument' at his disposal, however, was Bruck's plan for a vast customs union between the Lesser German *Zollverein* and the Habsburg empire. Economic factors now played a decisive part. Prussia and 'Third Germany' were industrially far more advanced than the Austrian lands. By moving steadily towards free trade, Prussia could force the other members of the *Zollverein* to do likewise and so turn against Austria, who because of her weaker economic position could not manage without high tariff walls.

Austria's absurd policy during the Crimean War further weakened her position in two ways. First, by mobilizing her army against Russia she drove that country onto the side of Prussia which had remained strictly neutral. Second, the mobilization itself put such a grave strain on Austria's economy that her currency collapsed. She was therefore in a particularly vulnerable position when the first world-wide recession occurred in 1857. Prussia, meanwhile, was flourishing as never before. In the space of three years the exports of the *Zollverein* reached a level four times as high as those of the Austrian empire. If the cry for still higher tariffs grew ever more insistent in Austria, Prussia could force the pace towards free trade, finally signing the 1862 trade treaty with France which spelled the end of Austria's hopes of breaking into the *Zollverein*. The middle states would for political reasons have preferred the leadership of Vienna; economic reasons forced them into ever-closer dependence upon Berlin.

This series of crises, coupled with the disasters in Italy in 1859, forced Vienna temporarily to make concessions to the historic nationalities within the empire by reviving the provincial diets. The idea of centralization triumphed again in 1861, however, when the *grossdeutsch* politician Schmerling (1805–93) established a Vienna parliament elected by a franchise distinctly favouring the German element. His aim, much like Schwarzenberg's, was to concentrate the power of the Habsburg monarchy under German leadership and then to establish Austria's supremacy over Germany. In 1863, the Emperor Francis Joseph travelled to Frankfurt cheered all the way by enthusiastic crowds, and presented to the German princes a plan for a five-man directorate under his own leadership, and for a German parliament composed of delegates from the state diets. The project was foredoomed to failure. It could hardly satisfy the German nationalists, yet the non-German nations of the Danube monarchy were already vociferously rejecting the idea of German hegemony. Bismarck ruined the entire scheme in any case by dissuading King William I from going to Frankfurt. And he anticipated later developments by proposing the election of an all-German parliament by universal suffrage—an appeal to the national-democratic principle which Austria could not possibly accept.

The accession of William in 1858, when Frederick William IV became insane, roused the quite unwarranted hope among German liberals that Prussia would reform herself and then proceed to make 'moral conquests' in Germany. Events in Italy during the following two years, together with the centenary celebrations of Schiller's birth in 1859, clearly revealed that the masses were becoming increasingly involved in politics: countless singing and gymnastic societies were formed, mass rallies held, and new political movements started. A series of elections to the Prussian diet reduced the Conservatives to a mere handful of deputies, and if Bismarck had not been there to save him, William I might well have abdicated in face of the popular storm against his reactionary Army Bill.

Bismarck and the Second Reich

Cavour had been taken unawares by the successes of the nationalist movement, but had managed at the last moment to capture the movement for his own ends. Bismarck, on the other hand, was always in supreme control of the situation. His invasion (with Austria) of Denmark in 1864 appealed to the nationalists in Germany now as in 1848. His summoning in 1866 of a Lesser German parliament elected by universal male suffrage was a direct challenge to the Liberal opposition, to the German princes, and especially to Austria. That the elections to the Prussian diet were held on a 'high-tide of national enthusiasm' on the very day of the battle of Königgrätz was not entirely an accident, and those Liberals who had proclaimed themselves 'sick of principles and doctrines' and interested only in 'Power, Power, Power' found little trouble in coming to terms with Bismarck after Prussia's decisive victory. Had the war against Austria gone badly for Prussia, Bismarck was quite prepared to call on the Italian, Serb, Roumanian, Polish, Magyar and Czech nationalists to rise against Vienna and St Petersburg.

If his aim four years later in 1870 was not to provoke a war against France at all costs, he certainly did nothing to avoid war when the opportunity presented itself. The annexation of Alsace and Lorraine was not, as historians have long believed, forced upon him by military and nationalist pressures: he himself gave the orders to begin the propaganda campaign in favour of annexation. And when even the massive popular enthusiasm unleashed by the Franco-Prussian war proved insufficient to persuade the Bavarian king to join the new Reich, Bismarck solved the problem simply by bribing him with money sequestered from the King of Hanover whose lands Prussia had annexed in 1866.

Bismarck's new Reich was, however, full of contradictions. By forcibly excluding the Austrian Germans, he had divided Germany rather than united her. As the Austrian poet Franz Grillparzer (1791–1872) bitterly observed, 'You think you have created an empire, when all you have really done is destroyed a nation.' Support within the Reich for separatism and the *grossdeutsch* solution disappeared with surprising rapidity after 1871, at least until the Pan-German League revived such ideas in an altered form towards the end of the century. Nevertheless, the separate states within the Reich mostly continued in existence, and both Bismarck and his successors were always acutely aware of the danger that Austria might yet attempt to prise the southern states away from Prussian control. The problem posed by the national minorities was no less grave. If the Lithuanians and Masurs who together made up 30 per cent of the population of East Prussia as yet had no national consciousness, this was hardly true of the nearly three million Poles living in West Prussia and Posen, and of the Danes who composed 15 per cent of the inhabitants of Schleswig. Inverting Herder's doctrine that states should be refounded on the basis of nations, the Prusso-German government attempted to Germanize the minority nationalities which fell within Prussia's frontiers. However, all its efforts—which began with the enforcement of German as the official language and ended with virtual acceptance of the programme of the racialist *Ostmarkenverein*—met with the reverse of success. In Alsace-Lorraine, linguistic and historical criteria supported the German annexation. The trouble was that the Alsatians felt themselves to be so much citizens of France that even at the Frankfurt National Assembly in 1848—where some delegates had proposed the extension of the German empire to include Rhodes, Cyprus and Crete—no one had seriously suggested that Alsace and Lorraine belonged to Germany. These internal tensions were so severe that Burckhardt feared as early as 1872 that there might be 'a new war as the only possible diversion from home affairs'.

The uncertain national identity of the Second Reich was reflected in its ceremonies and symbols. The subsidiary role played by the nationalist movement in creating a German state was epitomized by the exclusion of the elected representatives of the people from the ceremony at Versailles in which William I of Prussia was proclaimed 'German Emperor'. The constitution of 1871 was not only virtually unworkable; it was anything but designed to serve as a symbol of national unity in the manner of the American and French constitutions. There was not even at first a national flag. The revolutionary tricolour was obviously unacceptable to Bismarck, but the new Imperial tricolour of black-white-red (in which the Prussian colours of black and white significantly predominated) was not officially adopted until 1892, and when this national cockade was introduced into the army in 1897, there was a storm of protest from the Bavarians. There was similar uncertainty about the national anthem. Initially, the nationalist *Die Wacht am Rhein* was sung together with the Prussian monarchist anthem *Heil Dir im Siegerkranz*, which used the tune of *God save the King*. In the 1890s, *Deutschland über Alles* became increasingly popular, but it was not officially recognized as the German anthem until the Socialist president of the Weimar Republic proclaimed it as such in 1922. This particular song was in any event not exactly fitting to the Prussian-dominated Reich, its music having been composed by Haydn for a Habsburg emperor, and its words by a revolutionary nationalist on the British island of Heligoland in 1841.

The style of the national monuments which were now erected, like that to Hermann in the Teutoburg forest (1875), evoked the primitive Germanic past; others, like the statue of William I erected on the Kyffhäuser mountain and the countless Bismarck-towers which were put up after Bismarck's death, aimed at reviving medieval legends. There was not so much as an official national holiday in Germany. The celebration of Sedan Day (September 2nd) was begun by a group of Protestant pastors in 1873, but always met with strong protests from the Catholics and Socialists because of its militaristic connotations. The feast of January 18th, the anniversary of the Kaiser Proclamation of 1871, became popular only after the empire's disappearance in 1918. The Kaiser's birthday was probably the most widely-observed holiday, though the title of Kaiser was hated by William I himself.

International reactions: international relations

The emergence of so powerful yet so unstable an empire in the heart of Europe not unnaturally perturbed many observers. Benjamin Disraeli spoke in the English House of Commons of a 'German revolution' whose consequences would be at least as serious as those of the great French Revolution. No country, however, was more directly affected than Germany's multi-national neighbour to the south-east. It is true that Bismarck had prevented William I and the Prussian generals from establishing an 'East Roman empire'—as he sarcastically called it—at Austria's expense. It is equally true that the repercussions of Königgrätz did not fully emerge in Austria until after the end of the Liberal era in 1879. The Saxon Beust (1809–86), who dominated Vienna politics after 1866, actually tried to form an anti-Prussian coalition with France and Italy to wrest Silesia from Prussia and establish an Austrian protectorate over the South German states. And even after the failure of these plans—the execution of Francis Joseph's brother in Mexico in 1867 had hardly contributed to harmonious relations between Vienna and Paris—the Austrian Liberals were able to carry through an extensive modernization programme in the western cisleithanian half of the monarchy. Gradually, however, the Germans of Austria realized that the events of 1866 and 1871 had left them a minority in the Habsburg dominions, and as this realization grew, so did their susceptibility to a radical and racial nationalism which was to become all too familiar to the world in the twentieth century through the speeches and writings of a man who first saw the light of day in the Austrian-German border town of Braunau on 20 April 1889.

The Königgrätz disaster brought the negotiations between Vienna and Budapest for an *Ausgleich*, or Compromise, to a speedy conclusion. Francis Joseph agreed to his coronation in Budapest with the crown of St Stephen, and the Magyars gained full internal control over the eastern half of the empire. There, the moderate attitude of Déak and Eötvös, which had inspired the granting of autonomous status to the Kingdom of Croatia in 1868, soon gave way to a ruthless Magyarization policy whose only effect, however, was to stiffen the resistance of the Germans, Slovaks, Roumanians, Croats and Serbs who were its victims. Magyar nationalism reached its emotional climax in the celebration of the 'millennium' of Hungarian power on the Danube in 1896.

The 1867 Compromise may indeed have been, as the Hungarian historian Miskolczy has claimed, the only possible arrangement whereby Austria-Hungary might maintain the status of a Great Power. That it aggravated the nationality problem in the western half of the monarchy is, however, hardly to be doubted. By granting special status to Galicia in April 1871, Vienna succeeded in attracting the loyalty of the Poles. But the Czechs, who went into total opposition for a decade and a half after the signing of the *Ausgleich*, were not won over. The emperor promised to undergo coronation with the Crown of St Wenceslas in Prague, and announced a new Nationalities Bill which would give equal civil rights to Czechs and Germans in Bohemia. Yet the violent opposition of the Magyars and Germans, coupled with the danger that if the latter were disaffected they would look increasingly to Berlin, finally persuaded Francis Joseph to abandon his plans, to the bitter disappointment of the Czechs. German fears of the higher Czech and Slovene birthrate and of Slav immigration into hitherto German areas led to growing demands for a withdrawal from such Slav areas as Galicia and Dalmatia in the hope that the German element would then retain a dominant position vis-à-vis the Czechs, Slovenes and Italians in the remainder of Cisleithania. It was by opposing the occupation of Bosnia and Hercegovina out of such considerations that the Austro-German Liberals committed political suicide in 1879.

In opposition, the Austrian Germans became ever more radical. They strongly opposed the granting of equal status by Taaffe (1833–95), who was premier from 1879 to 1893, to the Czech language in Bohemia in 1880, and the partitioning of Prague university into a Czech and German half two years later. The full horror of the Czech-German conflict revealed itself in the mass violence provoked by the attempt of Badeni (1846–1909) in 1897 to introduce the principle of bilingualism into public administration in Bohemia and Moravia. The Germans of the Second Reich took a lively part in the controversy, the senile Professor Theodor Mommsen (1817–1903), historian of the Roman Empire, jettisoning his liberal principles to the point where he declared that Czech skulls were better suited to receiving blows than ideas. Nationalism was indeed, as Grillparzer observed, entering the 'phase of bestiality'. Frightened by the violence, Francis Joseph dismissed Badeni, prorogued Parliament and eventually withdrew the language ordinances. If the German nationalists were triumphant at their victory, the Czechs were now finally convinced that they would achieve nothing by looking to Vienna. The disgraceful scenes in parliament during the crisis contributed heavily to the lasting disaffection of many Central Europeans from the system of parliamentary democracy. One other result of the crisis was the flowering of an outstanding literature on the nationality problem, which was to make an impression—for good or ill—on the minds of such diverse inhabitants of Vienna as Hitler and Herzl, Trotsky and Stalin, Tito, Masaryk and De Gasperi. This was the Vienna which Karl Kraus (1874–1936) termed an *Experimentierlager für Weltuntergänge*, a camp for trying out ways of ending the world.

In the Russian empire, too, the principle of nationality was gaining ground. It was no coincidence that the Pan-Slav Congress met in Moscow in 1867, the year of the Austro-Magyar *Ausgleich*, or that the 'bible of Pan-Slavism', Danilevsky's *Russia and Europe*, was written at this same time. The policy of Russification, which Uvarov had applied to Lithuania after the 1839 Polish revolt, was extended into Poland itself after the 1863 rebellion. The Church, the courts, and the civil administration were brought under the direct control of the St Petersburg bureaucrats. Warsaw university was closed, and when it reopened in 1869 as a Russian university, Polish lecturers were given two years in which to learn the Russian language if they wished to go on teaching. By 1892, instruction in the Polish language was completely prohibited even in primary schools. Small wonder, perhaps, that the imaginative William II of Germany could now believe that 'in the event of a war with Russia the whole of Poland would revolt and come over to my side with the express intention of being annexed by me'. In the Ukraine, where the first stirrings of a cultural nationalism occurred in the 1870s, the authorities also clamped down by prohibiting all publications, dramas and song-recitals in Ukrainian.

The hardest hit of all the minorities in the Russian empire were the five million Jews who were compelled to live in the western area known as the Pale. Far from preventing the pogroms which broke out after the assassination of Alexander II (1818–81), the government added fuel to the flames by issuing the 'Temporary Rules' severely restricting the entry of Jews into schools and universities and the legal and medical professions. Count Pahlen's recommendations to the effect that the Jews could and should be emancipated and assimilated were ignored; instead, Pobedonostsev (1827–1907), bitterly opposed both to Western liberalism and to Russian nonconformity, seemed to speak for the government when he said that one third would be assimilated, another third emigrate, and the rest die. In these conditions it was hardly surprising that the Jewish intelligentsia should turn to revolutionary socialism or to the nationalism propagated by Theodor Herzl (1860–1904) at the first Zionist Congress in Basel in 1897 and in his booklet *Der Judenstaat* (1896).

The policy of Russification was applied to the Baltic provinces in the late 1880s. Russian was introduced as the teaching language in all but the lowest classes of the primary schools in 1887. In 1893, the old and famous German University at Dorpat was closed down, to be reopened with a Russian name and a largely Russian student body. A big drive by the Orthodox Church to convert the Baltic peoples, 90 per cent of whom were Protestants, succeeded in alienating the Latvians and Estonians who would otherwise have welcomed Russian support against the dominant German minority. Pobedonostsev even expressed the hope that Latvian mothers would one day sing Russian cradle-songs to their babies. When similar measure were enforced in Finland and Finland's autonomous status abolished by decree in 1899, both the Finns and the Swedes offered complete passive resistance; with the assassination

Until 1853 Japan was closed to all foreign shipping except the Dutch, who were allowed a limited right of trade. But in July of that year a US naval squadron under Commodore Perry entered Edo Bay (left). Next year he returned and a treaty of peace and friendship was signed.

Right: symbols of the new nationalism of Japan, nourished on the struggle against China (1894–95). Just as in Europe, this was a period of revived interest in early literature and sports (such as wrestling), of patriotic songs and of aggressive nationalist ideologies.

of the Russian General Bobrikov in 1904, Russia and Finland were practically at war. Finland, however regained her autonomy in 1905 (the year in which Norway achieved independence from Sweden).

The Ottoman Empire

The cultural and linguistic nationalism which appeared to threaten the integrity of the Russian empire at the end of the nineteenth century had by that time contributed considerably to the break-up of the weakest of the three great empires, Turkey. Serbian scholars like Karadžić (1787–1864) had won the admiration of Goethe and Jakob Grimm for their collection of folk songs, fairy tales and epic poems. Similar work was done by the Greeks Korais (1748–1833) and Rhigas (1760–98), who composed the Greek national anthem, both of whom had studied in Paris. Roumanian national consciousness was similarly awakened largely by wealthy students returning from the West and emphasizing the 'Latinity' of Roumanian culture. The Bulgarian language was virtually unknown even to philologists in 1800. The first modern work to appear in the language was a history of the Bulgarians written by the monk Paysios in 1762. The Slovak scholar George Venelin (1802–39) had the words 'Awakener of Bulgaria' inscribed on his tomb for his efforts to revive the dormant national awareness.

Nevertheless, religious and ethnic divisions in the mountainous Balkans were so confused that the Sultan might well have resisted demands for independence more successfully had it not been for the frequent rival intervention of the Great Powers. When the Serbs revolted against the unruly Janissaries in 1804, for instance, they were saved from being crushed by Turkish troops only by the intervention of the Russian army. A Greek rebellion begun by Prince Ypsilanti (1792–1828) in the Roumanian Principalities in 1821 failed (despite the support of the secret but numerically strong *Hetairia Philike* movement) because the Roumanians disliked the distant Sultan less than the Greek administrators and merchants close at hand. The rising in southern Greece in that same year enjoyed, it is true, an astonishing initial success. Soon, however, the Turks retaliated in the most brutal fashion. On Easter Sunday, 1821, the Greek Patriarch of Constantinople was hanged in his sacred vestments from his palace gates, and in the following year the entire population of the island of Chios was either slaughtered or sold into slavery. When the efficient Egyptian army under Ibrahim Pasha (1789–1848) reached Missolonghi, where Lord Byron had earlier died, thousands of Greeks lost their lives while trying to break out of the Turkish encirclement, and many others blew themselves up with gunpowder rather than surrender. This terrible bloodshed finally provoked the Powers to intervene. The Anglo-French navy sank the Egyptian fleet at Navarino, and when a Russian army once more bore down upon Constantinople in 1829, the Turks were forced to grant independence to a small Greek kingdom under a Bavarian monarch and to give autonomous status to the Serbs.

That foreign intervention could also work against national independence became evident when the Russian troops at first refused to leave Roumania after the invasion of 1829, and when a

Russian protectorate which was to last up to the Crimean War was established there. The Roumanians gained a staunch champion in Napoleon III, however, who was anxious both to demonstrate his concern for nationality and to strengthen the French position in Eastern Europe. French influence proved of great importance in securing the election in 1859 of Alexander Cuza as ruler of both Principalities. In 1866, when the Powers were again preoccupied with a major war, the name of Roumania was adopted by a national assembly, even though formal independence was not attained until 1877–78.

Great Power rivalry also proved decisive in the emergence of a Bulgarian state. Revolts in the remote Turkish provinces of Bosnia and Hercegovina in 1875 sparked off a massive wave of Pan-Slav enthusiasm in Russia. Countless nationalist meetings echoed writers like Dostoevsky in calling for the liberation of the Balkan peninsula, the destruction of Turkey, and the annexation of Constantinople and the Straits. The Russian government allowed even high-ranking officers to join volunteer forces. Eventually, in 1877, formal war began between Russia and Turkey and the latter was once again compelled to sue for peace. The Treaty of San Stephano momentarily gave Russia hegemony over the Balkans. Serbia, Montenegro and Roumania were declared independent; Russia advanced to the mouth of the Danube; a Great Bulgaria, stretching from the Black Sea almost to the Adriatic, was created; and Turkey was left with a few scattered and indefensible possessions. This settlement proved unacceptable to the other Powers, so that Russia was forced, under the threat of war against another Crimean coalition, to submit the Balkan question to the Congress of Berlin in 1878. There, Bulgaria was reduced to half its planned size, and divided into two halves, one of which gained autonomous status, the other (Eastern Roumelia) remaining a Turkish province under a Christian governor. This arrangement was undone in 1885, when a group of Bulgarian nationalists seized power in Eastern Roumelia and Alexander of Battenberg (1857–93) agreed—despite violent Russian hostility—to become ruler of a united Bulgaria.

Even after the emergence of these five new states in the Balkans, the situation remained tense and confused. The conflicting ambitions of Bulgaria, Greece and Serbia in Macedonia foreshadowed not only a further war against Turkey, but a war of all against all in which, in keeping with the Balkan tradition, countless innocents would die. Roumania had designs both on Russian Bessarabia and on Hungarian Transylvania. Serbia entertained the ambition of becoming the Piedmont of Dalmatia by uniting the Serbs, Croats and Slovenes of the Austro-Hungarian Monarchy under her rule. It was when the Great Powers for once proved unable or unwilling to control this situation that the lights went out all over Europe. When they went on again, the nation-state principle had triumphed —for the time being, at least—in Eastern Europe, too.

Japan: the East westernized

Outside Europe and North America there was only one country which could claim to be a modern nation state by the end of the 19th century, and this was Japan. The Tokugawa shoguns or military rulers had held effective power in the country since the early 17th century, but they had been able to maintain that power only by imposing social stagnation at home and almost complete seclusion in foreign affairs, and by the mid-19th century their position was being seriously undermined on both fronts. In July 1853, Commodore Matthew C. Perry (1794–1858) of the United States Navy dealt a fatal blow to feudalism in Japan by sailing his four 'black ships' into Edo Bay and insisting that the shogunate open its ports to foreign shipping. Before long an armed rebellion, led by the western clans of Choshu and Satsuma and supported by the new merchant class of Osaka as well as by the ancient nobility at the Imperial Court at Kyoto, succeeded in defeating the *samurai* armies of the shogun and restoring the emperor to his former glory. Early in 1869, the boy-emperor Meiji and his Court moved in procession from Kyoto to Edo, now renamed Tokyo, to the sound of *The British Grenadiers* played by the regimental band of the British garrison at Yokohama. This strange admixture of old and new, this 'highly nervous, vivid compound of love and hate' for Western civilization was to provide, as Richard Storry has said, the central theme of modern Japanese history.

Though starting from very different premises, the hectic modernization programme of the Meiji Restoration followed the European pattern remarkably closely. The first step was to abolish feudalism and establish central control. The lords of the western clans determined in 1869 to 'offer up all our feudal possessions . . . so that uniform rule may prevail throughout the Empire. Thus the country will be able to rank equally with the other nations of the world'. When the other feudal lords had done likewise, Japan was divided into prefectures administered by prefects appointed from Tokyo. Elected prefectural assemblies and town and village councils were introduced in 1878 and 1880 respectively. As the great statesman Prince Ito (1841–1909) put it, the Japanese people were 'slowly but steadily led to extend their vision beyond the pale of their village communities, to look upon the affairs of their districts and prefectures as their own, until finally they could interest themselves in the affairs of state and nation as strongly as, or even more strongly than, in the affairs of their own villages'. Finally, in 1890, a Constitution modelled in many respects on those of Prussia and Germany (Ito himself had visited Berlin to meet Bismarck and hear the lectures of Rudolf von Gneist) was granted by the Emperor. The electorate was strictly limited by tax qualifications to one per cent of the population; the assembly met for only three months in the year and possessed not even the right to reject the budget; the Cabinet was composed of the Emperor's nominees and was not responsible to parliament; and the Army and Navy departments were always headed by service officers. Nevertheless, the electorate gradually expanded as the country grew richer, and the government's early attempts to secure a majority by violence and bribery proved so unsuccessful that, in 1900, Ito felt compelled to step into the political arena and found his own party.

Japan's successful industrialization was largely the result of deliberate government policy. To avoid succumbing to foreign penetration, capital was raised by taxing the land rather than by borrowing abroad. At the same time, however, large numbers of foreign experts were induced to come to Japan as teachers and technical advisers, and Japanese students were sent abroad to learn foreign techniques. By 1884, most industrial enterprises were sufficiently established to allow the government to hand them over to the huge financial combines called *zaibatsu;* only the military industries were retained under state control. Conscription had been introduced in 1872, thus breaking the *samurai* monopoly of the military virtues while at the same time encouraging the feeling of national unity among the population at large. Of vital importance in the latter respect was the introduction, also in 1872, of compulsory primary education. By the beginning of the 20th century, 95 per cent of children of school age were receiving primary education—a remarkable achievement. The government at first banned many of the outward signs of the feudal past, prohibiting, for example, the wearing of swords and of the top-knot hairstyle. A British architect was commissioned to build the Hall of the Baying Stag which was to act as the centre for huge social gatherings of the Western type. In 1880, when it was discovered that all self-respecting Occidental nations had a national anthem, the German bandmaster of the British troops at Yokohama was invited to set the words of a 9th-century hymn to the Imperial House to music. Western dress was worn by many Japanese, and there were some who went so far as to advocate the substitution of bread for rice as the staple diet. By the late 1880s, a distinct reaction against Westernization set in, but even in seeking to return to indigenous values, Japan was following the Western pattern.

Modern Japanese nationalism had its origins in the late Tokugawa period, when several scholars worked to revive the ancient mythology centring around the Sun Goddess Amaterasu Omikami, from whom the emperors claimed descent: the imperial standard of the golden chrysanthemum was in all probability derived from the sun-symbol which featured in the national flag. The Shinto religion, which stressed undying obedience to the emperor, Japan's divine mission to conquer, and the superlative virtues of the Japanese nation, was given official sponsorship immediately after the Meiji Restoration; in 1899 the instruction of all other religions was banned. In 1890, the year in which the Constitution was granted, the Imperial Rescript on Education enshrined these principles as the basis of the entire Japanese educational system. The people were exhorted: 'offer yourselves courageously to the State' so as to 'guard and maintain the prosperity of Our Imperial Throne coeval with heaven and earth'. Each school was presented with a copy of the Rescript, which was kept in a shrine next to a portrait of the emperor and read to the pupils on national days. Military drill became part of the curriculum, and teachers were granted the status of civil servants. The new martial spirit was also evidenced in the publication of songs like 'Come, foes, come' (1888) and 'Though the enemy be tens of thousands strong' (1891), which gained enormous popularity in the feverish atmosphere produced by the Sino-Japanese war in 1894–95. The appearance of Ochiai's *Complete Collection of Japanese Literature* in 1890 revived interest in the classics and helped to shift the emphasis away from Westernization towards the preservation of national values. On a more mundane level, wrestling rather than baseball established itself as the national sport, and the old *samurai* ideology of *bushido* came to enjoy much popularity. After her recognition as an equal of the Great Powers in the Anglo-Japanese alliance of 1902, and her astonishing victories in the Russo-Japanese war of 1904–05, Japan became, for a time at least, the inspiration of nationalists elsewhere in Asia. Toyama Mitsuru, the fanatical leader of ultra-nationalist secret societies like the 'Genyosha' and 'The Black Dragon', was frequently visited in Tokyo by delegations from China, India and the Philippines. In Asia as in Europe, nationalism was Janus-faced, encouraging at one and the same time unbridled aggression and a burning desire for liberation from alien rule.

A German artist's impression of old and new Japan towards the end of the 19th century.

VII WAR AND PEACE

Mechanized warfare and the growth of pacifism

BRIAN BOND

*'We see, therefore, that War is not merely a
political act, but also a real political instrument,
a continuation of political commerce,
a carrying out of the same by other means.'*

CLAUSEWITZ: 'On War'

The French revolutionary spirit,

which created so much that was new in social and political institutions, also created a new concept of an army: 'the nation in arms'. In the hands of Napoleon the French army was to become the greatest instrument of conquest since the Roman Empire. Yet it began as a force for defence. By the summer of 1792 emigré nobles outside France were organizing troops and collecting allies for an invasion; the king was said to be plotting with the Habsburgs; the cry was *'la patrie en danger'* — and it was true. The first Revolutionary wars, against Austria and against Prussia, were waged by men lacking in discipline and training, but fired by the idea that the cause for which they were fighting was their own. Something of their enthusiasm is captured by Cogniet in his painting (opposite) of the volunteer National Guards under the authority of the city of Paris who took the place of the old Royal Guards in June 1792. It was the same enthusiasm which produced the *Marseillaise* and the victories of Valmy and Jemappes. These campaigns, under Dumouriez, are often taken to mark the beginning of modern warfare.

To turn the raw volunteer into the drilled and efficient National Guardsman was the work of several years. In 1796 the ragged army of the French (*above*, a sketch made '*d'après nature*') was no match for the Austrians. But by 1804, the Imperial Guard (*above right*) had been formed as the chosen instrument of the Napoleonic system. Napoleon was a military genius whose innovations affected every aspect of war. *Right*: he visits the siege works outside Danzig in 1807. His methods, however, could be learned and used against him, notably by Wellington in the Peninsula. *Below right*: the siege of Burgos in 1812.

The Crimean War ended forty years of peace in Europe. The generals were old and out of practice and neither England nor France had any experience of large-scale operations so far from home. As a result, the horrors off the battlefield eclipsed those on it. Sevastopol eventually fell, after nearly a year's siege, in September, 1855. *Opposite above*: one of the battered Russian gun-emplacements. The confusion in the Russian army was, if anything, rather worse than that among the Allies; it has been estimated that two out of every three recruits died before they reached the front. *Opposite below*: one of the British field kitchens, introduced towards the end of the war, when conditions generally improved.

Napoleon's battles became textbook examples for students of warfare throughout the century, remarkable both for the variety of problems they presented and for Napoleon's invention in solving them. At **Wagram**, in 1809 (*above*), the front was eight miles long and the fighting lasted for two days. **Jena**, 1806 (*opposite*, a detail from the painting by Vernet) was perhaps his greatest victory, decisively crushing the power of Prussia. But at **Waterloo**, 1815, (*below*) he faced Wellington, his temperamental opposite: calculating, cool, and inflexible.

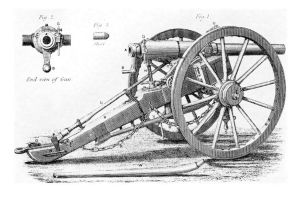

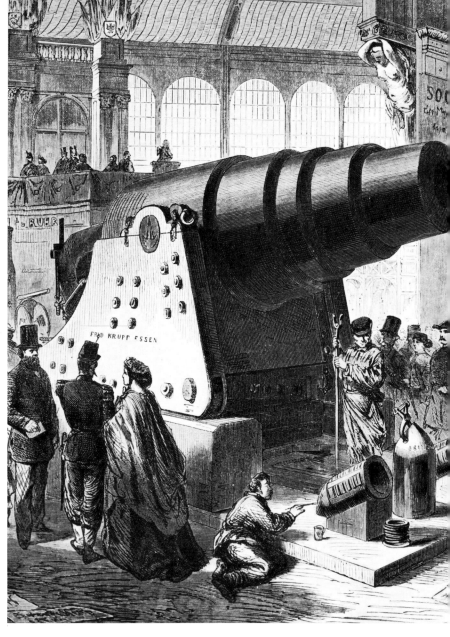

The Krupp Works at Essen provided Prussia with new weapons on an unprecedented scale. The huge gun shown at the Paris Exhibition of 1867 (*above*) was to be used against the city in another three years. A slightly later model introduced breech-loading.

The face of war changed more radically in the sixty years after Waterloo than it had done in the previous six hundred. In 1824, old-fashioned smoothbore, muzzle-loading cannons were still the rule. *Top*: a 32-pounder complete with its rammer and sponge. Before long, rifling and breech-loading was increasing speed and accuracy at long range. *Above centre*: Armstrong's 12-pounder field-gun of 1859. Rapid-fire weapons began as artillery (*above*: a French '*canon à balles*') but were to develop as small-arms, the forerunner of the modern machine-gun. *Right*: the French *mitrailleuse* might have turned the scales of the War of 1870 if the troops had been trained to use it.

The fire-power of machine-guns was not fully appreciated until 1914. In the Franco-Prussian war the French had used them like field-guns, where they were no match for the heavier pieces, rather than as infantry support weapons. These three examples show the machine gun's gradual development into an infantry weapon. *Left*: the French Montigny gun, 1870. *Centre*: the American Gatling, perfected in 1862 and used at the end of the Civil War; it fired 350 shots a minute. *Right*: the Maxim, the first truly automatic machine gun, invented in the eighties. The recoil movement ejected the spent cartridge, reloaded and fired.

War under the sea, attempted as early as 1800, was a practical possibility by mid-century, after which submarines evolved rapidly. The *Garrett* (below), invented by the Rev. G.W. Garrett, managed to remain under water for prolonged periods, its crew supplied with oxygen chemically. *Bottom left*: the *Holland*, an American model of 1898. By 1906 (*bottom right*), the familiar outlines of the submarine, with its periscope and conning tower, had already made its appearance.

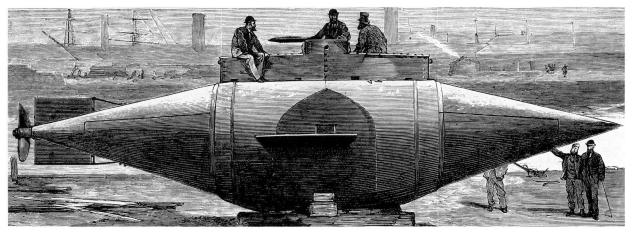

Steam and iron revolutionized naval strategy. The three battles illustrated here show the rapid replacement of wood by iron. *Top*: Lissa, 1866, the first large-scale encounter between iron-clads – eleven Italian and seven Austrian, ending in an Austrian victory. *Centre*: Santiago, 1898, when the United States defeated the Spanish Atlantic Fleet. *Bottom*: Tsushima, 1905, when the Russian Baltic fleet, having sailed round the world, was easily beaten by Japan's more modern navy.

Mechanized warfare and the growth of pacifism

BRIAN BOND

It was before the rise of the 19th-century nation state that Europe went through its most general and its most protracted war for a hundred years. Not surprisingly, contemporaries wondered whether the 19th century would be a century of war. Clausewitz, revising his manuscript *On War* shortly before his death from cholera in 1831, feared that barriers once torn down could never easily be set up again: provided great issues were at stake, fighting of Napoleonic intensity would probably recur.

In the short run this analysis seemed mistaken. Not a single great war occurred in the forty years after Waterloo, and even then the first conflicts involving major powers exhibited many of the characteristics of 18th-century warfare. Throughout the century Europe, for all its national wars, avoided cataclysm. A. J. P. Taylor has written of a 'perpetual quadrille of the balance of power' and has pointed out that for all the 'ups and downs' of individual countries, including the new nation states, there was no such 'whirligig of fortune' among the powers that mattered as there had been in the 18th century. 'The Great Powers who launched the First World War in 1914 were the Great Powers who had made up the Congress of Vienna in 1814. Prussia had changed her name to Germany. Apart from this, Metternich and Castlereagh, Talleyrand and Alexander I would have recognized the European landmarks'. Yet the landmarks were not all that mattered. The facts of power themselves were changing. Already during the last decade of the century there was scope for what Bernard Brodie has aptly called 'the dizzying impact of science and the industrial revolution upon tactics and strategy'.

The 19th century can be considered naturally in four phases— the Napoleonic Wars; the period of peace between 1815 and 1854, during which the industrial revolution exerted enormous influence on the tools of destruction; the years between 1854 and 1870 when the impact of these changes can be noted in a series of major wars; and the last thirty years of the century which, though generally peaceful, were characterized by military preparations of unprecedented scale and intensity.

The nation in arms

The French Revolutionary and Napoleonic wars cast a long shadow into the 19th century; indeed the French army was still obsessed with the Napoleonic myth in 1914. Though personal memories of these wars faded, their professional relevance was constantly reiterated in the writings of military historians and critics. Outstanding among these, both in his output and influence, was the Swiss-born Baron Antoine-Henri de Jomini (1779–1869) who had gained first-hand knowledge of war on the headquarters staff of a Napoleonic army corps. Jomini's primary interest in military history and the operational techniques and principles of war was more to the taste of professional students of the Crimean era than Clausewitz's more philosophical emphasis and concern with the non-rational elements of organized violence. In any case Clausewitz's works were not widely published and translated until his name was made fashionable by Prussia's victories in the 1860s.

Perhaps Clausewitz's most valuable perception was that the superiority of the French Revolutionary armies lay less in purely military innovations—important though those were—than in the release of the nation's energy and enthusiasm through the means of the *levée en masse*. In contrast to the 'clockwork figures and mechanical puppets' of the 18th-century dynastic armies, war for the French again became 'a matter for the people as a whole, took on an entirely different nature, or rather approached more nearly to its true nature, its absolute perfection'. Universal conscription, introduced in principle in France in 1793, though never in practice fully implemented, rapidly swelled the standing army from 255,000 in 1791 (including about 100,000 volunteers) to 732,000 men by April 1794. For several years, until their revolutionary idealism was eroded by war-weariness and the advent of military despotism, the French armies marched and fought with a speed and an *élan* which proved to be beyond the reach of their opponents.

Yet, vital though these qualities were, the basic soundness of the French military machine should not be under-estimated. Once the militarily incompetent or politically suspect officers of the Royalist army had been removed—and no less than 593 generals were cashiered in 1792–93—the remarkably young French generals, who included Napoleon, had in their hands the best military system in Europe. Mathematics and engineering were already proficiently taught at the cadet colleges, and the Revolutionary government founded the Ecole Polytechnique in 1794. Striking improvements had been made in communications by road and water, and up-to-date military maps were also available. The reforms of Gribeauval, when Inspector-General of Ordnance after 1763, had made French artillery second to none. He reduced the miscellaneous variety of cannon to a few basic types which were designed with interchangeable parts to facilitate mass production. Gun carriages were built to a standard model, and mobility was increased by harnessing the horses in pairs instead of in file. Without these and other reforms in organization and drill regulations the nation in arms of 1793–95 would have remained an armed horde.

The undisciplined characteristics of the early Revolutionary armies have received too much emphasis. Admittedly the earliest raw conscripts were thrown into battle inadequately drilled and disciplined; they could not be relied upon to carry out complicated tactical movements nor to maintain a stolid alignment while discharging volleys at point blank range. Their natural tendency was to advance in dense columns for mutual support and, under fire, to rush forward impetuously to get to grips with the enemy. Commanders moreover, conscious of the vast reservoir of man-power, were inclined to accept heavy casualties by launching repeated assaults which would have been unthinkable for the smaller and less easily replaceable armies of the era of Frederick the Great.

Recent research has laid more stress on the continuity of developments in military organization and tactics from the end of the Seven Years War in 1763. There was, for example, long before the Revolutionary skirmishers, a strong European tradition of élite light troops, such as Jägers and Pandours, who were privileged, as highly skilled scouts and marksmen with distinctive green uniforms, to fight in loose formations ahead or on the flanks of the main body. The essential point is that the Revolutionary armies did not remain an unskilled horde for very long. Shabbily dressed and ill-fed the troops may have been, but in essentials Napoleon inherited in 1796 a very efficient military machine.

The Napoleonic inheritance

Similarly there was nothing original about the organizational key to the mobility of Napoleon's armies. The Duc de Broglie had experimented with the permanent organization of his army into divisions at the end of the Seven Years War. A division was in effect an army in miniature which moved independently and was strong enough to defend itself until the rest of the army could come up in support. Napoleon's genius was displayed in the boldness with which he developed and applied this means to strategic flexibility. His independent columns advanced, in Liddell Hart's striking simile, 'like the waving tentacles of an octopus', and when one column was attacked or contacted the enemy the others would rapidly close upon their prey. This method added a new dimension to the commander-in-chief's functions in that his strategy had to be broadly determined before the strategic approach march began, and also because a great deal of responsibility devolved upon the column commanders and their staffs. In the hands of a master, like Napoleon or, later, Moltke (1800–91), this articulation of the mass army could be employed to paralyze the opposing commander's will by a calculated dispersion followed by concentration just before or even on the battlefield. Though only occasionally, as in the campaign of 1805, did strategic deception succeed in defeating the enemy without much hard fighting, it was always a vital element in Napoleon's more brilliant operations. With lesser commanders, or less efficient staff work, the attempt to outmanoeuvre the French frequently resulted in dislocation and loss of control. The Austrians in 1796, for example, the Prussians in 1806 and the Allies in 1815 were all deceived by Napoleon's strategic approach. The poor performance of the French marshals in Spain and Portugal serves also to underline the advantage of unity of command which Napoleon so often enjoyed against the commanders of coalition armies.

In the last resort Napoleon's military genius lay in his passionate devotion to the art of warfare and consequently it defies historical analysis. There is no mystery, however, about the skills that made him a great general. He supremely exemplified the adage that 'knowledge is power'. As a subaltern he had steeped himself in the history and theory of war, besides mastering the practice of his own arm, the artillery. As a youthful general he drove himself ruthlessly to master every aspect of his own army and to study a succession of opponents. Also, although there were obvious histrionic and propagandist elements in his relationship with his troops, it cannot be doubted that his charismatic appeal was in large measure genuine—and of enormous practical value.

Tactically Napoleon was not an innovator. It has been aptly said of him that he mastered Europe with weapons available to other men before he rose to power. He took remarkably little interest in certain new inventions such as observation balloons and shrapnel shells. Although he and Wellington only clashed at Waterloo, a strong case can be made that Wellington was superior to Napoleon as a tactician; certainly Wellington throughout his career had to take more care to husband his exiguous forces.

The military causes of Napoleon's eventual downfall are not particularly mysterious, though there is ample room for argument as to their order of importance. A study of his campaigns after the high-water mark of Jena in 1806 suggests that—until forced to return to a war of manoeuvre by inferior numbers in 1813–14—he came to take less trouble to catch the enemy off balance, and attempted rather to smash in his front with massed artillery and then overwhelm him by superior weight of infantry. Such tactics characterized the costly battles of Eylau, Friedland, Wagram—and Waterloo.

Secondly, as the supreme political and military authority, Napoleon depended too long and too exclusively on his own omni-competence. For example he neither created a responsible general staff system as did Prussia after Jena nor, with rare and brief exceptions, did he trust his marshals sufficiently to allow them to exercise independent command. Inevitably as the quality of his armies decreased through casualties, war-weariness and dilution with foreigners; and as his abler marshals became victims to old age, wounds, dissipation or political temptations, so the burden became too crushing even for Napoleon to bear. By contrast,

Napoleon's opponents in his last campaigns, generals like Kutusov (1745–1813), Schwarzenberg (1771–1820), Blücher (1742–1819) and Wellington (1769–1852) had far more limited responsibilities and could concentrate more single-mindedly on the military task in hand.

Nor of course must the reasons for Napoleon's eclipse be sought exclusively on the French side. The nations he had conquered adopted his methods; and the military institution of the nation in arms—though without its revolutionary ideology—was widely adopted on the Continent. The successive defeats suffered by Austria, Prussia and Russia, so far from crushing their resistance for good, provoked an upsurge of patriotism which, in the campaigns of 1812–14, was manifest in large and determined armies. Furthermore the political jealousies and conflicts which had repeatedly weakened the early coalitions were set aside just long enough for superiority of numbers and greater co-operation between the allied commanders-in-chief (as exemplified by Blücher's support of Wellington at Waterloo) to bring about Napoleon's defeats of 1814 and 1815.

Finally Napoleon, like Hitler later, failed because his brilliant military strategy was not equalled by his political or grand strategy. Too few of the 19th-century students of warfare who extolled Napoleon as the model general reflected on the salient fact that his political strategy was frequently inept (Egypt, Spain, Russia and the economic war against Britain), while his military victories twice ended in disaster, with his country defeated, impoverished and occupied by foreign armies.

Peace and professionalism

Although the popular notion that the period between 1815 and 1854 was one of unbroken peace is mistaken, the reality is still impressive. Though French troops invaded Spain (in 1823), Russia and Greece fought against Turkey (1827–28) and Holland against Belgium (1830), there were no long wars involving the major powers: this was a unique achievement in European history.

Another remarkable feature of the period was that peace movements sprang up in profusion and—in terms of membership and literature—flourished as never before in peace time. Not surprisingly most of the movements were inspired by Quakers like the founder of the British Peace Movement, William Allen (1770–1843), and other Christian pacifists, and the cynic might point out that they were concentrated principally in the two countries least threatened by invasion—Britain and the United States. Thus of the 324 delegates who attended the first international Peace Convention at the Freemasons Hall in London in 1843, 292 were British, 26 American and only 6 European.

Nevertheless the peace movements, though their practical achievements were small, were not an isolated phenomenon. Many of the leading classical political economists and political philosophers, such as David Ricardo (1772–1823), Jeremy Bentham (1748–1832) and James Mill (1773–1836), began to take the view that war, like other social and political evils, could be checked—if not abolished—by wise legislation and increased international co-operation. From a different standpoint, Saint-Simon (1760–1825) and, later, Auguste Comte (1798–1857), also took the extremely optimistic view that industrialization would gradually render warfare obsolete, in part because it would replace the traditional aristocratic and militaristic ruling class with industrialists, merchants and bureaucrats who would naturally be opposed to war.

In retrospect it can be seen that the long period of comparative tranquillity depended less on any new idealism than on general war-weariness and the remarkably successful peace settlement achieved by the conservative statesmen at Vienna. European state boundaries had been re-drawn and more or less settled for a generation; and ample safeguards were taken against a renewal of French aggression, while at the same time France had been conciliated by moderate terms and by prompt readmission to the small circle of great powers. More constructively the great powers' common interest in the peaceful settlement of international and (to some extent) internal conflicts found expression in the Congress system and—after its demise in the 1820s—the looser arrangement

English Quakers, led by Joseph Sturge, present a peace petition to Nicholas I on the eve of the Crimean War. In spite of such isolated attempts to keep the peace and the foundation of peace movements, there was during the 19th century a general feeling of the inevitability of wars. The Peace Conferences in the second half of the century aimed at providing rules for war rather than preventing it.

known as the Concert of Europe. Perhaps the outstanding achievement in international co-operation in this period was the almost bloodless separation of Holland and Belgium in 1830, and the guarantee of the latter's neutrality nine years later.

Though it would be unjust to deny an element of idealism in the European rulers and statesmen of the age of Metternich, the salient fact about the great powers is probably that all were monarchies and all were more or less in danger from nationalist movements and popular insurrection. For a generation they had lived in fear of a revival of the Jacobin terror, and the revolutions of 1830 were a timely reminder of the passionate aspirations for greater freedom and national self-determination that had been deliberately suppressed since 1815.

In this atmosphere it was not surprising that, in the rulers' eyes, the greatest virtue of a standing army was unquestioning loyalty to the regime. Thus as well as the suppression of political freedom by measures such as the Carlsbad Decrees of 1819—the resolutions of a conference of ministers of German states called by Metternich—there was also a tendency to reverse or erode those military reforms which had political implications. In particular, though the principle of conscription was retained in most countries, the related concepts of the nation in arms and the army as 'the school of the nation' were hastily abandoned. Thus in Prussia, where universal conscription had been adopted in 1813 after a long constitutional struggle, a sharp reaction set in after 1815. The standing army was reduced to 125,000 and only about a third of each annual class was called up for three years in the Colours—a period rapidly reduced in practice to two. By 1819 the military reformers, such as Boyen and Gneisenau, who were also advocates of constitutional reform, were all out of office. 'There grew up,' as Professor Gordon Craig has written, 'the concept of the army as a special calling, followed by technicians who were essentially separate from civilian society. . . . In the years between 1819 and 1840 everything that Scharnhorst and his disciples had done to reconcile the military establishment with civilian society had been destroyed; the army was once more regarded as the main barrier to social progress; and it was clear that, in the event of a major domestic upheaval, its existence would be in jeopardy.'

The French officer corps under the Bourbons was far less aristocratic than the Prussian, but there was a similarly sharp reaction after 1815. The standing army was reduced to 150,000 and was filled as far as possible by long-service professionals. Conscription was only employed in the form of the ballot from 1818 to supplement the volunteers. Substitutes were allowed for those who could afford to pay for them. The army remained essentially a conservative institution which was neither militarily nor politically progressive.

Whatever their military deficiencies the standing armies of the great powers had little difficulty, and no compunction, in suppressing the revolutionary and constitutional movements of 1848 and 1849. In June 1848 General Cavaignac (1802–57), who had earlier fought in Algeria, crushed the Parisian workers; in October General Windischgrätz (1787–1862) bombarded Vienna into submission, and in November General Wrangel (1784–1877) marched into Berlin and dispersed the National Assembly. The octogenarian Austrian commander, Field Marshal Radetzky (1766–1858) displayed the most brilliant generalship since Napoleon in twice defeating the Italian nationalists. The Tsar sent an army to assist Austria in putting down the Hungarian revolution.

New weapons

It is a remarkable fact that the means of waging war available in 1825 were almost identical with those of 1785. Consequently it still made sense to estimate a nation's military potential by the number of 'bayonets'—or infantry soldiers—that it could mobilize. The infantry's basic weapon remained the 'Brown Bess', a muzzle-loading musket fired by means of a flintlock with an accurate range of about 50 yards and a maximum of about 300. It was clumsy to load, since the soldier had to stand upright to ram home the charge and ball; two rounds per minute was a good rate of fire; and its usefulness was virtually limited to dry weather. Hence the necessity for rigid tactical formations learnt on the drill square: movement in dense columns, and deployment into two or three lines or squares for the face to face confrontation on the battlefield. Since artillery outranged the musket it could be massed in the front line to pound the opposing infantry as Napoleon had demonstrated so effectively. A series of innovations now placed a greater premium on the quality of the troops' arms and training, drove the artillery temporarily out of the front line, and gradually transformed the appearance of the battlefield.

The first reform improved the method of igniting the charge. In 1839 the British Ordnance Department replaced the flintlock by a percussion cap. This reduced misfires and also lessened the handicaps of firing in wet weather. The second innovation was the substitution of a cylindro-conoidal bullet for the round ball: the new elongated bullet had a hollow base which expanded when fired to fit grooves or rifling in the bore. It had been invented by Captain Norton in 1823 and improved by Greener, a London gunsmith in 1836. Rejected by the Ordnance Department it was taken up by Minié in France and adopted by the French army in 1849. The British government then paid Minié £20,000 for his patent and Greener £1,000 for his idea. The 'Minié's' effect on range and accuracy was quickly demonstrated, for in 1852 British troops were able to open fire effectively against the Kaffirs at 1,300

The development of small-arms between 1840 and 1890. In each of these diagrams (a) indicates the bullet, (b) the priming element, (c) the charge, (d) the spring (inside the bolt) and (e) the firing pin.

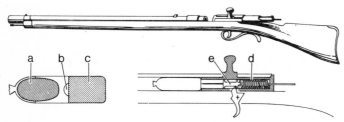

The needle gun, invented by Johann von Dreyse in 1836 and adopted by the Prussian army in 1842. It was the first breech-loading firearm to be generally used in warfare. Its cartridge consisted of an egg-shaped bullet (a), a priming pellet (b) and a charge of gunpowder (c). The breech-loading mechanism, which was of the 'bolt' type, contained a powerful spring (d) released by a trigger, and a firing pin (e) which in order to strike the priming pellet had to pass right through the charge and therefore had to be long and thin, like a needle.

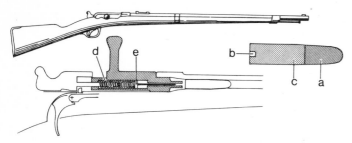

The Chassepot, adopted by the French army in 1867, after the efficiency of the needle gun had been demonstrated in the Austro-Prussian War of the previous year. It too was a breech-loader, but the priming element (b) was placed at the base of the cartridge, so that a shorter and blunter firing pin (e) could be used. The cartridge itself, however, was still made of paper, and no further improvement was possible until the evolution of a strong metallic cartridge-case.

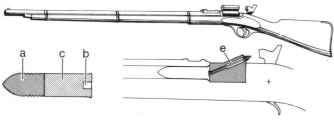

The Snider-Enfield rifle embodied several new features. The action of the firing pin was diagonally downwards; the cartridge was made of metal and the bullet itself of lead. The result was a faster and heavier bullet; the grooves on its side carried grease to lubricate the bullet as it passed down the barrel.

yards. Rifled muskets were being issued to the British army when the Crimean War began in 1854.

Meanwhile an even more momentous innovation was accepted in the Prussian army in 1841, namely Johann von Dreyse's 'needle gun': a breech-loading rifle with a bolt action and a metal 'needle' as striker. Breech-loading permitted the rate of fire to be increased to seven rounds per minute, and, at least equally important, the rifle could be loaded lying down. The needle was apt to break, however, and its range was considerably shorter than the Minié's, so that its significance was not widely appreciated until the war against Austria in 1866. By that date other armies were independently adopting breech-loading rifles: the United States army already had the Sharps breech-loader (hence sharpshooter), the British adopted a rifle designed by an American, Jacob Snider, in 1864 (replaced by the Martini-Henry in 1867), and the French had their excellent Chassepot by 1866.

Conservatism, doubtless due in part to the greater cost, was more evident in the history of artillery development. Although breech-

loading and rifled cannon were old as separate ideas and had even been brought together in a British experiment in 1745, it was not until exactly a century later that Cavalli in Italy and Whitworth in England independently constructed breech-loading rifled cannon with ranges of over 9,000 yards. Impressive though this sounds, smoothbores firing spherical shot remained more mechanically reliable and also more effective at short ranges. Thus there was some justification for the retention by the United States Navy of Dahlgren's smoothbore cannon from 1850 to 1880, and for the British Army's actually reverting to smoothbores after using Armstrong's breech-loading 12-pounder in the China War of 1860.

On the Continent, however, the pace of change was hastened by the ruthless test of battle. Napoleon III secured the adoption of a breech-loading field-gun which gave good service against the Austrians at Magenta and Solferino in 1859. In 1866 the Austrian artillery was more up-to-date than Prussia's: the former having over 700 rifled muzzle-loading cannon and only 58 smoothbores, and the latter less than 500 rifled cannon and over 300 smoothbores. Yet by 1870 Prussia had converted to Krupp's steel breech-loaders and these completely outdistanced the French artillery. Two other major developments in gunnery may be mentioned here though they were not perfected until the 1890s: namely an improved gun carriage and recoil mechanism which obviated re-aiming and so enabled as many as twenty shots to be fired per minute; and smokeless powder, which at last dispersed the fog of war, increased the projectile's penetrative power, and permitted a choice between longer ranges or heavier shells.

Machine guns, in the sense of repeating firearms, also had a long history, but only in the mid-19th century did they become really effective weapons of war. Their three vital advantages were that they fired more shots than a rifle, they could raise a 'curtain of fire' through which it was suicidal for infantry or cavalry to advance, and they made fewer demands on the steadiness and markmanship of the firer. Samuel Colt's machine gun—Colt (1814–62) gave his name to a species—was employed by the United States in the Mexican War and the Gatling in the Civil War, but its popularity and usefulness was limited by technical faults as well as by shortage of ammunition.

A much more impressive instrument was the mitrailleuse, which was developed under Napoleon III's patronage between 1851 and 1869. It possessed 37 barrels, weighed a ton and was mounted on a carriage pulled by four horses. Its rate of fire was approximately 370 rounds per minute. The mitrailleuse might have played a crucial role in the war of 1870, but unfortunately for the French they had kept it so secret that their own troops were insufficiently trained in its use. Worse still, instead of being used as an infantry support weapon it was employed as an artillery piece where it was no match for the Prussian guns. For this fiasco, and for a tendency to jam at critical moments, machine guns in general received a bad press and few armies fully grasped their enormous significance before 1914. Long before that, however, the first truly automatic machine guns such as the Maxim—invented in the 1880s—provided a preview of 20th-century war: the apparently deserted, lead-swept battlefield, and the concomitant problem for the attacker of how to obtain fire superiority so as to shield the infantry over the last half a mile to the enemy defences.

The steamship goes to war

The adoption of steam power for the warship effected the most far-reaching changes in naval power since the displacement of the galley by the sailing ship. Ships could now steam in a direct line and in any weather instead of being at the mercy of the winds. For the same reason the naval tactics even of Nelson's era were speedily rendered obsolete. But of course all was not gain. To offset this new mobility and virtual freedom from the dictates of weather, the need for coal supplies acted as a tether and presented strategic problems of acquiring overseas bases and coaling facilities.

The first steam-propelled armoured ship was built by Robert Fulton (1765–1815), an American inventor, in 1813—he had launched the first commercially successful steam-boat, the *Clermont* six years earlier—and within a few years mail boats and merchant shipping—at least on the great ocean routes—were converting to steam. Why then did admiralties lag behind in clinging to sail power for another thirty years? Three explanations are suggested. The British Admiralty deliberately adopted the policy of resisting innovations which were against their interest as the dominant naval power. From time to time this resulted in brief periods of qualitative inferiority and consequent scares of a French invasion; yet British conservatism rested on sound assumptions, notably the supremely confident Nelsonian legacy and an unrivalled shipbuilding capacity. Secondly, in the short term sail was still an advantage for scattered empires like those of Britain and France. Thirdly the early steamships were driven by paddle-wheels and could hardly have been less suitable for battle: they were cumbersome to manoeuvre and, with engines above the waterline, very vulnerable to gunfire.

Thus in 1840 the Royal Navy still possessed very few steamships and 'authorities' could still be found to argue that iron ships would not float. Within two decades the champions of wooden walls had been silenced for good.

A Swedish inventor, John Ericsson, successfully demonstrated screw propulsion on the Thames in 1836 but failed to convince the Admiralty. Seven years later he completed the first screw-propelled warship, the *Princeton*, in the United States. This development suggested that the days of the sailing ship of the line were numbered, and the incompatibility of sailing and steamships was further underlined in the Crimean War. Yet the Royal Navy retained sail as an auxiliary until 1873, the final abandonment probably being prompted by the capsizing of the fully-rigged H.M.S. *Captain* in a gale off Spain in 1870.

One curious tactical repercussion of introducing poorly protected steam warships while naval gunnery was still in a transitional stage, was that for a few years ramming was given the importance it had enjoyed in earlier centuries. Some minor successes were registered in the American Civil War, notably by the Confederate ironclad *Merrimac* in Hampton Roads; but the most spectacular feat was the sinking of the Italian flagship by the Austrian fleet under Admiral Tegethoff in the battle of Lissa in 1866.

The gradual development of the ironclad warship was the logical sequel to the invention of screw propulsion and shell guns. France led the way when in 1859 she launched *La Gloire*, a wooden frigate with a 4½ inch thick iron belt on her sides. Six years earlier the Russian Black Sea fleet's annihilation of the Turkish fleet at Sinope had demonstrated that wooden ships were as vulnerable as matchboxes against shell guns—and as inflammable. None of the British or French warships in the Crimean War was armoured, but both admiralties were persuaded of the superiority of ironclads by the epic battle of the *Merrimac* and *Monitor* in Hampton Roads in March 1862. The next twenty-five years witnessed an intense competition between naval gunnery and armoured protection.

Thus the maximum weight of the British naval gun increased from the 4 tons of the 68-pounder smoothbore to the 111 tons of the 16.25 inch rifled gun of 1884. During the 1870s recoil mechanism and revolving turrets added greatly to naval gunnery power. To offset this, armour plating increased from 4½ inches in 1860 to 24 inches in 1880—a thickness never exceeded.

The first submarine, with a one man crew, was built by an American, David Bushnell, in 1776. In 1801, Robert Fulton, the American pioneer of the steamship, experimented with his 'plunging boat' *Nautilus* which remained submerged in Brest harbour for over half an hour. There followed a lull before submarines made an unpropitious debut in warfare. In the war against Denmark in 1851 the Prussian submarine *Brandtaucher* sank in Kiel harbour with the loss of all its crew. The Confederate *Hunley*, operating awash, managed to sink the corvette *Housatomi* with a bomb rigged to the end of a pole, but the explosion also sank the submarine. Submarines did secure a few 'kills' in the Civil War but floating mines were far more deadly. By 1890 France and Britain each had several electrically-powered submarines in service. These were really effective instruments of war except for their extremely limited range (not much more than 80 miles) which right up to 1914 seemed to confine their role to inshore work. Also before the First World War it was hardly credible, except perhaps to a few extremists of the French *Jeune Ecole*, that submarines would sink unarmed merchant ships on sight.

Thus already by the 1860s technical changes had effected a revolution in naval tactics and strategy. Henceforth it would be extremely difficult for a weaker navy to keep to the seas, while tactically—as on land—it seemed likely that battles would be fought at ever greater distances. Since naval power was still reckoned largely in the number and size of capital ships, it was easier than with armies to assess a nation's position in the table. Until the 1880s the Royal Navy was stronger than any possible combination of enemies, and even after the potentially hostile Franco-Russian entente she was able to maintain the 'two power standard' embodied in the Naval Defence Act of 1889: the Royal Navy was to be kept at a strength in battleships equivalent to that of the combined fleets of the next two major powers. Nevertheless, rapid obsolescence permitted new or formerly weak naval powers such as the German Empire and Japan to vie for high positions, while even a small country like Chile was for a few years a power to be reckoned with in American waters.

Railroad strategy

Along with the application of steam to the warship, the coming of railroads was the most important of strategic developments in the 19th century. The railroad increased the pace and power of strategic manoeuvre, and transformed the problem of logistics.

German ammunition train in 1870. The Prussians were the first to recognize the importance of railways in strategy and when Moltke was appointed Chief of the General Staff in 1857 he insisted that military considerations should take precedence over civilian claims in the plotting of new tracks. The Prussians' ability swiftly to mobilize troops and supplies proved decisive in the Six Weeks War (1866) and again in the Franco-Prussian War of 1870.

Troops could be moved far more quickly to distant fronts—for journeys of less than a hundred miles it was still faster by road—and arrived in good condition to fight. Indeed without railways the huge conscript armies of the later 19th century could not have been moved and fed, hence General Fuller's pardonable hyperbole that 'it was George Stephenson (1781–1848) more so than Napoleon or Clausewitz who was the father of the nation in arms'.

Although Britain pioneered the civil use of railways, it was in Prussia that their strategic significance was first appreciated; indeed the first studies of their military value were published before Prussia had even a mile of track. The economist Friedrich List (1789–1846), for example, pointed out that from the position of a secondary military power whose weakness lay in her vulnerable central position between powerful potential enemies, Prussia could be raised by railways into 'a formidable defensive bastion in the very heart of Europe'. As a junior staff officer in the 1840s Moltke significantly chose to specialize in the study of railways, and military influence was strong in planning some of the main German lines. Yet the practical significance of these early studies must not be exaggerated. Apart from a few small-scale troop movements very little was done before 1859. In that year both France and Austria moved troops and supplies by rail to the theatre of operations in northern Italy. It was appropriate that it was in the American Civil War that railways first played a really crucial part since army engineers, including George B. McClellan (1826–85) and Robert E. Lee (1807–70), had had so much to do with surveying and building them. In the long run the Confederacy was crippled by the inadequacy of its railways and rolling stock, particularly as its access to the Middle and Far West was steadily eroded from 1863. Three years later Moltke demonstrated for the first time the decisive employment of railways in mobilization and strategic deployment by using five lines to spread an army of nearly a quarter of a million men on a front of some 275 miles. The Austrians, despite mobilizing first, never regained the initiative.

Yet, as with all military innovations, railways were not a panacea. Larger armies than ever before assembled could find themselves precariously dependent on fixed and vulnerable life-lines that provided an ideal target for guerrillas and cavalry raids. Tactically railways created more problems than they solved. The Germans calculated, for example, that an army corps would need 117 trains to transport it with all its supplies; and on a double track railway it could move 900 kilometres in 9 days. Beyond the railheads however, which might be scores of miles from the front, there was no improvement on horses and mules. By the end of the century military theorists were already wrestling with the problem of how to restore tactical mobility. Lastly, after Moltke's demonstrations of the vital importance of speedier and more efficient mobilization, the general staffs of the European armies devoted themselves to elaborating ever more detailed mobilization plans. By the time Count Schlieffen became Chief of the German General Staff in 1891, railways had come to dominate strategic planning and preparation for war.

The return of war: Crimea and Piedmont

Although the first of the mid-century conflicts between major powers revealed some of the features of modern war, they appear in the main as the last examples of limited 18th-century warfare. In the Crimean War (1854–56), fought by an alliance of Britain, France, Turkey and Piedmont against Russia, vital interests were not at stake and neither side could bring its full military weight to bear. Britain and France were operating some 3,000 miles from their home base while Russia, lacking a railway to the theatre of operations, was probably at an even greater disadvantage. In some of the Russian drafts sent to the Crimea during the winter as many as two-thirds of the men died en route from sickness or hunger.

The war has been called with justice 'one of the most ill-managed campaigns in modern history'. Lord Raglan (1788–1855), the reluctant British commander-in-chief, had never previously held a field command, and all but two of his divisional commanders were over sixty. They had lived too long under the shadow of the Duke of Wellington and were deeply imbued with the 'pipeclay

and polish' tradition. The army moreover now suffered the consequences of years of Parliamentary parsimony. The original expeditionary force consisted of veteran troops, but neither the men nor their officers had had much experience of field training, and behind them there existed no trained reserve. The French commanders were slightly younger and their army's performance a little more proficient. The Russians, in their weapons and tactics, were even more out of date than the allies, moving their troops about the battlefield—notably at Inkerman—in dense formations that were suicidal in the face of rifled muskets.

But if tactics were anachronistic, administration and staff work on both sides were lamentable and accounted for more of the privation and suffering than the actual effects of battle. In the British army much of the administrative responsibility was still in the hands of civilians and all too often the boundaries of their jurisdiction were obscure. This, along with pre-war neglect, goes far to account for the inadequacy of land transport, the failure to provide winter clothing, the breakdown in supplies and the appalling conditions in the field hospitals. As regards staff duties, a Senior Department of the Royal Military College had been founded as long ago as 1799 to train staff officers, and Wellington had made good use of its products in the Peninsula. But after 1820 it had fallen into neglect, and lost most of its prestige since few of its graduates received staff appointments. Many of the shortcomings, however, were less the fault of over-worked and undertrained staff officers than the Government's and War Office's lack of foresight. Thus intelligence concerning the Russian dispositions and the geographical and climatic conditions of the Crimea was completely inadequate, and no forethought was given to the possibility of winter operations.

Perhaps the most historically significant developments of the campaign were not strictly military at all. Florence Nightingale (1820–1910) by her heroic efforts in the hospitals at Scutari effected a revolution in both the public and official attitudes to military health and nursing. W. H. Russell (1820–1907) by his vivid—if sometimes indiscreet—reports to *The Times* brought home to the public for the first time the terrible conditions habitually endured by the common soldier, and the unromantic realities of war. This too was the first war to be widely photographed. Henceforth even the smallest military expedition seldom lacked a complement of journalists some of whom, like W. T. Stead (1849–1912), were to

The Battle of Solferino, at which there were 39,000 casualties. One spectator, Jean-Henri Dunant, was so horrified that in 1862 he published 'Un Souvenir de Solférino' in which he proposed the formation of voluntary services for the prevention and relief of suffering in peace and war and international agreement regarding those wounded in war. The book aroused much interest and led to the founding of the Red Cross at the Geneva Convention of 1864. In the Russo-Turkish War of 1877 (right) both sides had Red Cross units, those of the Turks taking the name of Red Crescent.

become even more famous than Russell himself. Russell's up-to-date reports had been made possible by the overland telegraph. As this means of communication was extended throughout the world in the second half of the century, so commanders in the remotest areas came under close surveillance by the political authorities and the public.

The Italian war of 1859 was fought by Piedmont with the support of a French army of 150,000 to liberate Lombardy and Venetia from Austria. Like the Crimean it was also a limited war, mainly because of the nature of Napoleon III's commitment, and because of French fears of a hostile Prussian army on the Rhine.

As mentioned above, the campaign saw the first serious use of railways in war. Both sides used them for the initial deployment, and the French used one of their lines in Piedmont to switch their weight from the right flank to the left to strike the Austrian flank at Magenta. The French had also profited from the administrative failures in the Crimea by organizing large transport echelons to carry reserve supplies of ammunition, and to maintain supplies from France.

The conduct of operations, however, revealed little improvement. The Austrians no longer had their great general Radetzky, and French movements were slow and ill co-ordinated. The latter failed to exploit their victory at Magenta by allowing the Austrians to escape to the Quadrilateral. Inept cavalry reconnaissance resulted in a head-on collision on June 24th and a day of carnage at Solferino. The Austrians withdrew, but the French had suffered almost as heavily and a compromise peace followed. One indirect effect of Solferino was the founding of the Red Cross, largely under the inspiration of a Swiss observer, Jean-Henri Dunant (1828–1910), who had been appalled by the suffering on the battlefield and the treatment of the wounded.

Rules for war and peace

The early 19th-century peace movement, with its pervading ideology of Christian pacifism, reached its climax in the Great Exhibition of 1851 before the disillusionment of the mid-century wars. Professor F. S. L. Lyons has noted ironically that while the Crystal Palace was described as 'the first Temple of Peace that modern hands have reared', one of the prizes was awarded to Krupps of Essen for a gun of cast steel of a superior quality. The propaganda efforts made by the peace movement had on the whole been very successful and, in practical terms, some fifty international disputes were settled by arbitration between 1794 and 1854. Nevertheless several serious weaknesses were by then apparent. First the movement had never resolved the problem of whether to condemn *all* war or to accept war as a necessary evil in certain circumstances. Secondly the movement had become deeply entangled with free-trade arguments and suffered accordingly when protectionism was revived in the 1860s. Much of its propaganda was also naive and wildly over-optimistic. Finally, pressure had been directed too much towards public opinion and too little towards governments.

The peace movement revived after 1870 and in 1889 received tremendous impetus from the publication of the passionate anti-war novel *Die Waffen Nieder* (translated as *Lay Down Your Arms*) by Baroness Bertha von Suttner (1843–1914): the novel was translated into at least eight languages and had gone through twelve editions by 1895. She poured scorn on the efforts of Dunant and other 'humanizers of war' and, like her friend and supporter Alfred Nobel—she was to be awarded the Nobel Peace Prize in 1905—looked prophetically to the perfection of an 'ultimate deterrent'. Nobel (1833–96), a Swedish chemist who had patented dynamite in 1866, thought that some kind of germ warfare would probably be the logical conclusion, but he also remarked pessimistically that Kant's 'perpetual peace' would probably be 'preceded by the peace of the cemetery'. Baroness von Suttner imagined the progress of artillery 'to such a point that any army could fire a shot which would smash the whole army of the enemy at one blow. Then, perhaps, all waging of war would be entirely given up.'

The efforts of Dunant, Gustave Moynier, Dufour and other Swiss supporters met with early success in the Geneva Conventions of 1864 and 1868. The former, which was eventually ratified by more than fifty countries, contained regulations governing the care of the wounded, the treatment of prisoners of war, and the protection of medical supplies and hospitals covered by the Red Cross flag.

Limitations and rules for naval warfare—neglected at Geneva—were particularly important because the rights of neutrals were always liable to infringement. By the Declaration of Paris (1856) the powers represented had urged that privateering be abolished; a neutral flag should be held to cover and protect all enemy goods except contraband of war; and neutral goods, except contraband of war, when carried in enemy ships should not be liable to confiscation. Henceforth, too, naval blockades had to be effective if they were to be recognized as legal, that is they had to close enemy ports permanently and not be conducted intermittently or at a distance.

The American Civil War speedily underlined the problems of maintaining a blockade if the Declaration of Paris was to be strictly observed. In fact the transformation of the means of war-making at sea, such as the development of submarines, mines, torpedoes and coastal artillery, was soon to render close blockade practically impossible. Distant blockades were again enforced, assisted by a great extension of goods listed as contraband of war.

The Civil War also provided an interesting example of successful arbitration. Britain had allowed the extremely destructive Confederate cruiser *Alabama* to be built and to sail from Birkenhead. In 1872 the United States' claims were submitted to arbitration; Britain lost and the liberal government headed by W. E. Gladstone (1809–98) agreed to pay £3,237,000 compensation. Although Britain's gesture greatly encouraged the advocates of compulsory arbitration, it remained a rare example of a sovereign state acknowledging itself to be in the wrong.

Arms limitation and disarmament were also much debated in the last quarter of the century. In 1898 the Russian government called for an international conference to halt the arms race and secure for all peoples the benefits of a real and durable peace. Nicholas II (1868–1918), the last Tsar of Russia, was probably sincere in his hopes, but there is no doubt too, that Russia was in dire financial straits through trying to keep up with German and Austrian armaments as well as constructing strategic railways.

So far as disarmament was concerned, the consequent Hague Conference of 1899 was a failure. Only three restrictions on armaments were approved, and of these the ban on soft-nosed bullets and asphyxiating gases met with protests from the British and United States delegations. The value of the Conference lay in two achievements: first, the revision and extension of the Geneva Convention of 1864 and the Brussels Declaration of 1874 ('Concerning the Laws and Customs of War'); second, the organization of a permanent Court of Arbitration with a secretariat to sit at the Hague.

Important though these international conventions were, they made little impression on the hard reality of absolute national sovereignty. Accordingly, in Professor Lyons' words, 'there was no permanent international league. There was no compulsory arbitration. There was no agreement on disarmament. Instead there were empty phrases, ambiguous gestures of friendship . . . and a steady preparation for war by the professional militarists.'

'Modern' warfare

Recognizably modern warfare first appeared in Europe in Prussia's astonishing victories over Austria and her South German allies in 1866, and over France in 1870. It would be little exaggeration to say that in the last resort both victories were due to the superiority of the German General Staff under the direction of Helmuth von Moltke.

The Six Weeks War of 1866 was a masterpiece in the history of military operations. Moltke exercised remote control by means of the electric telegraph, remaining in his Berlin office until June 30th —only four days before the decisive battle of Sadowa. Although Austria mobilized first, and although Moltke was hampered by his King's unwillingness to appear the aggressor, his daring strategic deployment bewildered the Austrian High Command—in which the commader-in-chief and chief of staff were at loggerheads.

Consequently the Austrians lost the opportunity of striking at either of the Prussian armies in isolation, fell back onto the defensive, and were overwhelmed by converging attacks from front and flank. Half a million troops clashed at Sadowa on July 3rd—the largest number since Leipzig in 1813—and the Austrians' west front, facing the Prussian First Army, was nine miles long. Pedantic critics were to accuse Moltke of taking unjustified risks by dispersing his forces so widely, but his correspondence during the campaign shows that he had taken his adversary into account. The keynote of Moltke's method of command, displayed again in 1870, was to utter only a few broad directives and then to rely on the initiative of his thoroughly trained staff officers in the headquarters of each field army.

Five points must suffice to illuminate Germany's even greater triumph over France in 1870. First, more efficient mobilization and early tactical successes again proved crucial. French mobilization was chaotic and she could only oppose 240,000 troops to the 370,000 with which Moltke crossed the frontier during the first week of August. Secondly, though the German generals made several major blunders, such as the abortive pursuit which Moltke ordered westwards along the Moselle after the battle of Wörth on August 6th, general headquarters never panicked or lost sight of the broader picture. Moreover, in contrast to the French, the German corps and divisional commanders generally supported their neighbours by marching to the sound of the guns. The French had no equivalent to Moltke, and Napoleon III made the disastrous decision to command his armies in person. Thirdly, the war confirmed what many experts had still questioned after 1866: that Prussia's three-year conscripts and reservists could more than hold their own against France's long service veterans. Fourthly, the war brought home to European armies the tactical changes already manifested in the American Civil War. Lastly, although the war was comparatively brief it was not concluded like that of 1866, by the defeat of the enemy's main armies at Sedan and Metz. On Napoleon III's personal surrender, the Third Republic was proclaimed in Paris and the provinces. Militarily French resistance was little more than irritating; politically it came near to depriving Bismarck of the fruits of victory. Here was an ominous preview of 20th-century 'total warfare' in which the enemy's people had to be defeated as well as his armed forces.

The lessons of America

If the American Civil War is mentioned after Prussia's wars for German unification it is only because transatlantic military experience had little immediate influence on European military theory or practice. This, in retrospect, appears a regrettable blind spot since in many ways the Civil War provided better clues to the future of warfare than Moltke's comparatively short and decisive campaigns.

The Civil War was unlimited in the sense that President Lincoln (1809–65) and his supporters believed they had no choice but to crush the Confederacy into unconditional surrender, or accept secession and the dissolution of the United States; also, simply because it was a civil war, slavery providing the ideological cause for passionate intolerance on either side.

Because of the unlimited issue at stake, and because neither side had the military capacity to crush the other in a short campaign in such a vast and thinly populated country, the outcome depended on a protracted struggle of attrition, symbolized by the North's blockade of Southern ports. Both sides were forced to resort to conscription and the Confederacy in particular mobilized almost to capacity. Total enlistments in the Union army numbered nearly three million, and in the Confederate army between a million and a quarter and a million and a half. In both industrial and manpower terms the Confederacy's effort was the more remarkable since it had to evolve a war industry out of practically nothing, and dared not employ its negroes as combatant soldiers.

The South's great inferiority in manpower and material was partly offset in the short run by the fact that, although most of the 16,000 regular soldiers of the United States army of 1861 remained loyal to the Union, some 200 officers including many of the ablest opted for the Confederacy. Consequently from 1861 to 1863 generals such as Lee (1807–70), Longstreet (1821–1904), 'Stone-wall' Jackson (1824–63) and Beauregard (1818–93) repeatedly frustrated Union attempts to invade Virginia and the mid-West. From 1863 not only did the North's superior strength begin to tell, but a more imaginative strategy was evolved which eventually ended the South's skilful use of interior lines. Ulysses S. Grant (1822–85) and William T. Sherman (1820–91), especially, appreciated the significance of the Western theatre, and once the former had taken Vicksburg (on July 4th, 1863) a broad strategy was planned to hold Lee's army fast in North Virginia while the Confederacy was divided from north to south by occupation of the whole line of the Mississippi, and then subdivided from west to east by a drive through Georgia. When Grant became Commander-in-Chief in March 1864 this strategy was implemented. Meade's Army of the Potomac by threatening Richmond gave Lee no respite, while Sherman took the more dramatic role of the march through Georgia to the sea. Sherman clearly understood that his task was as much psychological as narrowly military. By blazing a trail of destruction through the heart of the Confederacy he undermined the Confederate troops' morale and demonstrated to the citizens the futility of further resistance.

In no war before the 20th century were the tactical effects of the innovations discussed earlier so fully and dramatically displayed. Few contemporary European observers were acute enough to grasp that the tendency for troops to disperse behind cover and advance in short disorderly rushes was due neither to inexperience nor to the broken terrain. Rather such tactics paid tribute to the devastating effects of rifle fire and the superior strength of the concealed defender. With the fire fight now opening at 500 yards or more, individual marksmanship was more valuable than volley firing, bayonets were seldom crossed and few opportunities occurred for cavalry charges against demoralized infantry. Two tactical lessons stood out. Frontal infantry assaults against defended positions were sometimes unavoidable but they invariably resulted in heavy losses. Among the most bloody and fruitless were Burnside's attack on the Confederates at Fredericksburg (December 13th, 1862), Lee's at Gettysburg (July 3rd, 1863) and Grant's at Cold Harbor (June 3rd, 1864). Secondly, as the war progressed the spade became increasingly important, until in 1864 every action fought between Grant and Lee in Virginia was one of entrenchments. A few intelligent soldiers such as Colonel G. F. R. Henderson realized the implications of these developments for the huge European armies, but their ideas received all too little attention before 1914.

Armed peace: 1870–1914

After the rash of wars between 1854 and 1871, Europe enjoyed another long period of peace extending, if the Balkans are excluded, to 1914. Indeed the only large-scale wars anywhere in the world were those between Russia and Turkey (1877–78), Japan and China (1894), the United States and Spain (1898) and Britain and the Boer Republics (1899–1902).

Yet armed forces probably received more attention—and certainly cost more—than in any previous era. International and domestic tensions were reflected in virtually every aspect of military affairs. From 1871 Berlin generally superseded Paris as the centre of military ideas and fashions; in particular, Germany provided the model for the development of general staffs, short service conscription and annual manoeuvres. Military studies, professional journals and institutions burgeoned, and military attachés were established throughout the world. To counteract the momentous artillery developments already discussed, historic fortresses such as Verdun, Liège and Antwerp were converted into vast fortified areas, in large part subterranean and invisible. Apart from the aircraft and the motor car the weapons and instruments of war in 1914 were already to hand by the turn of the century. The few wars that did occur between 1870 and 1900 were closely observed by the major powers and exhaustively described in official histories, the earliest of which had been devoted to the Italian War of 1859.

The most striking feature of the Russo-Turkish War of 1877 was Osman Pasha's heroic defence of Plevna which held up the Russian advance into Bulgaria for five months. Significantly the defences of Plevna were not a fortress at all in the traditional sense, but a series of hastily improvised earthworks which time and again exposed the ineffectiveness of the Russians' high explosive shells and breech-loading rifles. Admittedly Russian tactics were crude: for example they threw away their advantage in numbers by launching unco-ordinated attacks, and did not select the weakest points in the perimeter. Nevertheless the superiority of the entrenched defender was again evident.

One solution for the tactical offensive, and that officially adopted in the German army after 1870, was to bombard the defences with shrapnel, mortars and howitzers as the prelude to a stage by stage advance of widely separated skirmishers. In sharp contrast, the French army, from the 1890s, reverted to the doctrine of a shoulder to shoulder advance, placing its faith in speed, high morale and the infantry's own rifle fire. Despite the penetrating criticisms of soldiers like Colonel Colin and Captains Mayer and Grouard, this emotional and unrealistic doctrine received increasing emphasis

The defence of Plevna by the Turks for five months against superior Russian forces foreshadowed the trench warfare of the First World War. For Russian high explosive shells (the giant battery is shown here) made no impression on the entrenched Turks who repulsed any Russian attempts to rush the 'no-man's land' between the two lines with deadly rifle fire. By the end of the war all the Russian infantry were equipped with entrenching tools.

from Colonel Foch (1851–1929) and his disciples. It was also adopted in Russia.

In naval warfare the most important conclusion to be drawn from the innovations and limited experience of the Crimean era was that henceforth the weaker fleet could not hope to cripple the stronger by superior tactics or the fortune of wind and weather. The fleet with the more powerful engines, guns and armour would annihilate its opponent or drive him from the seas. This deduction was borne out by the Sino-Japanese and Spanish-American wars which were both essentially decided by sea power. The numerically stronger Chinese fleet was defeated off the river Yalu in 1894 by superior gunnery: there was no need for the Japanese to attempt to board or ram.

After the Civil War the United States navy again consisted entirely of wooden ships, but in 1889 the Navy Department determined to construct a modern navy. The enormously influential book *The Influence of Sea Power* (1889) by Captain (later Admiral) A. T. Mahan (1840–1914) added impetus to this project and by 1898 five battleships were in service. The Spanish had only one battleship and their fleets were obsolete. Admiral Dewey (1837–1917) had no difficulty in smashing the Pacific fleet at Manila (May 1st) nor Sampson the Atlantic fleet at Santiago (July 3rd). Although the amphibious operations that followed exposed serious weaknesses in the United States army, the capture of Cuba and the Philippines followed as a matter of course.

Britain was not a military power in the Continental sense. She avoided compulsory service between the Napoleonic wars and 1916, and her standing army seldom exceeded 200,000 white troops, with only a small reserve of regulars. Nevertheless there was scarcely a year in the whole century when her troops were not in action in some remote part of the world. Thus her long service veterans—even Cardwell's so-called short service enlistment after 1870 was for seven years—gained uniquely varied experience against foes as different in temperament and tactics as the Sikhs, Maoris, Ashantis, Zulus, Dervishes and Boers. Though Britain almost invariably had great advantages in weapons and discipline, some of her small wars provided formidable tests. The ablest colonial generals, such as Sir Robert Napier (1810–90), Garnet Wolseley (1833–1913), Frederick Roberts (1832–1914) and H. H. Kitchener (1850–1916) had to combine a genius for improvization (there being no General Staff nor organized expeditionary force until after 1900) with the talents of an ambassador and proconsul. The fact remains that until the second South African War in 1899 none of them had commanded forces larger than about 25,000 men, and they had had few opportunities even for the substitute of peace-time manoeuvres. It is therefore fortunate that Wolseley's often-repeated wish to 'die with his boots on' in a great Continental war (presumably against France) was never realized.

The way to Armageddon

By 1900 the rival political alliances that were to fight the First World War were hardening but had by no means taken their final form. Germany's perennial fear of a two-front war against France and Russia simultaneously became more acute in the 1890s as both built strategic railways and strengthened their frontier defences. In this dilemma Count Schlieffen (1833–1913), Chief of the German General Staff from 1891 to 1905, reversed his predecessor's basic war plan by devising schemes for the rapid defeat of France entailing an attack on Belgium, before turning against Russia. Between 1871 and 1913 Germany increased her railway lines leading to the Franco-Belgian frontiers from nine to sixteen, while France increased hers to her eastern frontier from three to ten.

In 1900 Britain was still uncommitted to the Continental groupings. Her rivalry with France in the Mediterranean reached a climax in the Fashoda incident of 1898 and thereafter relations gradually improved until the entente of 1904. For the army, however, France and, even more, Russia remained potential enemies. For the Royal Navy on the other hand Germany was becoming the most likely antagonist. In 1894 Admiral von Tirpitz (1849–1930), Chief of the German Naval Staff, had outlined a policy designed to make Germany a considerable sea power. He evolved

the fallacious 'risk theory' which has been aptly summarized as 'a bid for sea power on the cheap'. If, so the theory ran, the German fleet met the Royal Navy in battle it should be strong enough to inflict such damage that the latter would be unable to meet the combined threat from France and Russia. By 1900 Tirpitz had abandoned the risk theory, under pressure from the Emperor and the powerful naval lobby, to aim for parity with Britain. This ambitious goal was embodied in the Navy Law of 1900 which provided for doubling the number of German capital ships. Britain could hardly avoid the conclusion that this programme was a direct challenge to her declared naval policy and national interests.

Indeed the balance of power at sea was changing not just in the North Sea but also in the Pacific and Atlantic. Between the war with Spain and the accession of the expansionist Theodore Roosevelt (1858–1919) to the Presidency in 1901, the United States launched a major building programme and by the latter year had seventeen battleships afloat or building.

In 1894 the British trained—and largely British built—Japanese fleet comprised only three obsolete ironclads and three more modern but unarmoured cruisers mounting heavy battleship guns. The following year a major expansion was approved including Japanese construction of one battleship and two armoured cruisers. Already by 1902 the alliance with Britain proclaimed that Japan was a considerable military and naval power. When war with Russia broke out in 1904 Japan possessed six first-class battleships and eight armoured cruisers. Tsushima, the greatest naval battle since Trafalgar, clearly signified the end of European hegemony in the Far East.

In contrast to our own time, war and the threat of war were not continuously subjects of popular dread and international debate during the 19th century. Then, as now, powerful armed forces and the will to use them were the ultimate safeguards of national frontiers and vital interests, but they could also be viewed, as was the German Navy, as objects of glamour and prestige. It is all too tempting to read history backwards from 1914 and both ante-date and exaggerate a general awareness of impending doom. It is true that the socialist movement struggled to raise international barriers against the outbreak of general war but it was an unequal struggle in an era of military conscription and state-controlled primary education, and when so many individuals and groups eagerly anticipated the challenge and excitement of war.

What may be thought surprising is that so few professional students of war seemed to have grasped what in retrospect appears to be the inexorable progress towards Armaggedon from the late 19th century. Finance, commerce, industry and an ever increasing segment of the population were all becoming entangled directly or indirectly in the apparatus of war. Most obvious of all, the armies of the major powers were swelling to a size never imagined since the myths of the Homeric era. By the end of the century Germany could put 3,400,000 men into the field, France 3,500,000, Austria 2,600,000 and Russia 4,000,000. What would be the effect on European civilization if these dinosaurs blundered into war?

No one investigated this question more thoroughly and acutely before 1900 than an amateur student of war, I. S. Bloch (1836–1902), by profession a Warsaw banker, the last of whose six volumes on *The Future of War* was published in 1898. Bloch was not an expert on military operations but his knowledge of finance and economics provided useful tools of analysis. In the next great war, he predicted, the tactical superiority of the defensive would prevent a quick decision (on which the general staffs banked) and trench warfare would set in. Eventually the conflict would end, not by a decisive military stroke but from the mutual exhaustion of the combatants and the internal collapse of their societies into revolution and class war. Bloch, like Sir Norman Angell (1874–1967) later, presumably believed that to demonstrate the futility of war would prevent it from occurring. He was wrong. It is now easy to understand, though none the less regrettable, why Bloch and those who agreed with his diagnosis had virtually no contemporary influence on policy and why his prescience was honoured only after his grimmest predictions had been fulfilled in the First World War.

VIII THE MAKING OF AMERICA

Opportunities and problems of a new world

MARCUS CUNLIFFE

'The old nations of the world creep on at a snail's pace; the Republic thunders past with the rush of an express'

ANDREW CARNEGIE, 1886

'Abraham, though very young, was large at his age,

and had an axe put into his hands at once; and from that till within his twenty-third year, he was almost constantly handling that useful instrument.' Abraham Lincoln's childhood and early life, thus described by himself in the third person, followed a pattern that was already becoming archetypal: birth in a log cabin, a background of pioneering poverty and manual labour, the struggle to raise himself in the world by his own efforts, the well merited success. It was the image surest of winning sympathy and support, and one which Lincoln himself did not hesitate to exploit. This life-size electioneering portrait (opposite, from the Chicago Historical Society) probably dates from 1858, when he was conducting his famous 'debates' with Stephen A. Douglas. Lincoln, the strong, God-fearing man of the people, is splitting wood to make a fence, a job he had actually done on his father's farm. In the background is the Mississippi river, with log rafts floating down it; in the far distance—the White House.

Freedom and equality were the two first and most fundamental American ideals. Both were unchallengeable ideologically, but in practice both, by Lincoln's time, were seriously compromised.

In the Illinois campaign of 1858, which was for a seat in the Senate, the main issue was that of slavery. Douglas argued that such Western territories as Kansas and Nebraska should be allowed to choose for themselves whether or not to admit slavery, Lincoln that slavery should be contained within its existing limits—a position that had been undermined by the Dred Scott decision of the previous year, when a runaway slave had been judged to be a slave even in a non-slave state. Douglas in fact won the election but Lincoln's reputation rose. He was chosen as Republican candidate in May 1860 and in the next year became the sixteenth president of the United States.

To Lincoln, as to most of his fellow countrymen, America represented a new kind of society, a land in which the corruption of the Old World could be avoided and where, for the first time, the government (in his own words) 'of the people, by the people, for the people' could flourish. The words *Novus ordo saeclorum*—a new order for the ages—had been inscribed on the federal seal. One of Lincoln's objections to slavery was that 'it deprives our republican example of its just influence in the world'.

The first industrialists where men of vision and faith. Samuel Slater set up his cotton mill at Pawtucket, Rhode Island (*below*), in the 1790s. By his death in 1835 he had built other textile mills and an iron foundry, and even founded a manufacturing village called Slatersville.

Andrew Carnegie, a penniless immigrant from Scotland, made his fortune in steel and used it to provide libraries for the masses.

Barn building in Ohio, 1880 (*below*): community spirit in action.

By the last quarter of the century the United States had outstripped the industrial capacity of the whole of Europe put together. This huge steel works (*below*), making railway track and using magnetic hoists, dates from about 1880. Most of the techniques of mass-production – mechanization, standardization of parts, the organization of unskilled labour – originated in Europe, but were applied on an increased scale in America.

Goods travelled by river, canal and, in the second half of the century, railway. *Top*: the Erie Canal, completed in 1825, linked the production areas of the Great Lakes with the Hudson river and thus with New York and the consumer areas of the East. The north-south line of the Mississippi was the country's first main axis, with St Louis (*above*) as its most important commercial centre. In 1840 the steamboat tonnage equalled that of the British merchant navy.

Selling was as important as producing, and became an American speciality. By the 1880s the old-style general store increasingly gave way to the large-scale merchandising of the department stores and the mail-order houses. This advertisement for one such house, Montgomery Ward and Co. (*opposite above*) reveals the inside of the 'hive'. But the small town store kept its usefulness. A Vermont shop (*right*) painted in 1873 sells most dry goods and incorporates a post office as well. By this date there is still little sign of mass production.

INDEX TO BUILDING — MADISON ST. FRONT

INDEX TO BUILDING — MICHIGAN AVE. FRONT

"A BUSY BEE-HIVE."
SECTIONAL VIEW OF THE ENORMOUS ESTABLISHMENT OF
MONTGOMERY WARD & CO.
MICHIGAN AVENUE, MADISON AND WASHINGTON STREETS, CHICAGO.

The men who fought: Private
Edwin Jennison, from Georgia.
Killed in action, July, 1862.

The South was equally prosperous, but its prosperity was different from, and at a deeper level incompatible with, that of the North. It depended upon slavery, and with the development of the cotton industry that dependence became more and more absolute. The South, indeed, had evolved a way of life that set it apart from the North – more leisured, more traditional, more structured. Beneath the slavery issue lay the fear that Northern culture would in time control the government and destroy that of the South altogether.

War came in April 1861, after first seven and then four more Southern States has seceded from the Union and formed a new nation, the Confederate States of America. Although the South started hostilities, it was throughout basically on the defensive against the North's superior wealth, industry and manpower. The Northern general, Ulysses S. Grant (*right*), victor of Shiloh, Vicksburg and Chattanooga, was chosen by Lincoln to lead the Federal armies in March 1864. After the war, in 1868, he was elected president. Robert E. Lee, the Southern commander, is a tragic figure, torn between loyalty to the Union and loyalty to his home state of Virginia, the last of the Confederate States to decide for secession.

Both sides improvised. Armies were thrown together hastily, raw volunteers forming new regiments without even a common uniform. *Left*: the Northern supply base at Cumberland Landing during McClellan's campaign of 1862. *Below centre*: men of the 9th Mississippi Regiment in the summer of 1861 at Pensacola, Florida.

The carnage of battle has been preserved for history by the new medium of photography. *Below*: Southern dead after the Battle of Antietam, September 17th, 1862, the bloodiest single day's fighting in the whole war.

The land of America seemed limitless. As settlement pushed further and further west, the 'Frontier' became a potent concept in the minds of Americans. A painting like that of the Rocky Mountains (*left*) by Bierstadt (1863), with its Indian encampment in a vast empty landscape untouched by civilization, gives such an attitude vivid and Romantic expression.

By dispossessing the Indians of land previously guaranteed them by treaty, the new states of the mid- and far West could build up their population and develop their resources. In 1890 South Dakota increased its attractions by opening the Sioux Reservation to settlement, and set about wooing immigrants by offers of free land and advertisements stressing the natural wealth of the region (*right*). The open book with its statistical records, the scroll illustrating public institutions, the plaques showing the local industries, held together by a 'chain' whose links represent different metals – all demonstrate civic responsibility and pride. Scotsmen, Frenchmen, Turks and every other nationality are shown crowding forward to make their home there.

Gold brought men west in 1849, filling the shanty towns of California with prospectors, adventurers and racketeers. *Left*: a gambling saloon at Sonora in 1855; among its clients are Mexicans and Chinese (though in a few years the latter were to be victimized). In the background a minstrel show is in progress.

A coast to coast railway network, complete by 1869 and run by private enterprise, gradually superseded rivers and canals, and made the move West comparatively easy. In this view of the marshalling yard of the Erie Railroad in New York State (*right*), passenger, mail and freight trains prepare to leave for every part of the Union.

The myth of the West, a strong ingredient in national consciousness, grew from the frontier situation, where toughness and self-reliance were necessary qualities for survival. Real life characters – the pioneer, the gunman, the cowboy – entered American folklore. *Left*: cowboys in Kansas with their chuck-wagon, a horse-drawn canteen that followed them on the range. *Below*: a wagon train halts at Denver, Colorado, in the 1860s. Supplies for the gold miners and settlers were carried in these convoys for safety: it was in similar covered wagons that the settlers themselves travelled. Denver was already an important staging post, with bank, land office and warehouses.

To the immigrant America offered both opportunity and freedom, as summed up in this cartoon of 1880, by Keppler, himself an immigrant. *Below*: saluting the flag in a New York school, *c.* 1889. *Bottom*: the Jewish quarter in New York in the 1880s, with signs in Hebrew script.

One city, Chicago, symbolizes the astonishing pace and scale of American growth better than any other. In 1831 (*top left*) it was merely a fort surrounded by a few houses at the mouth of the Chicago river, its only inhabitants troops and traders with the Indians. In 1832 the Indians were forced to move south and a town quickly developed. Its position made it a centre of water and, later, rail traffic. By 1870 it had a population of 300,000. The great fire of 1871 (*left centre*), which destroyed the whole business district and 18,000 private houses, served only as a spur to new achievements, especially in engineering and architecture. The last picture (*below*) shows the city in 1892, Lake Michigan crowded with shipping, the grid of streets dense with skyscrapers, railways bringing produce from all over the mid-West for transport and exchange.

Opportunities and problems of a new world

MARCUS CUNLIFFE

'IT SEEMS to have been reserved to the people of this country,' wrote Alexander Hamilton in 1787, 'to decide, by their conduct and example, the important question, whether societies of men are really capable or not of establishing good government on reflection and choice. . . .' He was at that time urging the acceptance of the new American Constitution. Duly ratified, though not without dissension, the Constitution took effect in 1789. The first president elected under its rubric, George Washington (1732–99), was sworn in, wearing a suit made of American broad-cloth; and the new bicameral Congress assembled to legislate for the United States. Few would have disagreed with Hamilton that they were embarked on what Washington himself called a 'great experiment'. Not all Americans were sanguine as to the outcome.

'A New Order'

On the negative side, it could be doubted whether the thirteen ex-colonies of Britain formed or would ever form a coherent nation. Local pride and sectional animosities were strong. Of a total population of just under four million, more than a sixth were Negroes held to slavery. Poor roads hindered the movement of men and of goods: the economy was localized, and dominated by agriculture. Hamilton's Society for Useful Manufactures, which he founded in order to promote industrial activity, languished and collapsed during the 1790s. As before the Revolution, imports and exports were closely tied to the mother country. The infant nation lacked even a name of its own: 'The United States' was only a general designation, to be shared before long with such other newly independent American nations as the United States of Mexico. Certain English observers prophesied a dismal, brief and factious future before the rebel colonies tumbled into anarchy. To judge from anti-administration newspapers in America during the first two decades, the nation's life under the new constitution might indeed be short and sour.

On the other hand, there were more cheerful predictions, and these magnified in volume and confidence as each year passed without bringing disaster. Their general theme was that the New World had escaped from the immemorial strife and vice of the Old World. God's divine purpose was discerned in the scheme of things. He had delayed the discovery of America until the moment was ripe, reserving this immense domain for Christianity's ultimate and prosperous triumph. That American evolution was providential had been an article of faith among the New England Puritans. In secularized versions it continued to seem self-evident throughout the 19th century. *Novus ordo saeclorum*—a new order for the ages—was inscribed on the seal of the federal government. It was a point of pride that the American government *was* federal: part of the 'great experiment' consisted in a dual system that conferred authority for some purposes upon the national government, yet reserved other matters to the control of the individual states. Such a division derived as much from practical scepticism as from constitutional theorizing. Americans counted it as a strength that they did not *need* to be closely governed, whether at state or federal level. 'That government is best which governs least' was a Jeffersonian motto that continued for many decades to seem axiomatic to a wide variety of Americans—from solid entrepreneurs to high-minded writers such as Henry David Thoreau (1817–62). In every

sense of the term, we may say, they believed in minding their own business. As Thoreau was to argue in his essay *Civil Disobedience* (1849):

> Government is at best but an expedient. . . . Yet this government never of itself furthered any enterprise, but by the alacrity with which it got out of its way. *It* does not keep the country free. *It* does not settle the West. *It* does not educate. The character inherent in the American people has done all that has been accomplished; and it would have done somewhat more, if the government had not sometimes got in its way.

In external affairs, victory in the War of Independence was thought to prove that not even a great maritime power could wage a successful war across the Atlantic. The actual lessons of the War of 1812, again fought between Britain and the United States, were equivocal. But they were taken by Americans to confirm the invulnerability of the young nation to foreign invasion. There were thus no reasons to recommend, and many to warn against, the forming of alliances with foreign powers. The treaty of 1778, binding the United States to France, was formally abrogated in 1800. In the 19th century, Americans signed no more such treaties, and took as their texts the phrases of Washington and Thomas Jefferson (1743–1826), to which they attached an eternal verity: 'The great rule of conduct for us in regard to foreign relations is, in extending our commercial relations, to have with them as little *political* connection as possible.' . . . 'Peace, commerce, and honest friendship with all nations—entangling alliances with none.'

Another item in early American doctrine also soon acquired something like the stature of holy writ. This was the decision, a logical one yet almost unique within its era, to substitute an elective presidency for an hereditary monarchy. True, the Constitution allowed for the re-election of the president, a provision that worried a number of libertarians, including Jefferson. But Washington as the first president retired at the end of two terms (eight years), and thus set a precedent not broken until 1940 (when Franklin D. Roosevelt was elected for a third term in office). Congress soon ruled that the portrait of neither Washington nor any incumbent president should be reproduced on the national currency. And the Constitution declared that

> No Title of Nobility shall be granted by the United States: And no Person holding any Office . . . under them, shall, without the Consent of the Congress, accept of any present, Emolument, Office, or Title . . . from any King, Prince, or foreign State.

The significance of these renunciations was clear, at home and abroad. The new nation was, in its own eyes, a different place. It had, under the protection of the Almighty, been vouchsafed a fresh start. In contrast to the ancient pattern of dynastic, hierarchical nation states, the United States launched its great experiment in federal, republican democracy. Europe was left in no doubt that America regarded the nations across the Atlantic as moral inferiors, whose corruption must be warded off as if it were a contagious disease. 'America, North and South,' Jefferson reiterated in 1823, 'has a set of interests distinct from Europe, and peculiarly her own. She should therefore have a system of her own, separate . . . from that of Europe. While the last is laboring to become the domicil of despotism, our endeavor should surely be to make our hemisphere that of freedom.'

American writers and orators echoed the notion long after Jefferson's day. Theirs was the 'sweet land of liberty': Europe was plunged in tyranny. America's was a classless society: Europe was layered into castes. America looked to the future while Europe remained obsessed with the past. America's literature, like her landscape, was (or at any rate would be, when men had leisure for such pursuits) generous, wholesome, untrammelled: the European scene was restricted and artificial.

In defining themselves as not-European, Americans occasionally drew parallels with other non-European nations. In the early years of independence comparisons with China were proposed. China was huge in extent, mainly agricultural, peaceable and self-enclosed. So Jefferson when president, and endeavouring to preserve American neutrality amid the Napoleonic wars, referred to his 'China policy'. Somewhat later in the century it became more common to suggest a parallel with Russia. Tocqueville gave the idea currency in his *Democracy in America* (1835–40). C. B. Boynton, a minor American patriot, writing in 1866 without fear and without research, produced a book entitled *The Four Great Powers*, which with a certain relish foretold the disintegration of Europe:

> Should this be so, then . . . Russia and America may . . . prove the salvation of the nations, presenting . . . two stable forms of government . . . both using alike political and religious power to . . . elevate the people. These two great powers will work in harmony with the spirit of the new age upon which we have entered, and, consequently, will be in alliance with each other. . . .

Boynton's book was composed in the immediate aftermath of the American Civil War of 1861–5, when Britain and France incurred considerable unpopularity for their supposedly hostile attitude to the American Union. According to legend, Russia had demonstrated its support for the Union. A second legend was that in purchasing Alaska from the Tsar in 1867 the United States paid a handsome price ($7,200,000) for apparently worthless terrain by way of demonstrating her gratitude. A Congressman in that year announced that one day 'the two great Powers on earth will be Russia and the United States'.

These however were fringe opinions, or prognostications. A more typical American conviction was that the United States was unique in world history: unique in its origins, in its present structure and in its destiny—a Christian, egalitarian, Anglo-Saxon civilization that had burst out of the European confines of its white settlers with irresistible energy, on a continent where opportunity was almost literally boundless. Most American historians have, consciously or unconsciously, interpreted the making of the nation in essentially the same terms as their 19th-century forebears. Nor can we deny that in several respects American development was quite sharply differentiated from that of the Old World.

Steps to democracy

Historians dispute the stages and the extent of democratic evolution in the United States. Some maintain that, at any rate for white males, a striking degree of political and social democracy prevailed even in the late colonial era. The two great exceptions, of course, were females and Negroes. Women acquired the vote in a few western states in the last third of the 19th century, but not for federal purposes, on a nationwide basis, until the passage of the 19th Amendment in 1920. Negro slaves were excluded from the franchise; so, in most states, were free Negroes. The 15th Amendment in 1870 sought to enfranchise the ex-slaves who had been freed as a result of the Civil War, and for a number of years Negroes did vote and hold office. But by 1900 those living in the former slave states had, through one expedient or another, been largely driven away from the polling stations.

Property qualifications for voting were low, and were in any case abolished in virtually all states by 1830. When two national political parties emerged in the 1790s, one of the contending groups, the Federalists, made a stand against the levelling tendency of the rival Republican party. A Federalist author, Thomas Green Fessenden (1771–1837), explained the conservative viewpoint in a

The Democratic Donkey and the Republican Elephant, created by the American cartoonist Thomas Nast in 1870 and 1874. ('Copperheads' were Confederate-sympathizing Democrats likened by their opponents to the dangerous copperhead snake.)

long Hudibrastic poem entitled 'Democracy Unveiled' (1805):

> There must be limits put to suffrage,
> Although the step excite enough rage,
> Lest men devoid of information,
> And honesty should rule the nation.

But much of the Federalist alarm was excited by fear of the French Revolution. Not even the Ultra-Federalists dreamed of establishing a monarchy in the United States, or seriously advocated what Europeans would have regarded as an 'aristocracy' (although the word was bandied about in American political controversy). And whatever dark designs were attributed to the Federalist gentry, Federalism disappeared as a national political force after 1815. By then, the term 'democracy' had lost its original pejorative connotations, and, having acquired an honorific tinge, was adopted by the Republicans as an alternative name for their party. When another national party with conservative inclinations was formed in the 1830s, it confused British observers by styling itself Whig—in part to emphasize that its aims were libertarian, not gentrified. Nor, despite the accusations of opponents, were the Whigs truly identifiable as a right-wing organization. For the remainder of the century, as American parties eventually took shape as Democrats and Republicans, 'the Donkey' and 'the Elephant', there was not a great deal to choose between them. As their names imply, American political organizations did not constitute a conservative-liberal alignment on the European model.

By the same token, except for a temporary exploitation of anti-Catholic feeling during the 1850s, religious divisions never played a prominent part in American politics. Here as in other respects politics mirrored social conditions. At least in theory, religious toleration was complete. There were no religious tests for public office, although in the first half of the century oath-takers were usually required to testify their belief in an unspecified deity. There

198

was no overt discrimination against Jews or Roman Catholics. They held commissions in the army and navy, served in Congress, and sometimes achieved high office. Roger B. Taney, for example, a devout Catholic, was a cabinet minister and then for nearly thirty years (1835–64) Chief Justice of the Supreme Court. In practice, religious prejudice did exist, and was intensified as the century wore on and the flow of immigration increased the proportion of non-Protestants. But, legally, religious discrimination did not exist. Moreover, the actual pluralism of American society had a powerful if accidental effect. For politicians, a Catholic vote was as good as a Protestant one; and the outcome of squabbles over such issues as financial support for sectarian education was a stalemate agreement that no special concessions should be made to any one group. Here, and in many fields of American life, a blend of principle and expediency led toward the creation of an open social order.

In politics, the evidence suggests that habits of deference survived for a generation or so after independence, but gradually evaporated in the atmosphere engendered by universal suffrage. All of the first six presidents, from George Washington to John Quincy Adams (1767–1848), could be described as gentlemen; so could a majority of the men who sought to enter Congress or State legislatures. A marked change was signalized by the election to the presidency of Andrew Jackson in 1828. Jackson (1767–1845) was a 'self-made' man (the expression seems to be an Americanism, dating from his era). So were several of his eminent political contemporaries: Daniel Webster (1782–1852), Henry Clay (1777–1852), Thomas Hart Benton (1782–1858), and Jackson's successor in the White House, Martin Van Buren (1782–1862). The presidency, said a Missouri newspaper in 1837, was 'within the reach of the humblest urchin that roams the streets of our villages. . . . *Liberty and Equality* is the glorious motto of our republic'. Politicians at the national level were expected to behave with a statesmanlike solemnity. Clay, Van Buren and the rest owed some of their success in public life to their social poise. Nevertheless, a too-obviously genteel manner became a decisive hindrance to political advancement. Candidates who could not claim truthfully, like Abraham Lincoln (1809–65), that they had been born in a log cabin, tried to persuade the electorate that they too had risen by their own exertions. Theodore Roosevelt (1858–1919), a member of an affluent New York family, was laughed at for his Harvard accent when he entered state politics in the 1880s, and had to plunge into a regimen of strenuous physical exercise in order to purge himself of the taint of gentility.

By 1830, then, candidates for public office were learning to attune themselves to the demands of their constituents. The belief, enshrined in the Declaration of Independence (1776), that all men are created equal, became an axiom of practical politics. Rotation in office, more cynically known as the spoils system, rested upon the Jacksonian conviction that any man could readily learn to perform any of the tasks of government; that no man had a right to hold appointive office indefinitely; and that a healthy political system must embrace a system of rewards for deserving adherents. God was still on the side of the American people; and the people were the voice of God. By 1830, too, the habit of selecting candidates within a small group or caucus had given way to the device of the national party convention, at which thousands of delegates from every state in the Union voted for their favourites, sometimes in as many as twenty or thirty ballots, until at last one of the candidates secured the necessary majority. Public opinion was expressed in, or spoken for, by a multitude of newspapers. A newspaper office, along with a church, a schoolroom, and a bar, was one of the first institutions in each newly established township. Libel law was extremely permissive, as public men discovered to their cost; practically every president from George Washington onward fulminated against the crimes of licence committed by the nation's journalism. Such impertinence was a standard complaint also among distinguished foreign visitors: Matthew Arnold in the 1880s was infuriated by unflattering newspaper accounts of his lectures (one of them said that, as he bent over his notes on the lectern, he resembled an elderly bird pecking at grapes).

Some historians have lately questioned whether social mores were as democratic as the political system appeared to suggest.

They contend that, especially in the north-eastern states, an ominous gap existed between rich and poor and by about 1850 was widening each year. In the second half of the century the gap was of course conspicuous. On the other hand—and this is probably the crucial element—the great majority of Americans seem to have continued to believe that theirs was a rags-to-riches, log-cabin-to-White-House society. In business, no less than in politics, success-stories were numerous enough to sustain the national myth. To cite the careers of a John Jacob Astor (1763–1848), a Joseph Pulitzer (1847–1911), a Commodore Vanderbilt (1794–1877) or an Andrew Carnegie (1835–1919) was enough to silence those who doubted the efficacy of the American gospel of wealth. Equally convincing was the reminder of the poverty and constriction of the life led by the average family in other lands.

Steps to wealth

The first American national census was taken in 1790. Successive decennial tabulations were eagerly scanned, and brought a glow of gratified pride. Moreover, the graphs began their dramatic rise almost immediately after the United States gained its independence—as if to prove that the colonies had been shackled by the mother country. Even before the 18th century was over, there were significant pointers to the future shape of American economic development.

One was the establishment of a cotton-spinning mill in Rhode Island, under the aegis of an English immigrant workman named Samuel Slater (1768–1835). It had been said that Slater was endowed with a 'photostatic' memory, which enabled him to recall the precise details of the textile machinery that he had tended in his native Derbyshire, and so to reproduce it in the United States. Slater's genius was certainly adaptive rather than inventive. In this respect it was to typify American practice. The New World supplied the stimulus. If Slater had remained in England he might never have risen above the status of a skilled workman. In the United States he rapidly became a captain of industry. With him began the American industrial revolution. 'I suppose that I gave out the psalm,' he said, 'and they have been singing the tune ever since.'

Others could claim a comparable pioneering importance. The idea of standardized, interchangeable parts in order to simplify and cheapen the production of small arms probably originated in France, where Jefferson saw such a process in operation. It was taken far more seriously in the United States, however, where the New Englander Eli Whitney (1765–1825) introduced the technique with immediate success. Also in the 1790s, Whitney demonstrated his ingenuity by devising a simple 'gin' (engine, or machine) for separating cotton fibre from the seeds and so permitting a prodigious saving in labour. At the same time the British powered cotton mill and the railroad and steamboat opened up the inland areas and made it possible to get cotton from upland farms to British mills. These developments revolutionized the production of raw cotton —the South's great staple crop, and, indeed, the basis of the American export economy during the first half of the 19th century. In 1793, when Whitney patented his gin, the cotton plantations produced a mere 10,000 bales. Thirty years later the figure had soared to an annual 400,000 bales, and by 1860 to a staggering total of over 3½ million bales.

Again, the United States did not originate any of the means by which communications were so markedly accelerated. Turnpikes, canals, steamboats, railroads were European in conception. But improved methods of transportation were so essential to a nation of continental extent, and so eagerly welcomed, that such 'internal improvements' (to use the American term) came in with a rush; one economic historian defines the period 1815–60 in the United States as that of 'the Transportation Revolution'. Thus, 1825 saw the completion of the 363 miles of the Erie Canal, linking New York City with the Great Lakes: an astonishing and highly profitable enterprise. By 1840 there were over three thousand miles of canals in the United States, and about the same mileage of railways—double the amount of lines in continental Europe. In 1840, too, the steamboat tonnage on the Mississippi river system equalled that of the British merchant navy. An animated map

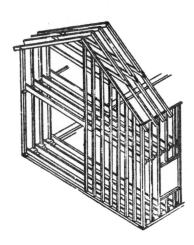

Two labour-saving inventions: the cotton gin (left) and the balloon frame (right). Whitney's cotton gin could clean 50 lb of cotton fibre a day. A manually turned wooden cylinder has fine spikes set half an inch apart, which protrude through teeth when the lid is closed. Raw cotton is fed into the gin on the right: the lint is pulled through the teeth by the spikes, leaving the seeds behind, and is finally cleaned from the spikes by revolving brushes. In the balloon-frame system of building, planks run continuously from sill to roof, giving an exterior shell—itself nailed together—to which the rest of the structure can be nailed. Skilled joiners are no longer needed.

would show tendrils of travel reaching out from the eastern seaboard with a tropical luxuriance, hastening and at times anticipating the surge of westward settlement. As a New England orator declared in 1835:

> The country, by nature or art, is traversed, crossed, reticulated, (pardon me, sir, this long word; the old ones are too short to describe these prodigious works,) with canals and railroads, rivers and lakes. The entire west is moving to meet us; by water, land, and stream, they ride, they sail, they drive, they paddle, they whiz,—they do all but fly down towards us.

By 1860 there were 30,000 miles of railroad. The figures continued to increase. By the end of the century no less than five railroad routes, in a total national mileage of nearly 200,000, spanned the continent from east to west. Communication-centres mushroomed from nothing. Chicago, in 1830 a tiny settlement on the edge of Lake Michigan, became in seventy years, as was noted in Chapter IV, a metropolis of over a million people; and this despite a fire which in 1871 had reduced a large part of the city to ashes. Every statistic seemed a national triumph. Between 1815 and 1860 the value of American manufactures multiplied tenfold, from $200 million to $2,000 million. In 1900 the figure stood at over $13,000 million. American ingenuity had produced several new devices— the telegraph, the telephone, the typewriter—to quicken the pace of economic life. And in the last third of the century, to the jubilant satisfaction of America-firsters, the United States outstripped the industrial capacity of Europe. The steel-magnate Andrew Carnegie, a Scottish-born immigrant, declared on behalf of his *pays d'adoption*, in his book *Triumphant Democracy* (1886) that 'the old nations of the world creep on at a snail's pace; the Republic thunders past with the rush of an express'.

Why had this happened? In the view of Carnegie, and of most Americans, it had come about because the United States was a democratic nation. The only restrictions were those that sheltered the American economy, in the shape of a protective tariff. Otherwise every way lay open: no hindrances to inter-state commerce, no insurmountable barriers between class and class. The United States did not consume its wealth in maintaining royalty, or such costly appendages as a large army and navy. In 1835, indeed, it had actually paid off the entire national debt; and while this freedom had proved temporary, indebtedness remained trivial by European standards. The very disadvantages that perturbed the Founding Fathers had turned out to be blessings in disguise. The shortage of labour (a constant reality except in brief interludes of economic depression), and particularly of craftsmen, had placed a premium on labour-saving devices and on mass-production. Every feature of American life had revealed the same tendencies. Standardization and simplification had for instance revolutionized building construction: the balloon-frame enabled houses to be

built by unskilled carpenters in a quarter of the time needed with conventional methods.

The results were already noticeable by mid-century, when the United States was still a good way behind Britain in economic maturity. At the Great Exhibition of 1851, the visitors who thronged London's Crystal Palace were awed by the industrial might of the host-country, and charmed by the artistic displays of some of the other nations. The exhibits entered by the United States were not at first sight impressive. The Americans had laid claim to more space than they could fill. This, and the huge sculpture of an American eagle surmounting their section, led to unfriendly comment on the American propensity to brag. 'They don't "whip all nature hollow",' *The Times* acidly observed. But it went on to add, with some acuteness, that the Americans 'have several very interesting machines, and the useful character of their display as a whole, forms a really striking contrast to the showy attributes of the national industries developed around them'. Or in the words of Samuel Cox (1824–89), an ardently patriotic Middle Western tourist, 'America had her own absolutely necessary work to do since she whipped her mother. She has been at home doing it, like a good housewife.' The equipment he delighted in included a McCormick reaper (a decisive contribution to agricultural productivity), and such achievements of mass-production as the Yale lock, the sewing-machine and the Colt revolver. Cox concluded in fairly characteristic Yankee-Doodle vein, that 'as in the young Hercules the astrologers read the lines of after-strength, so in the lineaments of America may now be read those of Empire. God has written them, in great mountains, rivers, lakes, men and energies, all over the face of the Union.'

The frontier

Equally characteristic was Cox's invocation of the American landscape. As with American manufacturing and agricultural production, the key themes were size, variety, growth. For all of these the geography of North America provided abundant metaphors. By 1850, through war and purchase, the United States had successfully asserted its claim to a domain extending from Maine to Florida, and from Oregon to New Mexico—roughly three thousand miles from ocean to ocean. The original thirteen states had been joined by eighteen others. It was widely assumed that in the fullness of time the whole of North America, including Canada and Cuba, would fall under the sway of the Stars and Stripes. In fact, a book entitled *The New Rome; or, the United States of the World* (1853) explained that the US would eventually absorb the entire hemisphere, not by conquest but rather by a natural gathering-in— much as ancient Rome had extended the mantle of its civilization over most of the known world. Such dreams of empire have inclined scholars to argue, in retrospect, that the United States was no less expansionist than Europe. The difference, on which

'The World is my market: my customers are all mankind' — so brags 'Y. Doodle' in 1877. In every sphere of competition America is shown eclipsing the Old World. But the brag was justified, and might indeed have been extended, had the cartoonist thought of heavy industry.

Americans were so fond of expatiating, was that the European nations had perforce to expand overseas: the United States, in common with Russia, could expand into a contiguous land-mass. Certainly we must note that, from the time of the Monroe Doctrine (1823), which warned the Old World not to interfere in the concerns of the New World, the United States took for granted that 'America, North and South' (Jefferson's revealing phrase) was its special sphere of influence. Another, more chimerical vision, that

of Pan-Americanism, co-existed with the US dream of empire. It nourished the hopes of some of the newly independent nations of Latin America. But the United States showed little interest in schemes for Pan-American unity. Its war with Mexico (1846–58) and its general air of Anglo-Saxon superiority, built up a lasting resentment at 'Yanqui' aggressiveness among the nations of the former Spanish empire.

There is no doubt, however, that westward expansion made the

United States turn its back on Europe, figuratively as well as literally. In 1848, the year of revolutions in the Old World, no comparable events occurred in the United States. The nation was preoccupied with events west of the Mississippi: campaigns against the Mexicans, the occupation of California, the drama of covered waggons along the Oregon trail. The discovery of gold in California, in the same year, supplied a further stimulus. 'Go West, young man, and grow up with the country': this famous exhortation by the journalist Horace Greeley (1811–72) was obeyed by millions (though not, incidentally, by Greeley himself). It became a commonplace—emphasized by Tocqueville, and by the influential Scottish pundit James Bryce (1838–1922) in his *American Commonwealth* (1888)—that the West was more truly American than the East through being newer, closer to nature, and further away from Europe. True, in 1853 the New Englander Thoreau told a friend:

> The whole enterprise of the nation, which is not an upward, but a westward one, toward Oregon, California, Japan etc., is totally devoid of interest to me, whether performed on foot, or by a Pacific railroad. . . . What aims more lofty have they than the prairie dogs?

But Thoreau was a wayward individual. A few years earlier he revealed that, at least as a metaphor, the idea of the frontier haunted his thoughts:

> Eastward I go only by force; but westward I go free. . . . Let me live where I will, on this side is the city, on that the wilderness, and ever I am leaving the city more and more and withdrawing into the wilderness. I should not lay so much stress on this fact if I did not believe that something like this is the prevailing tendency of my countrymen. I must walk toward Oregon, and not toward Europe.

With each decade the geographical and metaphorical definitions altered. In the early part of the century 'the West' was a farmer's frontier in fertile areas like Ohio. As settlement pushed across the Mississippi other types emerged: the cattle frontier of the Great Plains; and the mining frontier, frenetic in its quest for gold, silver and copper in Colorado, Nevada, or Montana. Whatever their precise quality, they were all 'West'; and the West was, in myth, the land of the tall tale, of the rugged pioneer, of the wide open spaces and the wide open towns. Where once the United States had been symbolized by such figures of folklore as the Yankee peddler and the Southern planter, it now began to prefer Western images of Americanism: the pioneer in his Conestoga wagon, vigilant to ward off marauding Indians; the Indian himself, implacable in warpaint (represented, along with the buffalo, on the national coinage); the miner with his washbowl; the badman (Jesse James, Billy the Kid) equivocally both a hero and a villain; and of course, eventually and pre-eminently, the cowboy. In trying his luck as a Dakota cattle-rancher, and in later christening a volunteer regiment 'The Roughriders', Theodore Roosevelt revealed a true instinct for the rhythms of American sentiment. So did *The Luck of Roaring Camp* (1870) and *Roughing It* (1872), early works of Bret Harte (1836–1902) and Mark Twain (1835–1910) that managed to romanticize the miners' frontier in the guise of unblinking realism.

They and most Americans, cherishing the special Western legend of red-blooded individualism, were indulgent toward its violence and lawlessness. In this way, they implied yet another contrast between America and Europe. Paradoxically, the nation that purported to lay the highest stress on the worth of every human being also tolerated a homicide rate far higher than that of Britain, France or Germany. Brawling with knife and gun, feuding, private wars, vigilantism and lynching, also entered into the American legend. Americans often complained that this was a malignant caricature invented by Europeans. Their suspicions would have been confirmed if they had known at the time that Queen Victoria, examining Sheffield wares at the Great Exhibition, was fascinated by some long 'Bowie' knives. 'Americans,' she noted in her journal, 'never travel without one.' Yet these knives *were* manufactured for the American market, or at any rate for the Western

Lynching was a kind of rough justice (or sometimes injustice) which prevailed in areas like California during the Gold Rush era, when the forces of law were deemed insufficient to control crime. Vigilance Committees were formed and with popular support either hanged offenders or drove them out of town.

and South-western states; and she could be forgiven for taking American national legends at their face-value.

The legend of the frontier, long current in various guises, found its most eloquent chronicler in the historian Frederick Jackson Turner (1861–1932). His celebrated essay, *The Significance of the Frontier in American History* (1893) asserted that the United States possessed a distinct national character, and that it had been formed not by traits or institutions brought from Europe, but by the interaction between man and his new environment. Forced to accommodate himself to novel circumstances, the settler was reduced to primitivism. Having been thus psychologically stripped naked, Americans then—according to Turner—over and over again, in each of the innumerable tiny communities founded in the wilderness, established democracy from first principles. The experience, he conceded, made them impatient of authority, sometimes insensitive to the arts and amenities, and sometimes brutal.

Turner's 'frontier thesis' can easily be challenged. One might ask, for example, why the process of settling 19th-century frontiers elsewhere in the world had not brought about identical developments, though Turner might have pointed to Australia and Canada as confirmatory examples. It could be asserted, too, that he neglected urbanization and industrialization as major factors in American evolution. Turner was well aware of the complexity of national and world history. But he thought he had found the essential key to the *initial formation* of the American character; and, himself a Westerner from Wisconsin, he was in some sense signalling the end of an era, when he took as his text the bitter-sweet announcement of the 1890 census that there was no longer a continuous belt of free land available for settlement. In his America of swarming cities and polyglot immigration, the word 'frontier' was already heavy with nostalgia. There had always been something ambivalent in the activity of pioneering. The newcomers might love the wilderness; yet the more successful they were in taming it, the more rapidly they transformed it into another kind of place. Once they had consolidated their gains they began to wonder what they had lost. While the frontier seemed illimitable, however, the word itself symbolized the edge of the unknown and not, as in Europe, the line across which rival sovereignties confronted one another.

The tide of immigration

American population statistics were as spectacular as those for industrial and agricultural production. Increase was geometric rather than arithmetical. In other words, the population of the United States more than doubled every thirty years. The 1790 figure of 4 million rose to over 9 million in 1820. By 1850 the total was 23 million. By 1900 it was 76 million. At first the growth was accounted for chiefly through natural increase: only a quarter of a million immigrants entered the United States between 1790 and 1820. The birth-rate remained high among the native-born population; a diet rich in meat and a generally comfortable standard of living gave white Americans a life-expectation somewhat above that of western Europeans. It was noted that the native-born, even those of foreign parentage, seemed to have developed unmistakably American physical characteristics. The American physique and physiognomy were depicted by cartoonists: while John Bull was invariably thickset to the point of corpulence, renderings of Uncle Sam showed him to be thin and wiry to the point of emaciation. A theory commonly believed by Americans—though without medical foundation—was that their pulse-rate was more rapid than that of Europeans: the habit of 'hustle' was supposed to have induced a metabolic change. In the last third of the 19th century some concern was expressed. A book entitled *The American Nervousness* (1881) suggested that the pace of life in the United States had produced new nervous ailments. The popular American clergyman, Henry Ward Beecher, said the same thing in 1886. His countrymen were pressing 'nature to her utmost limits till the very diseases of our land are changing'; Americans were 'dropping dead' through 'the violence done to the brain by excessive industry, through excessive hours, and through excessive ambition'. But even this supposition could be a source of pride: restlessness was the attribute of conquerors, somnolence that of backward peoples.

With the 1840s there began an immense influx of immigrants from overseas which was to continue almost unabated, except for occasional fluctuations, until the 1914–18 War. Half the population of Ireland moved to the United States, together with sizeable contingents from other parts of Great Britain. At mid-century there was also a large flow from Germany and Scandinavia, and (on the Pacific coast) from China. No world-migration on such a scale, claimed the *Democratic Review* in 1852, had occurred since the barbarian invasions of Rome. 'In a single week we have again and again received into the bosom of our society, numbers as great as a Gothic army,' it maintained, echoing Disraeli's long-term historical comparison. Thus, in the single peak-year of 1854, no less than 430,000 immigrants arrived. Though this figure was not surpassed again until 1880, thereafter the annual inflow frequently exceeded half a million. In 1880, two-thirds or more of the inhabitants of Western farm-states like Wisconsin and Minnesota were of foreign parentage. Then and later, the centres of American cities formed a kaleidoscope of ethnic groups.

The comparison drawn by the *Democratic Review* is perhaps equivocal: are barbarian invasions desirable or not? Americans remained of two minds. On the one hand, the growth of the nation depended upon an increase of population; most immigrants

An American view of England: John Bull and Uncle Sam in 1898.

An English view of America: hotel manners in 1856, from 'Punch'.

were eager to 'Americanize' themselves; few, including the Irish, were politically radical; employers welcomed the prospect of cheap labour, and the households of the affluent relied upon the services of a legion of Bridgets and Berthas. The desire of people from other lands to settle in the United States bolstered national self-esteem. There was moreover an emotional commitment to the old idea of America as an 'asylum for the oppressed', a nation of all nations. Until the early 19th century some European countries prohibited the emigration of certain categories of citizens, above all of skilled workmen; and some maintained the principle of 'indefeasible' citizenship. Against such limitations the United States upheld the principle of free choice and transfer of citizenship. *Ubi panis, ibi patria* was the immigrant's credo: why attempt to thwart him? According to Hector St Jean de Crèvecœur, the author of *Letters from an American Farmer* (1782), himself a Frenchman by birth, the American was a 'new man' evolved from the possible mingling of several different racial stocks. The promise of American hospitality for Europe's 'huddled masses, yearning to breathe free' was restated a hundred years after Crèvecœur, as we have seen in the words of the poem by Emma Lazarus inscribed on the base of the colossal Statue of Liberty in New York harbour.

On the other hand, Americans began to argue with growing vehemence that a nation of nations was not a nation at all. There must be a limit to the inflow of immigrants, at any rate from certain nations which were deemed 'unassimilable'—i.e. un-American. It was said against the Irish that they were ignorant, shiftless, and prisoners of the Roman church. Chinese immigration was in fact ended in 1882, though not until San Francisco and New York had acquired their 'Chinatowns'. The so-called 'new immigration' of the last two decades of the century seemed even more unassimilable than the Irish. At least the Irish spoke English. But Jews from the ghettos of eastern Europe, Poles, Hungarians, Slovaks, Italians, Greeks: these seemed immitigably alien to 'old-stock' Americans, by which might be understood Americans who had arrived anything over thirty years ago. Crèvecœur's panegyric was actually not much quoted during the 19th century, and Emma Lazarus' lines did not warm the hearts of portions of White Anglo-Saxon Protestant (WASP) America. The expatriate novelist Henry James (1843–1916), returning to his country after a long absence, was horrified by the polyglot swarm of New York life, and admitted his craving for some 'sweet, whole' national consciousness like that of the Swiss or the Scots.

But whether dismayed or exhilarated (or both) by the process, the citizens of the United States knew that this was how America had been peopled. Except for perhaps half a million Indians, the territory that was later to be known as the United States was initially a vast, uncharted emptiness. In this respect, every American was an immigrant; and so, though priority of arrival became a measure of relative status—in fact, the basis of an American class-system—their common origin implied a kind of kinship. Though they might differ from one another in nationality, religion, language, complexion, they believed themselves to be more adventurous than the stay-at-homes of the Old World.

Nor did they tend to stay put on arrival in the New World. Millions of families were lured inland from their first homes by the prospect of cheaper or more fertile land, the promotional activities of railroad companies and boom towns, the extravagant rumours of discoveries of mineral wealth, or because they had made

An anti-immigration cartoon of the end of the century showing German Socialists, Russian anarchists, Italian brigands and English convicts flooding into America.

a mess of things and wanted a fresh start. One piece of doggerel asked new arrivals in the Western territories:

> *Say, what was your name in the States?*
> *Was it Smith, was it Jones, was it Bates?*
> *Did you murder your wife?*
> *Did you flee for your life?*
> *Say, what was your name in the States?*

American fiction abounded in stories of mysterious strangers, men who had changed their identities, taciturn characters who declined to talk about their previous careers. One of the most vivid indicators in the decennial census was the map that showed the imaginary balancing-point of the nation's population. In 1790 this centre was in Maryland, only a few miles from the Atlantic. By 1850 it was in Ohio, several hundred miles inland: by 1900 in Indiana, a thousand miles from the seaboard. The process was epitomized in the steady accretion of new states, as each territory acquired enough population to qualify for statehood. It was even symbolized on the national flag, which (to the profit of the flag-makers) added a new star each time a new state was admitted to the Union.

Slavery and Civil War

To many foreign observers and to a growing number of Americans during the first half of the century, the most singular, contradictory and repellent feature of the United States was the institution of slavery. The Anglo-Irish poet Thomas Moore (1779–1852), visiting the country in the early years of nationhood, poured scorn on the 'piebald polity' of 'slaving blacks and democratic whites'. If the Constitution of 1787 had tacitly recognized the 'peculiar institution', the Declaration of Independence had in 1776 roundly announced that all men were endowed with fundamental rights—among which were 'life, liberty, and the pursuit of happiness'. Apologists tried in vain to explain away the discrepancy, their arguments becoming more extreme and more belligerent with each decade. Thus, they insisted, it was the British government—and British slave traders operating out of Glasgow and Bristol—who had fastened the curse upon North America. Slavery might have been extinguished peaceably and gradually if it had not been for Whitney's cotton-gin, and for the insatiable appetite of the British cotton-textile industry. The 'white slaves of England' or of the manufacturing towns in Northern states, ill-paid, ill-housed, and liable to be thrown out of work without notice, were worse off than Negro slaves on the paternally administered plantations of the South. As for the Declaration of Independence, it was sentimental nonsense. Men were simply not equal to one another; the promise of America had never extended to the idle or stupid, but only to the energetic and able. Nor were Negroes 'men' in the full understanding of the term. They were innately inferior; those who manifested exceptional ability were nearly always of mixed descent. But while Negro stock might be improved with white blood, miscegenation would lead to an inevitable deterioration in the quality of white 'Anglo-Saxons'. The emancipation of the slaves in the British West Indies, in 1833, had ruined their economy without any appreciable compensations. Whites did not like to work with blacks: hence the relative absence of immigration in the slave states. Negroes were not only childish, they were also (puzzlingly enough) vicious creatures who must be kept under strict discipline.

And so on. Some of these contentions were not altogether baseless. Outside the South, for instance, most Americans were not so much anti-slave as anti-Negro. Except for a small minority of radical abolitionists, even those who fancied themselves as men of goodwill confined their activities to schemes for keeping Negroes away from their own doorsteps, by re-colonizing them in Africa (a move that has left one historical landmark, the black nation known as Liberia) or by passing legislation to debar them from various Northern states.

But whatever extenuations could be offered, by white Southerners or by Americans as a whole, the 'piebald polity' remained a conundrum of ever-widening complexity and tension. If slavery had been abolished, say, by 1820, it is conceivable that the United

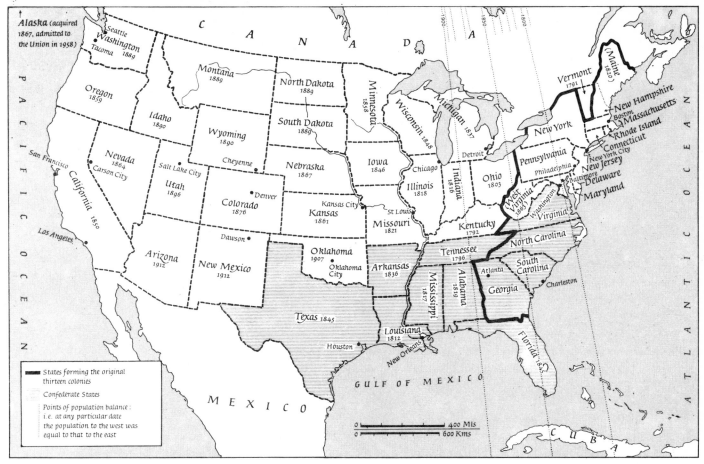

The United States of America, showing the dates when each State was admitted to the Union and the 'points of balance' of population during the 19th century. The western Mississippi–Missouri basin ('Louisiana') was purchased from

France in 1803; the territories of California, Utah, Arizona and New Mexico were acquired from defeated Mexico in 1848. Alaska was purchased from Russia in 1867 for $7,200,000.

States might have pursued an appreciably more aggressive colonial policy, along the lines recommended by 'manifest destiny' orators of the 1840s and 1850s. Instead, the mutual suspicion of North and South tended to block such schemes. The problem of slavery became obsessive, affecting every area of American life. In national politics it shattered the Whig party during the 1850s, broke the Democratic party into sectional wings, and—in the North—brought about the creation of the Republican party, whose first President (elected in 1860) was Abraham Lincoln. Following the victory of the 'Black Republican' candidate, seven states of the lower South seceded from the Union and established themselves as a separate nation, the Confederate States of America. Their attempt was challenged; four more slave states in the upper South joined them; and so began the Civil War. Unsympathetic or pessimistic witnesses, especially those of conservative temperament, concluded that the conflict was the last act of an American melodrama: a society whose only cement was money could not expect to hold together. The United States was sliding into the same corrupt disarray as its neighbours in Latin America. Nor could the war be regarded as a crusade to end slavery, since Lincoln's government at first remained silent on the issue, and then merely proclaimed the abolition of slavery in those parts of the South over which it had no control.

The fighting dragged on for four years, at a cost of a million lives, North and South. The eventual defeat of the South, the formal freeing of the slaves and the hallowing of Lincoln's reputation by means of an assassin's bullet, seemed to prove that the great experiment had been justified after all. Patriotic fervour *was* strong even in a nation that appeared a mere aggregate of self-centred individuals. Despite initial setbacks, and the lack of a strong tradition of military professionalism, the Union had forged a formidable war-machine. The wrong of slavery had been removed. Within a few years, the obvious scars healed over; the economy prospered as never before. A moralist might say that the Civil War

settled nothing, except that the Union would not allow any portion to secede. Otherwise, the bloodletting was a mere ritual, peculiar to the American psychology. The North was more intent than ever on its magic graphs of productivity, the South on restoring—as it rapidly did—the previous acceptance of white supremacy. The United States was still a piebald polity, a curious blend of an open society and of one shut fast within the walls of racial prejudice.

America defined

Previous pages have sketched a picture of a country which deliberately repudiated its European heritage, and which as a matter of circumstance evolved a culture of its own—or possibly three cultures, if one considers the North, the West and the South as distinct regions. This cultural distinctness was illustrated in the emergence of new forms of religion such as Mormonism and Christian Science; and of a vernacular literary style, as well as of a mass of special word-coinages, that went some way toward the formulation of an American language. 'There is no such thing as the Queen's English,' Mark Twain declared. 'The property has gone into the hands of a joint-stock company, and we own the bulk of the shares.' American society might be wistfully admired by European liberals, and heartily detested by the European upper classes. Both concurred, however, in feeling that it was a novel social order, and a portent for other societies: America, for good or ill, was their probable future. American nationalism seemed to contain additional ingredients that differentiated it from the patriotic ardour of other nations. There was a tincture of what might be called ideology: an assertion that the United States had found the key to the future. The ideological resonance could be detected in any number of American utterances, from the high-toned to the frankly jingoistic. 'Ours is a country,' said Ralph Waldo Emerson, 'of beginnings, of projects, of vast designs and expectations. It has no past; all has an onward and prospective look.' Twenty years later, in his book *Spread-Eagleism*, which appeared on the eve of the Civil War, a promoter named George Francis Train (1829–1904), a pioneer of the tramway, assured his readers that 'Egypt gave Industry, Greece Liberty . . . leaving American to combine the whole and represent the Progressive Idea.' The ideological element, reminiscent in some ways of the later tone of Soviet Russia, may be seen in the theory about the American pulse-rate, and in a bizarre notion propounded by settlers in the arid Western plains, that building and tree-planting would increase the rainfall.

Americans and non-Americans alike, enthusiastically or critically, conceived of the United States as a nation diametrically opposed to those of western Europe. Several prominent historians, from George Bancroft (1800–91) in the 1830s to Daniel Boorstin in the 1960s, have likewise defined the United States as a different place.

We have seen that there were indeed important differences; and *belief in difference* itself becomes an important factor in the balance. Yet in perspective the emphasis seems to have been exaggerated. It has led, for one thing, to an American assumption that 'Europe' was all of a piece, instead of being a collection of states encompassing a wide variety of social and economic systems. It has encouraged also a relative neglect of the long-settled (and most densely populated) areas of the North-East, out of a belief that they were somehow less 'American' than regions further west.

Present-day historians of the New Left persuasion appear to be redressing the balance, out of a desire to show the fallacy of the time-honoured legends of American social mobility. Even in the 19th-century United States, they contend, the race was (as elsewhere) to the swift: the children of the well-to-do thrived, while the poor mostly remained near the bottom of the ladder. They suggest, too, that in foreign affairs the United States—always a trading nation—was an aggrandizing power on essentially the same scale as Britain or France. As soon as it suited their purposes, Americans began to seize possessions overseas with the greedy alacrity of an imperialist power: Hawaii, the Philippines, Puerto Rico (the last two as a result of the unnecessary Spanish-American War of 1898). Even the allegedly virtuous 'Open Door' policy toward China, enunciated in 1844, is now asserted to have meant very little: at the end of the century the United States was as eager as any other western nation to exact concessions in the Far East.

Economic historians, less revisionist in temper, have likewise insisted that the United States belonged to and benefited from a larger, Atlantic economy. Immigration conferred upon America a copious supply of young adult labour, without the social costs of preliminary rearing and training. European investments, particularly from Britain and France, financed New World enterprises. European invention and technology was an indispensable adjunct to American economic growth. If the Old World had been as retrogressive as some of the more rabid American xenophobes pretended, the American economic miracle would probably have been delayed by half a century. The United States, it is true, was quick to improve on European techniques, and began to contribute its own innovations to the Atlantic economy.

In this view, then, the United States bore close resemblances to Western Europe—far closer than to Latin America or China or Russia. Perhaps it was slightly more than a coincidence though, in the deeper tides of world development, that the United States freed its slaves at almost exactly the same time as the Tsar emancipated the serfs. Other possible parallels are intriguing. One may for example envisage the American Civil War as a final, forcible phase in unification, since it was waged to consolidate the Union. In the same decade of the 1860s the unification of Italy and Germany was also being effected to the sound of gunfire. And as far as the West was concerned, the American frontier was only one of several world regions in which white settlers were trekking inland, and thrusting aside the aborigines. Canada, the Argentine, South Africa, New Zealand, Australia: each was at the pioneer stage of exploitative enterprise. Australia's gold-rush in Victoria came within a few years of the first gold-strike in California. The mineral wealth of South Africa was uncovered soon after. Both the initial impetus and the repercussions can be seen within a world-wide context.

The closest comparison, not surprisingly, is that between the United States and the United Kingdom. The parallel was in fact often drawn during the 19th century. Michel Chevalier (1806–79), an intelligent Frenchman who visited the United States in the 1830s, felt that the two nations displayed a similar innovatory spirit because of their similarity of background: both were predominantly Protestant, enjoyed limited constitutional governments and were acquisitive and libertarian in outlook. Turner's contention that American democracy grew out of the American forest, and was not brought over by the early English settlers, was in part an answer to those numerous commentators on both sides of the Atlantic who had preferred to base American evolution on ideas of heredity rather than of environment. Even George Bancroft, whose history of the colonies was considered almost vulgarly 'American' in approach, postulated a steady progression in which the furthest moral advance—until the Americans became independent—was that of the mother-country. If the Americans thought their pace of life alarmingly hectic, some British observers felt the same about the whirl of their own existences. 'We have got into a habit of valuing speed *as* speed,' wrote W. R. Greg, a member of a Manchester cotton-mill family, in 1875. 'We are growing feverishly impatient in temperament.'

In some respects, therefore, Turner and his environmentalist followers have distorted the American self-image as it obtained during the 19th century. Along with declamations of American prowess and American uniqueness went an intimate if ambivalent and emulatory awareness of Britain. The connections were most obvious in social and cultural matters. A French 19th-century joke, that the United States was a country with two hundred and fifty religions and only one soup, was probably adapted from the 18th-century jest of the Neapolitan, Francesco Caraccioli: 'There are in England sixty different religious sects, but only one sauce.' The great evangelists of the Anglo-American world seemed equally at home on either side of the Atlantic. Reform impulses—abolitionism, temperance, the peace movement, women's rights, mechanics' institutes, co-operative societies, penal codes, treatment of the insane, the Y.M.C.A, the Salvation Army, single-tax, slum settlement-houses, garden cities—sprang up in response to the same problems. Often they originated in Britain, because of the time-lag in American industrialization and urbanization. For this reason, British trade unionism was established a whole generation before that of the United States. But once the need was felt, the two countries readily introduced one another's remedies. Most of the American public's favourite authors were British. Scott, Burns, Bulwer-Lytton, Carlyle, Dickens, Thackeray, Matthew Arnold, Browning, Ruskin, Kipling and R. L. Stevenson were household names. One of the American exhibits at the Crystal Palace was a statuette of Oliver Twist, a character whose story, according to an American traveller, was 'far more familiar in America than in England'. To a lesser extent, such American authors as Emerson, Longfellow, Oliver Wendell Holmes and Mark Twain, enjoyed a comparable reverse celebrity.

Some American scholars maintain that there *was* a cultural contrast, exemplified in the United States by those great, strange writers Herman Melville (1819–91) and Walt Whitman (1819–92). Yet this is a latter-day judgement. In their own day Melville and Whitman were regarded as minor oddities. Although they did not use the term, most 19th-century Americans subscribed to the value-system summed up in 'Victorianism': self-help, thrift, piety, energy. The comment of an English contemporary on the American Civil War puts the comparison into perspective. It was, he said, as if the younger sons of the Irish or Scottish nobility (i.e., the South) were fighting against the tradesmen of Leeds (i.e., the North). A somewhat supercilious opinion, but it suggests to us that in truth the United States was a Victorian society—omitting Queen Victoria, her court, the Brigade of Guards and various other appendages. North of the home counties, Britain and the United States had a surprising amount in common; and, allowing for differences of language and social behaviour, with all those middle-class zones of Europe in which share certificates and company prospectuses were more impressive than deeds to farm property (unless held as mortgages), or than the *Almanach de Gotha*.

IX THE EXPANSION OF RUSSIA

Reaction, reform and revolution

HUGH SETON-WATSON

'*Placed between the two great divisions of the world,*
between East and West, our head on Germany
and our feet in China, we ought to have combined
within ourselves the two great principles of human life—
imagination and reason.
Destiny has given us no such role. . . . We are alone,
we have given nothing to the world.'

CHAADAEV, 1836

'We feed you':

the cry of the people, at the bottom of the social pyramid, sounds like a ground-bass through the history of 19th-century Russia. No country had a more consistent tradition of revolutionary activity, though in fact no revolution took place—not in 1825, when the Decembrists made their ill-judged bid for power; nor in 1830, when France, Belgium and Poland had risen; nor in 1848, when almost every European throne seemed to be tottering; nor in 1881, when Alexander II was assassinated. When this propaganda poster (opposite) was issued—abroad—by the 'Union of Russian Socialists' about 1900, there was still no immediate prospect of change.

At the top, framed under the imperial eagle, sit the Tsar and Tsarina, supreme autocrats of all the Russias—the motto: 'We rule over you'. Beneath them is the Court ('We govern you'), supported by the Church ('We deceive you') and the Army ('We shoot you'). Under them come the nobility and gentry, a rigid hereditary caste, enjoying the wealth of the land in idleness: 'We eat for you'. At the bottom—'We work for you. We feed you'— are partly peasants and partly the new class of industrial workers.

The working classes in Russia were in fact probably not more exploited than in many other European countries, nor were their rulers necessarily harsher or more callous. What made Russia appear the pattern of monolithic, reactionary conservatism was the relative absence of a middle class, due to the fact that the Tsars had succeeded in rendering the landed gentry politically powerless. This had the effect that reform, if it came at all, had to come from the top, and was usually resisted by the gentry (the prime example is the abolition of serfdom). Liberalism made little headway in such conditions, and revolution seemed to be the only solution.

Marx, it is true, saw no hope of successful revolution in Russia, since besides lacking a bourgeoisie it also lacked a proletariat; and in fact most of the active revolutionaries before 1900 were intellectuals in revolt against their own class. But as soon as industrialization did produce a proletariat (minute though it was in comparison with those of England and Germany), the two elements—workers and intelligentsia—could fuse, under the pressure of military disaster, and the long expected revolution take place.

Мы царствуемъ надъ вами.

Мы правимъ вами

Мы морочимъ васъ

Мы стрѣляемъ въ васъ.

Мы ѣдимъ за

Работаемъ за васъ.

Мы кормимъ васъ

Но настанетъ пора — возмутится народъ.
Разогнетъ онъ согбенную спину
И дружнымъ, могучимъ напоромъ плечъ
Опрокинетъ онъ эту махину.

Two Tsars dominate the first half of the 19th century, setting the pattern of autocratic rule that was to stamp Russia in the eyes of the world. Alexander I (*above*) led his country to victory against Napoleon, giving it a sense of nationhood hitherto unknown, and becoming a sort of father figure to most of his people. But in later life he became preoccupied with a mystic sense of his mission as the saviour of Europe. *Right*: a military parade in front of the Winter Palace, St Petersburg, in 1812. On the left is the Admiralty. Alexander's successor, Nicholas I (*above right*), feared change and tried to arrest it. His reign is marked by a tightening of government control, increased censorship and the suppression of individual freedom. In both the army and the civil service a network of ranks, rules and precedents hampered efficiency. A sequence began to be established between military failure and successful demands for reform. *Above centre*: a hussar, from part of Nicholas's imperial dinner service.

Any opposition brought down the full weight of official punishment, and the road to exile (*below*), was to be trodden by thousands during the course of the century. For the poorer political prisoners it meant hardship or death. For wealthier revolutionaries it often meant little more than a change of residence and an unattractive climate.

Serfdom ended with the accession of Alexander II. It was a slow process, lasting from 1857 to 1861, and it did little to improve the peasant's lot. Legally free, he was all the more securely bound economically. The former serfs, burdened with new debts, were disappointed and bewildered. This painting by G.G. Miasoyedov (*below*) shows a village group listening in a barn while one of their number reads the decree of February 19th, 1861.

Assassination became the weapon of the revolutionaries. During the 1870s and 80s acts of terrorism increased all over Russia, forcing Alexander II, 'the Tsar Liberator', into a policy of suppression. In March 1881 he was himself murdered. Members of the 'People's Freedom' Group threw a bomb at his coach as it was crossing a bridge in St Petersburg. He stepped down from his carriage – the moment shown in the drawing *above* – and spoke to the wounded. As he turned to re-enter the carriage a second bomb exploded. His death caused a wave of repression. Five of the assassins were hanged (*below*), the rest sent to Siberia.

In the villages (*left*) civilization had hardly progressed since the Middle Ages. The peasants were by nature conservative. A few landowners tried to 'improve' their estates in the English manner, but most left things to their managers, a state of affairs immortalized in Goncharov's novel *Oblomov*. The actual conditions of rural life went mostly unnoted in fiction.

Russian society – the society of the landowning classes and the higher officials – existed in a state of tension unlike that in any other European country: tension between power and impotence, between boredom and energy, between aimlessness and idealism. Hence the fascination of Russian 19th-century literature, which is partially reflected in art. Yaroshenko's *Girl Student* (*right*) might have stepped out of Kushchevsky's *Nikolai Negorev*, a picture of life at a provincial university and of the gradual reimposition of political control after the emancipation. *The Young Widow* (*far right*) by P.A. Fedotov combines sentimentality with a hint of satire in a way that looks back to Pushkin.

Holy Russia (*left*): a religious procession in the Kursk district, depicted by Repin about 1880.

A precarious charm hangs over Russian life during the last years of the old order, a charm epitomized in such paintings as *On the Banks* (*right*) by Repin, 1876, and above all in the plays of Chekhov. It was a society which realized that it was doomed, yet was powerless to change.

In 1905 the 'dark people' for the first time erupted on to the stage of Russian history. Defeat in the Russo-Japanese War led to strikes, mutinies and dissatisfaction, not only among the intelligentsia but among the workers themselves, including those in the new factories of St Petersburg. Men gathered outside the Putilov works early in January (*top*) and students (*above*) marched through the streets carrying red flags; troops refused to enforce order. For a few months it seemed as if this 'First Revolution' had succeeded, but by October the government had regained control and the Tsar revoked most of the concessions he had made.

Reaction, reform and revolution

HUGH SETON-WATSON

THE RELATIONSHIP between Russia and the West during the 19th century was complex: it can only be understood, indeed, in terms of a longer time span. The first Russian state, with its capital at Kiev, had maintained links not only with Byzantium but with central and western Europe, and the city state of Novgorod prospered for three hundred years in trade with Germany and Scandinavia. Yet more than two centuries of the Tatar yoke destroyed most of these links, and neither the princes nor the prelates of Moscow, which rose to be the new centre of the Russian land, had much detailed knowledge of Europe. The further great divide came in the 17th century when Peter the Great (1672–1725), following more hastily and more brutally in the footsteps of his father, carried through reforms which, while neither as original nor as effective as has been conventionally suggested, administered a rude shock both to the people of Russia and to the courts of Europe. The traumatic effect of his actions on the Russian mind remains one of the main facts of Russian history.

Artificial modernization

Peter was what may be called an 'artificial modernizer', and the theory and practice of 'artificial modernization' offers a key to Russian history even in the 19th century. Whereas in north-western Europe and its offshoots in the lands of white settlement overseas, notably North America and Australasia, 'modernization' was the product of a multitude of individual initiatives, in Russia, following Peter, the will of the ruler was decisive. The ruler sought to select those features of foreign experience which he believed would strengthen his power while rejecting those which in his view might damage the minds of his subjects or the fabric of Russian society. The process was, of course, more painful and more complex than the ruler could foresee. The erection of European structures on traditional foundations created dangerous social strains and distortions, and it was never possible for long to exclude the subversive general ideas to which modern Europe gave birth.

Throughout the 19th century Russia was engaged in a process of painful, erratic and often interrupted 'artificial modernization'. Yet what distinguished her from other countries of 'artificial modernization' then and since was that she remained a 'Great Power' in the process. Japan emerged as a Great Power only after the first modernizing measures taken there; Turkey had ceased to be a Great Power before modernizing Mahmud II (1784–1839) became sultan; Egypt's period of modernization under Mehemet Ali (1769–1849) was followed by decline and foreign occupation. After Peter the Great Russia was always a Great Power: for the rulers of Europe her alliance was a valued prize, her enmity a danger.

Even European commentators, who questioned her modernizing tendencies, did not doubt her power. 'There was a country a century ago which excited little interest,' a writer in the English radical periodical, *The Westminster Review* remarked in 1824, 'it was known and thought of only as the land of strange and distant barbarians. . . . Things are altered now; and Russia, barbarous still, has aspired to and has obtained a dictatorship over the states of Europe. She sits like a huge *incubus* upon the rest. . . . Russia in the great struggle which is going on between improvement and barbarism is the commanding champion as well as the efficient repre-

sentative of the latter.' There was enough 'Russiaphobia' in 19th-century Britain for such a comment not to seem out of place. 'A very general persuasion has long been entertained by the Russians,' another editorial commentator had declared in 1817, 'that they are destined to be the ruler of the world, and this idea has been more than once stated in publications in the Russian language.' 'Russia's prayer is for TIME,' wrote another in 1840, 'and Europe kindly offers it to her; *time* to be ready for the splendid inheritance.' For Marx and Engels the main object of Russian foreign policy was to dominate the world, or if not the world, at least Europe. 'In our times only a civilized government ruling over barbarian masses can hatch out such a plan and execute it.'

The interrelation between foreign and internal policy profoundly affected the process of modernization in Russia, even more in the 19th century than in the 18th. The fact of Great Power status was of undoubted advantage, in so far as it allowed Russia's rulers to make their own plans without seeking permission from foreigners, and strengthened the pride and self-confidence of the Russian political class. However, it was not an unmixed blessing. The power of the Russian armies and the splendour of the Russian court, from the time of Empress Elizabeth (1709–62) onwards, contrasted with the backwardness of Russian villages and the poverty and ignorance of Russian subjects. The resources available for modernization were limited, and they were enormously reduced by the cost of the armed forces and of the various civil expenditures required to maintain Great Power prestige. Thus, if the backwardness of the economy set limits to the effectiveness of foreign policy, the demands of foreign policy were a brake on internal development. An analogous contradiction may be observed in regard to the results of Russia's 19th-century wars. Defeat in war brought a crisis of the regime in 1855 and in 1905, but both these crises were followed by important social and political reforms which strengthened Russia. In 1917 the crisis proved incurable, and led to the disappearance of the monarchy. On the other hand the great victory of 1814 led to a glorification of the regime, the whitewashing of its cruelties and the preservation of its abuses and its obsolescence: the result was that the pace of modernization was relaxed, and by 1855 it faced collapse.

The making of the Russian army

Peter the Great's military and naval reforms had been the most successful of all his modernizing measures. His army beat the Swedes at Poltava in 1709, and his navy made its presence felt in the Baltic. The Russians also held their own with European armies in the Seven Years War, and during the last quarter of the 18th century produced a military genius in Alexander Suvorov (1729–1800). Despite bitter opposition from his superiors, and frequent conflicts with the court, Suvorov succeeded in reversing the priorities of the time: perfection on the parade-ground was to be less important than effectiveness in battle. Suvorov studied his enemies and their countries, and showed special brilliance in the rapid movement of his forces. He also transformed the relationship between officers and men, even within the framework of serfdom. The culmination of his career were his great victories against the French in North Italy in 1799 and his retreat, in fantastically difficult conditions, through Switzerland in the autumn of that

Michail Semenovich Vorontsov (1782–1856) exercising his troops in the Caucasus. Commander-in-Chief and governor in the Caucasus from 1844–53, he led the campaign against the Caucasian patriot Shamil. By 1848 he had conquered two-thirds of Daghestan, for which feat he was given the title of prince.

year. His successor Mikhail Kutuzov (1745–1813) achieved immense popularity as the ultimate victor against Napoleon in 1812. Like Suvorov, Kutuzov had the gift of winning the adoration of his troops. Second only to him in national acclaim was the much younger Prince Bagration (1765–1812), who died of wounds sustained at the Battle of Borodino. Throughout the Napoleonic wars the Russian army was the equal in every sense of any in the world. Though badly defeated at Austerlitz, it inflicted crushing losses on the French at Eylau, Friedland and above all Borodino, drove the French out of Russia and covered itself with glory in Europe.

During the next forty years Russia's military efforts were directed not against Europeans but against Asians, including both the regular armies of once great empires and the smaller but more war-like forces of free mountain peoples. Superior numbers and weapons told in the end, but it cannot be said that during this period the Russian military record was very brilliant. Paskevich captured Erivan from the Persians in 1827, but the opposition was hardly formidable. The war of 1828 with Turkey began badly, but Diebitsch's advance along the Black Sea in July 1829 was a substantial achievement. During the 1830s and 1840s Russia was more or less permanently engaged in hostilities in the Caucasus, against either the Circassians in the west or the Chechens in Daghestan. These campaigns had the advantage of giving battle-training to the regular army: in this they may be compared with the hostilities on the North-West Frontier of British India. However, the achievement of the Chechens, under the Imam Shamil, in defying the Russian Empire for more than twenty years, is more impressive than the final victory of his opponents. The combination of precipitous mountains and thick forests, Chechen bravery and deep religious conviction long proved more than a match for the Russian commanders and their serf soldiers.

When the Russian army again faced European armies, in the Crimea in 1854–55 (see above, Chapter VII), the men fought bravely as ever but the commanders were for the most part mediocre —in this resembling their French and British adversaries. The exception were the defenders of the naval base of Sevastopol, which stood a siege of almost a year. Admiral Nakhimov (1802–55) was a brilliant commander, and the fortifications were planned by General Totleben (1818–84), one of the outstanding military engineers of the century. The war ended without a major disaster, but the fact remained that Russia had been defeated and humiliated. Since 1815 Russia had been generally regarded both by soldiers and by revolutionaries like Marx and Engels as the greatest of the European land powers. The events of 1848, which had shaken all the other Continental states but had left Russia untouched, increased the admiration or hatred in which Tsar Nicholas I (1796–1855) had

been held. But the Crimean War suggested that the Russian colossus had feet of clay. During the next twenty years Russia counted for less than France or even Austria, and after 1870 there could be no doubt that the leading Continental power was the new German Empire.

Serious reform of the Russian army was the work of a great Minister of War, Dimitri Milyutin (1816–1912), who held office from 1861 to 1881. It was he who introduced regular conscription, now made both possible and necessary by the abolition of serfdom in 1861 (see below). He also did much to improve military training and specialized education, and placed the branches of the service on a more systematic basis. He met with bitter opposition from influential senior officers and Grand Dukes who saw their privileges doomed, but on the whole he was supported by the Tsar, and his work had practical results. The war against Turkey of 1877–78 came before his reforms had had much effect, but it was on the whole well conducted. In this war the great heroic siege was endured not by the Russians but by the Turks: Plevna in north Bulgaria was defended by Osman Pasha for five months in the face of several attacks by Russian and Roumanian troops. The crossing of the Balkan mountains and the capture of Kars on the Caucasian front were memorable achievements by the Russians.

During the third quarter of the century frontier wars in Asia continued, no longer in the Caucasus—where Shamil had surrendered in 1859 and Circassia had been pacified in 1864—but in Central Asia. Turkestan was conquered in the 1860s and early 1870s with little serious fighting. More formidable opponents were the Turcomans of the eastern coast of the Caspian. In 1879 they defeated a Russian force sent against them. It was not till January 1881 that General Skobelev (1843–82) captured their fortress, and dishonoured his victory by a deliberate massacre of the male population within its walls and in flight across the steppe.

In the Far East the Russian government made great gains at the expense of China without having to fight at all. At the end of the century, however, an opponent of different quality appeared in the shape of the Japanese. The St Petersburg government threw away more than one opportunity of agreement with Japan in the decade 1894–1904. Having forced the Japanese to relinquish the strategic Liaotung peninsula in 1895, the Russians seized the same territory from China three years later. The Japanese might reluctantly have accepted Russian domination of southern Manchuria if Russia had been willing to recognize Japanese hegemony in Korea. The Russian government was both divided and irresolute, but in 1904 it was not prepared to give the Japanese what they wanted. War began on the night of 8–9 February with a Japanese surprise attack on the Russian naval base of Port Arthur. The war was disastrous for Russia. The defence of Port Arthur for five months was a fine achievement, though not equal to that of Sevastopol. Elsewhere the Russian forces did not distinguish themselves. Inadequate communications had been one of the main causes of the Crimean failure. Since then railways had been built on a substantial though still insufficient scale in European Russia, but contact with the Far East was dependent on a single enormously long Trans-Siberian line, begun in 1891. The Japanese defeated the Russian Far Eastern fleet, the Black Sea fleet was unable (because of the Convention of 1841) to pass through the Straits, and when the Baltic fleet arrived after steaming halfway round the world it was quickly sunk by the enemy in the Straits of Tsushima. The Japanese, whose basic resources were incomparably smaller than those of Russia, mobilized men and materials far more efficiently, and had the advantage of being much closer to the theatre of war. When hostilities ended, Japan was not far from exhaustion, but the Russian Empire faced the danger of internal collapse.

During the following decade new efforts were made to improve the organization, equipment and transportation of the Russian army. They were not without effect, but when the test came in 1914 the Russian army could not meet it. It had to face the most efficient army in the world; its own economy and transport system were still very backward; its supplies from abroad were cut off by Turkey's entry into the war on the side of the Central Powers and the Allies' failure to force the Dardanelles; its ill-planned mobilization system and ruthless requisitioning of transport disorganized industrial manpower and civilian food supplies; and it had the supreme misfortune to be ruled by a monarch and a team of ministers who were not so much bad rulers as men incapable of ruling at all. The Russian army had its moments of grandeur as well as of misery, yet the war as a whole was a disaster for Russia, and it brought the monarchy to its end. For Russia both the 19th century and the age of Peter and St Petersburg ended in March 1917.

Peoples of Russia: the west and the south

Ever since the principality of Moscow began to emerge from vassalage to the Tatar khans in the 14th century, the history of Muscovy and Russia had been one of conquest. The list of victims is long: Novgorod, Kazan, Astrakhan, Estland, Livonia, Poland, Georgia, Bashkiria, Bessarabia, Armenia, Kazakhstan, the Amur, the Ussuri, Turkestan, Turkmenia are among the more important. Russia became the greatest, territorially contiguous, land empire in history, and such it remained into the third quarter of the 20th century. The first systematic modern census, held in 1897, showed that 55% of the population of the Empire were not Russians. The Tsar's 19th-century subjects consisted of many different peoples, peoples with their own distinctive history, some with a sense of distinctive history in the making.

A large part of the once great Polish Commonwealth had gone to Russia as a consequence of the 18th-century Partitions. Yet the inhabitants of these lands were for the most part not Poles. In 1815 the ambitious, but also generous, plan of Tsar Alexander I (1777–1825) to unite all Poland in a single Kingdom, to be loosely linked with Russia under his Crown, was prevented first by the opposition of the other Great Powers at the Congress of Vienna, and then by rising national intolerance on both the Polish and the Russian sides. The rump Kingdom which did come into being, and which had a compact Polish population, revolted against Russia in 1830 and in

1863, and was deprived of virtually all its autonomy. Although there were times in the 19th century when Poles tried to make the best of membership of the Russian Empire, latent feeling remained predominantly anti-Russian. The Poles not only resented Russian rule in Warsaw, but continued to reject in their hearts the annexation by Russia of the broad belt of borderlands extending from the Baltic to the Black Sea, the historical Grand Duchy of Lithuania, founded in the 14th century, whose culture had for centuries been Polish, but the majority of whose people were neither Poles nor Russians. In the north there was a complex love-hate relationship between Poles, Lithuanians, Belorussians and Jews: in the south the contestants were Poles, Ukrainians and Jews. The ethnic diversity was overlaid by the rivalry between the Catholic, Orthodox and Uniate churches. As the Lithuanians, Belorussians and Ukrainians acquired during the century a stronger national consciousness based on their languages, the situation grew still more difficult. Perhaps the only certain fact is that all these communities disliked the regime of the Tsars.

In the south-west, the province known as Bessarabia was ceded to Russia by the Ottoman Empire in 1812. This was simply the eastern half of the historic principality of Moldavia, the home of the Roumanian people. In the first half of the 19th century it was widely expected that Russia, whose armies repeatedly occupied Moldavia and Wallachia, would eventually annex both. However, this process was arrested by Russia's defeat in 1856. The creation of an independent Roumania was perhaps the most important single effect of the Crimean War: it certainly proved more lasting than the other provisions of the Treaty of Paris, although Russian possession of Bessarabia (South Bessarabia was taken back by Russia in 1878) remained an obstacle to the completion of Roumanian unity. It was not only resented in the Kingdom of Roumania, but was becoming less acceptable to the Bessarabians

'Gentlemen,' says Nicholas I, the bear, to the Polish revolutionaries of 1830, 'I know that you wish to address me; but to spare you from delivering a pack of lies, I desire that you hold your tongues.' The Polish rebellion of 1830–31 was brutally suppressed by the Russians. However, this brutality reinforced Polish national sentiment (the Poles rebelled again in 1863) and engaged the sympathy of the West for the Poles—as this English cartoon shows.

themselves: at the end of the 19th century Roumanian national consciousness was growing, and the beginnings of a national movement were visible.

In the north-west, the provinces of Estland, Livonia and Kurland were annexed by Russia during the 18th century as part of the process of 'opening a window on to Europe' of which the foundation of the city of St Petersburg itself by Peter the Great was the most striking symbol. These provinces had a German ruling class, of landowners and prosperous burghers, whose Protestant religion extended to the subject majorities of Estonians and Latvians. The German upper classes loyally served the Tsars as soldiers and bureaucrats, and their social privileges were assured in return. During the century both Estonians and Latvians developed national movements, led by their incipient social élite of Protestant pastors and school teachers and directed rather against the Germans than the Russians. Although these national movements received some encouragement from Russian nationalist opinion, Russian nationalists had no real sympathy for Estonian or Latvian aspirations: their concern was to weaken German influence and to ensure Russian control over the strategic Baltic coastline.

Russification did not become official Russian policy until the 1890s, and it then antagonized each community in turn: Estonians, Latvians and Germans quarrelled bitterly with each other, but all detested Russian rule. Something similar developed in Finland, which in 1809 was ceded by Sweden and became a distinct Grand Duchy, with its own institutions but with the Russian Emperor as its Grand Duke. The Finnish majority, in its struggle against the Swedish upper classes, whose position was analogous to that of the Germans in the Baltic provinces, to some extent regarded the Russians as protectors. However, during the 1890s the Russian government began to interfere with Finnish institutions and to impose Russian officials and Russian language. It succeeded only in uniting Finns and Swedes in hatred of all things Russian.

The most dangerous national problem in the Russian Empire was the Ukrainian. In the Russian view these were not a nation at all, but merely Russians with an uncouth 'Little Russian' dialect who had had the misfortune to be separated from the rest of Russia since the 14th century when the Lithuanians had conquered Kiev, the first capital of Russia, and the lands west of the lower Dnieper valley. These were recovered by Russia only by the partitions of Poland in the late 18th century. By this time the speech, culture, legal and social institutions of the people were widely different from those of the Muscovites. The problem was further complicated by the nature of the lands to the east of the Dnieper. For centuries this broad steppe land had been sparsely populated by warlike Tatar nomads and by runaway Russian serfs escaping from Muscovite or Polish rule. It was a vast no-man's-land, economically undeveloped, subject to sporadic cavalry raids and constant minor guerrilla warfare, with no stable sovereignty and a great variety of ethnic groups. By the end of the 18th century the whole area had been conquered by Russia, systematic agricultural settlement was beginning, and its black soil, perhaps the most fertile in Europe, began to produce rich crops which formed the basis of Russia's growing grain trade through the Black Sea, and one of the main foundations of the Russian economy. Later in the 19th century iron ore and coal were developed, and in the first decade of the 20th southern Russia, or the Ukraine—the word meant 'borderland'—was not only the main granary but also far the most important metallurgical area of the whole Russian Empire.

By this time the inhabitants of this huge area were overwhelmingly of 'Little Russian' speech, with cultural and social traditions distinct from those of the Great Russians, and regarding the 'Muscovites' *(moskaly)* as aliens. In the mid-19th century there appeared a great poet, Taras Shevchenko (1814–61), who made of the Little Russian dialect a literary Ukrainian language. Secondary literature developed in this language, it came to be used increasingly by educated people of the region in preference to Great Russian, and, on the basis of the language, a modern Ukrainian national consciousness began to crystallize. The process was greatly assisted by the growth of Ukrainian nationalism in neighbouring Galicia, under Austrian rule. Whereas Ukrainian nationalism was fiercely repressed by the Russian government, the Vienna authorities

protected it as a political weapon to be used both against the Poles of the Habsburg monarchy and against Russia.

At the end of the 19th century a strong, organized Ukrainian nationalist movement existed in Galicia, which gave help to struggling Ukrainian nationalists in Russia and a refuge to their leaders. During the last years of the Russian Imperial regime, indeed, Ukrainian nationalism had acquired a wide following among both the educated élite and the peasants. The cities of the Ukraine still had a predominantly Great Russian character, but even this was changing: if the influx into industry from the Ukrainian peasantry tended to be subjected to Russian urban culture, it is also true that the peasant immigrants tended to Ukrainianize the working class of such rapidly growing industrial centres as Ekaterinoslav, Yuzovka and even Kharkov.

South of the Caucasus were two Christian nations of older civilization than the Russians—the Georgians and the Armenians, who tended from the 18th century onwards to regard the Russians as their protectors against Turks or Persians. In 1801 the main Georgian kingdom voluntarily joined the Russian Empire, but neighbouring Georgian principalities and tribes had to be conquered by Russian arms in the following years. The Persian part of Armenia was annexed by Russia in 1828, but the largest part of the Armenian homeland remained under Ottoman rule, while communities of Armenian merchants and craftsmen were scattered through the cities of the Caucasus, south Russia and the Middle East. During the 19th century both Georgians and Armenians remained basically loyal to Russia, but they had good grounds for discontent. The Georgian peasants were oppressed by their landlords, and the terms on which serfs were emancipated in Georgia after 1861 were even more onerous than those applied to Russian peasants. In Armenia at the end of the century the Russian government started interfering in the administration of the Armenian Church and of its cultural fund, which was based on voluntary contributions from the Armenian population and maintained a most impressive system of schools. Thus by the beginning of the century in Transcaucasia, as in the Baltic provinces and Finland, the bureaucrats of St Petersburg had succeeded in turning Russia's natural loyal friends into discontented subjects or even enemies.

The Empire had more than fifteen million Muslim subjects. Outstanding among them were the Tatars of the middle Volga valley, who possessed a prosperous business class, a system of privately financed modern schools, numerous well-educated teachers and the beginnings of other modern intellectual professions. At the end of the century there developed a vigorous political movement, which combined loyalty to Islam with acceptance of European democratic ideas, including social progress and the emancipation of women. The city of Kazan on the Volga was an important centre of Russian culture, the seat of a Russian university since 1805, but it was also the centre of a flourishing Tatar counter-culture, which more than held its own against Russian pressures. In 1900 the Volga Tatars had advanced further in political and cultural modernization than any Muslim people in the world, including the Egyptians and the Indian Muslims. The same tendencies were also making themselves felt among the Crimean Tatars and the Azeri Turks of Azerbaidjan, but Central Asia was barely beginning to be affected.

Turkestan and Turkmenia were Russian colonies, not unlike British or French colonies in Muslim lands. Russian administration was roughly comparable in purpose, if not in style, with the 'indirect rule' instituted by Lugard in Northern Nigeria: the traditional rulers were allowed to carry on much as before, except where specific Russian interests were involved. Yet the position at the end of the century was beginning to change for two main reasons: Turkestan began to be a major source of raw cotton for the Russian textile industry, and Russian peasants began to settle on a mass scale in parts of Central Asia. Both processes were favoured by the authorities. The encouragement of cotton at the expense of other crops was on a similar scale, and led to similar results, as the encouragement of cotton cultivation by the British rulers of Egypt. Settlement of Russians was officially welcomed by the authorities as a means both of relieving population pressure in European Russia and of securing Russian possession of a potentially vulnerable borderland. However, it was bitterly resented by

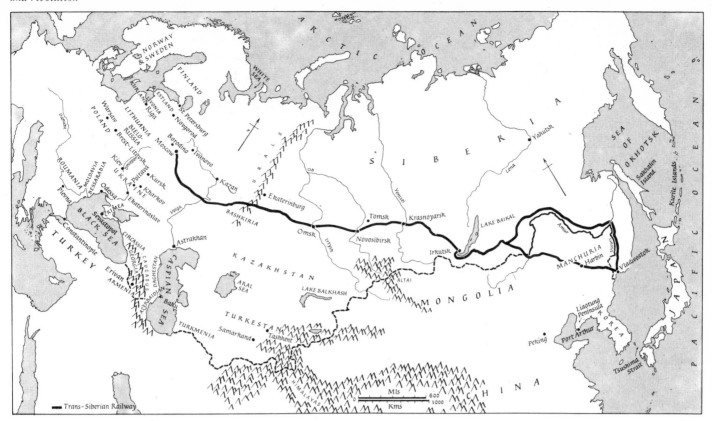

The Russian Empire in the 19th century. The thick black line indicates the Trans-Siberian Railway.

the people of Turkestan, and was a main cause of a series of disorders, culminating in a bloody rising in 1916.

The expansion eastwards

Russian exploration of the north Pacific, both by land and by sea, began in the 18th century, but was taken seriously in hand only in the mid-19th, under the leadership of an energetic governor-general of Eastern Siberia, Count N. N. Muravyov-Amursky (1809–81). In 1849 the mouth of the Amur and the coast of Sakhalin island were explored and small Russian settlements established. In 1860 a brilliant Russian diplomat, Count N. P. Ignatyev (1832–1908), exploited the weakness of China, then faced by an Anglo-French expedition against its capital, to obtain by the Treaty of Peking a vast expanse of Pacific coast-line between the Amur and the Ussuri. Here was founded the future base of Russian naval power in the Pacific, the arrogantly named port of Vladivostok ('ruler of the East'). In 1875 a treaty with Japan allocated Sakhalin to Russia and the Kurile islands to Japan, thus preserving a strategic balance in the Sea of Okhotsk.

Twenty years later, however, the Russian government embarked on a career of systematic imperialism at the expense of China, obtaining effective control first of northern Manchuria, with the Russian-owned Chinese Eastern Railway crossing it, then of the rest of that province, with the South Manchurian Railway going from Harbin south to the sea. There were plans also for the control of Korea. Defeat by Japan cost Russia the SMR and half Sakhalin, but she kept the CER and was able in 1912, with Japanese consent, to establish a protectorate over Outer Mongolia. Russia's relations with Japan and with the European Great Powers in the Far East thus fluctuated, as did the fortunes of Russian imperialism. The one factor which it never occurred to Russian rulers to take into account was the interest of China. When the sleeping giant awoke from its slumbers, it was to administer a rude shock to the Russians, who had treated it with greater greed and brutality than any of the Powers. More than a century after Muravyov-Amursky's first triumphs, it was clear that the process of retribution had only begun.

The largest single area of Russian expansion was Siberia. Here from the 16th century onwards Russian explorers, religious exiles or runaway serfs had begun to open up lands of sparse population, rigorous climate and great natural resources. It was only in the late 19th century that large-scale immigration began, with official encouragement. The indigenous peoples were thinner on the ground, and even less capable of resistance, than the North American Indians. The southern belt of Siberia contained land magnificently suitable for agriculture. From the 1890s Siberia began to develop as Russia's Canada, not separated from the homeland by an ocean. There even developed in Siberia something not unlike the farming communities of the American Mid-West; a new breed of self-reliant, enterprising farmers, with plenty of land at their disposal, developed an interest in efficient production and marketing. Siberian co-operatives, selling their butter on world markets on the eve of the First World War, were an outstanding example of successful capitalist agriculture.

'Russification'

Tsars and ministers had long been accustomed to rule over subjects of many languages, creeds and customs. Discrimination on grounds of religion existed: Orthodox were favoured, Jews and Moslems victimized, and Catholics and Protestants reluctantly tolerated. But by the end of the 18th century there was less collective discrimination than before; Alexander I and Nicholas I required from their subjects obedience, not abandonment of their culture. Russian absolutism had a certain impartiality, even if this did not always penetrate down to the lower levels of the bureaucracy.

At the end of the 19th century there was a marked change, connected with the growth of industry and schools and with the influx of the children of noble landowners into the cities and into jobs in the bureaucracy and the professions. Though it is not possible precisely to pinpoint all the causes of the change, the phenomenon itself is quite clear—the growth of Russian nationalism. A vocal public opinion was demanding, not only that subjects should obey the Tsar, but that they should become Russians. The basis of the legitimacy of government was being extended, for to God and the Tsar was now added the Russian nation. In a sense this may be regarded as a 'democratization' of legitimacy, corresponding to the entry of much larger numbers (even if still only a small minority of society) into the political class. But this kind of

democratization meant not greater liberty but a denial of the residual liberties of half the population of the Empire. During the 1890s this new intolerant climate of opinion spread to the higher levels of the bureaucracy, and under Alexander III (1845–94) and Nicholas II (1868–1918) Russification became official policy. Not only Poles, long regarded as seditious, and Jews, a traditional object of popular hostility, but loyal Baltic Germans, Georgians and Armenians were subject to cultural aggression. Ukrainians and Tatars were objects of particular hatred: 'Little Russian separatism' and 'Pan-Islamism' were denounced in waves of official rhetoric and repressed by zealous bureaucrats.

There was of course an element of benevolence in this policy. Russian nationalists genuinely believed in the superiority of Russian culture, and felt that they were doing the non-Russians a service by helping them to abandon their barbarous dialects and parochial habits and to enter the great Russian nation and take part in its glorious destiny. In this they closely resembled the champions of the other main contemporary example of 'official nationalism', the exponents of Magyarization in Hungary. The result was similar in both countries: the process was self-defeating. Russian and Magyar culture exercised a genuine attraction on the more primitive nations, especially on peasants entering the cities. But brutal Russification and Magyarization antagonized them, and reversed the natural tendency to cultural absorption. Kiev and Kazan were centres of Russian culture, but they also became centres of Ukrainian and Tatar counter-culture, just as in Hungary Kolozsvár and Kassa were not only centres of Magyar culture but also centres of Roumanian and Slovak counter-culture. At the end of the 19th century all the main non-Russian nations of the Empire developed nationalist movements, and national resentment in all the non-Russian areas provided a still more favourable climate for revolutionary ideas of all types than was to be found in areas of Russian population.

Both in Russia and in Hungary there were acute observers—notably P. B. Struve (1870–1944) in Russia and the sociologist Oszkár Jászi in Hungary—who believed that, if official nationalism and persecution were abandoned, the dominant culture would peacefully absorb the lesser cultures. Comparisons were made with the United States: the ethnic crucibles of Pittsburg and Chicago could be reproduced, it was argued, in the Urals or the Ukraine. But the arguments are unconvincing, for the cases were basically different. In America, fragments of different ethnic origins, torn out of their old homes, transported thousands of miles across the ocean and thrown into the American industrial melting-pot, were indeed forged together into a new American nation in a new land. But the nations of Russia or Hungary continued to live in compact communities in their ancestral lands, and those who sought work in the new industrial cities did not lose contact with their fellow nationals at home.

Landowners, peasants and serfs

Russia in the 19th century was an agrarian society, and of the farming population half were serfs owned by private landowners and half were state peasants living in somewhat less irksome bondage to the government. There were some improving landlords, eager to introduce European techniques and livestock on their estates, and the growth of the grain trade from New Russia through the Black Sea provided incentives for greater efficiency. Yet as a whole Russian agriculture was immensely backward.

The case for abolition of serfdom rested partly on moral or political and partly on economic arguments. Tactical use of different arguments by different groups makes it difficult to identify their real motivation, and it is still harder to relate the arguments to social or economic realities. The main reason given by Tsar Nicholas I against abolition was political. If the power of the landowner over the serf were removed, what would replace it? This was a real problem, and there was no easy answer. It can of course be asserted that Nicholas was a reactionary champion of serfdom, who used the argument about public order as an excuse. This view, though widely held at the time and later, is unconvincing. The Tsar himself spoke forcefully of the evil nature of serfdom. He decided to prepare the ground by setting up what was a more efficient

Scene at a village tavern—an idealized view of Russian peasants by F. P. Tolstoi. In fact they were mostly ignorant and illiterate and lived in the most primitive conditions.

system of administration at least for the regions inhabited by state peasants. This task was carried out by Count P. D. Kiselyov (1788–1872), beginning in 1836.

During the reign, private discussion of serfdom grew, though official consideration was confined to a series of ineffective secret committees, and no public agitation for emancipation was permitted. However, the climate of opinion gradually changed. Within the St Petersburg high bureaucracy, especially within the Ministry of the Interior, abolitionist feeling was strong, and a substantial number of landowners were moving to the same conclusion, whether from humanitarian motives or from a conviction that free wage labourers would bring them more profit than serfs or from a combination of these beliefs.

Defeat in the Crimean War brought the problem to a critical stage. The argument about public order operated now in favour of emancipation, for maintenance of the old order seemed more likely to bring collapse than change. A new Emperor had come to the throne. Reorganization of the army and the reconstruction of Russia's defences required the replacement of reluctant contingents of serfs by citizen soldiers. Meanwhile minor riots by peasants were increasing on an alarming scale. Alexander II decided to set in motion the machinery for the enactment of reform.

The process of enactment lasted from 1857 to 1861. It was mainly the work of the Ministry of the Interior, especially of its Deputy-Minister, Nicholas Milyutin (1818–72). Individual enlightened landowners, such as Yury Samarin (1819–76) and Prince V. A. Cherkassky (1824–78), had a big part to play. The result was a compromise. The peasants were to be obliged to pay annual sums to the government for forty-nine years, and the government was to pay compensation to the landowners for the land which was to pass into the possession of the former serfs. In practice, the sums paid to the landowners exceeded the value of the land, and the plots transferred to the peasants were in many cases smaller than those of which they had had the use as serfs. Many landowners had to use the compensation to pay off debts accumulated in the previous decades, while others spent the money in various unproductive ways. Only a minority used the opportunity to improve their estates, or invested it wisely in the industrial enterprises which were now rapidly developing. For their part, the peasants were bitterly disappointed, and many of them expressed their feelings in riots, some on quite a large scale.

If neither landowners nor peasants had much ground for joy, the gainer was the state. The condition required by Nicholas I was on the whole fulfilled: the central administration was extended down to the village level, and a bureaucratic system was set up in place of the serf-owner's authority. The essential instrument was the peasant commune *(obshchina)*, an institution of controversial origin but of long standing, which, among other factors, determined the rotation of crops, allocated land to individual households, collected taxes, issued passports for those seeking work in the towns, and in various ways regulated the life of the peasants. It was governed partly by its members and partly by appointed officials. During the 1880s the power of the officials was substantially increased. In practice the commune exercised a depressing effect on agricultural output, artificially protecting the least efficient and making improved methods of cultivation more difficult. Its supporters upheld it essentially on the grounds that its economic defects were more than compensated for by its administrative convenience: they also claimed that it corresponded to peasant ideas of social justice. In the last decades of the century the commune was the centre of lively controversy at various levels—in the press, in the central ministries and in the provincial assemblies (*zemstvos*) set up by law in 1864 to handle local problems of social welfare. On the whole the Ministry of the Interior defended the commune, on grounds of public order, while the Ministry of Finance opposed it, on grounds of economic efficiency. Among radical political writers, Marxists opposed it, because they believed that capitalism must spread in the villages before the conditions for socialism could be created, while the agrarian socialists or Populists defended it in the belief that the commune could, after a successful revolution, be transformed into the basic rural unit of a socialist society.

Whatever the merits or defects of the commune, Russian agriculture did not prosper in the late 19th century. Population rose while agricultural output remained almost unchanged. Some regions, such as Kursk or Poltava provinces, suffered from serious relative overpopulation. Meanwhile the direct and indirect taxes paid by the peasants were not used to improve agriculture: they went either to the armed forces or to the development of industry and railways. It was only after 1905 that priorities began to change. P. A. Stolypin (1862–1911), Prime Minister from 1906 to 1911, introduced a series of measures which encouraged the replacement of communes by private holdings and the consolidation of scattered small plots into single farms. At the same time both the central government and the *zemstvos* increased their expenditure on agricultural improvement and rural schools. Although these measures could not bring much direct advantage to the poorest section of the peasantry, they did give promise of benefit to the whole economy, from which all would gain in the end. The development was cut short, however, first by war in 1914 and then by revolution.

The three middle classes

Already Peter the Great had encouraged industry, if only to produce weapons and uniforms for his armies. During the 18th century Russia became an important producer of iron ore, and in the 19th textiles made some progress in the central provinces, especially Moscow and Ivanovo. The next big advance was the railway boom of the 1870s, and in general the abolition of serfdom stimulated industry by removing obstacles to growth. It was during the 1890s that a real industrial revolution set in, based on the metallurgy of the Ukraine, the petroleum of Baku, and various branches of engineering located in St Petersburg and Riga, with a few ministers, particularly S. Y. Witte (1849–1915) seeking through industrialization to enhance the greatness of the Russian state. Russian industry was supported by high protective tariffs, and foreign capital played an important part in its growth. The city population increased in consequence, not only in St Petersburg and Moscow but also in the industrial centres and ports of the south. It included not only a new factory working class, with a growing minority of skilled workers, but also a much larger number of urban poor, casual labourers and raw recruits from the countryside, an inescapable feature of the first stages of industrialization in so many countries in modern times. The low wages and hideous living conditions within the new urban agglomerations, most of which hardly merit the name of city, were much the same in Russia about 1900 as they had been in England a century earlier or were to be in Cairo or Calcutta at a later date.

Russia had its urban middle classes, but hardly, as in Western Europe, a single homogeneous middle class, or *bourgeoisie*. The three categories of business men, government officials and intellectual professions remained essentially separate. They had no common outlook, and for most of the 19th century there was little sign of the individualist civilian *bourgeois* ethos of the West. Russian capitalists shared none of the political liberalism of their European counterparts. Material interest had driven English capitalists into opposition to the government in the cause of Corn Law Repeal during the 1830s and 40s: material interest inclined Russian capitalists of the 1890s to support the government which supplied them with huge tariffs and high prices. The partnership between capitalists and autocracy was mutually beneficial. The government

P. A. Stolypin. Hated by revolutionaries and reactionaries alike, due to his insistence on peaceful reforms (of which his agrarian reforms were the most notable), he was assassinated in 1911.

got what it wanted, an industrial development which would directly strengthen Russia's military power, and for this it was prepared to pay by assuring high profits and by repressing labour protest. Russian capitalists not only supported the government, but were content to leave the business of governing to the bureaucrats. In the late 19th century the bureaucracy was filled with sons of noble landowners for whom there was no place on the family estate, and with former landowners who had sold their land to peasants and moved to the towns. These men strengthened the paternalist and military ethos which had always been predominant in the government service, and contributed to the growth of the Russian nationalism which coincided with, but was largely outstripping in importance, the old loyalty to autocracy and Orthodoxy, which had been proclaimed in slogan form earlier in the century ('autocracy, orthodoxy and national principle—*narodnost'*) by Count S. S. Uvarov (1786–1855), Minister of Education from 1833 to 1849.

The third middle class, the intellectual professions, occupied a position of peculiar importance in Russian social structure and political life. The appearance of a secular intellectual élite, educated in the mode of contemporary Europe, dates essentially from the reforms of Peter the Great. At first such men were few, and they were sure of high positions in the state service. By the end of the 18th century European culture had become attractive to the nobility as a whole, and the abolition of compulsory state service by Peter III in 1762 made possible a life of cultured leisure. Persons not of noble origin also began to climb the educational ladder. Most important were the children of Orthodox priests, who were entitled to free education in church seminaries: if they showed intellectual ability they might be able, though this was not always easy, to transfer to the secular education system, pass through the university and make a wordly career. By the mid-19th century priests' sons (*popovichi*) formed a quite disproportionate share of non-noble educated Russians, and later in the century provided an equally disproportionate share of revolutionary leaders. Still later, children of minor officials and shopkeepers entered the educated élite. Another important element were Jews. Virtually excluded from government service or from agricultural occupations, Jews could only go into business or intellectual professions, and the whole Judaic tradition inclined them towards intellectual activity.

The predicament of the modern intellectual élite in Russia long appeared to be unique. Yet it can now be seen to be typical of societies undergoing artificial modernization. Educated in the values of contemporary Europe, familiar with the most advanced social and political ideas of their time, the members of the élite saw in their own country a backward economy, an unjust society and a brutal form of government. Filled with generous compassion for their compatriots in the villages or factories, they could find no common language with them. The cultural gap between élite and people, inevitable at the beginning of artificial modernization, was made worse in Russia than it need have been, and was prolonged for longer, by the failure adequately to develop primary education in relation to universities and secondary schools. This was due largely to the sheer poverty of Russia, and to the obsession of the Tsars with military expenditure and the trappings of Great Power status, but it was due also to a conviction, which actually increased as economic possibilities improved, that the lower orders were best left in ignorance. As late as 1887 the Minister of Education was urging that 'children of coachmen, servants, cooks, washerwomen, small shopkeepers and persons of a similar type' should not be educated above their station. Only after 1905 was a serious attempt made to speed up and improve primary education.

The isolation of élite from people was aggravated by its isolation from the government machine. An educated Russian could only make a career in state service if he would give up his democratic ideas and place himself at the disposal of the autocracy. This fewer and fewer were willing to do, whether of noble or plebeian origin. The word *intelligentsia*, first invented in Russia, acquired the implication of basic hostility to the regime as such. It was from this alienated *intelligentsia* that the leaders of radical groups, and later of active revolutionary parties, were recruited.

Autocracy

The foundation of government in Russia, from the emergence of Muscovy to the downfall of the Romanovs, was the principle of autocracy. For most of the time autocracy appeared immutably rigid, but sometimes it brought violent upheavals dictated from above. The initiative, whether for conservation or change, belonged to the autocrat alone.

Russian and European monarchies have of course a common ancestry, in the Roman Empire and more remotely in the great despotisms of Asia Minor, Mesopotamia and Iran to which Rome was heir. But the institutions and culture of most of Europe were transformed by two great struggles that were protracted for centuries on end: between Church and State and between the monarchical power and a series of social élites, from feudal barons through city burghers to modern capitalists. In the first Russian state, Kiev Rus, these forces were present: in particular the nobles enjoyed some independence in relation to the Grand Prince. But after the Mongol conquest of the mid-13th century and the shift of the centre of gravity of Russian life to Moscow, all this changed.

In Muscovy all power was concentrated at the top. The nobles were the servants of the Grand Duke, their privileges closely linked to their service. Individual magnates, or boyars, at times dominated weak rulers. But the rights of the boyars were never firmly institutionalized, no corporate consciousness of the noble class in relation to the sovereign emerged, and there was no equivalent of the long association of leading noble families with a particular region or city or castle which formed so large a part in the power of the medieval nobility of England or France. The influence of the political system of the Tatar khans may account in part for the divergence from European patterns. Possibly more important is the physical nature of the Russian land, devoid of protective natural barriers, an 'open frontier' to the steppes in the south and east, offering not, as in North America, opportunity and freedom but insecurity and fear, making necessary a militarization of the whole society, a strict vertical hierarchy of command even in civil life.

When the Tatar power broke up, the raids of the southern nomads grew less frequent, and Muscovy's territory expanded in all directions, there was still no internal challenge to autocracy. It survived the invasions and anarchy of the early 17th century. The assemblies of the land (*zemskii sobor*) summoned by the first Romanovs showed no inclination to turn themselves into parliaments. Further disorders at the end of the century produced the most brutal and most revolutionary autocrat of all, Peter the Great, who laid the foundations for regular armed forces and a civil bureaucracy in which the nobility was firmly harnessed to the chariot of state.

The Grand Dukes of Moscow largely owed their success to the support of the Church. Russian archbishops interpreted Byzantine doctrine on autocracy in terms which perhaps owed more to Tatar models than to those of Constantinople, with which only rather superficial contact could be made in the two centuries between the conquest of Russia by the Mongols and the fall of the Imperial City to the Turks. Support of Church and State was mutual, but in the course of time it was the Tsar who became the stronger partner. Opinion in the Church was divided between the champions of pious poverty and those of wealth and power: as in the history of other churches, it was the latter who won. Latent opposition remained, and in the mid-17th century a tremendous crisis rent

Russian society. The Patriarch was determined to introduce European methods of scholarship into church life, and to reform the liturgy by purging accretions of popular legend and superstition. He aroused fanatical opposition from a part of the clergy. There was a mass exodus of the faithful into the forests of the east and north. When the Tsar's forces caught up with them, whole communities would burn themselves to death rather than surrender. Many thousands escaped into the wilderness, and from the Schism numerous sects were born. Nobody ever knew how many Russians were sectarians. In 1850 official estimates varied between less than one million persons and more than nine million: the true number may have been far greater still. The 17th-century Patriarch Nikon won a Pyrrhic victory, and when he then tried to assert claims to a share of temporal power, he was broken by the Tsar. Half a century later Peter the Great abolished the office of Patriarch, and simply placed the Church under a department of the civil government.

During the 18th century there were Russian noblemen who wished to secure constitutional rights for their class. England or Sweden were their models. They received little support from the bulk of the Russian nobility. In 1785 Catherine II granted a Charter to the nobility, intended not only to assure them social privileges but to encourage them to play a more active and progressive part in the management of local affairs. The response was extremely lukewarm. When during the first half of the 19th century various projects of social and political reform were discussed, both within the government hierarchy and before a wider public, a division of opinion repeatedly emerged between those who believed that reform should be the work of an enlightened and politically responsible social élite and those who maintained that it should be left solely to the autocrat.

At the beginning of the reign of Alexander I, liberal aristocrats believed that constitutional limitations on the Tsar were a necessary part of political and social progress. Within the intimate circle of the young Emperor's friends—the so-called 'Unofficial Committee' of 1801–03—Prince Adam Czartoryski (1770–1861) had some sympathy for this view, but Count Paul Stroganov (1772–1817) was against, on the ground that if the Tsar gave up any of his power, '*il pourrait bien se lier les bras de manière qu'il ne pourrait plus exécuter ce qu'il projette en faveur de la nation*'. Alexander's most brilliant adviser, the humbly born Michael Speransky (1772–1839), was well aware of the sinister interdependence of the two institutions of autocracy and serfdom. 'I find in Russia,' he wrote in 1802, 'two classes: the slaves of the sovereign and the slaves of the landowners. The first are called free only in relation to the second, but there are no truly free persons in Russia, except beggars and philosophers.... The interest of the nobility is that the peasants should be placed in their unlimited power; the interest of the peasants is that the nobility should be in the same degree of dependence on the throne.' Speransky realized that reform had to be gradual. He contented himself with working for what he called 'monarchical government', or royal absolutism operating through regular channels according to known rules, in place of the arbitrary and unpredictable rule that had hitherto prevailed. Yet even this was too much to expect. Speransky was disgraced for some years, and when he returned to activity it was as a high-level bureaucrat administering a system that remained virtually unchanged.

Fifty years later, in connection with the abolition of serfdom, there was renewed debate between the spokesmen for autocracy and those for constitutional government. The outstanding social reformer of the time, the great Nicholas Milyutin, was utterly opposed to any participation of organized groups of unofficial persons in the emancipation. Individual landowners, partly elected by the nobility and partly chosen by provincial governors, were allowed to comment on matters of detail, but the main lines of the reform were to be decided by the bureaucrats. Reforming bureaucrats suspected all noblemen of a mere reactionary desire to preserve things as they were: any central representative institutions would merely enable these selfish men to frustrate the noble zeal of the Tsar for his subjects' welfare. Yet the truth was that there was an important group among the gentry no less devoted to social justice than the reforming bureaucrats. These men were silenced in the 1860s, some were persecuted, and the chance of introducing the beginnings of parliamentary government in Russia was lost, with fateful results. The dogma of autocracy set liberal reformers and reforming bureaucrats against each other: the only gainers were the entrenched obscurantists who soon got rid of such men as Milyutin, reasserted their briefly contested grip on the state machine, and led the Russian monarchy on to its ultimate ruin.

Religious and political thinking

In the mid-19th century little could be expected in the way of spiritual or cultural leadership from the Orthodox Church. The educated youth of Russia, increasingly numerous and increasingly attracted by European democratic ideas, viewed the Church with contempt. The words written by the philosopher V. G. Belinsky (1810–48) to Gogol in 1847 sum up the attitude of the Radicals of the 1860s and their successors: the Church 'has always been the bulwark of the whip and the handmaid of despotism'. Belinsky added, 'Look a little closer and you will see that this is by its nature a profoundly atheistic people.' Though emotionally understandable in the circumstances in which Belinsky wrote, neither statement was true. Right up to the Revolution and beyond it, millions of Russians remained Christians, both within official Orthodoxy and in the schismatic and sectarian communities derived from it. Their piety was no less real because it often lacked much intellectual content; no less significant a part of Russian life because Russian priests and laymen, like those of other Christian communities, often led sinful and brutish lives.

In a more specific sense we may say that the Russian political mind and political activity were influenced by Orthodoxy in two ways, one direct and the other indirect.

The members of the first modern political group to take its stand on Orthodoxy were the Slavophils. Their thinking was conservative and religious, but they were no hide-bound defenders of the established order. On the contrary, they stood for social and legal reform and the abolition of serfdom. They were humane and cultured Europeans, who rejected not European culture as such, but what they regarded as the desire of the radical Westernizers slavishly to imitate Western models on Russian soil. One of them, A. S. Khomyakov (1804–60), was an eminent theologian. In his learned writings on Orthodoxy he stressed the unity of the whole body of Christians in the Holy Spirit *(sobornost)* contrasting this with the hierarchical subordination of laymen to priests and of priests to the Pope which he claimed to see in the Catholic Church. He emphasized the piety and humility *(smirenie)* of the Orthodox as against the cold legalism of the Catholics. Of Khomyakov's devotion to these virtues, and of his efforts to practise them in his own life, there can be no doubt. But like romantic nationalists in other countries, he distorted his nation's history, exaggerating the role of noble men and lofty principles and passing over in silence the triumphs of the ungodly.

Even the best of the Slavophils propagated the extraordinary view that conquest and oppression of other nations were something alien to Russian history but characteristic of the Roman-Germanic world. It was one thing to extol Christian humility and brotherly love, another simply to identify these virtues with the will of Russian rulers. Yet in later generations the doctrines of the original Slavophils became perverted into precisely this odious hypocrisy. No one more eloquently exposed the error than the Christian philosopher Vladimir Solovyov (1853–1900), who showed that Slavophil doctrine must lead to the conclusion that the Russian people was 'some sort of Pharisee, righteous in its own eyes, extolling its virtues in the name of humility, despising and condemning neighbour peoples in the name of brotherly love, and ready to wipe them off the face of the earth to ensure the complete triumph of its own gentle and pacific nature'. The elements of saintliness and humility on the one hand and of self-righteous arrogance on the other seem to have been more profoundly rooted in the spiritual traditions of Russia than in those of any other nation, and even the cataclysm of 1917 was too slight to dislodge them.

Towards the end of the 19th century the combination of Orthodoxy and Russian nationalism contributed not only to the new official policies of Russification, but to the growth of militant anti-

Jews in Samarkand. The Jews, more than any other minority groups in the Russian Empire, aroused suspicion and hatred. During Easter 1881 there were outbreaks of violence against them and their property throughout Russia. Consequently a 'temporary order concerning the Jews' was passed which resulted in their being driven into the towns and their rural property being confiscated.

semitism and to the emergence of movements which can best be described as proto-fascist. The 'black hundreds', gangs of toughs who smashed Jewish shops and beat students and school-children in the years 1903–06, and the Union of the Russian People which put across their views in more respectable form, enjoyed the active support of many Orthodox priests and bishops. Like the fascist parties of a later age, they sought to combine the propagation of reactionary ideas with a modern technique of mass mobilization and popular slogans. In this they had a large measure of support from Russian shopkeepers, bureaucrats, workers and peasants.

More indirect, yet unmistakably present, is the influence of Orthodoxy on the opposite extreme of Russian political life, on the movements for social revolution. A large proportion of those who entered the *intelligentsia* from below in the 19th century were children of priests. They lost the faith in which they had been raised, but needed something to take its place. In Western Europe the decline of religious belief was a slow process, and led to scepticism; in Russia, as in Spain and southern Italy, it was sudden and produced *ersatz* religion. The revolutionary programmes of the 1860s and 1870s were not just plans for political action: their aim was a New Jerusalem. Another contributory factor, which can never be estimated with precision, is the influence of the sects. Since the Schism millions of Russians had believed that the Russian state was in the hands of Anti-Christ. This belief did not lead them to violent rebellion: Anti-Christ could dispose of their bodies in this life, they would be justified in the world to come. It did however lead to complete contempt for worldly institutions and laws.

When a more activist generation arose in the late 19th century, including the children of sectarians, they took with them into their political struggles the messianism and maximalism of the sects. Piecemeal reforms could not interest them: revolution must achieve all or nothing. It is of course arguable that the sects were products of social conflicts and oppression, yet it is also true that the way that sectarians reacted to social situations was influenced by their religious and moral outlook. Again, it is difficult, when one finds sectarian religious phrases in revolutionary literature, to say to what extent this was due to the revolutionaries' tactical aim of arousing support among sectarian peasants or to the influence on their political thinking of their childhood beliefs. Undoubtedly, however, a religious attitude to political issues was characteristic of the first generations of Russian revolutionaries, and many of the leading figures of the People's Will and the earlier Socialist Revolutionaries, including perhaps especially the assassins among them, showed a quality which can only be described as personal saintliness. Although the Marxists, who began to acquire an intellectual ascendancy among revolutionary youth during the 1890s, prided themselves on their scientific outlook and practical efficiency, many of them too shared something of the religious attitude of their Populist predecessors. Yet another element which contributed to the revolutionary movement was Jewish messianism. The large proportion of Jews among the revolutionaries was due of course to the special social structure of the Jewish community, to its traditional respect for learning which led young Jews still more than young Russians to seek higher education, and to the special discriminations against Jews built into the Russian political system which gave them even more grounds to oppose it than had the Russians themselves.

Law and revolution

Revolution gained a hold on young Russian minds not only because they were inclined to messianism and maximalism, but also for the perfectly practical reason that the rulers not only refused reforms but broke their own laws. The very concept of the rule of law, as understood in Europe, was alien to the Russian political tradition. Lawyers were despised as dreary formalists obsessed with meaningless rituals and dusty papers. The notion that law should establish standards against which actions should be measured, regardless of person, was rejected as soulless Roman rationalism. In its place the Slavophils held up the ideal of collective common sense: good, decent, humble, kindly Russian men and women should sit down together and talk like brothers and sisters, and a sense of the meeting would emerge in the end, so much sounder and more valuable than the edicts of inhuman pen-pushers.

Nevertheless, during the 1860s a great judicial reform was carried out. The initiative came from within the bureaucracy, for the existing system of courts was so incompetent that it impeded the operation of the autocracy. The new system was based on that of Western Europe, and in the following half-century it worked reasonably well. It also brought into being a modern legal profession. No group did more to spread liberal ideas and liberal practices, to develop in Russia a *bourgeois* ethos in the European sense. When in 1905, under the impact of military defeat and revolutionary upheaval, Nicholas II granted a Constitution, and a Russian Parliament, the State Duma, came into existence, there were hopes, at least in liberal circles, that the rule of law would prevail. Yet the hopes were disappointed. Not only was there no responsible parliamentary government—for ministers were chosen by the Emperor without regard to the majority in the Duma, and the military estimates and the sums allocated to the Imperial Court were out of the Duma's control—but even the powers granted by law were not observed. Nicholas II considered his autocratic will to be above the law. Even the comparatively enlightened conservative Stolypin (1862–1911), Prime Minister from 1906 to 1911, twice broke the law: in 1907 he altered the franchise in the interval between the dissolution of the Second Duma and the new election, and in 1911 he arbitrarily prorogued the Third Duma for three days in order to enact by decree a reform of the local government system which the upper chamber had rejected. As for the provincial governors and police chiefs, they frequently ignored or perverted

the law, and prevented their subjects from exercising legally guaranteed rights. Not surprisingly, from their side the revolutionaries poured contempt, not only on the existing laws, the class bias of which was often undeniable, but on the very principle of the prevalence of law. The interests of 'the working class', or 'the masses', that is, the will of the revolutionary leaders who claimed to speak on behalf of these abstractions, must take precedence, they argued, over any formal rules. Fundamentally, the attitude to law of Imperial bureaucrats and Marxist or Populist leaders was the same.

In the last fifty years of Imperial Russia there was progress not only in industry and trade, but also in education, social welfare, science and culture. The tendency to *embourgeoisement* was visible, and even the incomplete and lopsided series of reforms had a civilizing effect on growing sections of the people. Yet there still seemed to be good grounds for holding the view that revolution was the only way to achieve liberty or justice, and in consequence revolutionary movements remained strong. Revolutionary action began in the 1860s. At this time there were only small groups of young *intelligentsia*, first discussing the most radical ideas imported from the West and then seeking conspiratorial methods to put them into effect. A second stage began during the late 1870s when the revolutionaries sought mass support among the peasants, had virtually no success, but found instead a real though restricted mass base among the workers of a few large cities: a specifically Marxist discussion group existed in St Petersburg in 1885, in correspondence with G. V. Plekhanov (1856–1918) in Switzerland, and the Populists also tried to make contact with the workers. During the 1890s a mass working-class movement developed: a Social Democratic Labour Party was founded in 1898, and groups of Social Revolutionaries, never large or well-disciplined, survived the harrying of the police. Both Social Democrats and Social Revolutionaries were torn by internal conflicts, which became more acute after the failure of the 1905 Revolution. The split of the Social Democrats became final in 1912, and V. I. Lenin (1870–1924), the most powerful personality amongst them with the finest feeling for revolutionary tactics and timing, went on to build up his own small but resolute Bolshevik party. The Socialist Revolutionaries remained nominally one party, but this fictitious unity barely concealed an inner confusion which proved a source of fatal weakness when opportunity came in 1917.

A combination of *intelligentsia* and city workers could not suffice to take power in agrarian Russia. Decisive mass support required the involvement of the peasants. The experience of 19th-century Russia, which has been reinforced subsequently by the later experience of such countries as China, Yugoslavia and Mexico, suggests that the involvement of peasants in mass revolutionary action is not a cause but a consequence of the dissolution of the state power. In 1905 defeat in war, mass strikes and numerous mutinies shook the machinery of government to its foundations, and it was at this point that peasant risings became widespread. The Tsar's generals and ministers were able to restore order, and in the relative economic prosperity of the following years the peasants were quiet again. Yet the pattern was to repeat itself. In 1917 military defeat and economic troubles in the city brought down the monarchy, whose leading servants had displayed an incompetence amounting almost to political paralysis which hardly has a parallel in human history. The fall of the monarchy was followed by a disintegration of the machinery of government itself. It was at this point that the peasants, both those in uniform in the army and those who remained on the land, were involved in the revolutionary process which engulfed the whole of Russia and which separates the 19th from the 20th centuries—not only in Russia but in the world—as sharply as the French Revolution of 1789 had separated the 18th from the 19th centuries.

Select Bibliography

I The shape of the century

ASHTON, T. S. *The Industrial Revolution* (London, 1948)

CAMERON, R. *France and the Economic Development of Europe, 1800–1914* (Oxford and Princeton, 1961)

CHEVALIER, L. *Classes laborieuses et classes dangereuses à Paris pendant la première moitié du XIXᵉ siècle* (Paris, 1958)

CIPOLLA, C. M. *The Economic History of World Population* (Harmondsworth, 1962)

CLAPHAM, J. H. *The Economic Development of France and Germany, 1815–1914* (4th ed. Cambridge, 1936)

DUPEUX, G. *La société française, 1789–1960* (Paris, 1964)

HENDERSON, W. O. *The Industrialisation of Europe, 1780–1914* (London, 1969)

HOBSBAWM, E. *The Age of Revolution* (London and New York, 1962)

HOUGHTON, W. E. *The Victorian Frame of Mind* (New Haven, Conn. and Oxford, 1957)

LANDES, D. S. *The unbound Prometheus: Technological Change and Industrial Development in Western Europe from 1750 to the Present* (Cambridge, 1969)

MORAZE, C. *La France bourgeoise* (Paris, 1946)

MORAZE, C. *Les Bourgeois conquérants* (Paris, 1957)

REINHARD, M. R. *Histoire de la population mondiale de 1700 à 1948* (Paris, 1949)

STEARNS, P. N. *European Society in Upheaval* (London and New York, 1967)

THOMPSON, E. P. *The Making of the English Working Class* (London, 1963; New York, 1964)

YOUNG, G. M. *Victorian England, Portrait of an Age* (Oxford, 1936)

ALTINCK, R. D. *The English Common Reader: A Social History of the Mass Reading Public* (Cambridge and Chicago, 1957)

BERNAL, J. D. *Science in History* (London, 1954)

BRINTON, C. C. *A History of Western Morals* (London and New York, 1959)

CLARK, K. *The Gothic Revival* (London, 1962; New York, 1963; paperback edition, Harmondsworth, 1964)

EINSTEIN, A. *Music in the Romantic Era* (London and New York, 1947)

FRIEDELL, E. *Kulturgeschichte der Neuzeit*, 3 vol. (Munich, 1927–31)

FRIEDELL, E. *A Cultural History of the Modern Age.* Translation of the above by C. F. Atkinson. 3 vol. (New York, 1930–32)

GOMBRICH, E. H. *The Story of Art* (London and New York, 1950)

HILLIS MILLER, J. *The Disappearance of God: Five Nineteenth-Century Writers* (Harvard and Oxford, 1963)

HITCHCOCK, H. R. *Architecture in the Nineteenth and Twentieth Centuries* (Harmondsworth, 1958)

HUGHES, S. *Consciousness and Society* (London, 1959)

JACKSON, H. *The Eighteen nineties* (London, 1913)

LANG, P. H. *Music in Western Civilisation* (New York, 1941; London, 1942)

LESTER, J. A. *Journey Through Despair, 1880–1914* (Princeton, 1968; Oxford, 1969)

MASON, S. F. *A History of the Sciences* (London, 1953). Same book published in New York, 1954, with the title *Main Currents of Scientific Thought*

MOSSE, G. L. *The Culture of Western Europe in the Nineteenth and Twentieth Centuries* (New York, 1961; London, 1963)

NOVOTNY, F. *Painting and Sculpture in Europe, 1780–1870* (Harmondsworth, 1960)

STERN, F. *The Politics of Cultural Despair* (Cambridge and Berkeley, 1961)

TALMON, J. L. *Romanticism and Revolt* (London and New York, 1967)

WILLIAMS, R. *Culture and Society* (London, 1958; New York, 1959)

II Revolution and improvement

ARTZ, F. B. *Reaction and Revolution 1814–1832* (London and New York, 1934; London, 1963)

BERKELEY, G. F. H. *Italy in the making* (Cambridge, 1932)

BRIGGS, A. *The Age of Improvement* (London, 1959)

CROCE, B. *History of Europe in the Nineteenth Century*, trans. H. Furst (London, 1934)

LANGER, W. L. *Political and Social Upheaval*

LEFEBVRE, G. *La révolution française* (3rd ed. Paris, 1963)

LEFEBVRE, G. *The French Revolution*, 2 vol., translation of the above (London, 1962; New York, 1964)

LEFEBVRE, G. *Napoléon* (6th ed. Paris, 1969)

LEFEBVRE, G. *Napoleon*, translation of the above (London, 1969)

RAMM, A. *Germany 1789–1914* (London and New York, 1967)

ROBERTSON, P. *Revolutions of 1848: A social history* (Princeton, 1952; re-issue, New York, 1960)

SCHNERB, R. *Le XIXᵉ siècle* (Paris, 1955)

TALMON, J. L. *Romanticism and Revolt* (London and New York, 1967)

III Authority and protest

BRIGGS, A. *The Age of Improvement* (London, 1959)

CLAPHAM, J. H. *The Economic Development of France and Germany, 1815–1914* (4th ed. Cambridge, 1936)

COLE, G. D. H. *A History of Socialist Thought:* Vol. II *Marxism and Anarchism, 1850–1890* (London, 1954); Vol. III *The Second International 1889–1914* (London, 1956)

HEARDER, H. *Europe in the Nineteenth Century* (London and New York, 1966)

JOLL, J. *The Anarchists* (London, 1964; New York, 1966)

LANDES, D. S. *The unbound Prometheus: Technological Change and Industrial Development in Western Europe from 1750 to the Present* (Cambridge, 1969)

LICHTHEIM, G. *Marxism* (London and New York, 1961)

MOSSE, G. L. *The Culture of Western Europe in the Nineteenth and Twentieth Centuries* (New York, 1961; London, 1963)

RAMM, A. *Germany 1789–1919* (London and New York, 1967)

REWALD, J. *The History of Impressionism* (New York, 1949)

REWALD, J. *Post-Impressionism* (New York, 1956)

SETON-WATSON, C. *Italy from Liberalism to Fascism, 1870–1925* (London and New York, 1967)

WRIGHT, G. *France in Modern Times, 1760 to the present* (Chicago, 1960; London, 1962)

IV Cities

BRIGGS, A. *Victorian Cities* (London, 1963; Chester Springs, Pa., 1964; paperback edition, Harmondsworth, 1968)

DICKINSON, R. E. *The West European City* (2nd rev. ed. London, 1962)

GUTKIND, E. A. *International History of City Development*, 3 vol. (New York, 1964–67)

HALL, P. *The World Cities* (London and New York, 1966)

HOWARD, E. *Garden-Cities of To-morrow* (London, 1902; reprint, 1946)

LAVEDAN, P. *Histoire de l'urbanisme*, vol. 3 (Paris, 1952)

LAVEDAN, P. *Géographie des villes* (2nd ed., Paris, 1960)

MEURIOT, P. *Des agglomérations urbaines dans l'Europe contemporaine* (Paris, 1897)

MUMFORD, L. *The City in History* (London and New York, 1961; paperback edition, Harmondsworth, 1966)

PETERMANN, T. (ed.) *Die Grosstadt* (Dresden, 1903)

REPS, J. W. *The Making of Urban America: a history of city planning in the U.S.* (Princeton, 1965)

WEBER, A. *The Growth of Cities in the XIXth Century* (New York, 1899; reprint, 1965)

V Countrysides

a) Contemporary accounts:

CAIRD, J. *English Agriculture in 1850–51* (London, 1852; reprinted 1968)

COLMAN, H. *The Agricultural and Rural Economy of France, Belgium, Holland and Switzerland* (London, 1848)

LAVELEYE, E. de, *Etudes d'économie rurale: la Lombardie et la Suisse* (Paris, 1869)

POLLARD, S. and C. Holmes (ed.) *Documents of European Economic History, 1750–1870* (London, 1968)

RIDER HAGGARD, H. *Rural Denmark and its Lessons* (London, 1911)

b) Recent works:

CHAMBERS, J. D. and G. E. Mingay, *The Agricultural Revolution, 1750–1880* (London and New York, 1966)

CONZE, W. 'The Effects of 19th-century Liberal Agrarian Reforms in Central Europe', in Crouzet, Chaloner and Stern (ed.), *Essays in European Economic History, 1789–1914* (London, 1969)

DOVRING, F. 'The Transformation of European Agriculture', in *Cambridge Economic History of Europe*, Vol. VI, Part II (Cambridge, 1965)

JONES, E. L. and S. J. Woolf (ed.), *Agrarian Change and Economic Development* (London, 1970)

THOMPSON, F. M. L. *English Landed Society in the Nineteenth Century* (London and Toronto, 1963)

YOUNGSON, A. J. 'The Opening up of New Territories', in *Cambridge Economic History of Europe*, Vol. VI, Part I (Cambridge, 1965)

VI Nation building

ACTON, W. 'Nationalism', in *The History of Freedom and other Essays* (London, 1907)

BOEHME, H. (ed.) *Probleme der Reichsgründungszeit, 1848–1879* (Cologne and Berlin, 1968)

BURY, J. P. T. 'Nationalities and Nationalism', in *The New Cambridge Modern History*, Vol. X, pp. 213–45 (Cambridge, 1960)

HANTSCH, H. *Die Nationalitätenfrage im alten Österreich* (Vienna, 1953)

HOLTOM, D. C. *Modern Japan and Shinto Nationalism* (revised ed., Chicago, 1947)

KANN, R. A. *The Multinational Empire: Nationalism and National Reform in the Habsburg Monarchy, 1848–1918*, 2 vol. (New York, 1950; Oxford, 1951)

KEDOURIE, E. *Nationalism* (London and New York, 1960)

KOHN, H. *Prelude to Nation-States. The French and German Experience, 1789–1815* (Princeton, 1967)

LEMBERG, E. *Nationalismus*, 2 vol. (Reinbeck, 1964)

MACARTNEY, E. A. *National States and National Minorities* (London, 1934)

MACK SMITH, D. *Cavour and Garibaldi, 1860* (Cambridge, 1954)

MACK SMITH, D. *Italy, A Modern History* (London and Ann Arbor, 1959)

MINOGUE, K. R. *Nationalism* (London, 1967)

NAMIER, L. 'Nationality and Liberty', in *Avenues of History* (London and New York, 1952)

SCHIEDER, R. *Das deutsche Kaiserreich von 1871 als Nationalstaat* (Cologne and Opladen, 1961)

SETON-WATSON, H. *The Decline of Imperial Russia* (re-issue, London, 1964)

STORRY, R. *A History of Modern Japan* (Harmondsworth, 1960)

VII War and peace

BEALES, A. C. F. *The History of Peace* (London, 1931)

BOND, B. (ed.) *Victorian Military Campaigns* (London and New York, 1967)

BRODIE, B and F. *From Crossbow to H-Bomb* (New York, 1962)

BURY, J. P. T. (ed.) *The New Cambridge Modern History*, Vol. X (Cambridge, 1960), Chapters XI and XII

CRAIG, G. A. *The Politics of the Prussian Army, 1640–1945* (New York, 1964)

CRAIG, G. A. *The Battle of Königgrätz* (London and New York, 1964)

FULLER, J. F. C. *The Conduct of War, 1789–1961* (London and New Brunswick, 1961)

HINSLEY, F. H. (ed.) *The New Cambridge Modern History*, Vol. XI (Cambridge, 1962) Chapter VIII

HOWARD, M. *The Franco-Prussian War* (London and New York, 1961)

LYONS, F. S. L. *Internationalism in Europe, 1815–1914* (Leyden, 1963)

PRESTON, R. A., S. F. Wise and H. O. Werner, *Men in Arms* (revised ed., London and New York, 1962)

ROPP, T. *War in the Modern World* (New York, 1962)

VIII The making of America

ALLEN JONES, M. *American Immigration* (Cambridge and Chicago, 1960)

BOORSTIN, D. J. *The Americans: The National Experience* (Harmondsworth, 1970)

CUNLIFFE, M. *The Literature of the United States* (Harmondsworth, 1954; 3rd edition, 1967)

FRANKLIN, J. H. *From Slavery to Freedom. A History of Negro Americans* (3rd edition, New York, 1967)

GLAAB, C. N. and A. Theodore Brown, *A History of Urban America* (New York, 1967)

HABAKKUK, H. J. *American and British Technology in the Nineteenth Century* (Cambridge, 1962)

HOFSTADTER, R. *The American Political Tradition* (London, 1962; paperback edition, London, 1967)

NASH SMITH, H. *Virgin Land: The American West as Symbol and Myth* (Cambridge, Mass., 1950)

POTTER, D. M. *People of Plenty: Economic Abundance and the American Character* (Chicago, 1954; Cambridge, 1955)

TAYLOR, W. R. *Cavalier and Yankee: The Old South and American National Character* (New York, 1961)

TOCQUEVILLE, A. de, *Democracy in America*, ed. J. P. Mayer and M. Lerner, 2 vol. (London, 1968)

VANN WOODWARD, C. *The Burden of Southern History* (Baton Rouge, 1960)

IX The expansion of Russia

BLUM, J. *Lord and Peasant in Russia* (Princeton, 1961)

CURTISS, J. S. *The Russian Army under Nicholas I* (Durham, N.C., 1965)

EMMONS, T. *The Russian landed gentry and the Peasant Emancipation of 1861* (Cambridge, 1968)

KEEP, J. L. H. *The Rise of Social Democracy in Russia* (Oxford, 1963)

KUCHEROV, S. *Courts, Lawyers, and Trials under the last three Tsars* (New York, 1953)

RAEFF, M. *Origins of the Russian Intelligentsia* (New York, 1961)

RAEFF, M. *Michael Speransky, Statesman of Imperial Russia* (The Hague, 1957)

RIASANOVSKY, N. V. *Nicholas I and Official Nationality in Russia* (Cambridge and Berkeley, 1959)

ROBINSON, G. T. *Rural Russia under the old regime* (London, 1929)

SETON-WATSON, H. *The Russian Empire, 1801–1917* (Oxford, 1967)

TREADGOLD, D. W. *The Great Siberian Migration* (Princeton, 1957; Oxford, 1958)

VENTURI, F. *Roots of Revolution* (London and New York, 1960)

VON LAUE, T. *Sergei Witte and the Industrialization of Russia* (New York, 1963)

ZENKOVSKY, S. A. *Pan-Turkism and Islam in Russia* (Oxford and Harvard, 1960)

Pictures are listed spread by spread, from top left to bottom right

9 ● John Martin: *The Bard*; 1817. Laing Art Gallery, Newcastle-upon-Tyne. Photo *Philipson Studios Ltd*

10–11 ● Bed; First Empire style. Palazzo Mansi, Lucca. Photo *Georgina Masson*

● Brass four-poster bed 'in Renaissance style'; English, manufactured by R. W. Winfield and shown at the Great Exhibition, 1851. From Matthew Digby Wyatt, *Industrial Arts of the Nineteenth Century*, London 1851

● Oak four-poster bed, lacquered white; designed by Charles Rennie Mackintosh for his own flat in Glasgow, c. 1900. Glasgow University, Mackintosh collection. Photo *Annan, Glasgow*

● Napoleon I bronze and ormolu mantel clock; French, early 19th C. Formerly in the René Fribourg Collection. Photo *courtesy Sotheby & Co.*

● The 'Hours' clock-case; electroplate, designed by John Bell and made by Elkington, Mason & Co. of London and Birmingham, shown at the Great Exhibition in 1851. From *The Illustrated London News*, 9 August 1851

● Clock; designed by H. M. Baillie Scott and made by J. P. White of Bedford, illustrated in a catalogue of 1901. *Victoria and Albert Museum, London (Crown copyright)*

● Woven silk tissue; French, 1800–1815. *Victoria and Albert Museum, London (Crown copyright)*

● Woven silk on satin ground; German, shown at the Great Exhibition of 1851. From *The Art Journal Illustrated Catalogue*, London 1851

● Printed cotton chintz; designed by C. F. A. Voysey, c. 1896. *Victoria and Albert Museum, London (Crown copyright)*

● Detail of main doors of the Altes Museum, Berlin; bronze, designed by Karl Friedrich Schinkel, c. 1823. Photo *Staatliche Museen zu Berlin*

● Detail of choir screen of Hereford Cathedral; iron, copper and brass, designed by Sir George Gilbert Scott and made by Skidmore of Coventry, 1862. The screen was dismantled by the Cathedral authorities in 1967 and is now in store in Coventry Museum. Photo *National Monuments Record*

● Detail of railing round Metro entrance, Paris; cast iron painted green, designed by Hector Guimard, c. 1900. Photo *André Martin*

● 'Kensington Garden Dresses'; from *Le Beau Monde*, London, June 1808

● Day and evening dresses; from *Le Courier des Dames*, Paris, May 1855. *Victoria and Albert Museum, London (Crown copyright)*

● Waiting dress; from *La Mode Artistique*, Paris 1900. Photo *courtesy Verlag Georg D. W. Callwey*

12–13 ● Great Exhibition, London, 1851; the Crystal Palace, designed by Joseph Paxton, in Hyde Park; coloured lithograph from *Dickinson's Comprehensive Pictures of the Great Exhibition of 1851 from the originals painted ... for H.R.H. Prince Albert*, London 1854. Courtesy Professor Sir Nikolaus Pevsner. Photo *John Webb (Brompton Studio)*

● Exposition Universelle, Paris, 1867: bird's-eye view of exhibition grounds in the Champ de Mars; lithograph by Van Geleyn, 1867. Bibliothèque Historique de la Ville de Paris. Photo *Giraudon*

● Exhibition Building, Melbourne, 1880; from the *Illustrated Australian News*, October 1880. The State Library of Victoria, Melbourne. Photo *Nigel Buesst*

14–15 ● Detail of membership certificate of the National Union of Gas Workers and General Labourers 1889. Trades Union Congress, London. Photo *R. B. Fleming*

● Percy Pit, Percy Main Colliery; detail of engraving from T. H. Hair, *Sketches of Coal Mines in Northumberland and Durham*, 1839. Science Museum, London

● Oil wells at Tarr Farm, near Oil Creek, Pennsylvania, c. 1860; detail of engraving from L. Simonin, *Mines et mineurs, la vie souterraine*, Paris 1867. Bibliothèque Nationale, Paris. Photo *Holzapfel–Documentation Française*

● Palais de l'Électricité at the Paris Exposition Universelle of 1900, illuminated at dusk; from a contemporary photograph. *Collection of Georges Sirot, Paris*

● Interior in the Forth Banks Power Station in the region of Newcastle-upon-Tyne, Northumberland, showing 75kw Parsons steam turbines; detail of a photograph of 1892. *Science Museum, London*

16–17 ● Rome: Monument to Victor Emmanuel II; designed by Count Giuseppe Sacconi in 1884, built 1885–1911. Photo *Scala*

● Munich: Glyptothek, seen from the Königsplatz; by Leo von Klenze, begun 1816. Photo *Werner Neumeister*

● London: Houses of Parliament from the south, with the Victoria Tower on the left; by Sir Charles Barry and A. W. N. Pugin, 1840–65. Photo *Eileen Tweedy*

● St Louis, Missouri: Wainwright Building (detail); by Dankmar Adler and Louis Sullivan, 1890–91. Photo *Savage Studio, St Louis*

● Barcelona: façade of the Nativity transept, Sagrada Familia church; by Antoni Gaudí, 1891–1926. Photo *Mas*

● Paris: Eiffel Tower; by Gustave Eiffel, begun 1887 for the Exposition of 1889. Photo *Scala*

18–19 ● Vignette representing the various peoples of the Russian Empire: engraving from E. Ukhtomsky, *Travels in the East of Nicholas II Emperor of Russia*, London 1896. British Museum, London. Photo *John R. Freeman*

● The Germans as colonizers: caricature from *Jugend*, Munich, 1896. British Museum, London. Photo *John R. Freeman*

- Franz Krüger: portrait of Frederick William IV of Prussia; c. 1852. In the background are the gardens of the palace of Sans Souci, Potsdam. Schloss Charlottenburg. Photo *Staatsbibliothek, Berlin*
- Henri Baron: *Soirée at the Tuileries, given in honour of the visit of the Czar of Russia and the King of Prussia to the Paris exhibition of 1867*; watercolour. Palais de Compiègne. Photo *Bulloz*

82–83
- James Cafferty and Charles Rosenberg: *Bank Crash in Wall Street, New York, 13 October 1857, at half past 2 p.m.* Museum of the City of New York
- The Bank of England, Consols Office; from a photograph of 1894. Photo *Brompton Studio*
- Dover elections; from a photograph of 1865. *Gernsheim Collection, University of Texas*
- London dockers on strike; from a photograph of 1889. *Transport and General Workers' Union*
- 'Assassination' of Generals Clément Thomas and Jules Lecomte at 6, rue des Rosiers, Montmartre, Paris, 18 March 1871, at 4 p.m.; from a photograph staged after the event for propaganda purposes. Victoria and Albert Museum, London. Photo *John R. Freeman*
- Statue of Napoleon from the top of the Vendôme column, Paris, after being pulled down by Communards, 16 May 1871; from a contemporary photograph. Gustave Courbet eighth from the right. *Gernsheim Collection, University of Texas*
- The Socialist League, Hammersmith; formerly a branch of the Social Democratic Federation; from a photograph of c. 1885. *Victoria and Albert Museum, London, Crown Copyright*

84
- Membership certificate of the Associated Shipwrights Society. Trades Union Congress, London. Photo *R. B. Fleming*

86
- *A Good Offer*; drawing by Sir John Tenniel from *Punch*, 29 September 1860

87
- Caricature of Bismarck's *Kulturkampf* against the Roman Catholic Church, 1874. Photo *Staatsbibliothek, Berlin*

88
- Ornamental effect of the hair of a monkey; illustration from Charles Darwin, *The Descent of Man*, London 1871

89
- *A Socialist Parable: Absolute Monarchy; Constitutional Monarchy; Middle-Class Democracy; Socialist Democracy*. From C. E. Jensen, *Karikatur Album*, Copenhagen 1904–8, II

90
- *The Socialist Menace*; drawing by Bertall, 1850

91
- Portrait of Friedrich Engels. *Mansell Collection*

93
- Map of Europe after the Congress of Berlin, 1878

94
- Aubrey Beardsley: *Return of Tannhäuser to the Venusberg*; 1895

97
- Gustave Doré: 'A City Thoroughfare'; engraving from G. Doré and B. Jerrold, *London. A Pilgrimage*, London 1872

98–99
- Gaetano Gigante: *View of the Via Toledo in Naples*; c. 1830. Museo Nazionale di San Martino, Naples. Photo *A. Parente*
- William Ibbit: *South-East View of Sheffield*; watercolour. c. 1854. *Sheffield City Museums*
- View of Barcelona in the second half of the 19th century; chromolithograph. Museo de Historia de la Ciudad, Barcelona. Photo *Mas*

- Charles Graham: *The Skyline of New York*; chromolithograph, 1896. The New York Public Library
- E. Heswert: *View of the Port of Rotterdam*; 1904. *Gemeentearchiv, Rotterdam*

100–101
- Demolition for the building of the new Rue des Ecoles, Paris; engraving by Félix Thorigny, 1858. Bibliothèque Nationale, Paris. Photo *Roger-Viollet*
- Bird's eye view of Paris before Haussmann; lithograph after Testard. Photo *La Documentation Française*
- Building works at the Rue de Rivoli, Paris; engraving from *L'Illustration*, 1854. Photo *La Documentation Française*
- Caricature of Baron Haussmann; from *Le Trombinoscope*, Paris 1872
- Plan of Paris showing the Haussmann boulevards
- Grands Magasins du Printemps, Paris; detail of print after M. Berteault, 1889. *Archive de la Documentation Française*

102–103
- Atkinson Grimshaw: *Liverpool Quay by Moonlight*; 1887. The Tate Gallery, London. Photo *John Webb (Brompton Studio)*
- Berry F. Berry: *Bath Road, looking East*; from a series of chromolithographs of Bedford Park (Chiswick, Middlesex), 1882. Collection T. A. Greeves, Esq. Photo *Eileen Tweedy*
- Milan: Victor Emmanuel Gallery; by Giuseppe Mengoni, 1863–7. Photo *F. A. Mella, Milan*
- Interior of a bazaar in Constantinople; watercolour, probably English, first quarter of the 19th C. Victoria and Albert Museum, London. Photo *John Webb (Brompton Studio)*

104–105
- W. M. Egley: *Omnibus Life in London, 1859*. The Tate Gallery, London
- *View on the Metropolitan Railway: Baker Street Station*; chromolithograph, 1868. *Science Museum, London*
- New York: elevated railway in the Bowery; from a photograph by J. S. Johnston, 1895. *Prints and Photographs Division, Library of Congress, Washington, D.C.*
- 'Night Refuge for the London Poor'; engraving from the *Illustrated Times*, 1859
- Gustave Doré: Devil's Acre, Westminster; engraving from G. Doré and B. Jerrold, *London. A Pilgrimage*, London 1872
- George Scharf: *Building the Common Sewers at Tottenham Court Road*; pencil drawing, 1845. British Museum, London. Photo *John R. Freeman*
- The Sewers of Paris; from Belgrand, *Les Travaux Souterrains de Paris*, 1887. Bibliothèque Nationale, Paris. Photo *La Documentation Française*

106–107
- G. Veith: *View of the Ringstrasse*; chromolithograph, 1873. *Historisches Museum der Stadt Wien, Vienna*
- View of Collins Street; lithograph from the *Melbourne Album*, London 1864. British Museum, London. Photo *John R. Freeman*
- *View of Oklahoma City in Indian Territory*; lithograph by T. M. Fowler, 1890. *The New York Public Library, Stokes Collection*

110
- Table showing the growth of cities throughout the world

111
- View of Lyons; from E. Reclus, *Nouvelle Géographie Universelle*, II Paris 1877

- View of Buda and Pest; from E. Reclus, *Nouvelle Géographie Universelle*, III Paris 1877

112
- St Helens, Lancashire in the 19th C.; from Barker and Harris, *A Merseyside Town in the Industrial Revolution*, Liverpool 1959

113
- View of Le Creusot; from E. Reclus, *Nouvelle Géographie Universelle*, II Paris 1877

115
- A street scene in Philadelphia; engraving from George Sala, *America Revisited*, London 1888

116
- The five storeys of a typical house in Paris; engraving from Edmond Texier, *Tableau de Paris*, Paris 1852–3

121
- John Constable: *The Cornfield*; 1826. The scene is Norfolk, near East Bergholt. National Gallery, London. Photo *John Webb (Brompton Studio)*

122–123
- Three of four ploughs advertised by Ransomes, Sims & Head of Ipswich, England. They are the Newcastle Plough (so called after it won four first prizes at the Agricultural Show in Newcastle, in 1864; it could be used with two wheels, one wheel, or as a swing, i.e. without wheels); the Improved Wood Beam Plough (which could be fitted with the same breasts and shares as the metal prize ploughs); and the Patent General Purpose Double Plough. From *The Implement Manufacturers' Review*, 3 October 1877. *Museum of English Rural Life, University of Reading*
- Fowler's steam-ploughing apparatus at work. In 1858 John Fowler won a prize for the successful application of steam to ploughing; by 1864 his Leeds factory employed 900 workmen. From S. Copland, *Agriculture, Ancient and Modern*, London 1866
- Steam threshing machinery by Ransomes, Sims & Head of Ipswich, England (portable steam engine, double blast finishing machine and straw elevator); engraving, mid-19th C. *Mansell Collection*
- Reaping machine invented by the Rev. Patrick Bell of Forfarshire in Scotland, first used in 1827. From J. M. Wilson, *Rural Cyclopaedia*, 1847–9, IV, who comments that it is 'passing into oblivion. ... The very best of the many reaping machines hitherto constructed ... are but a degree better than mere curiosities.'
- Joseph Wilhelm Wallander: *Rapethreshing in Skåne*; 1888. *Nordiska Museet, Stockholm*
- English seed-drill; from a mid-19th C. engraving. *Radio Times Hulton Picture Library*
- Hay-mowing team at Wenham Grange, Suffolk; from a photograph of c. 1880. *Suffolk Photographic Survey, by courtesy of Gordon Winter, Esq., and the Abbot's Hall Museum of Rural Life of East Anglia, Stowmarket, Suffolk*
- Benjamin Holt combine harvester of 1887 drawn by 33 horses at work near Walla Walla, Washington; from a photograph of 1902. *Prints and Photographs Division, Library of Congress, Washington, D.C.*

124–125
- Richard Ansdell: *Country Meeting of the Royal Agricultural Society of England at Bristol, 1842* (detail). City Art Gallery, Salford, on loan to the Royal Agricultural Society. Photo *John Webb (Brompton Studio)*
- 'A Train of Carriages with Cattle'; aquatint by S. G. Hughes after a drawing by J. Shaw, from the series

Travelling on the Liverpool and Manchester Railway published by Ackermann & Co., London 1831. British Museum, London. Photo *R. B. Fleming*
- *The Rhine at Ruhrort*; steel engraving by J. M. Kolb after L. Rohbock, c. 1845. *Das Topographikon Verlag Rolf Müller, Hamburg*
- Agricultural Implements Section in the Crystal Palace, London, for the Great Exhibition of 1851; lithograph from *Dickinson's Comprehensive Pictures of the Great Exhibition of 1851 from the originals painted ... for H.R.H. Prince Albert*, 1854. British Museum, London. Photo *R. B. Fleming*
- View of part of the Halles Centrales in Paris, completed in 1862 by V. Baltard and F. E. Callet; detail of engraving by Myrbach, 1885. Bibliothèque Nationale, Paris. Photo *Arts Graphiques de la Cité*

126–127
- Russian peasant ploughing; from a photograph of 1880. *Radio Times Hulton Picture Library*
- Detail of plate showing the market at Batha in Hungary; from R. Bright, *Travels from Vienna through Lower Hungary*, London 1818
- Agricultural labourers on a farm in the south Midlands of England; from a photograph by William Grundy, 1857. *Radio Times Hulton Picture Library*
- Fritz von Dardel: *Morning Awakening at Orsa Sn, Dalarna*; watercolour, 1893. The superposed beds were common in Dalarna but not in other parts of Sweden; the clock, with its rounded case, is typical of Mora (a large parish in Dalarna); the bread hanging on a pole was most characteristic in the middle and northern parts of Sweden; the stove is of local shape. (Information kindly supplied by Mr Rut Liedgren, of the Nordiska Museet, Stockholm.) Photo *Nordiska Museet, Stockholm*
- Interior of the Nordiska Museet, Stockholm, showing an exhibition devoted to the region of Skåne; engraving, 1890s. *Nordiska Museet, Stockholm*
- Kila, Sweden: view from the village, showing strip-cultivation; from a photograph of 1913. *Nordiska Museet, Stockholm*

128–129
- G. Lepaulle (1804–86): *Equipage du prince de Wagram*. Musée de la Chasse et de la Nature, Paris. Photo *Eileen Tweedy*
- William Powell Frith: *Ramsgate Sands* (detail); 1851–3. Reproduced by gracious permission of Her Majesty Queen Elizabeth II. Copyright Reserved
- Asher B. Durand: *Kindred Spirits* (detail); 1849. The two men are the poet William Cullen Bryant and the painter Thomas Cole. The New York Public Library, Astor, Lenox and Tilden Foundations
- Music cover the *Cook's Excursion Galop*, a song by Musgrave; by Alfred Concanen, 1870. *Courtesy Messrs Thomas Cook & Son Limited*
- Poster for the Chemins de Fer Vicinaux (local railways) of Haute-Saône; lithograph by Misti printed by R. Carvin, Paris, 1903. Folkwangschule, Essen. Photo from H. Schardt, *Paris 1900*, 1968, by courtesy of Chr. Belser Verlag, Stuttgart

130–131
- Rasmus Christiansen: *Milk-preparation on a Danish farm about 1880*; watercolour, 1919. A trough for butter-kneading, with a wooden pail and butter cask beneath it, stands

against the back wall; on the bench to the right two tubs contain cheese weighted down with stones, while above them is a rack for keeping small special cheeses. *Landbrugsmuseet, Lyngby, Denmark*

● Hjeding, western Jutland: interior of the restored co-operative dairy. To the left is a balance; behind this is a big milk-vessel, for the milk received and weighed; at the back a cheese-press is partly visible. Machinery includes a centrifuge, at the right (of 'Maglekilde' manufacture), powered by a vertical steam engine visible behind. Photo *Landbrugsmuseet, Lyngby, Denmark*

● R. W. Whitford: 'The most celebrated flock of Cotswold Sheep in the World the property of Wm. Lane of Northleach [Gloucestershire] Sold to U.S.A.'; 1860/61. Photo *Mansell Collection*

● Co-operative dairy set up in the old rural deanery of Stege Church, on the island of Møn in Denmark; from a photograph of c. 1889. Museum of Møn, Stege. Photo *Dansk Folkemuseum, Nationalmuseet, Lyngby, kindly supplied by the Royal Library, Copenhagen*

● Preparation of Edam cheese on a farm in north Holland, c. 1850. Photo *courtesy the Dutch Dairy Bureau*

● Thomas Weaver: *Portrait of the Holstein or Friesian Bull*; 1806. The bull, imported from Holstein via Newcastle, was presented to Mr Thorold of Syston Park near Grantham in Lincolnshire on his retirement from farming at the age of 80. Private Collection. Photo *courtesy Frost & Reed Limited*

● View of experimental cultivation fields surrounding the castle at Hohenheim, the Royal Agricultural and Forestry Institute of Württemberg; from E. Royer, *L'Agriculture allemande*, Paris 1847. In addition to this area of intensive cultivation (which, according to Royer, 'titillated visitors'), Hohenheim possessed fields, pastures, plantations, gardens and seed-beds; it consisted of institutes of agriculture (producing 'gentlemen farmers'), of forestry, and for *Landbaumänner* (giving the actual workers practical training)

132 ● Paul Seifert: *Wisconsin Farm Scene*; c. 1880. At this time the region was turning from grain-farming to dairying (the farmer's fine herd are probably Devons). The buildings are, from left to right: house; summer kitchen (needed in the high temperatures of the Mid-West); outhouse; well-house or tool-shed; probably a chicken house; corn-crib; barn. Domestic buildings are painted white; work-buildings red. Seifert emigrated to Wisconsin from Germany in his twenties. (Information kindly supplied by Mr Robert W. Sherman, of the State Historical Society of Wisconsin.) *New York State Historical Association, Cooperstown, N.Y.*

● Tom Roberts: *Shearing the Rams*; 1890. Painted from life at Brocklesby Station, Riverina, New South Wales. *National Gallery of Victoria, Melbourne*

135 ● Sanfoin and red clover; from J. Donaldson, *British Agriculture*, London 1860. *Museum of English Rural Life, University of Reading*

136 ● Garrett's portable threshing machine, from Richard N. Bacon, *The Report on the Agriculture of Norfolk to which the Prize was awarded by the Royal Agricultural Society of England*, London 1844

137 ● Le Butt's 'Champion' double-action haymaker or hay-tedder; from *The Implement Manufacturers' Review*, 2 May 1876. *Museum of English Rural Life, University of Reading*

139 ● Charolais bull, Shorthorn cow, Hereford bull and Angus bull; from Victor Borie, *Animaux de la ferme*, Paris 1863–7

140 ● English poster advertising a pig exhibited in Oxford; c. 1840. *Museum of English Rural Life, University of Reading*

● Trout-fishing in Scotland; from John Sherer, *Rural Life described and illustrated*, London 1868/9

141 ● Cover of a pamphlet inviting settlement in Manitoba; 1882. From a copy in the British Museum, London

142 ● Haslam's Dry-Air Refrigerator; from R. Wallace, *The Rural Economy of Australia and New Zealand*, London 1891

145 ● Napoleonic flag; 1815. Invalides, Paris. Photo *Bulloz*

146–147 ● *Le Soutien de la France*, contemporary allegory on the government in 1799; engraving. *Bibliothèque Nationale, Paris*

● *Stufenleiter der Grösse und des Sturzes Napoleons*; engraving caricature, 1814. *Historisches Museum der Stadt Wien, Vienna*

● Confederation of the Rhine, 1806; lithograph. British Museum. Photo *John R. Freeman*

● M. Bacciarelli: *Napoleon handing over the constitution document of the Duchy of Warsaw to the Poles, 1807*. National Museum, Warsaw. Photo *CAF, Warsaw*

● Francisco de Goya: *The Shooting of May 3rd 1808*; 1814. Prado, Madrid. Photo *Mas*

● Nicholas André Monsiaux: *Proclamation of the Italian Republic, 1802*. Château de Versailles. Photo *Musées Nationaux*

148–149 ● Revolutionary scene in Palermo, 1848; lithograph. Collection Bertarelli, Milan. Photo *Scala*

● Garibaldi and his army arriving at Marsala, 1860; lithograph. Collection Bertarelli, Milan. Photo *Saporetti*

● Anton von Werner: *Proclamation of the German Empire at Versailles, 1871*. Photo *Staatsbibliothek, Berlin*

150–151 ● A Hercegovinian delegation received by Francis Joseph I, 1878; from a drawing by V. Katzler. *Österreichische Nationalbibliothek – Bildarchiv, Vienna*

● General Jellačić and his troops near Hegyes; lithograph by J. Lancelli, 1848–49. *Historisches Museum der Stadt Wien, Vienna*

● *Divan ad hoc*; lithograph by C. Popp de Szathmary, 1857. *Library of the Rumanian Academy, Bucharest*

● *Auto-da-fé* at the Wartburg festival, 18 October 1817; from a drawing by Ludwig Burger. Photo *Staatsbibliothek, Berlin*

● *Free Bulgaria*; lithograph by Georgi Dančov, 1879. *National Library, Sofia*

● Angry scenes in the Viennese Parliament; engraving from *Leipziger Illustrierte Zeitung*, 9 December 1897

● Anton von Werner: *The Congress of Berlin, 1878*. From *Bismarck Album*, Berlin 1895

152 ● Eugène Delacroix: *Greece Expiring on the Ruins of Missolonghi*; 1827. Musée des Beaux Arts, Bordeaux

● Peter von Hess: *King Otto of Wittelsbach enters Athens*; 1839. Bayerische Staatsgemäldesammlungen, Munich. Photo *J. Blauel*

155 ● Portrait of Count Camillo Cavour; engraving. *Mary Evans Picture Library*

● *The Boy's Magic Horn*; title-page from C. Brentano and L. A. von Arnim *Des Knaben Wunderhorn*, Heidelberg and Frankfurt 1806–08, II

158 ● *The Three Props of the Austro-Croat Civilization*; French caricature from *Revue Comique*, Paris 1849. British Museum. Photo *John R. Freeman*

161 ● A US naval squadron under Commodore Perry enters Edo Bay; from J. E. J. Papinot *Dictionnaire d'Histoire et de Géographie du Japon*, Paris 1889

● Symbols of the new nationalism of Japan; Japanese woodcut from *Japanese-Chinese War*, 1895. British Museum

162 ● 'Westernized' Japanese; from P. Lindenberg, *Um die Erde in Wort und Bild*, Berlin 1899–1900, II

165 ● Léon Cogniet: *The National Guard of Paris leaving for the Army, September 1792*; 1836. Château de Versailles. Photo *Giraudon*

166–167 ● Benjamin Zix: *Volunteer returning from the Army of the Rhine*; watercolour, 20 October 1796. Musée Historique, Strasbourg. Photo *Franz*

● F. Bastin: *The Imperial Guard of Napoleon I, 1809–1815*; engraving. *National Army Museum, Camberley*

● J. F. J. Swebach: *The Emperor visiting the siege works outside Danzig, 9 May 1807*; engraving. British Museum

● Siege of Burgos, August 1812; engraved by Aubert *fils* after a painting by Heim. British Museum, London

● Russian gun emplacement in the Crimean War; from a contemporary photograph. *Victoria and Albert Museum, London*

● Field kitchen of the 8th Hussars, Crimean War; from a contemporary photograph by R. Fenton. *Gernsheim Collection, University of Texas*

168–169 ● W. v. Kobell: *Battle of Wagram, 1809*; 1811. Residenzmuseum, Munich. Photo *Blauel*

● A. Alken: *Cavalry Charge at Waterloo*; watercolour, c. 1816. *National Army Museum, Camberley*

● Horace Vernet: *Battle of Jena* (detail); 1830s. Château de Versailles. Photo *Giraudon*

170–171 ● Garrison shell gun with carriage; engraving, 1824. *Mary Evans Picture Library*

● Armstrong 12-pounder field-gun and carriage; engraving, 1859. *Mary Evans Picture Library*

● Field gun of the Reffye type; 1867. *Musée de l'Armée, Paris*

● Krupp gun exhibited in the Paris Exhibition of 1867; Photo *Ullstein Bilderdienst*

● French *mitrailleuse*, 1870; engraving. *Mary Evans Picture Library*

● Montigny gun, 1870; engraving. *Mary Evans Picture Library*

● Gatling gun, c. 1862; engraving. *Mary Evans Picture Library*

● Maxim gun, 1880s; engraving. *Mary Evans Picture Library*

● French submarine *Plongeur*, 1863; engraving. *Mary Evans Picture Library*

● *Garrett* submarine, 1880; engraving. *Mary Evans Picture Library*

● *Holland* submarine, 1898; engraving. *Mary Evans Picture Library*

● French submarine, 1906; *Mansell Collection*

172 ● *Battle of Lissa, 1866*; lithograph. National Maritime Museum, Greenwich. Photo *John Webb (Brompton Studio)*

● Alfonso Saenz; *Battle of Santiago, 3 July 1898*; 1899. *Department of the Navy, Washington, D.C.*

● *Battle of Tsushima, 1905*; Japanese woodcut. British Museum, London. Photo *R. B. Fleming*

175 ● English Quakers present a peace petition to Nicholas I; engraving, c. 1854. *Mary Evans Picture Library*

176 ● Diagram of a needle gun by David Eccles

● Diagram of a French Chassepot rifle by David Eccles

● Diagram of a Snider-Enfield rifle by David Eccles

177 ● German ammunition train in 1870; engraving from Cassell's *Illustrated History of the War between France and Germany*, London 1871–72

178 ● Battle of Solferino; engraving from *The Illustrated London News*, 16 July 1859

179 ● Russian Red Cross hospital and ambulances; engraving from Cassell's *History of the Russo-Turkish War*, Vol. 1, London 1877–79

181 ● Gun battery at Plevna; engraving from Cassell's *History of the Russo-Turkish War*, London 1877–79

185 ● *The Railsplitter*, life-size portrait of Abraham Lincoln; artist unknown, thought to have been painted in 1858 during the Lincoln-Douglas debates. *Courtesy Chicago Historical Society*

186–187 ● Pawtucket, Rhode Island: Samuel Slater's cotton-spinning mill; from an old but undated scrapbook photograph. *The Rhode Island Historical Society*

● Andrew Carnegie in his library; detail of an old photograph. *United States Information Service, London*

● Barn-raising on the farm of Jacob Roher, near Massillon, Ohio; from a photograph by Theodore Teeple, 1888. The Massillon Museum, Massillon, Ohio. Photo *American Heritage*

● Rails awaiting transport at an American steel mill; from a photograph of c. 1880. *U.S. War Department General Staff photograph in the National Archives, Washington*

188–189 ● John Hill: *Junction of the Erie and Northern (Champlain) Canals*; coloured proof in aquatint, c. 1830–32. *Courtesy of The New-York Historical Society, New York City*

● *View of St Louis, Missouri, from Lucas Place* (detail); lithograph, c. 1850–60. *Courtesy Chicago Historical Society*

● *A Busy Bee-Hive*, advertisement for Montgomery Ward & Co. of Chicago; chromo-lithograph by the Forbes Company of Boston, probably 1899 (the building shown was erected then). *Courtesy Chicago Historical Society*

● Thomas Waterman Wood: *The Village Post Office*; 1873. The location is thought to be Ainsworth's Store in Williamstown, Vermont. The store serves as a social centre, as well as selling clothing, yardgoods, pottery, such sophisticated products as hair restorer and bitters, and probably food. The clothes worn are mostly old-fashioned for the period; the country shirts worn by an old man and a boy near the counter are of 18th-

C. type. (Information kindly supplied by the New York State Historical Association.) *New York State Historical Association, Cooperstown, N.Y.*

190–191 ● Supply base of the Army of the Potomac (Union) at Cumberland Landing on the Pamunkey River, Virginia, used during McClellan's Peninsular Campaign of May 1862; from a photograph by James F. Gibson. *Prints and Photographs Division, Library of Congress, Washington, D.C.*

● Edwin Francis Jennison, in Company C of the 2nd Louisiana Cavalry, killed at Malvern Hill on 1 July 1862. Photo *Library of Congress, Washington, D.C.*

● Camp of Company B, 9th Mississippi Regiment (Confederate), at Warrington Navy Yard, Pensacola, Florida; detail of a photograph by J. D. Edward, 1861. *Prints and Photographs Division, Library of Congress, Washington, D.C.*

● Major-General Ulysses S. Grant; detail of a photograph taken in the autumn of 1863. *Prints and Photographs Division, Library of Congress, Washington, D.C.*

● Brigadier-General Robert E. Lee; detail of a photograph by Julian Vannerson, taken at Richmond in 1863. *Prints and Photographs Division, Library of Congress, Washington, D.C.*

● Confederate dead in a field on the west side of Hagerstown Pike, after the Battle of Antietam in Maryland; from a photograph by Alexander Gardner, September 1862. *Prints and Photographs Division, Library of Congress, Washington, D.C.*

192–193 ● Albert Bierstadt: *The Rocky Mountains* (detail); 1863. *The Metropolitan Museum of Art, New York, Rogers Fund, 1907*

● Bar of a gambling saloon in Sonora, California, c. 1850–52; from F. S. Marryat, *Mountains and Molehills*, London 1855. The American Museum in Britain, Claverton Manor, Bath. Photo *Eileen Tweedy*

● Poster promoting settlement in South Dakota, issued by the Commissioner of Immigration at Aberdeen, S.D.; lithograph by the Forbes Lith. Mfg. Co., 1890. *Prints and Photographs Division, Library of Congress, Washington, D.C.*

● *An American Railway Scene, at Hor-nellsville, Erie Railway*; lithograph by Currier & Ives, used as an advertisement by the Erie Railway, 1872. *The Harry T. Peters Collection, Museum of the City of New York*

194–195 ● Cowboys and chuckwagon near Ashland, Kansas; detail of a photograph of 1898. *Courtesy Kansas State Historical Society, Topeka*

● Wagon-train coralling in Market Street, Denver, Colorado; from a photograph by W. C. Chamberlain, 20 June 1868. The wagon train was that of David Bruce Powers of Leavenworth, Kan., who freighted between the two towns, carrying manufactured goods, coffee, sugar, etc. *Courtesy Western History Department, Denver Public Library*

● *'Welcome to all!'*, pro-immigration cartoon by Joseph Keppler, himself an immigrant; lithograph from *Puck*, 1880

● Saluting the Flag in the Mott Street Industrial School, New York City; detail of a photograph by Jacob A. Riis, c. 1889. *The Jacob A. Riis Collection, Museum of the City of New York*

● Hester Street, on the Lower East Side of New York City; from a photograph of the mid-1880s. Los Angeles County Museum of Natural History. Photo *Robert Wernstein, courtesy American Heritage*

196 ● View of Chicago from Lake Michigan in 1831, showing Fort Dearborn; from S. Morton Peto, *The Resources and Prospects of America*, London and New York 1866

● The great Chicago fire; lithograph by Currier & Ives, 1871. *Prints and Photographs Division, Library of Congress, Washington, D.C.*

● View of Chicago from Lake Michigan in 1892; lithograph by Currier & Ives, 1892. *Courtesy of The New-York Historical Society, New York City*

198 ● Thomas Nast: Donkey of the Democratic Party; detail of cartoon from *Harper's Weekly*, 15 January 1870

● Thomas Nast: Elephant of the Republican Party; detail of cartoon from *Harper's Weekly*, 7 November 1874

200 ● Eli Whitney's cotton gin, in the open position; wood-engraving from a 19th-C. history. *Mansell Collection*

● Isometric diagram of the balloon frame; from George E. Woodward, *Woodward's Country Homes*, 1865

201 ● '*"The World is my market: my customers are all mankind" – Y. Doodle*'; caricature from *The Daily Graphic*, 20 March 1877. *Courtesy of the New-York Historical Society, New York City*

202 ● Lynching by the Vigilance Committee in San Francisco; detail of wood-engraving from *The Illustrated London News*, 15 November 1851, based on a sketch sent from California. *Mansell Collection*

203 ● *Life in an American hotel?*; cartoon from *Punch*, 26 June 1856

● Cartoon of Uncle Sam and John Bull, captioned 'UNCLE SAM: "My, Johnny, but it dew please me to have you on my side for once"'; from *The New York Journal*, 5 May 1898. *Radio Times Hulton Picture Library*

204 ● *The Evils of unrestricted immigration*; detail of cartoon by Hamilton from *Judge*, 28 March 1891. *Radio Times Hulton Picture Library*

205 ● Map of the United States showing the dates of admission to the Union of the various States, and the westward movement of the population indicated by 'points of balance' published every ten years by the Census Bureau (given here from 1800 to 1900)

209 ● Caricature of Russian society issued by the Union of Russian Socialists; c. 1900. *Saltykov Schedrin Public Library, Leningrad*

210–211 ● Portrait of Tsar Alexander I by George Dawe RA (1781–1829). *Reproduced by gracious permission of Her Majesty Queen Elizabeth II. Copyright Reserved*

● Plate decorated with the type of military scene especially admired by Nicholas I. It bears the cypher of Nicholas I and the mark of the Imperial Porcelain Factory, St Petersburg. Mrs Herbert A. May Collection, Washington D.C. Photo *James R. Dunlop Inc.*

● Military parade in front of the Winter Palace; coloured print by Du Mornay, Paris, 1812. British Museum, London. Photo *John R. Freeman*

● Portrait of Nicholas I; watercolour by George Dawe. British Museum, London. Photo *John R. Freeman*

212–213 ● I. Yakov: *The Halt of the Prisoners*; painting in the Tretyakov Gallery, Moscow, reproduced from a facsimile in the British Museum, London. Photo *John R. Freeman*

● G. G. Miasoyedov: *19 February 1861*; painting in the Tretyakov Gallery, Moscow, reproduced from a facsimile in the British Museum, London. Photo *John R. Freeman*

● The assassination of Alexander II and the execution of the assassins; from the *Illustrated London News*, 1881. British Museum, London. Photo *John R. Freeman*

214–215 ● Fjodor Alexandrovitch Vassiliev: *The Village Street*; 1868. Tretyakov Gallery, Moscow. Photo *Novosti Press Agency*

● I. Repin: *Religious Procession*; c. 1880. Tretyakov Gallery, Moscow. Photo *Novosti Press Agency*

● N. A. Yaroshenko: *A Girl Student*; 1883. *Museum of Russian Art, Kiev*

● P. A. Fedotov: *The Little Widow*; 1851. District Land Museum, Ivanov

● I. Repin: *On the Banks*; 1876. Russian State Museum, Leningrad. Photo *Novosti Press Agency*

216 ● Student demonstration in St Petersburg; from a photograph of 1905. Photo *Novosti Press Agency*

● Workers outside the Putilov works, St Petersburg; from a photograph of 1905. Photo *Novosti Press Agency*

218 ● M. S. Vorontsov exercising his troop in the Caucasus; popular Russian woodcut of the second half of the 19th C. From a facsimile in the British Museum. Photo *John R. Freeman*

219 ● English cartoon of Nicholas I. British Museum, London. Photo *John R. Freeman*

221 ● Map of the Russian Empire in the 19th C.

222 ● Silhouette of a village scene by F. P. Tolstoi. From a facsimile in the British Museum, London. Photo *John R. Freeman*

223 ● P. A. Stolypin; lithograph after a contemporary caricature. *Novosti Press Agency*

225 ● Jews in Samarkand; engraving after V. V. Vereshchagin. British Museum, London. Photo *John R. Freeman*

Index

Page numbers in italics refer to illustrations